LEVITICUS

Kabbalah Publishing is a registered DBA of
The Kabbalah Centre International, Inc.

For further information:

The Kabbalah Centre
155 E. 48th St., New York, NY 10017
1062 S. Robertson Blvd., Los Angeles, CA 90035

1.800.Kabbalah
www.kabbalah.com

First Edition
January 2009
ISBN13: 978-1-57189-625-4

Design: HL Design (Hyun Min Lee) www.hldesignco.com

THE KABBALISTIC BIBLE

LEVITICUS

TECHNOLOGY FOR THE SOUL™

www.kabbalah.com™

EDITED BY **YEHUDA BERG**

TABLE OF CONTENTS

INTRODUCTION

For more than 80 years, The Kabbalah Centre has been the leading force in bringing the once-hidden wisdom of Kabbalah to the world. This volume of the Kabbalistic Bible that you now hold in your hands is one of the most important initiatives in that effort because in it, the wisdom of the *Zohar*, which decodes and gives deeper meaning to the Bible, is revealed for the first time. For centuries, these secrets were available only to the great kabbalists; now they are before your eyes, too. These monumental disclosures give us the essential tools for removing chaos from our lives.

Since its founding in 1922, The Kabbalah Centre's teachers have sacrificed their own security and well-being to reveal the life-enhancing tools of Kabbalah and the *Zohar*. In spite of many difficulties, their passion and commitment to delivering this knowledge has never wavered. The decision of The Kabbalah Centre to open its doors to teach Kabbalah to anyone with the desire to learn was an unprecedented break with tradition and aroused great antagonism. Some people said it would be impossible to bring forth a universally accessible interpretation of so deep and complex a tradition. In addition, The Centre was perceived as having mistakenly taken this bold step toward inclusiveness at a time when the study of Kabbalah was still prohibited—as if the mere existence of a widespread prohibition was reason enough to keep Kabbalah's sublime teachings from all who are in search of them. The prohibition that The Centre was accused of violating had existed for centuries, but it was actually revoked some 450 years ago by the great Kabbalist Rav Avraham Azulai (1570–1643). Nevertheless, when we reflect on the lives of many courageous kabbalists over the four centuries since the time of Rav Azulai, we realize that these pioneering individuals all underwent the same abuse that still greeted the founders of The Kabbalah Centre more than 80 years ago.

Today, things are rapidly changing for the better, and Kabbalah is now widely recognized as a powerful methodology for improving one's life. How did this change take place? As you will see in the lessons of this third volume of the Five Books of Moses, the greatest sacrifices bring the greatest rewards—and there were many great kabbalists who sacrificed their lives to bring the gifts of the *Zohar* and Kabbalah to all humankind.

Why has the widespread dissemination of kabbalistic wisdom been the target of such anger and negativity? The answer to this perplexing question, like the answer to all others, appears clearly and simply in the teachings of the *Zohar* itself. When we examine the *Zohar*, as I have with the assistance of my master, Rav Brandwein, and his master, Rav Ashlag, before him, this becomes apparent. The teachings and disciplines of the *Zohar* are clearly intended for the removal of chaos from this planet. Therefore, the metaphysical force behind the suppression of the *Zohar's* wisdom is none other than Satan—the Opponent, our ego—for if chaos were permanently eliminated, he would be out of a job.

Satan exists only to preserve the chaotic condition that has engulfed mankind since the beginning of time. He has used the familiar tools of greed, envy, jealousy, and doubt to achieve this end. Though some may question the existence of such an evil force, observation of our own daily lives clearly reveals the presence of a very powerful force of darkness surrounding and even within us. How many times have we realized that we shouldn't be doing something, yet we've gone ahead and done it anyway? How many times have we known that we should be acting for the benefit of our soul, but an inner voice whispers, "Why bother?" That little coercive whisper is what Satan is all about. Make no mistake: Satan is alive and well. He is working every moment to continue his domination of our lives, attempting to thwart our hopes of liberation from chaos, pain, and suffering.

But even if we understand what's behind the recent forces working to prevent the revelations of Kabbalah today, the original prohibition of the study of Kabbalah still needs to be explained, as does Rav Azulai's repeal of that prohibition some 450 years ago. The *Zohar* tells us that the original prohibition was not a prohibition as we currently understand the word. The teachings of Kabbalah were deemed so advanced that prior to the 20th century, there was no framework to provide the layperson with a real-life context for the insights that Kabbalah offers.

This began to change with the advent of Newtonian physics some 300 years ago. Science began to break free from its dogmatic view of the nature of the material world and started moving toward a realization and acceptance of the existence of entities and forces beyond the physical realm. This shift in awareness made some of the disciplines stated in Kabbalah more accessible. A century and a half earlier, however, Rav Azulai had already foreseen the developments in science that would make Kabbalah more easily understood. The original prohibition against Kabbalah's widespread lay study had been merely a device to caution the student of Kabbalah that its teachings could not yet be grasped nor fully understood.

The *Zohar* states that all its teachings and disciplines will be revealed during the Age of Aquarius, an age that has already begun and that has ushered in phenomena that no one had even dreamed of even 100 years ago, like the Internet, cellular phones, nanotechnology, and the scientific discovery of mind over matter, which proves that our consciousness determines our reality. This all took place during the 20th century, when the environment for the *Zohar*'s revelations was supported by the revelations of modem physics. In addition, some 80 years ago, Rav Yehuda Ashlag presented a comprehensive explanation of the disciplines of Kabbalah in his book, *Ten Luminous Emanations* (*Talmud Eser Sfirot*), whose insights go far beyond even those of modem science. Rav Ashlag's presentation revealed the origin and meaning of all existence; his explanations uncovered truths not available to our five very limited senses.

Like other kabbalists before him, Rav Ashlag was condemned and physically abused for making the wisdom of Kabbalah more accessible. Through his notorious translation and commentary of the entire *Zohar* from Aramaic to Hebrew (HaSulam; in English, The Ladder), Rav Ashlag provided all the necessary tools for removing chaos from our midst. For the very first time, the complete compendium of Kabbalah's primary source was available to all those who sought its teachings. And for the first time, humanity had a method that it could use to free itself from the clutches of Satan. Since this created a serious problem for our Opponent, he enlisted the aid and support of many leaders to quietly—or not so quietly—remove the so-called heretical Rav Ashlag from their midst. Fortunately, they did not succeed, and the world now benefits from Rav Ashlag's accomplishments.

Now we can understand why this particular spiritual discipline—Kabbalah—was so emphatically concealed from the world. The revelation of this knowledge would have brought an end to the chaos that had prevailed over so many millennia. The power behind the effort to keep the *Zohar* concealed from humanity was none other than Satan using his vast arsenal of chaotic interference tools, tools that unfortunately still continue to perpetuate his reign. He knows exactly when and where to strike to have the maximum impact and to take full advantage of any and all human vulnerabilities.

However, with the advent of the Age of Aquarius, the prophetic assurances by Rav Shimon bar Yochai, the author of the *Zohar*, have become a reality. We are now experiencing the revelation of this vast body of knowledge. At no time in history has Kabbalah reached out to and touched so many millions of people as at this present moment. Life without chaos has never before been within reach of all of humanity.

As we acknowledge The Kabbalah Centre's tremendous progress over the last 18 years in bringing this wisdom to the people, we realize the sublime clarity of the *Zohar*'s insight regarding the elimination of Satan. Of course, this wisdom, like the corresponding breakthroughs in science, was deemed nonsensical daydreaming by many until very recently. But today, the consciousness of humanity has become so elevated that kabbalistic teachings—along with scientific "miracles" such as the rejuvenation of cells and nanotechnology—are becoming wholly acceptable realities.

This dramatic change in global consciousness may be difficult for most people to understand. However, from a kabbalistic perspective, it can be explained by the infusion of Light experienced by the many millions who either read or scan the *Zohar*. The Light that has been revealed has opened the door for the many seemingly futuristic concepts expressed in the *Zohar*. This period in which we now fortunately and meritoriously find ourselves shows great promise for the elimination of chaos in general, and specifically for the elimination of illness and chaotic health conditions. At no previous time in history have so many progressive ideas emerged, leading all humanity to the understanding that we can indeed live in eternal good health and without fear of mortality.

Why is this positive transformation taking place at the present time? In the absence of any alternative explanation, the *Zohar* can and should be considered the force behind such good fortune and hope. The power of the *Zohar* does it all. We can, for the very first time, honestly look forward to a fundamental improvement in our lives. While some may have difficulty understanding how the scanning and reading of this precious document can so deeply stimulate the momentous changes in our lives, this is precisely what was prophesied some 2000 years ago in the *Zohar*'s very pages.

We must recognize another way that Satan diverts us from the true path. I am referring here to the purely academic approach to the *Zohar*, which deflects its teachings from their true purpose. Some scholars—none of them kabbalists—have labeled the disciplines and teachings of the *Zohar* as a philosophy, thereby completely ignoring the real-world changes and immense practical benefits that can result from its study. Others have attempted to place the *Zohar* in the category of religion, as an adjunct to or by-product of Judaism. Yet the *Zohar* and its predecessor, *The Book of Formation* (*Sefer Yetzirah*) authored by Abraham the Patriarch, existed long before any formal religion came into being, clearly and unquestionably demonstrating the universality of these teachings. Whether or not one is versed in Aramaic—and most of mankind is not—scanning this awesome compendium can and will, without any doubt, reveal the Lightforce of the Creator for each of us and for the entire world.

Early on, The Kabbalah Centre's concept of scanning sources of scripture without reading or understanding the text was met with harsh and extreme criticism. This radical idea was branded as yet another attempt by The Centre to mislead people. However, scanning has been an integral part of many spiritual traditions. Take, for example, the long-standing prohibition by Jewish religious authority against pronouncing the four-letter Name of God (the Tetragrammaton). When the need arose to recite the Tetragrammaton as written in prayer books and elsewhere, the rabbis stipulated that this Name should only be scanned, not spoken out loud. In fact, they substituted another word composed of an entirely different combination of letters, instructing us to recite this other Name of God in place of the Tetragrammaton.

Throughout the Torah Scroll (the Bible), we find words that are written but not recited. Sometimes, the words that are recited are completely different from those that are written. The purpose of this highly unusual procedure is to connect us through visual scanning to the unspoken, written word in the Bible. In this way, we tap into the awesome Light of the Creator that is available within the unspoken word. Scanning the *Zohar* and other important texts, including the Torah Scroll itself, has always been considered a more powerful connection to the Light than the mere physical, oral recitation of the words.

The methodology of scanning is the most powerful single force that we can activate to realize the hope of a chaos-free universe. Therefore, to turn away millions of seekers who want to improve their lives solely on the pretext that they do not understand and cannot read the language of the *Zohar* must be considered a great travesty. This certainly could not have been the intent of Moses when he instructed Rav Shimon bar Yochai about the purpose of creating the *Zohar* that of realizing humanity's dream of eliminating chaos from the entire universe. To indulge in philosophical speculations about what constitutes "real" Kabbalah is an exercise in futility. Discussion as to who possesses the "true" Kabbalah and who should be considered the "authentic" authority is merely another trick by Satan to divert our attention from the *Zohar*'s true purpose.

There is no dispute or conflict surrounding the validity or credibility either of the *Zohar* itself or of most of the works written by famed kabbalists of the past. The *Zohar* is and always will be the ultimate tool for all of us to use in our efforts to improve our own lives and the lives of all of humanity.

In closing, let me emphasize the truly astonishing transformation that is now occurring with respect to the *Zohar*'s presence in the everyday world. Just 20 years ago, it would have been difficult for anyone, regardless of their scholarly qualifications or financial resources, to gain access to the authentic teachings of the *Zohar* or to the text itself. Now all that is changed. The *Zohar*, the teachings of Kabbalah, and the Kabbalistic Bible are available to everyone. This is as it should be—indeed, as it must be. The need to reveal the Lightforce of the Creator has never been greater than in our time, as we face the dreadful possibility of impending environmental meltdown and the threat of nuclear warfare that could obliterate life from the face of the Earth. Confronted with this terrible reality, it is incumbent upon all mankind to infuse our environment with as much Light as possible. The true purpose of Kabbalah and all its teachings is not simply to provide knowledge—it is to reveal the Light that will banish chaos from our lives and from all the world.

Rav Berg

VAYIKRA

LESSON OF VAYIKRA
(Leviticus 1:1-5:26)

"The power of the eyes"

When children come to learn the Five Books of Moses, Vayikra is the first chapter of the Bible we teach them. The lessons of this reading should stay with the children throughout their lives, just as those lessons should be paramount in our own awareness right now, regardless of our age. The Book of Vayikra is the beginning and the basis of all teachings because it is here that we realize the importance of our intense devotion to the Creator's Light. This is the first time in the Bible that such devotion is discussed. Of course, this devotion can take—and has taken—many different forms throughout history. In this reading, devotion is manifested as the Tabernacle and the sacrifices, while in our time, when the Tabernacle and the Holy Temple no longer exist, our connection to the Light comes about, not through sacrifices but through prayer.

We know that the desire of the Light to share with us is even greater than our desire to receive from the Light. Yet we create barriers such as ego, jealousy, and other forms of negativity that undermine our connection with the Light. Let us consider, for example, the jealousy that Joseph's brothers felt toward Joseph. We cannot assume that the brothers were like us, since they were the sons of our Patriarch Jacob and thus chariots for the Light in their own right. But at the very least, their jealousy created a barrier between them and the Light.

And what was the cause of the jealousy? Are we to believe that the brothers sold Joseph into slavery because of the special coat that Jacob had made for Joseph? Neither the Midrash nor the *Zohar* state that Jacob loved Joseph more than his other sons, yet after the brothers sold Joseph, it is written that they were afraid "because he was the one that their father loved."

From this we can learn an important lesson. We can see the damage our limited perception of reality can cause, and therefore, how careful we should be about the misperceptions we trigger in others. For example, there are people who flaunt their wealth and power, thus causing the illusion that those around them are inferior. This misperception, which we pick up when we rely only on our five senses, gives rise to negativity that can, in turn, manifest as jealousy and perhaps even hatred. As a result, the ostentatious person who ignited those feelings may end up losing all that he had.

It is written in the Bible: "Do not put an obstacle in front of a blind man." But when we stand by and allow people to be deceived by their own limited perceptions, it's as if we ourselves were actively putting "obstacles in the path of the blind." Furthermore, if people behave wrongly as a result of something we have done, then we are just as responsible for their negative behavior as they are—and we will be affected equally by whatever judgment comes to them. Likewise, if someone causes us harm in response to something we did—or even in response to something we said or to a thought that was in our consciousness—then we must share in the responsibility for the harm done to us.

Here is a case in point. Our sages have written: "Dress as well as other people dress so that you will not cause them to feel superior to you." This shows us the great power of the act of seeing, as well as the responsibility we must take for what others see in us. It is said that the sense of hearing is nothing compared to the sense of sight, for "the eyes are the windows to the soul." A person's eyes are also windows to his or her inner wisdom; when someone is truly wise, the Light of Wisdom (*Or deChochmah*) shines through their eyes.

> *This is because a man's eyes reflect the world and contain all the colors. The white color in them is like a great sea which surrounds the world on all sides. Another is like the ground dug out from the water. The ground stands in the midst of the water and so does the color in the midst of the water; NAMELY IN THE MIDST OF THE WHITE COLOR WHICH INDICATES THE WATER OF THE OCEAN. The third color in the middle of the eye is Jerusalem, the center of the world. The fourth color in the eye is where the power of sight dwells; NAMELY THE BLACKNESS IN THE EYE. It is called "the apple of the eye" (Psalms 17:8), where the face is seen and the most dear sight of all, Tzion, the innermost point of all, where the whole world is seen, where the Shechinah dwells, which is the beauty and sight of all.*
> — *The Zohar, Vayechi 32:341-342*

Unfortunately, most of us don't make use of the spiritual power of our eyes, so we see only the physical dimension. We need to start using our eyes to perceive the spiritual reality, to see the good in other people and in the world as a whole.

Tikkun HaNefesh

Kabbalah teaches that the *Tikkun HaNefesh* (the Correction of the Soul), which is the healing meditation involving the chakras of the body, should be done every day. This was revealed to us by Rav Isaac Luria (the Ari) in *The Gate of Divine Inspiration*. There are specific locations in our body where the Light enters, and these points replicate the kabbalistic Tree of Life. The Ari wrote:

> *"It is worthy for a man always to guide himself and to appreciate himself as the seat of Divine Emanation. Through his eyes, he will meditate and receive the merit to see holiness."*

Tikkun HaNefesh has special powers, not only to heal but also to reveal the Light in our eyes, our ears, and all throughout our body. By using the *Tikkun HaNefesh* for our meditation, we can banish spiritual darkness, thereby ending physical illness as well, for if there is no darkness, illness can not exist.

SYNOPSIS OF VAYIKRA

Vayikra, the first chapter in the Book of Leviticus, includes a discussion of the *korbanot* (sacrifices). Because we have no Tabernacle or Temple today, it's difficult to relate to this concept. While it may appear that the sacrifices involved cruelty to animals, the kabbalists explain that the animals actually lined up to be sacrificed because they knew that this process was part of their *tikkun* (correction).

The root of the word *korban*, which can be translated as "sacrifice" or "offering," actually means "to come near," and so the offering itself was seen as the way to draw near to God. Indeed, the *Zohar* says that the offerings were made in order to draw near the holy *Sefirot*, so that they would form a perfect unity and ultimately awaken mercy instead of judgment (*Vayikra 51-52*). Today, many of our sacrifices are internal; we sacrifice whenever we face and overcome obstacles or difficulties on behalf of others. Reading this chapter gives us the energy to make the sacrifices that are required of us every day in order to increase our proximity to the Light.

FIRST READING - ABRAHAM - CHESED

1:1 The Lord called to Moses and He spoke to him from the Tent of Meeting. He said, *2* "Speak to the Children of Israel and say to them: When any of you brings an offering to the Lord, bring as your offering an animal from either the herd or the flock.

3 If the offering is a burnt offering from the herd, he is to offer a male without defect. He must present it at the entrance to the Tent of Meeting so that it will be acceptable to the Lord.

FROM THE RAV

Kuf and *Reish*

According to Rav Shimon, everything is crouched in mystery, like a code. This is how the *Zohar* processes the whole Torah—as a code for something more, something higher.

The word *vayikra* is made up of five letters—*Vav, Alef, Yud, Kuf,* and *Reish.* Two of these letters—the Kuf and the *Reish*—together make the word *kar* (cold). Cold, the way a body is cold when it's dead. Why is it when a person is dead that the body goes cold? Is it because it is cold outside? What if a person dies on the equator? Does the body get warm? No, the body still goes cold.

The *Zohar*, in explaining the cold of *Kuf* and *Reish* and why a dead body is cold, refers to cold as the energy of Satan. The soul has left. That is why the body is cold. What do we mean when we say that people are cold to each other? It means that we forget to love our neighbors as ourselves; that we forget to treat others with human dignity, and that the expression of the soul is gone. We are alive, but it's as if our soul is gone. We are alive, but we live as if we have no soul.

The chapter of Vayikra helps us understand what the Torah is about. It's about the battle against Satan's playing field—against chaos. We learn from Vayikra that we can remove the chaos, but we must make a sacrifice. We must sacrifice our Satan-consciousness. Who is the sacrifice for? Is it for us? What do we have to sacrifice today? Human beings? No, it's not the human being that needs to be sacrificed; it is those two letters—the *Kuf* and the *Reish*—that are concealed in the word *vayikra.*

Remember, Satan is within each of us, and we live under his direction as long as we don't follow the rules of the Light—to treat our neighbors with human dignity. But sometimes we refuse to surrender our ego and so we remain in Satan's playing field. We hold onto our ego for stupid things and we are reactive and lose control. The only way we can be outside of the control of Satan is by acting like God—and to act like God, we have to share. When we don't share like God, we are acting like Satan—and we are stuck in his playing field.

When we are living in Satan's playing field, we are controlled and we have no choice, we are making judgments about other people. To remove chaos from our lives, we have to give up Satan. We have to act like the Light, like God, to be in God's playing field. It's merely a test. If you act like God, then you have a brain; if you act like Satan, then you are cooked.

FIRST READING - ABRAHAM - CHESED

וַיְדַבֵּ֣ר רָאה יְהֹוָה אל שדי מהע, אותיות אֶל־מֹשֶׁ֑ה ב"פ קס"א - ה 1 1

אֵלָ֛יו מֵאֹ֥הֶל לאה מוֹעֵ֖ד לֵאמֹֽר׃ 2 דַּבֵּ֞ר ראה אֶל־בְּנֵ֤י יִשְׂרָאֵל֙ וְאָמַרְתָּ֣

אֲלֵהֶ֔ם מ"ה כִּֽי־יַקְרִ֥יב מִכֶּ֛ם קָרְבָּ֖ן לַֽיהֹוָ֑ה מִן־הַבְּהֵמָ֗ה

מִן־הַבָּקָר֙ ב"ן, לכב, יבמ וּמִן־הַצֹּ֔אן מלוי אהיה דיודין ע"ה תַּקְרִ֖יבוּ אֶת־קׇרְבַּנְכֶֽם׃

3 אִם־ יווהך, ע"ה מ"ב עֹלָ֤ה קׇרְבָּנוֹ֙ מִן־הַבָּקָ֔ר זָכָ֥ר תָּמִ֖ים יַקְרִיבֶ֑נּוּ אֶל־

וַיִּקְרָא

Leviticus 1:1 – A small *Alef* appears at the end of the word *vayikra* (and He called). Vayikra refers to God calling to Moses. The *Zohar* says that both the great letters and the small letters were transmitted to Moses at Sinai, and we know that Moses was able to hear God speaking to him.

This is because each and every letter (Ot) that was transmitted to Moses was crowned and rose over the heads of the holy supernal living creatures, THE SECRET OF THE SUPERNAL CHARIOT, WHICH ARE CHESED, GEVURAH, TIFERET, MALCHUT. All the living creatures were crowned WITH THE LETTERS, EVEN THE LIVING CREATURES OF THE LOWER CHARIOT, WHICH IS IN MALCHUT. They flew in the air OF YISRAEL, SABA AND TEVUNAH, which descends from the supernal air that is fine and unknown, WHICH IS IN THE SUPERNAL ABA AND IMA. Both the great letters and the small letters went up and down, the great letters descending from the supernal chamber which is concealed from all, BINAH, and the small letters descending from another lower chamber, MALCHUT. All of these were transmitted to Moses at Sinai. The joining of the letters, which secretly join together in every letter, such as Alef, which is a single letter secretly joined by two other letters, namely, Lamed and Pei, IN PRONOUNCING THE LETTER. So, TOO, IN ARTICULATING THE NAME OF THE LETTER BET, IT IS JOINED BY YUD AND TAV. They were all transmitted to Moses at Sinai as well…
— *The Zohar, Vayikra 1:2-4*

Many times, we are called by God; the Creator frequently gives us messages in dreams and through other people, but we don't always hear them. The small *Alef* is a reminder that we must reduce our ego in order to hear the Voice of God.

עֹלָה

Leviticus 1:3 –The first type of offering, cattle, represents the energy of death and helps us remove death from our lives.

Sacrificing is to the Name of Elohim, which is the side of Gevurah so that the spirit of Judgment will be perfumed and broken and Judgment thus be weakened, thus bringing Mercy to overpower Judgment. Therefore, IT IS WRITTEN, "The sacrifices of Elohim" to break the strength and power of harsh Judgment, as it is written, "A broken spirit." This implies that the strong spirit of Judgment is broken, and its spirit and power shall not be overpowering. Thus, man is to stand by the altar with a broken spirit and feel remorse for his actions, in order that this strong spirit is broken, so that Judgment may be softened and Mercy overpower Judgment.
— *The Zohar, Vayikra 6:53*

Whenever good things of any kind come to an end, the cause of "the end" is the Angel of Death. This reading is a powerful weapon to weaken the Angel of Death everywhere, until ultimately we will achieve the death of death itself, resulting in immortality for ourselves and for the world.

⁴ He is to lay his hand on the head of the burnt offering, and it will be accepted on his behalf to make atonement for him.

⁵ He is to slaughter the young bull before the Lord, and then Aaron's sons, the priests, shall bring the blood and sprinkle the blood against the altar on all sides at the entrance to the Tent of Meeting.

⁶ He is to skin the burnt offering and cut it into pieces.

⁷ The sons of Aaron the priest are to put fire on the altar and arrange wood on the fire.

⁸ Then Aaron's sons, the priests, shall arrange the pieces, including the head and the fat, on the burning wood that is on the altar.

⁹ He is to wash the inner parts and the legs with water, and the priest is to burn all of it on the altar. It is a burnt offering, an offering made by fire, an aroma pleasing to the Lord.

¹⁰ If the offering is a burnt offering from the flock, from either the sheep or the goats, he is to offer a male without defect.

¹¹ He is to slaughter it at the north side of the altar before the Lord, and Aaron's sons the priests shall sprinkle its blood against the altar on all sides.

¹² He is to cut it into pieces, and the priest shall arrange them, including the head and the fat, on the burning wood that is on the altar.

¹³ He is to wash the inner parts and the legs with water, and the priest is to bring all of it and burn it on the altar. It is a burnt offering, an offering made by fire; an aroma pleasing to the Lord.

הַצֹּאן

Leviticus 1:10 – Sheep and goats, the second type of offering, are connected to ego. Our ego is the voice that convinces us that we are right even when we are wrong. Our ego makes us feel that we are free-thinking individuals when, in fact, we are robots following our own pre-programmed selfish desires. Denying that we have an ego is itself a demonstration of our ego hard at work. The ego blocks our spiritual growth and is the basis for all forms of misery. But reading this verse helps us to control the influence of ego in our lives, giving us a chance to escape the bondage of ego-based desires—the "me first" mentality—and to gain a life of happiness, meaningful relationships, and true freedom.

פֶּתַח אֹהֶל לאה מוֹעֵד יַקְרִיב אֹתוֹ לִרְצֹנוֹ לִפְנֵי וחכמה בינה יְהוָֹהאדניאהדונהי:

4 וְסָמַךְ יָדוֹ עַל רֹאשׁ רבוע אלהים ואלהים ביודין ע״ה הָעֹלָה וְנִרְצָה לוֹ לְכַפֵּר מצפצ עָלָיו: 5 וְשָׁחַט אֶת־בֶּן הַבָּקָר לִפְנֵי יְהוָֹהאדניאהדונהי וחכמה בינה וְהִקְרִיבוּ בְּנֵי אַהֲרֹן ע״ב ורבוע ע״ב הַכֹּהֲנִים מלה אֶת־הַדָּם רבוע אהיה וְזָרְקוּ אֶת־הַדָּם רבוע אהיה עַל־הַמִּזְבֵּחַ זן, נגד סָבִיב אֲשֶׁר־פֶּתַח אֹהֶל לאה מוֹעֵד: 6 וְהִפְשִׁיט אֶת־הָעֹלָה וְנִתַּח אֹתָהּ לִנְתָחֶיהָ: 7 וְנָתְנוּ אבי״ג ית״ן, וער, אהבת חנם בְּנֵי אַהֲרֹן הַכֹּהֵן מלה אֵשׁ אלהים ביודין ע״ה עַל־הַמִּזְבֵּחַ זן, נגד וְעָרְכוּ עֵצִים עַל־הָאֵשׁ שאה: 8 וְעָרְכוּ בְּנֵי אַהֲרֹן ע״ב ורבוע ע״ב הַכֹּהֲנִים מלה אֵת הַנְּתָחִים אֶת־הָרֹאשׁ רבוע אלהים ואלהים ביודין ע״ה וְאֶת־הַפָּדֶר עַל־הָעֵצִים אֲשֶׁר עַל־הָאֵשׁ שאה אֲשֶׁר עַל־הַמִּזְבֵּחַ זן, נגד: 9 וְקִרְבּוֹ וּכְרָעָיו יִרְחַץ בַּמָּיִם וְהִקְטִיר הַכֹּהֵן מלה אֶת־הַכֹּל ילי הַמִּזְבֵּחָה עֹלָה אִשֵּׁה רֵיחַ־נִיחוֹחַ לַיהוָֹהאדניאהדונהי:

10 וְאִם יוהך, ע״ה ב״פ מלוי אהיה דיודין ע״ה ☐מִן־הַצֹּאן☐ קָרְבָּנוֹ מִן־הַכְּשָׂבִים אוֹ מִן־הָעִזִּים לְעֹלָה זָכָר תָּמִים יַקְרִיבֶנּוּ: 11 וְשָׁחַט אֹתוֹ עַל יֶרֶךְ הַמִּזְבֵּחַ צָפֹנָה לִפְנֵי יְהוָֹהאדניאהדונהי וחכמה בינה זן, נגד וְזָרְקוּ בְּנֵי אַהֲרֹן ע״ב ורבוע ע״ב הַכֹּהֲנִים מלה אֶת־דָּמוֹ עַל־הַמִּזְבֵּחַ זן, נגד סָבִיב: 12 וְנִתַּח אֹתוֹ לִנְתָחָיו וְאֶת־רֹאשׁוֹ וְאֶת־פִּדְרוֹ וְעָרַךְ הַכֹּהֵן מלה אֹתָם עַל־הָעֵצִים אֲשֶׁר עַל־הָאֵשׁ שאה אֲשֶׁר עַל־הַמִּזְבֵּחַ זן, נגד: 13 וְהַקֶּרֶב וְהַכְּרָעַיִם יִרְחַץ בַּמָּיִם וְהִקְרִיב הַכֹּהֵן מלה אֶת־הַכֹּל ילי וְהִקְטִיר הַמִּזְבֵּחָה עֹלָה הוּא אִשֵּׁה רֵיחַ נִיחוֹחַ לַיהוָֹהאדניאהדונהי:

SECOND READING - ISAAC - GEVURAH

[14] *If the offering to the Lord is a burnt offering of birds, he is to offer a dove or a young pigeon.* [15] *The priest shall bring it to the altar, wring off the head and burn it on the altar; its blood shall be drained out on the side of the altar.*

[16] *He is to remove the crop with its contents and throw it to the east side of the altar, where the ashes are.* [17] *He shall tear it open by the wings, not severing it completely, and then the priest shall burn it on the wood that is on the fire on the altar. It is a burnt offering, an offering made by fire, an aroma pleasing to the Lord.*

[2:1] *When someone brings a meal offering to the Lord, his offering is to be of fine flour. He is to pour oil on it, put incense on it*

[2] *and to bring it to Aaron's sons the priests. The priest shall take a handful of the fine flour and oil, together with all the incense, and burn this as a memorial portion on the altar, an offering made by fire, an aroma pleasing to the Lord.*

[3] *The rest of the meal offering belongs to Aaron and his sons; it is a most holy part of the offerings made to the Lord by fire.* [4] *If you bring a meal offering baked in an oven, it is to consist of fine flour: unleavened cakes and mixed with oil, or unleavened wafers and spread with oil.*

[5] *If your meal offering is prepared on a griddle, it is to be made of fine flour mixed with oil, and without yeast.* [6] *Crumble it and pour oil on it; it is a meal offering.*

הָעוֹף

Leviticus 1:14 – Birds were the third type of offering. It is part of human nature to make decisions that, while gratifying the ego, may injure others. But here, the example of the bird's gravity-defying ability to fly gives us the power to transcend the limits of our own nature. Reading or hearing this section helps us cleanse our selfish behavior and overcome our *Desire to Receive for the Self Alone*, allowing us to elevate the "self" so that we can connect to the Light, the source of all happiness.

וְנֶפֶשׁ

Leviticus 2:1 – Food, the next kind of offering, provides us with strength to do our work; in addition, it reveals to us that eating is a major responsibility. There is a soul within every piece of food. The souls trapped within the food are unable to elevate through any kind of action on their part, but once we eat and the food becomes part of us, then our actions—both positive and negative—become connected to the actions of the souls in the food. Awareness of the responsibility we have when we eat is very important.

A food offering does not necessarily take place at an altar. For example, the *Zohar* talks about the great worth of the poor man who brings what he can, even though he has little or nothing to eat.

The poor man's offering is of great worth before God, as he brings before Him two offerings: the one is his fat and blood and the other is the sacrifice he is offering.

SECOND READING - ISAAC - GEVURAH

14 וְאִם יוהך, ע״ה מ״ב גי״פ ב״ן, יוסף, ציון מִן־הָעוֹף עֹלָה קָרְבָּנוֹ לַיהֹוֶׂאֱדִנִיֶאהדונהי

וְהִקְרִיב מִן־הַתֹּרִים אוֹ מִן־בְּנֵי הַיּוֹנָה כ״י מ״ה אֶת־קָרְבָּנוֹ: 15 וְהִקְרִיבוֹ

הַכֹּהֵן מלה אֶל־הַמִּזְבֵּחַ יוה, נגד וּמָלַק אֶת־רֹאשׁוֹ וְהִקְטִיר הַמִּזְבֵּחָה וְנִמְצָה

דָמוֹ עַל קִיר הַמִּזְבֵּחַ יוה, נגד: 16 וְהֵסִיר אֶת־מֻרְאָתוֹ בְּנֹצָתָהּ וְהִשְׁלִיךְ

אֹתָהּ אֵצֶל הַמִּזְבֵּחַ יוה, נגד קֵדְמָה אֶל־מְקוֹם יהוה ברבוע, ר״פ אל הַדָּשֶׁן: 17 וְשִׁסַּע

אֹתוֹ בִכְנָפָיו לֹא יַבְדִּיל וְהִקְטִיר אֹתוֹ הַכֹּהֵן מלה הַמִּזְבֵּחָה עַל־הָעֵצִים

אֲשֶׁר עַל־הָאֵשׁ שאא עֹלָה הוּא אִשֵּׁה רֵיחַ נִיחוֹחַ לַיהֹוֶׂאֱדִנִיֶאהדונהי:

2 1 וְנֶפֶשׁ רמ״ח ﬞﬞﬞ ﬞ הוויות כִּי־תַקְרִיב קָרְבַּן מִנְחָה ע״ה ב״פ ב״ן לַיהֹוֶׂאֱדִנִיֶאהדונהי סֹלֶת

יִהְיֶה יהוה קָרְבָּנוֹ וְיָצַק עָלֶיהָ פהל שֶׁמֶן י״פ טל, י״פ כוז״ו, ביט וְנָתַן אבגית״ץ, ושר, אהבת חנם

עָלֶיהָ פהל לְבֹנָה: 2 וֶהֱבִיאָהּ אֶל־בְּנֵי אַהֲרֹן ע״ב ורבוע ע״ב הַכֹּהֲנִים מלה וְקָמַץ

מִשָּׁם יהוה שדי מְלֹא קֻמְצוֹ מִסָּלְתָּהּ וּמִשַּׁמְנָהּ עַל כָּל־יבק לְבֹנָתָהּ וְהִקְטִיר

הַכֹּהֵן מלה אֶת־אַזְכָּרָתָהּ הַמִּזְבֵּחָה אִשֵּׁה רֵיחַ נִיחוֹחַ לַיהֹוֶׂאֱדִנִיֶאהדונהי:

3 וְהַנּוֹתֶרֶת מִן־הַמִּנְחָה ע״ה ב״פ ב״ן לְאַהֲרֹן ע״ב ורבוע ע״ב וּלְבָנָיו קֹדֶשׁ קָדָשִׁים

מֵאִשֵּׁי יְהֹוֶׂאֱדִנִיֶאהדונהי: 4 וְכִי תַקְרִב קָרְבַּן מִנְחָה ע״ה ב״פ ב״ן מַאֲפֵה תַנּוּר

סֹלֶת חַלּוֹת מַצֹּת בְּלוּלֹת בַּשֶּׁמֶן י״פ טל, י״פ כוז״ו, ביט וּרְקִיקֵי מַצּוֹת מְשֻׁחִים

בַּשָּׁמֶן י״פ טל, י״פ כוז״ו, ביט: 5 וְאִם יוהך, ע״ה מ״ב מִנְחָה ע״ה ב״פ ב״ן עַל־הַמַּחֲבַת

קָרְבָּנֶךָ סֹלֶת בְּלוּלָה בַשֶּׁמֶן י״פ טל, י״פ כוז״ו, ביט מַצָּה ע״ב ס״ג תִהְיֶה: 6 פָּתוֹת

אֹתָהּ פִּתִּים וְיָצַקְתָּ עָלֶיהָ פהל שֶׁמֶן י״פ טל, י״פ כוז״ו, ביט מִנְחָה ע״ה ב״פ ב״ן הִוא:

Though he has no food for himself, he still brings an offering. The offering of the poor is the lightest, two young turtledoves or two young pigeons, or he may even bring a little flour and he is forgiven. At that time, a proclamation resounds, saying, "For he has not despised nor abhorred the affliction of the poor." Why is that? Because the offering of the poor man is the worthiest of all.
— The Zohar, Vayikra 20:129

The poor man's offering may be the smallest of everyone's, yet his sins will be forgiven because it is as if he has offered his own soul in sacrifice.

THIRD READING - JACOB - TIFERET

7 If your meal offering is cooked in a pan, it is to be made of fine flour and oil.

8 Bring the meal offering made of these things to the Lord; present it to the priest, who shall take it to the altar.

9 He shall take out the memorial portion from the meal offering and burn it on the altar as an offering made by fire, an aroma pleasing to the Lord.

10 The rest of the meal offering belongs to Aaron and his sons; it is a most holy part of the offerings made to the Lord by fire.

11 Every meal offering you bring to the Lord must be unleavened, for you are not to burn any yeast or honey in an offering made to the Lord by fire.

12 You may bring them to the Lord as an offering of the first fruits, but they are not to be offered on the altar as a pleasing aroma.

13 All your meal offerings should be seasoned with salt. Do not leave the salt of the covenant of your God out of your meal offerings; add salt to all your offerings.

14 If you bring a meal offering of first fruits to the Lord, offer crushed heads of new meal roasted in the fire.

15 Put oil on it and put incense on it; it is a meal offering.

16 The priest shall burn the memorial portion of the crushed meal and the oil, together with all the incense, as an offering made to the Lord by fire.

בְּמֶלַח

Leviticus 2:13 – In ancient times, salt was supposed to be included in every offering. The numerical value of the Aramaic word for salt (*melach*) is three times that of the Tetragrammaton: 3 x 26 = 78, the four-letter Name of God. Biologically, salt is an important substance; it even moves the blood in our bodies through the process of osmosis. Salt is considered an inanimate object, so it helps us to elevate the souls that are trapped in inanimate objects; there is no other way for us to do this. We can help elevate the souls of animals by eating them or by having them as pets, and we can elevate the souls of plants by eating them or having them as house-plants or tending them in the garden. But the only way to elevate the souls of inanimate objects is through eating salt. The true purpose of everything in this world is to elevate and transform, and we have an obligation to help even inanimate objects in that process.

THIRD READING - JACOB - TIFERET

7 וְאִם יוהך, ע״ה מ״ב ־מִנְחַת ע״ה ב״פ ב״ן מַרְחֶשֶׁת קָרְבָּנְךָ סֹלֶת בַּשֶּׁמֶן י״פ טל, י״פ כוז״ו, ביט תֵּעָשֶׂה: 8 וְהֵבֵאתָ אֶת־הַמִּנְחָה ע״ה ב״פ ב״ן אֲשֶׁר יֵעָשֶׂה מֵאֵלֶּה לַיהוָׁואדניאהדונהי וְהִקְרִיבָהּ אֶל־הַכֹּהֵן מלה וְהִגִּישָׁהּ אֶל־הַמִּזְבֵּחַ הן, נגד: 9 וְהֵרִים הַכֹּהֵן מלה מִן־הַמִּנְחָה ע״ה ב״פ ב״ן אֶת־אַזְכָּרָתָהּ וְהִקְטִיר הַמִּזְבֵּחָה אִשֵּׁה רֵיחַ נִיחֹחַ לַיהוָׁואדניאהדונהי: 10 וְהַנּוֹתֶרֶת מִן־הַמִּנְחָה ע״ה ב״פ ב״ן לְאַהֲרֹן ע״ב ורבוע ע״ב וּלְבָנָיו קֹדֶשׁ קָדָשִׁים מֵאִשֵּׁי יְהוָׁואדניאהדונהי: 11 כָּל יל ־הַמִּנְחָה ע״ה ב״פ ב״ן אֲשֶׁר תַּקְרִיבוּ לַיהוָׁואדניאהדונהי לֹא תֵעָשֶׂה חָמֵץ כִּי כָל יל ־שְׂאֹר ג׳ מווזין דאלהים דקטנות וְכָל יל ־דְּבַשׁ לֹא־תַקְטִירוּ מִמֶּנּוּ אִשֶּׁה לַיהוָׁואדניאהדונהי: 12 קָרְבַּן רֵאשִׁית תַּקְרִיבוּ אֹתָם לַיהוָׁואדניאהדונהי וְאֶל־הַמִּזְבֵּחַ הן, נגד לֹא־יַעֲלוּ לְרֵיחַ רמ״ח נִיחֹחַ: 13 וְכָל יל ־קָרְבַּן מִנְחָתְךָ בַּמֶּלַח ג״פ יהוה תִּמְלָח וְלֹא תַשְׁבִּית מֶלַח ג״פ יהוה בְּרִית אֱלֹהֶיךָ ילה מֵעַל מִנְחָתֶךָ עלם עַל כָּל יל ־קָרְבָּנְךָ תַּקְרִיב מֶלַח ג״פ יהוה: 14 וְאִם יוהך, ע״ה מ״ב ־ תַּקְרִיב מִנְחַת בִּכּוּרִים לַיהוָׁואדניאהדונהי אָבִיב קָלוּי בָּאֵשׁ אלהים דיודין ע״ה גֶּרֶשׂ כַּרְמֶל תַּקְרִיב אֵת מִנְחַת בִּכּוּרֶיךָ: 15 וְנָתַתָּ עָלֶיהָ פהל שֶׁמֶן יפ טל, י״פ כוז״ו, ביט וְשַׂמְתָּ עָלֶיהָ פהל לְבֹנָה מִנְחָה ע״ה ב״פ ב״ן הִוא: 16 וְהִקְטִיר הַכֹּהֵן מלה אֶת־אַזְכָּרָתָהּ מִגִּרְשָׂהּ וּמִשַּׁמְנָהּ עַל כָּל יל ־לְבֹנָתָהּ אִשֶּׁה לַיהוָׁואדניאהדונהי:

FOURTH READING - MOSES - NETZACH

3:¹ If someone's offering is a peace offering, and he offers an animal from the herd, whether male or female, he is to present before the Lord an animal without defect.

² He is to lay his hand on the head of his offering and slaughter it at the entrance to the Tent of Meeting. Then Aaron's sons, the priests, shall sprinkle the blood against the altar on all sides.

³ From the peace offering he is to bring a sacrifice made to the Lord by fire: all the fat that covers the inner parts and the fat that is connected to the inner parts,

⁴ both kidneys with the fat on them near the loins, and the covering of the liver, which he will remove with the kidneys.

⁵ Then Aaron's sons are to burn it on the altar on top of the burnt offering that is on the burning wood, as an offering made by fire, an aroma pleasing to the Lord.

⁶ If he offers an animal from the flock as a peace offering to the Lord, he is to offer a male or female without defect.

⁷ If he brings a lamb for his offering, he is to present it before the Lord.

⁸ He is to lay his hand on the head of his offering and slaughter it in front of the Tent of Meeting. Then Aaron's sons shall sprinkle its blood against the altar on all sides.

⁹ From the peace offering he is to bring a sacrifice made to the Lord by fire: its fat, the entire fat tail cut off close to the backbone, all the fat that covers the inner parts and the fat that is connected to the inner parts,

¹⁰ both kidneys with the fat on them near the loins, and the covering of the liver, which he will remove with the kidneys.

זֶבַח שְׁלָמִים

Leviticus 3:1 – Here, we read about peace offerings. The only way to bring about peace in this world is by treating everyone with tolerance and respect for their human dignity.

. . . These are peace offerings that are slaughtered on the south side of the altar—THE SIDE OF CHESED, RIGHT—

because they bring peace to everyone, peace to the Upper and Lower beings, AS PEACE OFFERINGS (HEB. SHLAMIM) BRINGS PEACE (HEB. SHALOM) AND PERFECTION (HEB. SHLEMUT). They are the perfection of the directions of the world, overall perfection from the aspect of Faith, MALCHUT. Since peace offerings are overall peace, the owners eat of them and enjoy them, for it gives

FOURTH READING - MOSES - NETZACH

3 וְאִם־ זֶבַח שְׁלָמִים קָרְבָּנוֹ אִם מִן־הַבָּקָר הוּא
מַקְרִיב אִם־זָכָר אִם־נְקֵבָה תָּמִים יַקְרִיבֶנּוּ לִפְנֵי
יְהוָה: 2 וְסָמַךְ יָדוֹ עַל־רֹאשׁ קָרְבָּנוֹ
וּשְׁחָטוֹ פֶּתַח אֹהֶל מוֹעֵד וְזָרְקוּ בְּנֵי אַהֲרֹן הַכֹּהֲנִים
אֶת־הַדָּם עַל־הַמִּזְבֵּחַ סָבִיב: 3 וְהִקְרִיב מִזֶּבַח הַשְּׁלָמִים
אִשֶּׁה לַיהוָה אֶת־הַחֵלֶב הַמְכַסֶּה אֶת־הַקֶּרֶב וְאֵת כָּל־
הַחֵלֶב אֲשֶׁר עַל־הַקֶּרֶב: 4 וְאֵת שְׁתֵּי הַכְּלָיֹת וְאֶת־הַחֵלֶב אֲשֶׁר עֲלֵהֶן
אֲשֶׁר עַל־הַכְּסָלִים וְאֶת־הַיֹּתֶרֶת עַל־הַכָּבֵד עַל־הַכְּלָיוֹת יְסִירֶנָּה:
5 וְהִקְטִירוּ אֹתוֹ בְנֵי־אַהֲרֹן הַמִּזְבֵּחָה עַל־הָעֹלָה אֲשֶׁר עַל־
הָעֵצִים אֲשֶׁר עַל־הָאֵשׁ אִשֵּׁה רֵיחַ נִיחֹחַ לַיהוָה: 6 וְאִם
מִן־הַצֹּאן קָרְבָּנוֹ לְזֶבַח שְׁלָמִים לַיהוָה
זָכָר אוֹ נְקֵבָה תָּמִים יַקְרִיבֶנּוּ: 7 אִם־כֶּשֶׂב הוּא־
מַקְרִיב אֶת־קָרְבָּנוֹ וְהִקְרִיב אֹתוֹ לִפְנֵי יְהוָה: 8 וְסָמַךְ
אֶת־יָדוֹ עַל־רֹאשׁ קָרְבָּנוֹ וְשָׁחַט אֹתוֹ לִפְנֵי
אֹהֶל מוֹעֵד וְזָרְקוּ בְּנֵי אַהֲרֹן אֶת־דָּמוֹ עַל־הַמִּזְבֵּחַ
סָבִיב: 9 וְהִקְרִיב מִזֶּבַח הַשְּׁלָמִים אִשֶּׁה לַיהוָה חֶלְבּוֹ הָאַלְיָה
תְמִימָה לְעֻמַּת הֶעָצֶה יְסִירֶנָּה וְאֶת־הַחֵלֶב הַמְכַסֶּה אֶת־הַקֶּרֶב וְאֵת
כָּל־הַחֵלֶב אֲשֶׁר עַל־הַקֶּרֶב: 10 וְאֵת שְׁתֵּי הַכְּלָיֹת וְאֶת־הַחֵלֶב

---

one peace and everyone is on the same level. Sin offerings and guilt offerings are eaten by the priests alone, NOT BY THE PEOPLE WHO BROUGHT THEM, since it is for the priests to atone for them and to commute their sins. Of all offerings, the peace offerings are the most beloved by the Holy One, blessed be He, because they bring peace to the Upper and Lower beings.
—The Zohar, Vayikra 24:164

¹¹ *And the priest shall burn it on the altar, a food offering made to the Lord by fire.*

¹² *If his offering is a goat, he is to present it before the Lord.*

¹³ *He is to lay his hand on its head and slaughter it in front of the Tent of Meeting. Then Aaron's sons shall sprinkle its blood against the altar on all sides.*

¹⁴ *From what he offers he is to make this offering to the Lord by fire: all the fat that covers the inner parts and the fat that is connected to the inner parts,*

¹⁵ *both kidneys with the fat on them near the loins, and the covering of the liver, which he will remove with the kidneys.*

¹⁶ *The priest shall burn them on the altar as food, an offering made by fire, a pleasing aroma. All the fat is the Lord's.*

¹⁷ *This is a lasting ordinance for the generations to come, wherever you live: You must not eat any fat or any blood."*

FIFTH READING - AARON - HOD

4:¹ The Lord said to Moses, saying, ² "Say to the Children of Israel the following: When anyone sins unintentionally and does what is forbidden in any of the Lord's commands:

³ *If the anointed priest sins, bringing guilt on the people, he must bring to the Lord a young bull without defect as a sin offering for the sin he has committed.*

⁴ *He is to present the bull at the entrance to the Tent of Meeting before the Lord. He is to lay his hand on its head and slaughter it before the Lord.*

Leviticus 4:3 – The priests also had to give sin offerings. No matter how elevated their souls were, even priests committed negative actions occasionally. Their sin offerings were different from those of the people because of their priestly power to affect others—any negative action on their part had an impact on everyone they acted on behalf of. We learn here that the Universal Law of Cause and Effect is more stringent for those who have greater responsibility.

Rav Yitzchak said, "If the priest that is anointed does sin..." [This] refers to the priest Below, who prepares himself for service IN THE TEMPLE and a sin is found in him, it "brings guiltiness of the people," FOR THE PEOPLE WILL BE BLAMED FOR IT, BECAUSE woe to those who rely ON HIS SERVICE. Similarly, if a

אֲשֶׁר עֲלֵהֶן אֲשֶׁר עַל־הַכְּסָלִים וְאֶת־הַיֹּתֶרֶת עַל־הַכָּבֵד עַל־הַכְּלָיֹת

יְסִירֶנָּה: 11 וְהִקְטִירוֹ הַכֹּהֵן מלה הַמִּזְבֵּחָה לֶחֶם ג"פ יהוה אִשֶּׁה לַיהֹוָה‎אלהים‎אהדונהי:

12 וְאִם יוהך, ע"ה מ"ב עֵז קָרְבָּנוֹ וְהִקְרִיבוֹ לִפְנֵי חכמה בינה יְהֹוָה‎אלהים‎אהדונהי: 13 וְסָמַךְ

אֶת־יָדוֹ עַל־רֹאשׁוֹ וְשָׁחַט אֹתוֹ לִפְנֵי חכמה בינה אֹהֶל לאה מוֹעֵד וְזָרְקוּ בְּנֵי

אַהֲרֹן ע"ב ורבוע ע"ב אֶת־דָּמוֹ עַל־הַמִּזְבֵּחַ זן, נגד סָבִיב: 14 וְהִקְרִיב מִמֶּנּוּ

קָרְבָּנוֹ אִשֶּׁה לַיהֹוָה‎אלהים‎אהדונהי אֶת־הַחֵלֶב הַמְכַסֶּה אֶת־הַקֶּרֶב וְאֵת

כָּל־ ילי הַחֵלֶב אֲשֶׁר עַל־הַקֶּרֶב: 15 וְאֵת שְׁתֵּי הַכְּלָיֹת וְאֶת־הַחֵלֶב

אֲשֶׁר עֲלֵהֶן אֲשֶׁר עַל־הַכְּסָלִים וְאֶת־הַיֹּתֶרֶת עַל־הַכָּבֵד עַל־הַכְּלָיֹת

יְסִירֶנָּה: 16 וְהִקְטִירָם הַכֹּהֵן מלה הַמִּזְבֵּחָה לֶחֶם ג"פ יהוה אִשֶּׁה לְרֵיחַ רמ"ח

נִיחֹחַ כָּל־ ילי הַחֵלֶב לַיהֹוָה‎אלהים‎אהדונהי: 17 חֻקַּת עוֹלָם לְדֹרֹתֵיכֶם בְּכֹל

בין, לכב, יבמ מוֹשְׁבֹתֵיכֶם כָּל־ ילי הַחֵלֶב וְכָל־ ילי ־דָּם רבוע אהיה לֹא תֹאכֵלוּ:

FIFTH READING - AARON - HOD

4 1 וַיְדַבֵּר ראה יְהֹוָה‎אלהים‎אהדונהי אֶל־מֹשֶׁה מהש, אל שדי לֵּאמֹר: 2 דַּבֵּר ראה

אֶל־בְּנֵי יִשְׂרָאֵל לֵאמֹר כִּי־תֶחֱטָא בִשְׁגָגָה מִכֹּל ילי רמ"ח ־ ז הויות נֶפֶשׁ

מִצְוֹת יְהֹוָה‎אלהים‎אהדונהי אֲשֶׁר לֹא תֵעָשֶׂינָה וְעָשָׂה מֵאַחַת מֵהֵנָּה מ"ה, יה:

3 אִם יוהך, ע"ה מ"ב הַמָּשִׁיחַ יֶחֱטָא לְאַשְׁמַת הָעָם וְהִקְרִיב עַל מלה הַכֹּהֵן

חַטָּאתוֹ אֲשֶׁר חָטָא פַּר בזֶוֹהֶר, ערי, סנדלפון בֶּן־בָּקָר תָּמִים לַיהֹוָה‎אלהים‎אהדונהי

לְחַטָּאת: 4 וְהֵבִיא אֶת־הַפָּר בזֶוֹהֶר, ערי, סנדלפון אֶל־פֶּתַח אֹהֶל לאה מוֹעֵד לִפְנֵי

חכמה בינה יְהֹוָה‎אלהים‎אהדונהי וְסָמַךְ אֶת־יָדוֹ עַל־רֹאשׁ ריבוע אלהים ואלהים דיודין ע"ה הַפָּר

בזֶוֹהֶר, ערי, סנדלפון וְשָׁחַט אֶת־הַפָּר בזֶוֹהֶר, ערי, סנדלפון לִפְנֵי חכמה בינה יְהֹוָה‎אלהים‎אהדונהי

---

sin is found in the cantor, woe to those who count on him. Rav Yehuda said, All the more so the priest, to whom all Israel

Above and Below look and expect to be blessed by.
— The Zohar, Vayikra 43:298

5 Then the anointed priest shall take some of the bull's blood and carry it into the Tent of Meeting.

6 The priest is to dip his finger into the blood and sprinkle some of it seven times before the Lord, in front of the curtain of the sanctuary.

7 The priest shall then put some of the blood on the horns of the altar of fragrant incense that is before the Lord in the Tent of Meeting. The rest of the bull's blood he shall pour out at the base of the altar of burnt offering at the entrance to the Tent of Meeting.

8 He shall remove all the fat from the bull of the sin offering—the fat that covers the inner parts and the fat that is connected to the inner parts,

9 both kidneys with the fat on them near the loins, and the covering of the liver, which he will remove with the kidneys –

10 just as the fat is removed from the ox sacrificed as a peace offering. Then the priest shall burn them on the altar of burnt offering.

11 But the hide of the bull and all its flesh, as well as the head and legs, the inner parts and offal –

12 that is, all the rest of the bull—he must take outside the camp to a place ceremonially clean, where the ashes are thrown, and burn it in a wood fire on the ash heap.

13 If the whole Israelite community sins unintentionally—that is, the matter is not known to the community that they have sinned—and does what is forbidden in any of the Lord's commands, they are guilty.

14 When they become aware of the sin they have committed, the assembly must bring a young bull as a sin offering and present it before the Tent of Meeting.

15 The elders of the community are to lay their hands on the bull's head before the Lord, and the bull shall be slaughtered before the Lord.

כָּל־עֲדַת

Leviticus 4:13 – Sometimes a whole group or generation of people performs the same negative action, indicating that Satan is exerting extra force. If one person does something negative, it is usually caused by circumstances particular to that individual, but if many people fall, it reflects a greater influence by Satan. Whenever there is a critical mass of negativity, the negativity must be countered with a critical mass of positive energy of love and sharing.

5 וְלָקַ֛ח יהוה אהיה יהוה אדני הַכֹּהֵ֥ן מלה הַמָּשִׁ֖יחַ מדם רבוע אהיה מִדַּ֣ם הַפָּ֑ר בֵּזֶּזֶּךְ, עֲרִי, סְנְדַּלְפוֹן

וְהֵבִ֥יא אֹת֖וֹ אֶל־אֹ֥הֶל לאה מוֹעֵֽד׃ 6 וְטָבַ֧ל הַכֹּהֵ֛ן מלה אֶת־אֶצְבָּע֖וֹ בַּדָּ֑ם

רבוע אהיה וְהִזָּ֨ה והו מִן־הַדָּ֜ם רבוע אהיה שֶׁ֤בַע ע״ב ואלהים דיורין פְּעָמִים֙ וזְכְמָה בינה לִפְנֵ֣י

יְהֹוָ֔הֽואדניאהדונהי אֶת־פְּנֵ֖י וזכמה בינה פָּרֹ֥כֶת הַקֹּֽדֶשׁ׃ 7 וְנָתַ֣ן אבניתך, ושׂר, אהבת חנם

הַכֹּהֵ֡ן מלה מִן־הַדָּ֣ם רבוע אהיה עַל־קַרְנ֩וֹת מִזְבַּ֨ח ז״ן, נגד קְטֹ֜רֶת הַסַּמִּ֗ים י״א אדני

ע״ה קנ״א, אלהים אדני לִפְנֵ֤י וזכמה בינה יְהֹוָה֙ואדניאהדונהי אֲשֶׁ֣ר בְּאֹ֣הֶל לאה מוֹעֵ֔ד וְאֵ֣ת ׀

כָּל־יְלִי דַּ֣ם׀ רבוע אהיה הַפָּ֗ר בֵּזֶּזֶּךְ, עֲרִי, סְנְדַּלְפוֹן יִשְׁפֹּךְ֙ אֶל־יְסוֹד֙ ההע מִזְבַּ֣ח ז״ן, נגד

הָעֹלָ֔ה אֲשֶׁר־פֶּ֖תַח אֹ֥הֶל לאה מוֹעֵֽד׃ 8 וְאֶת־כָּל־יְלי חֵ֛לֶב פַּ֥ר בֵּזֶּזֶּךְ, עֲרִי, סְנְדַּלְפוֹן

הַֽחַטָּ֖את יָרִ֣ים מִמֶּ֑נּוּ אֶת־הַחֵ֙לֶב֙ הַֽמְכַסֶּ֣ה עַל־הַקֶּ֔רֶב וְאֵת֙ כָּל־יְלי הַחֵ֔לֶב

אֲשֶׁ֖ר עַל־הַקֶּֽרֶב׃ 9 וְאֵת֙ שְׁתֵּ֣י הַכְּלָיֹ֔ת וְאֶת־הַחֵ֙לֶב֙ אֲשֶׁ֣ר עֲלֵיהֶ֔ן אֲשֶׁ֖ר

עַל־הַכְּסָלִ֑ים וְאֶת־הַיֹּתֶ֙רֶת֙ עַל־הַכָּבֵ֔ד עַל־הַכְּלָי֖וֹת יְסִירֶֽנָּה׃ 10 כַּאֲשֶׁ֣ר

יוּרַ֗ם אבניתך, ושׂר, אהבת חנם מִשּׁ֥וֹר זֶ֣בַח הַשְּׁלָמִ֑ים וְהִקְטִירָם֙ הַכֹּהֵ֔ן מלה עַ֖ל

מִזְבַּ֣ח ז״ן, נגד הָעֹלָֽה׃ 11 וְאֶת־ע֤וֹר הַפָּר֙ בֵּזֶּזֶּךְ, עֲרִי, סְנְדַּלְפוֹן וְאֶת־כָּל־יְלי בְּשָׂר֔וֹ

עַל־רֹאשׁ֖וֹ וְעַל־כְּרָעָ֑יו וְקִרְבּ֖וֹ וּפִרְשֽׁוֹ׃ 12 וְהוֹצִ֣יא אֶת־כָּל־יְלי הַפָּ֡ר בֵּ

בֵּזֶּזֶּךְ, עֲרִי, סְנְדַּלְפוֹן אֶל־מִח֣וּץ לַֽמַּחֲנֶה֩ אֶל־מָק֨וֹם יהוה ברבוע ר״פ אל טָה֜וֹר ר״פ אכא אֶל־

שֶׁ֣פֶךְ הַדֶּ֗שֶׁן וְשָׂרַ֤ף אֹתוֹ֙ עַל־עֵצִ֣ים בָּאֵ֔שׁ אלהים דיורין ע״ה עַל־שֶׁ֥פֶךְ הַדֶּ֖שֶׁן

יִשָּׂרֵֽף׃ 13 וְאִ֤ם יוהך, ע״ה מ״ב כָּל־יְלי עֲדַ֣ת יִשְׂרָאֵל֙ יִשְׁגּ֔וּ וְנֶעְלַ֣ם דָּבָ֔ר ראה

מֵעֵינֵ֖י ריבוע מ״ה הַקָּהָ֑ל ע״ב ס״ג וְעָשׂ֗וּ אַחַ֤ת מִכָּל־יְלי מִצְוֺת֙ יְהֹוָ֔הואדניאהדונהי

אֲשֶׁ֖ר לֹא־תֵעָשֶׂ֑ינָה וְאָשֵֽׁמוּ׃ 14 וְנֽוֹדְעָה֙ הַֽחַטָּ֔את אֲשֶׁ֥ר חָטְא֖וּ עָלֶ֑יהָ

פהל וְהִקְרִ֣יבוּ הַקָּהָ֗ל ע״ב ס״ג פַּ֣ר בֵּזֶּזֶּךְ, עֲרִי, סְנְדַּלְפוֹן בֶּן־בָּקָר֙ לְחַטָּ֔את וְהֵבִ֣יאוּ

אֹת֔וֹ לִפְנֵ֖י וזכמה בינה אֹ֥הֶל לאה מוֹעֵֽד׃ 15 וְסָ֨מְכ֜וּ זִקְנֵ֧י הָעֵדָ֛ה אֶת־

יְדֵיהֶ֖ם עַל־רֹ֣אשׁ ריבוע אלהים ואלהים דיורין ע״ה הַפָּ֑ר בֵּזֶּזֶּךְ, עֲרִי, סְנְדַּלְפוֹן לִפְנֵ֣י וזכמה בינה

יְהֹוָ֑הואדניאהדונהי וְשָׁחַ֥ט אֶת־הַפָּ֖ר בֵּזֶּזֶּךְ, עֲרִי, סְנְדַּלְפוֹן לִפְנֵ֥י וזכמה בינה יְהֹוָֽהואדניאהדונהי׃

16 וְהֵבִ֛יא הַכֹּהֵ֥ן הַמָּשִׁ֖יחַ מדם רבוע אהיה הַפָּ֑ר בֵּזֶּזֶּךְ, עֲרִי, סְנְדַּלְפוֹן אֶל־אֹ֥הֶל

¹⁶ Then the anointed priest is to take some of the bull's blood into the Tent of Meeting.

¹⁷ He shall dip his finger into the blood and sprinkle it before the Lord seven times in front of the curtain.

¹⁸ He is to put some of the blood on the horns of the altar that is before the Lord in the Tent of Meeting. The rest of the blood he shall pour out at the base of the altar of burnt offering at the entrance to the Tent of Meeting.

¹⁹ He shall remove all the fat from it and burn it on the altar,

²⁰ and do with this bull just as he did with the bull for the sin offering. In this way the priest will make atonement for them, and they will be forgiven.

²¹ Then he shall take the bull outside the camp and burn it as he burned the first bull. This is the sin offering for the community.

²² When a leader sins, and unintentionally does what is forbidden in any of the commands of the Lord his God, he is guilty.

²³ When he is made aware of the sin he committed, he must bring as his offering a male goat without defect.

²⁴ He is to lay his hand on the goat's head and slaughter it at the place where the burnt offering is slaughtered before the Lord. It is a sin offering.

²⁵ And the priest shall take some of the blood of the sin offering with his finger and put it on the horns of the altar of burnt offering and pour out the rest of the blood at the base of the altar.

²⁶ He shall burn all the fat on the altar as he burned the fat of the peace offering. In this way the priest will make atonement for the man's sin, and he will be forgiven.

נְשִׂיא יֶחֱטָא

Leviticus 4:22 – The Bible recognizes the great probability that rulers will sin, which is why it uses the phrase "when a ruler sins" rather than "if a ruler sins." Rulers often tend to think of themselves first, but those who think only of themselves will inevitably fall. To be successful, rulers must free themselves from the domination of their ego.

In the *Zohar*, we learn why it was the rulers who were to bring onyx and precious stones for the *Ephod* (breastplate) that the priest customarily wore over his heart. The *Zohar* text says:

מוֹעֵד: 17 וְטָבַל הַכֹּהֵן אֶצְבָּעוֹ מִן־הַדָּם וְהִזָּה שֶׁבַע

פְּעָמִים לִפְנֵי יְהֹוָה אֵת פְּנֵי הַפָּרֹכֶת:

18 וּמִן־הַדָּם יִתֵּן | עַל־קַרְנֹת הַמִּזְבֵּחַ אֲשֶׁר לִפְנֵי

יְהֹוָה אֲשֶׁר בְּאֹהֶל מוֹעֵד וְאֵת כָּל־הַדָּם יִשְׁפֹּךְ

אֶל־יְסוֹד מִזְבַּח הָעֹלָה אֲשֶׁר־פֶּתַח אֹהֶל מוֹעֵד: 19 וְאֵת כָּל

חֶלְבּוֹ יָרִים מִמֶּנּוּ וְהִקְטִיר הַמִּזְבֵּחָה: 20 וְעָשָׂה לַפָּר

כַּאֲשֶׁר עָשָׂה לְפַר הַחַטָּאת כֵּן יַעֲשֶׂה־לּוֹ וְכִפֶּר עֲלֵהֶם

הַכֹּהֵן וְנִסְלַח לָהֶם: 21 וְהוֹצִיא אֶת־הַפָּר אֶל־מִחוּץ

לַמַּחֲנֶה וְשָׂרַף אֹתוֹ כַּאֲשֶׁר שָׂרַף אֵת הַפָּר הָרִאשׁוֹן

חַטַּאת הַקָּהָל הוּא: 22 אֲשֶׁר]נָשִׂיא יֶחֱטָא[וְעָשָׂה אַחַת מִכָּל

מִצְוֹת יְהֹוָה אֱלֹהָיו אֲשֶׁר לֹא־תֵעָשֶׂינָה בִּשְׁגָגָה וְאָשֵׁם:

23 אוֹ־הוֹדַע אֵלָיו חַטָּאתוֹ אֲשֶׁר חָטָא בָּהּ וְהֵבִיא אֶת־קָרְבָּנוֹ שְׂעִיר

עִזִּים זָכָר תָּמִים: 24 וְסָמַךְ יָדוֹ עַל־רֹאשׁ הַשָּׂעִיר

וְשָׁחַט אֹתוֹ בִּמְקוֹם אֲשֶׁר־יִשְׁחַט אֶת־הָעֹלָה לִפְנֵי

יְהֹוָה חַטָּאת הוּא: 25 וְלָקַח הַכֹּהֵן מִדַּם

הַחַטָּאת בְּאֶצְבָּעוֹ וְנָתַן עַל־קַרְנֹת מִזְבַּח

הָעֹלָה וְאֶת־דָּמוֹ יִשְׁפֹּךְ אֶל־יְסוֹד מִזְבֵּחַ הָעֹלָה: 26 וְאֶת־כָּל

חֶלְבּוֹ יַקְטִיר הַמִּזְבֵּחָה כְּחֵלֶב זֶבַח הַשְּׁלָמִים וְכִפֶּר עָלָיו הַכֹּהֵן

מֵחַטָּאתוֹ וְנִסְלַח לוֹ:

"God said, 'Let the rulers, whose heart is proud, come and bring these stones that are on the priest's heart, and their heart's pride will be atoned for.' This is why the rulers brought the onyx stones, to atone for themselves."
— The Zohar, Vayikra 60:391-392

SIXTH READING - JOSEPH - YESOD

27 If a member of the nation sins unintentionally, doing what is forbidden in any of the Lord's commands, he is guilty. 28 When he is made aware of the sin he committed, he must bring as his offering a female goat without defect for the sin he committed.

29 He is to lay his hand on the head of the sin offering and slaughter it at the place of the burnt offering. 30 Then the priest is to take some of the blood with his finger and put it on the horns of the altar of burnt offering and pour out the rest of the blood at the base of the altar.

31 He shall remove all the fat, just as the fat is removed from the peace offering, and the priest shall burn it on the altar as an aroma pleasing to the Lord. In this way the priest will make atonement for him, and he will be forgiven.

32 If he brings a lamb as his sin offering, he is to bring a female without defect. 33 He is to lay his hand on its head and slaughter it for a sin offering at the place where the burnt offering is slaughtered.

34 Then the priest shall take some of the blood of the sin offering with his finger and put it on the horns of the altar of burnt offering and pour out the rest of the blood at the base of the altar.

35 He shall remove all the fat, just as the fat is removed from the lamb of the peace offering, and the priest shall burn it on the altar on top of the offerings made to the Lord by fire. In this way, the priest will make atonement for him for the sin he has committed, and he will be forgiven.

5:1 If a person sins because he does not speak up when he hears a public charge to testify regarding something he has was witness to, or seen or learned about, he will be held responsible.

נֶפֶשׁ

Leviticus 4:27 – When people sin, it is not enough that they just correct their negative action; they must also feel the pain of those whom they have hurt. This sometimes means that the perpetrator and the injured party will have to meet face to face. Correcting ourselves and promising better behavior in future must be supplemented by erasing the pain we've caused other people by our negative actions.

In *Vayikra* 36:263, the *Zohar* discusses the meaning of "he shall restore," saying that someone who corrects his sinful action will restore the springs of water—that is, the abundance Above in the Supernal Realms—to their proper places, where they can water the plants that are the *Sefirot*.

SIXTH READING - JOSEPH - YESOD

27 וְאִם יוהך, ע״ה מ״ב רמ״ח ± ד׳ הוויות **נֶפֶשׁ** אַחַת תֶּחֱטָא בִשְׁגָגָה מֵעַם הָאָרֶץ

אלהים דההין ע״ה בַּעֲשֹׂתָהּ אַחַת מִמִּצְוֹת יְהוֹ^{אדני}אהדונהי אֲשֶׁר לֹא־תֵעָשֶׂינָה

וְאָשֵׁם: 28 אוֹ הוֹדַע אֵלָיו חַטָּאתוֹ אֲשֶׁר חָטָא וְהֵבִיא קָרְבָּנוֹ שְׂעִירַת

עִזִּים תְּמִימָה נְקֵבָה עַל־חַטָּאתוֹ אֲשֶׁר חָטָא: 29 וְסָמַךְ אֶת־יָדוֹ עַל

רֹאשׁ ריבוע אלהים ואלהים דיודין ע״ה הַחַטָּאת וְשָׁחַט אֶת־הַחַטָּאת בִּמְקוֹם

יהוה ברבוע, ר״פ אל הָעֹלָה: 30 וְלָקַח יהוה אהיה אהוה אדני הַכֹּהֵן מלה מִדָּמָהּ בְּאֶצְבָּעוֹ

אבגית״ץ, ועטר, אהבת חנם וְנָתַן עַל־קַרְנֹת מִזְבַּח זן, נגד הָעֹלָה וְאֶת־כָּל־ יּלי דָּמָהּ

יִשְׁפֹּךְ אֶל־יְסוֹד ההע הַמִּזְבֵּחַ זן, נגד: 31 וְאֶת־כָּל־ יּלי חֶלְבָּהּ יָסִיר כַּאֲשֶׁר

הוּסַר חֵלֶב עלם מֵעַל זֶבַח הַשְּׁלָמִים וְהִקְטִיר הַכֹּהֵן מלה הַמִּזְבֵּחָה

לְרֵיחַ רמ״ח נִיחֹחַ לַיהוֹ^{אדני}אהדונהי וְכִפֶּר מצפצ עָלָיו הַכֹּהֵן מלה וְנִסְלַח לוֹ:

32 וְאִם יוהך, ע״ה מ״ב ב״פ קס״א **כֶּבֶשׂ** יָבִיא קָרְבָּנוֹ לְחַטָּאת נְקֵבָה תְּמִימָה

יְבִיאֶנָּה: 33 וְסָמַךְ אֶת־יָדוֹ עַל רֹאשׁ ריבוע אלהים ואלהים דיודין ע״ה הַחַטָּאת

וְשָׁחַט אֹתָהּ לְחַטָּאת בִּמְקוֹם יהוה ברבוע, ר״פ אל אֲשֶׁר יִשְׁחַט אֶת־הָעֹלָה:

34 וְלָקַח יהוה אהיה יהוה אדני הַכֹּהֵן מלה רבוע אהיה מִדַּם הַחַטָּאת בְּאֶצְבָּעוֹ וְנָתַן

אבגית״ץ, ועטר, אהבת חנם עַל־קַרְנֹת מִזְבַּח זן, נגד הָעֹלָה וְאֶת־כָּל־ יּלי דָּמָהּ יִשְׁפֹּךְ

אֶל־יְסוֹד ההע הַמִּזְבֵּחַ זן, נגד: 35 וְאֶת־כָּל־ יּלי חֶלְבָּהּ יָסִיר כַּאֲשֶׁר יוּסַר

וְחֵלֶב־הַכֶּשֶׂב ב״פ קס״א מִזֶּבַח הַשְּׁלָמִים וְהִקְטִיר הַכֹּהֵן מלה אֹתָם הַמִּזְבֵּחָה

עַל אִשֵּׁי יְהוֹ^{אדני}אהדונהי וְכִפֶּר מצפצ עָלָיו הַכֹּהֵן מלה עַל־חַטָּאתוֹ אֲשֶׁר־חָטָא

וְנִסְלַח לוֹ: 5 1 וְנֶפֶשׁ רמ״ח ± ד׳ הוויות כִּי־תֶחֱטָא וְשָׁמְעָה קוֹל ע״ב ס״ג ע״ה אָלָה וְהוּא

עֵד אוֹ רָאָה ראה אוֹ יָדָע ב״פ מ״ב אִם יוהך, ע״ה מ״ב לוֹא יַגִּיד וְנָשָׂא עֲוֹנוֹ: 2 אוֹ

נֶפֶשׁ רמ״ח ± ד׳ הוויות אֲשֶׁר תִּגַּע בְּכָל־ בן, לכב, יבם דָּבָר ראה טָמֵא אוֹ בְנִבְלַת

חַיָּה טְמֵאָה אוֹ בְּנִבְלַת בְּהֵמָה בן, לכב, יבם טְמֵאָה אוֹ בְּנִבְלַת שֶׁרֶץ טָמֵא

² Or if a person touches anything ceremonially unclean—whether the carcass of an unclean wild animal or the carcass of an unclean livestock or the carcass of an unclean creature that moves along the ground—even though he is unaware of it, he has become unclean and is guilty.

³ Or if he touches human uncleanness—anything that would make him unclean—even though he is unaware of it, when he learns of it he will be guilty.

⁴ Or if a person thoughtlessly takes an oath to do anything, whether good or evil—in any matter one might carelessly swear about—even though he is unaware of it, in any case when he learns of it, he will be guilty.

⁵ When anyone is guilty in any of these ways, he must confess in what way he has sinned

⁶ and, as a penalty for the sin he has committed, he must bring to the Lord a female lamb or goat from the flock as a sin offering; and the priest shall make atonement for him for his sin.⁷ If he cannot afford a lamb, he is to bring, as a penalty for his sin, two doves or two young pigeons to the Lord—one for a sin offering and the other for a burnt offering.

⁸ He is to bring them to the priest, who shall first offer the one for the sin offering. He is to wring its head from its neck, not severing it completely,

⁹ and he is to sprinkle some of the blood of the sin offering against the side of the altar; the rest of the blood must be drained out at the base of the altar. It is a sin offering.

¹⁰ The priest shall then offer the other as a burnt offering in the prescribed way and make atonement for him for the sin he has committed, and he will be forgiven.

SEVENTH READING - DAVID - MALCHUT

¹¹ If he cannot afford two doves or two young pigeons, he is to bring as an offering for his sin a tenth of an ephah of fine flour for a sin offering. He must not put oil on it and he must not put incense on it, because it is a sin offering.

תִּשָּׁבַע

Leviticus 5:4 – Speech has tremendous power. If we say we're going to do something, it's as though we've already done it. Not following through with a promise that we make creates a metaphysical space between our words and our uncompleted action. Because empty space is inhabited by Satan, it's important to deliver on our promises to avoid making an opening for him. This reading gives us an opportunity to annihilate the spaces that we generate from our broken promises. But

וְנֶעְלַם מִמֶּנּוּ וְהוּא טָמֵא וְאָשֵׁם: 3 אוֹ כִי יִגַּע בְּטֻמְאַת אָדָם מ״ה לְכֹל

טֻמְאָתוֹ אֲשֶׁר יִטְמָא בָּהּ וְנֶעְלַם מִמֶּנּוּ וְהוּא יָדַע בי״פ מ״ב וְאָשֵׁם:

4 אוֹ נֶפֶשׁ רמ״ח - ז הויות כִּי תִשָּׁבַע לְבַטֵּא בִשְׂפָתַיִם לְהָרַע | אוֹ לְהֵיטִיב

לְכֹל אֲשֶׁר יְבַטֵּא הָאָדָם מ״ה בִּשְׁבֻעָה וְנֶעְלַם מִמֶּנּוּ וְהוּא־יָדַע בי״פ מ״ב

וְאָשֵׁם לְאַחַת מֵאֵלֶּה: 5 וְהָיָה יהוה כִי־יֶאְשַׁם לְאַחַת מֵאֵלֶּה וְהִתְוַדָּה אֲשֶׁר

חָטָא עָלֶיהָ פהכל: 6 וְהֵבִיא אֶת־אֲשָׁמוֹ לַיהוה אדני־אהדונהי עַל חַטָּאתוֹ אֲשֶׁר

חָטָא נְקֵבָה מִן־הַצֹּאן כִּשְׂבָּה אוֹ־שְׂעִירַת עִזִּים לְחַטָּאת

וְכִפֶּר מצפצ עָלָיו הַכֹּהֵן מלה מֵחַטָּאתוֹ: 7 וְאִם עה״ך, יוהך, עֹה מ״ב לֹא תַגִּיע יָדוֹ דֵּי

שֶׂה וְהֵבִיא אֶת־אֲשָׁמוֹ אֲשֶׁר חָטָא שְׁתֵּי תֹרִים אוֹ־שְׁנֵי בְנֵי־יוֹנָה כ״ו מ״ה

לַיהוה אדני־אהדונהי אֶחָד אהבה, דאגה לְחַטָּאת וְאֶחָד אהבה, דאגה לְעֹלָה: 8 וְהֵבִיא

אֹתָם אֶל־הַכֹּהֵן מלה וְהִקְרִיב אֶת־אֲשֶׁר לַחַטָּאת רִאשׁוֹנָה וּמָלַק אֶת־

רֹאשׁוֹ מִמּוּל עָרְפּוֹ וְלֹא יַבְדִּיל: 9 וְהִזָּה רבוע אהיה מִדַּם וֹהוּ הַחַטָּאת עַל־

קִיר הַמִּזְבֵּחַ זן, גגד וְהַנִּשְׁאָר בַּדָּם רבוע אהיה יִמָּצֵה אֶל־יְסוֹד ההע הַמִּזְבֵּחַ זן, גגד

חַטָּאת הוּא: 10 וְאֶת־הַשֵּׁנִי יַעֲשֶׂה עֹלָה כַּמִּשְׁפָּט עה הי אלהים וְכִפֶּר מצפצ

עָלָיו הַכֹּהֵן מלה מֵחַטָּאתוֹ אֲשֶׁר־חָטָא וְנִסְלַח לוֹ:

SEVENTH READING - DAVID - MALCHUT

11 וְאִם יוהך, עֹה מ״ב לֹא תַשִּׂיג - יָדוֹ לִשְׁתֵּי תֹרִים אוֹ לִשְׁנֵי בְנֵי־יוֹנָה כ״ו מ״ה

וְהֵבִיא אֶת־קָרְבָּנוֹ אֲשֶׁר חָטָא עֲשִׂירִת הָאֵפָה אלהים סֹלֶת לְחַטָּאת לֹא־

---

it is certainly easier to avoid creating those spaces in the first place, which is why we must always do what we say we will do.

לֹא תַשִּׂיג

Leviticus 5:11 – Our sacrifices should be commensurate with what we are able to give.

If we can't afford a costly sacrifice, we should offer a less expensive one. However, if we give less than our capacity, it's as though we gave nothing. On the other hand, if we have very little to offer but give anyway, it's as though we have given a million dollars. What matters is the effort we make, as well as the consciousness behind our sacrifice.

12 He is to bring it to the priest, who shall take a handful of it as a memorial portion and burn it on the altar on top of the offerings made to the Lord by fire. It is a sin offering.

13 In this way the priest will make atonement for him for any of these sins he has committed, and he will be forgiven. The rest of the offering will belong to the priest, as in the case of the meal offering." 14 The Lord spoke to Moses, saying:

15 "When a person commits a violation and sins unintentionally in regard to any of the Lord's holy things, he is to bring to the Lord, as a penalty, a ram from the flock, one without defect and of the proper value in silver, according to the sanctuary shekel. It is a guilt offering.

16 He must make restitution for what he has failed to do in regard to the holy things, add a fifth of the value to that and give it all to the priest, who will make atonement for him with the ram of the guilt offering, and he will be forgiven.

17 If a person sins and does what is forbidden in any of the Lord's commands, even though he does not know it, he is guilty and will be held responsible.

18 He is to bring to the priest as a guilt offering a ram from the flock, one without defect and of the proper value. In this way the priest will make atonement for him for the wrong he has committed unintentionally, and he will be forgiven.

19 It is a guilt offering; he has been guilty of wrongdoing against the Lord." 20 The Lord spoke to Moses, saying: 21 "If anyone sins and is unfaithful to the Lord by deceiving his neighbor about something entrusted to him or left in his care or stolen, or if he cheats him,

22 or if he finds lost property and lies about it, or if he swears falsely, or if he commits any such sin that people may do – 23 when he thus sins and becomes guilty, he must return what he has stolen or taken by extortion, or what was entrusted to him, or the lost property he found,

---

בִּשְׁגָגָה

Leviticus 5:15 – Whether we do negative things intentionally or unintentionally is irrelevant—the law of Cause and Effect still applies. It was the lowering of our spiritual consciousness so that Satan could enter that enabled us to commit the negative action in the first place. Therefore, even if our action wasn't intentional, we are still responsible for it.

וּמָעֲלָה

Leviticus 5:21 – A certain amount of money is allotted to us each year. If we act dishonestly to get more, the money we were supposed to receive in the first place won't come to us. Thus, not only will we lose the profit from our theft, but we will get even less than we originally deserved. Stealing is a way of trying to circumvent the laws of the universe—laws that cannot be broken.

יָשִׂים עָלֶיהָ שֶׁמֶן פהל י"פ טל, י"פ כוו"ו, ביט וְלֹא־יִתֵּן עָלֶיהָ פהל לְבֹנָה כִּי חַטָּאת

הִוא: 12 וֶהֱבִיאָהּ אֶל־הַכֹּהֵן מלה וְקָמַץ הַכֹּהֵן מלה | מִמֶּנָּה מְלוֹא קֻמְצוֹ

אֶת־אַזְכָּרָתָה וְהִקְטִיר הַמִּזְבֵּחָה עַל אִשֵּׁי יְהוָׁ אהדני ﬞ זﬞ הויות אהדני וְחַטָּאת הִוא:

13 וְכִפֶּר מצפצ עָלָיו הַכֹּהֵן מלה עַל־חַטָּאתוֹ אֲשֶׁר־חָטָא מֵאַחַת מֵאֵלֶּה

וְנִסְלַח לוֹ וְהָיְתָה לַכֹּהֵן כַּמִּנְחָה מלה ע"ה ב"פ בﬞן 14 וַיְדַבֵּר ראה יְהוָׁ אהדני אהדני

אֶל־מֹשֶׁה מהﬞע, אל שדי לֵּאמֹר: 15 נֶפֶשׁ רמ"ח ﬩ זﬞ הויות כִּי־תִמְעֹל מַעַל עלﬞם וְחָטְאָה

בִּשְׁגָגָה מִקָּדְשֵׁי יְהוָׁ אהדני אהדני וְהֵבִיא אֶת־אֲשָׁמוֹ לַיהוָׁ אהדני אהדני אַיִל

תָּמִים מִן־הַצֹּאן מלוי אהיה דיודין ע"ה בְּעֶרְכְּךָ כֶּסֶף־שְׁקָלִים בְּשֶׁקֶל־הַקֹּדֶשׁ

לְאָשָׁם: 16 וְאֵת אֲשֶׁר חָטָא מִן־הַקֹּדֶשׁ יְשַׁלֵּם וְאֶת־חֲמִישִׁתוֹ יוֹסֵף

ציﬞון, ר"פ יהוה עָלָיו וְנָתַן אביﬞת"ﬞ, וﬞער, אהבﬞת ﬞ חﬞם אֹתוֹ לַכֹּהֵן וְהַכֹּהֵן מלה יְכַפֵּר

עָלָיו בְּאֵיל הָאָשָׁם וְנִסְלַח לוֹ: 17 וְאִם־ יוﬞהﬞר, ע"ﬞה ﬞ נֶפֶשׁ רמ"ח ﬩ זﬞ הויות כִּי

תֶחֱטָא וְעָשְׂתָה אַחַת מִכָּל־ יﬞלﬞי מִצְוֹת יְהוָׁ אהדני אהדני אֲשֶׁר לֹא תֵעָשֶׂינָה

וְלֹא־יָדַע ב"פ מ"ב וְאָשֵׁם וְנָשָׂא עֲוֹנוֹ: 18 וְהֵבִיא אַיִל תָּמִים מִן־הַצֹּאן

מלוי אהיה דיודין ע"ה בְּעֶרְכְּךָ לְאָשָׁם אֶל־הַכֹּהֵן מלה וְכִפֶּר מצפצ עָלָיו הַכֹּהֵן

מלה עַל שִׁגְגָתוֹ אֲשֶׁר־שָׁגָג וְהוּא לֹא־יָדַע ב"פ מ"ב וְנִסְלַח לוֹ: 19 אָשָׁם

הוּא אָשֹׁם אָשַׁם לַיהוָׁ אהדני אהדני: 20 וַיְדַבֵּר ראה יְהוָׁ אהדני אהדני אֶל־

מֹשֶׁה מהﬞע, אל שדי לֵּאמֹר: 21 נֶפֶשׁ רמ"ח ﬩ זﬞ הויות כִּי תֶחֱטָא וּמָעֲלָה מַעַל עלﬞם

בַּיהוָׁ אהדני אהדני וְכִחֵשׁ בַּעֲמִיתוֹ בְּפִקָּדוֹן אוֹ־בִתְשׂוּמֶת יָד אוֹ בְגָזֵל אוֹ

עָשַׁק אֶת־עֲמִיתוֹ: 22 אוֹ־מָצָא ק"ל ﬞ ע"ה אֲבֵדָה וְכִחֶשׁ בָּהּ וְנִשְׁבַּע עַל־

שֶׁקֶר עַל־אַחַת מִכֹּל יﬞלﬞי אֲשֶׁר־יַעֲשֶׂה הָאָדָם מﬞה לַחֲטֹא בָהֵנָּה מ"ה, יﬞהﬞ:

23 וְהָיָה יהוה כִּי־יֶחֱטָא וְאָשֵׁם וְהֵשִׁיב אֶת־הַגְּזֵלָה אֲשֶׁר גָּזָל אוֹ אֶת־

הָעֹשֶׁק אֲשֶׁר עָשָׁק אוֹ אֶת־הַפִּקָּדוֹן רביﬞע ﬞ ע"ב אֲשֶׁר הָפְקַד אִתּוֹ אוֹ אֶת־

הָאֲבֵדָה אֲשֶׁר מָצָא ק"ל ﬞ ע"ה:

MAFTIR

²⁴ or whatever it was he swore falsely about. He must make restitution in full, add a fifth of the value to it and give it all to the owner on the day he presents his guilt offering.

²⁵ And as a penalty he must bring to the priest, that is, to the Lord, his guilt offering, a ram from the flock, one without defect and of the proper value.

²⁶ In this way, the priest will make atonement for him before the Lord, and he will be forgiven for any of these things he did that made him guilty."

HAFTARAH OF VAYIKRA

This Haftarah is about cleansing all sins. The Creator speaks to Jacob saying, "I have swept away your offenses like a cloud, your sins like the morning mist. Return to me, for I have redeemed you." (*Isaiah 44:22*)

Isaiah 43:21 – 44:23

43:²¹ "The people I formed for Myself that they may proclaim My praise.

²² Yet you have not called upon Me, Jacob, you have not wearied yourself for Me, Israel.

²³ You have not brought Me sheep for burnt offerings, nor honored Me with your sacrifices. I have not burdened you with a meal offering nor wearied you with frankincense.

²⁴ You have not bought Me any sweet cane with money, nor have you satisfied Me with the fat of your sacrifices; but you have burdened Me with your sins, you have wearied Me with your iniquities.

²⁵ I, even I, am He who blots out your transgressions for My Own Sake, and remembers your sins no more.

²⁶ Review the past for Me, let us plead together; declare you, so that you may be justified.

MAFTIR

24 אוֹ מִכֹּל יﭏﭏ אֲשֶׁר־יִשָּׁבַע עָלָיו לַשֶּׁקֶר וְשִׁלַּם בﭏﭏ רבוע עﭏﭏ אֹתוֹ בְּרֹאשׁוֹ

וַחֲמִשִׁתָיו יֹסֵף עָלָיו לַאֲשֶׁר הוּא לוֹ יִתְּנֶנּוּ בְּיוֹם עﭏﭏ = נגד, זן, מזבח אַשְׁמָתוֹ:

25 וְאֶת־אֲשָׁמוֹ יָבִיא לַיהוָֹהיאהדונהי אַיִל תָּמִים מִן־הַצֹּאן מלוי אהיה דיודין עﭏﭏ

בְּעֶרְכְּךָ לְאָשָׁם אֶל־הַכֹּהֵן מלﭏה: 26 וְכִפֶּר מצפצ עָלָיו הַכֹּהֵן מלﭏה לִפְנֵי וﭏחכמה בינה

יְהוָֹהיאהדונהי וְנִסְלַח לוֹ עַל־אַחַת מִכֹּל יﭏﭏ אֲשֶׁר־יַעֲשֶׂה לְאַשְׁמָה בָהּ:

HAFTARAH OF VAYIKRA

מָחִיתִי כָעָב פְּשָׁעֶיךָ וְכֶעָנָן חַטֹּאותֶיךָ שׁוּבָה אֵלַי כִּי גְאַלְתִּיךָ

This teaches us that as long as we are still in the physical world, we always have the chance to correct and transform ourselves and to reconnect with God.

יְשַׁעְיָהוּ פֶּרֶק מג' – מד'

43 21 עַם־זוּ יָצַרְתִּי לִי תְּהִלָּתִי יְסַפֵּרוּ: 22 וְלֹא־אֹתִי קָרָאתָ יַעֲקֹב

זﭏﭏ יהוה, יאהדונהי אידהנויה כִּי־יָגַעְתָּ בִּי יִשְׂרָאֵל: 23 לֹא־הֵבֵיאתָ לִּי שֵׂה עֹלֹתֶיךָ

וּזְבָחֶיךָ לֹא כִבַּדְתָּנִי לֹא הֶעֱבַדְתִּיךָ בְּמִנְחָה עﭏﭏ בﭏﭏ בﭏﭏ וְלֹא הוֹגַעְתִּיךָ

בִּלְבוֹנָה אדון יוﭏﭏ (אור מקיף) 24 לֹא־קָנִיתָ לִּי בַכֶּסֶף קָנֶה עﭏﭏ = יוסף, ציון, וﭏﭏ יהוה

וְחֵלֶב זְבָחֶיךָ לֹא הִרְוִיתָנִי אַךְ אהיה הֶעֱבַדְתַּנִי בְּחַטֹּאותֶיךָ הוֹגַעְתַּנִי

בַּעֲו‍ֹנֹתֶיךָ: 25 אָנֹכִי איע אָנֹכִי איע הוּא מֹחֶה פְשָׁעֶיךָ לְמַעֲנִי וְחַטֹּאתֶיךָ

לֹא אֶזְכֹּר: 26 הַזְכִּירֵנִי נִשָּׁפְטָה יָחַד כﭏﭏ אתון סַפֵּר אַתָּה לְמַעַן תִּצְדָּק:

27 אָבִיךָ הָרִאשׁוֹן חָטָא וּמְלִיצֶיךָ פָּשְׁעוּ בִי: 28 וַאֲחַלֵּל שָׂרֵי

קֹדֶשׁ וְאֶתְּנָה לַחֵרֶם יַעֲקֹב זﭏﭏ יהוה, יאהדונהי אידהנויה וְיִשְׂרָאֵל לְגִדּוּפִים:

27 Your first father sinned; and your intercessors have transgressed against Me.

28 Therefore, I have profaned the princes of the sanctuary, and I have given Jacob to condemnation and Israel to reviling.

44:1 Yet now hear, Jacob, My servant, Israel, whom I have chosen.

2 This is what the Lord who made you and who formed you in the womb, and who will help you, says: Fear not, Jacob, My servant and yours, Jeshurun, whom I have chosen.

3 For I will pour water on the thirsty land, and streams upon the dry ground; I will pour My Spirit upon your seed, and My Blessing upon your offspring,

4 and they shall spring among the grass, like willows by flowing streams.

5 One shall say, 'I am the Lord's;' and another shall call himself by the name of Jacob; and another shall write with his hand to the Lord and surname himself by the name of Israel."

6 This says the Lord, the King of Israel and his Redeemer, the Lord of Hosts: I am the first and I am the last; and beside me there is no God.

7 And who, as I, can proclaim—let him declare it and lay it out before Me, since I appointed the ancient people, and what is yet to come and that shall come to pass, let them declare.

8 Do not fear, nor be afraid, have I not announced to you of old and declared it? And you are My witnesses. Is there a God besides me? Yea, there is no other Rock; I know not any.

9 They that fashion a graven image are all of them vanity, and their delectable things shall not profit, and their own witnesses see not, nor know that they may be ashamed.

10 Who has fashioned a god, or a molten image that is profitable for nothing?

11 See, all the fellows thereof shall be ashamed; and the craftsmen skilled above men, let them all be gathered together, let them stand up; they shall fear and they shall be ashamed together.

12 The blacksmith makes an axe and works with it in the coals; and fashions it with hammers, and works it with his strong arm; yea, he is hungry and his strength fails; he drinks no water and is faint.

44 1 וְעַתָּה שְׁמַע יַעֲקֹב ז"פ יהוה, יאהדונהי אידהנויה עַבְדִּי וְיִשְׂרָאֵל בָּחַרְתִּי בוֹ:

2 כֹּה הי -אָמַר יְהֹוָהאידיאהדונהי עֹשֶׂךָ וְיֹצֶרְךָ מִבֶּטֶן יַעְזְרֶךָּ אַל-תִּירָא עַבְדִּי יַעֲקֹב ז"פ יהוה, יאהדונהי אידהנויה וִישֻׁרוּן בָּחַרְתִּי בוֹ: 3 כִּי אֶצָּק-מַיִם עַל-צָמֵא וְנֹזְלִים עַל-יַבָּשָׁה אֶצֹּק רוּחִי עַל-זַרְעֶךָ וּבִרְכָתִי עַל-צֶאֱצָאֶיךָ:

4 וְצָמְחוּ בְּבֵין חָצִיר כַּעֲרָבִים עַל-יִבְלֵי-מָיִם: 5 זֶה יֹאמַר לַיהֹוָהאידיאהדונהי אָנִי אני, טדה"ד כוז"ו וְזֶה יִקְרָא בְשֵׁם יהוה שדי -יַעֲקֹב ז"פ יהוה, יאהדונהי אידהנויה וְזֶה יִכְתֹּב יָדוֹ לַיהֹוָהאידיאהדונהי וּבְשֵׁם יהוה שדי יִשְׂרָאֵל יְכַנֶּה: 6 כֹּה הי -אָמַר יְהֹוָהאידיאהדונהי מֶלֶךְ-יִשְׂרָאֵל וְגֹאֲלוֹ יְהֹוָהאידיאהדונהי צְבָאוֹת נתה ורבוע אהיה אָנִי אני, טדה"ד כוז"ו רִאשׁוֹן וַאֲנִי ב"פ אהיה יהוה אַחֲרוֹן וּמִבַּלְעָדַי אֵין אֱלֹהִים מום, אהיה אדני ; ילה: 7 וּמִי ילי -כָמוֹנִי יִקְרָא וְיַגִּידֶהָ וְיַעְרְכֶהָ לִי מִשּׂוּמִי עַם-עוֹלָם וְאֹתִיּוֹת וַאֲשֶׁר תָּבֹאנָה יַגִּידוּ לָמוֹ: 8 אַל-תִּפְחֲדוּ וְאַל-תִּרְהוּ הֲלֹא מֵאָז וּמב הִשְׁמַעְתִּיךָ וְהִגַּדְתִּי וְאַתֶּם עֵדָי הֲיֵשׁ אֱלוֹהַּ מִבַּלְעָדַי וְאֵין צוּר אלהים דההן ע"ה בַּל-יָדָעְתִּי: 9 יֹצְרֵי-פֶסֶל כֻּלָּם תֹּהוּ וַחֲמוּדֵיהֶם בַּל-יוֹעִילוּ וְעֵדֵיהֶם הֵמָּה בַּל-יִרְאוּ וּבַל-יֵדְעוּ לְמַעַן יֵבֹשׁוּ: 10 מִי ילי -יָצַר אֵל יאא"י וּפֶסֶל נָסַךְ לְבִלְתִּי הוֹעִיל: 11 הֵן כָּל ילי -חֲבֵרָיו יֵבֹשׁוּ וְחָרָשִׁים הֵמָּה מֵאָדָם מ"ה יִתְקַבְּצוּ כֻלָּם יַעֲמֹדוּ יִפְחֲדוּ יֵבֹשׁוּ יָחַד כ"ב אתוון: 12 חָרַשׁ בַּרְזֶל ר"ת בלהה רחל זלפה לאה מַעֲצָד וּפָעַל בַּפֶּחָם וּבַמַּקָּבוֹת יִצְּרֵהוּ וַיִּפְעָלֵהוּ בִּזְרוֹעַ כֹּחוֹ גַּם-רָעֵב ע"ג ע"ב ורבוע אלהים וְאֵין כֹּחַ לֹא-שָׁתָה מַיִם וַיִּיעָף: 13 חָרַשׁ עֵצִים נָטָה קָו יְתָאֲרֵהוּ בַשֶּׂרֶד יַעֲשֵׂהוּ בַּמַּקְצֻעוֹת וּבַמְּחוּגָה יְתָאֳרֵהוּ וַיַּעֲשֵׂהוּ כְּתַבְנִית אִישׁ ע"ה קנ"א קס"א כְּתִפְאֶרֶת אָדָם מ"ה לָשֶׁבֶת בָּיִת ב"פ ראה: 14 לִכְרָת-לוֹ אֲרָזִים וַיִּקַּח תִּרְזָה חֹעם וְאַלּוֹן וַיְאַמֶּץ-לוֹ בַּעֲצֵי-יָעַר עֹרי נָטַע אֹרֶן וְגֶשֶׁם יְגַדֵּל: 15 וְהָיָה יהוה לְאָדָם מ"ה לְבָעֵר וַיִּקַּח חֹעם מֵהֶם וַיָּחָם אַף-יַשִּׂיק וְאָפָה לָחֶם אלהים גֹ"פ יהוה אַף-יִפְעַל-אֵל יאא"י וַיִּשְׁתָּחוּ

¹³ The carpenter stretches out a line and he marks it out with a pencil; he fits it with planes and he marks it with compasses; and he makes it after the figure of a man, according to the beauty of a man, to dwell in the house.

¹⁴ He cuts down cedars, and takes a cypress and the oak, and he strengthens for himself one among the trees of the forest, he planted a bay tree, and the rain nourishes it.

¹⁵ Then a man uses it for fuel, and he takes thereof and warms himself, yea, he kindles it and bakes bread, yea makes a god and worships it; he makes it a graven image and bows down to it.

¹⁶ Half of it he burns in the fire; half of it he uses to eat meat, he roasts meat and is satisfied, yea, he warms himself and says, 'Ah! I am warm; I have seen the fire.'

¹⁷ And from the rest he makes a god, even his graven image; he bows down to it and worships and prays to it and says, 'Deliver me; you are my god.'

¹⁸ They know nothing, nor do they understand for their eyes are bedaubed so they cannot see, and their hearts so that they cannot understand.

¹⁹ No one considers in his heart, nor has the knowledge or understanding to say, 'I have burned half of it in the fire, yea I even baked bread over its coals, I have roasted meat and eaten it; and shall I make an abomination from what is left? Shall I bow down to a block of wood?'

²⁰ He strives after ashes; a deceived heart misleads him so that he cannot deliver his soul, or say, 'Is there not a lie in my right hand?'

²¹ Remember these things, Jacob and Israel, for you are My servant; I have made you, you are My own servant; Israel, you should not forget Me.

²² I have blotted out, as a thick cloud, your transgressions and as a cloud, your sins, return to me, for I have redeemed you.

²³ Sing, you heavens, for the Lord has done this; shout you lowest parts of earth; burst into song, you mountains, forests and every tree, for the Lord has redeemed Jacob, and does glory Himself in Israel."

עַל־וְחֶצְיוֹ עָשָׂה פֶסֶל וַיִּסְגָּד־לָמוֹ: 16 וְחֶצְיוֹ שָׂרַף בְּמוֹ־אֵשׁ אלהים דיודין ע״ה

בְּשָׂר יֹאכֵל יִצְלֶה צָלִי וְיִשְׂבָּע אַף־יָחֹם וְיֹאמַר הֶאָח חַמּוֹתִי רָאִיתִי

אוּר: רז, אין סוף (כתיב: יסגוד) 17 וּשְׁאֵרִיתוֹ לְאֵל יא״י עָשָׂה לְפִסְלוֹ יִסְגָּד־

לוֹ וְיִשְׁתַּחוּ וְיִתְפַּלֵּל אֵלָיו וְיֹאמַר הַצִּילֵנִי כִּי אֵלִי אָתָּה: 18 לֹא יָדְעוּ

וְלֹא יָבִינוּ כִּי טַח מֵרְאוֹת עֵינֵיהֶם ריבוע מ״ה מֵהַשְׂכִּיל לִבֹּתָם: 19 וְלֹא־

יָשִׁיב אֶל־לִבּוֹ וְלֹא דַעַת וְלֹא־תְבוּנָה לֵאמֹר חֶצְיוֹ שָׂרַפְתִּי בְמוֹ־

אֵשׁ אלהים דיודין ע״ה וְאַף אָפִיתִי עַל־גֶּחָלָיו לֶחֶם ג״פ יהוה אֶצְלֶה בָשָׂר וְאֹכֵל

אל יהוה וְיִתְרוֹ לְתוֹעֵבָה אֶעֱשֶׂה לְבוּל עֵץ ע״ה קס״א אֶסְגּוֹד: 20 רֹעֶה רהע אֵפֶר

סוזיך ע״ה לֵב הוּתַל הִטָּהוּ וְלֹא־יַצִּיל אֶת־נַפְשׁוֹ וְלֹא יֹאמַר הֲלוֹא שֶׁקֶר

בִּימִינִי: 21 זְכָר־אֵלֶּה יַעֲקֹב ז״פ יהוה, יאהדונהי אידהנויה וְיִשְׂרָאֵל כִּי עַבְדִּי־אָתָּה

יְצַרְתִּיךָ עֶבֶד־לִי אַתָּה יִשְׂרָאֵל לֹא תִנָּשֵׁנִי: 22 מָחִיתִי כָעָב פְּשָׁעֶיךָ

וְכֶעָנָן חַטֹּאותֶיךָ שׁוּבָה הווז אֵלַי כִּי גְאַלְתִּיךָ: 23 רָנּוּ שָׁמַיִם י״פ טל, י״פ כוזו

כִּי־עָשָׂה יְהֹוָהאההאהדונהי הֵרִיעוּ תַּחְתִּיּוֹת אָרֶץ אלהים דאלפין פִּצְחוּ הָרִים

רִנָּה יַעַר ערי וְכָל־עֵץ ילי בּוֹ כִּי־גָאַל ע״ה בוכ״ו, ע״ה אלד יְהֹוָהאההאהדונהי

יַעֲקֹב ז״פ יהוה, יאהדונהי אידהנויה וּבְיִשְׂרָאֵל יִתְפָּאָר:

TZAV

LESSON OF TZAV
(Leviticus 6:1 – 8:36)

It is written in the *Gemara*: "In the future, God will take the sun out of His pocket, and the *tzaddikim* (the righteous) will be healed by it and the wicked will be harmed by it." (*Nedarim* 8b) In this verse, the sun is a symbol for the Light of the Creator. In the presence of the Light, a *tzaddik* will be "healed," which here means "fulfilled." He has desired the Light throughout his life; now the Light is within him, and any fear that had been tarnishing his life is now eliminated.

We don't often think of *tzaddikim* as living in fear, but the thought of "maybe I am not doing enough" is always with them. This is the only thing that frightens a truly righteous human being, as it is written: "Joyous will be the man who is always afraid." (Proverbs 28:14) He knows that he has to work to receive the Light. That knowledge motivates him to take righteous action, which results in his receiving the Light. The wicked, however, are neither fearful nor courageous; they're simply indifferent. A wicked person might say to himself, "I don't care about anything. It doesn't matter whether I receive the Light or not." But he is wrong, of course. When the Light comes to him, it will be like the coming of death itself, as it is written in the *Gemara*: "The wicked will be harmed." This is because the positive intensity of the Light cannot be borne by anyone who is resonating to darkness.

A person may be a *tzaddik* or a sinner, but the truth of his spiritual attainment cannot be hidden. Who and what we are will always be revealed in the end. By using the sun as a symbol for the Light, the *Gemara* reminds us how we can learn the truth about people. We can learn that someone who seems quite negative is, in fact, a tzaddik, or that someone who seems righteous is actually a very destructive individual.

Rav Brandwein once said something very important to Rav Berg: "When we come to the world of truth, we are asked to name the greatest accomplishment of our lives. Sometimes, people say, 'Everybody loved me.' But those people are deeply in error. They are saying that they did nothing in their lives except what others wanted them to do, and whatever that may have been, they were willing to do it." We must learn to act always in accordance with the Light, even if the true nature of our actions may not be apparent to others.

Angels

Of the angels it is written: "And their legs are a straight leg." It is also written that people should seek to be like angels. If we are trying to emulate the angels, we need to understand this teaching about a "straight leg."

Angels move straight ahead. Angels look neither to the right nor to the left, being completely unaffected by what is said or thought about them. Nothing deters an angel from its work, and this is the level we should desire to attain in our own spiritual work. We can reach this level by performing actions that we know to be correct, rather than by succumbing to the influence of other people.

> "And their feet were straight feet" (Ezekiel 1:7). For the feet of the demons are crooked, while about their feet, namely about the feet of the holy beings, it is said: "And their feet were straight feet." And this is why "their feet were straight feet," "for the ways of God are straight." (Hosea 14:10). The sages of the Mishnah said: 'One who prays should arrange his feet during his prayer as do the ministering angels,' NAMELY HIS FEET SHOULD BE STRAIGHT "like the sole of a calf's foot," namely to be THUS recorded with them. And for this reason the sages taught: "When one prays, he should place his feet in proper position, as it says: 'And their feet were straight feet'." And the Holy One, blessed be He, said TO THE MINISTERING ANGELS: 'Those who are thus noted in their prayer, that they place their feet as you do, for them open the gates of the temple to enter this appearance.'
> — The Zohar, Pinchas 51:317-321

Most people live as if they were running for political office. To get as many votes as possible, they say only those things they think others want to hear. So we should take ourselves "out of the running." We should learn from angels, not from political candidates.

The chapter of Tzav contains a passage where the Creator instructs Moses on the manner in which the *kohenim* (priests) should perform their sacrifice of the burnt offering: "He is to take off these clothes and put on others, and carry the ashes outside the camp, to a place that is ceremonially clean." (*Leviticus 6:4*) What do we learn from the fact that both the *Kohen HaGadol* (the High Priest) and the other priests took their clothes off? And why did they have to wear different clothes for the different ceremonies they performed?

The following story about a spiritual teacher provides a metaphorical explanation. When people would visit this teacher and ask his advice, he was known to sweat profusely. One day, one of his students asked why his master was always sweating. After all, he wasn't performing any physical labor; he was just sitting in his house all day, meeting with one person after another.

Patiently, the teacher answered, "Whenever someone comes to ask for a blessing or for advice or the solution to a problem, I can't be of help to them if I can't feel where they are. To be able to really listen to the problem, I have to take off my spiritual clothes and put on those of the person who needs the help. Then after hearing the question, I have to put my own clothes back on to give the answer. And that's how it is every day. After changing clothes ten times an hour, who wouldn't be sweating?"

The *Kohen HaGadol* and the other priests were not just changing their physical clothes, by removing their mundane clothing and donning the clothing of the priests, they were altering their level of consciousness. In our case, our negativity forms a covering that separates us from the Light and from others. We have to learn how to free ourselves from this covering (metaphorically "taking off our clothes") to make progress in our spiritual work and relate proactively to other people.

It is said that when the holy Maggid of Mezritch (Rav Dov Ber, 1704–1772) was about to leave this world, he decided to present something to each of his students. To one, he gave his righteousness; to another, his wisdom. But to Rav Elimelech, the Maggid gave the work of "fixing the world."

After the Maggid passed away, Rav Elimelech went around to all the nearby villages, trying to bring people closer together by giving them ways to connect to the Light of the Creator. Two years went by, when one day he found himself sitting in his home and wondering whether he was really doing the work that had been entrusted to him. That night, while he was sleeping, the Maggid came to him in a dream and said, "You have traveled very far as you try to change the whole world, but how far have you traveled in trying to change yourself?"

It's much easier for us to see what's wrong with others than to see our own faults, but our real work begins with our internal process of correction, our individual tikkun. The purpose of The Kabbalah Centre is simply to help people with the work of tikkun and personal transformation, using the technology of Kabbalah in all its forms.

A short narrative illustrates this point. A man was sent by his employer to deliver a truckload of merchandise to a distant location. After a few days, the man returned with a smile on his face and said, "I successfully completed the task you assigned me." The employee counted on his fingers so as not to leave anything out: "First of all, I went the whole way without getting a single traffic ticket. I didn't kill anyone and didn't even hurt anyone. I had no flat tires or breakdowns of any kind." "But what about the delivery?" his employer asked. "Oh, the delivery. By chance, I forgot to load the truck..." Needless to say, his employer was very disappointed!

Every day, we behave just like this worker. Were we really put in this world just to avoid getting any traffic tickets? Our mission in life is so much more than that: We are here to manifest the Light within us so that the world as a whole can reveal its Light as well. This is our true purpose—and the purpose for which Rav Ashlag founded The Kabbalah Centre.

SYNOPSIS OF TZAV

The numerical value of the word *tzav*, (command), equals the number of verses—96—in this chapter of the Bible. This numerical matching of the name of a chapter with its length does not happen anywhere else in the Bible. In this chapter, God told Moses to instruct Aaron and his sons on the correct practice for the burnt offerings. The lesson here is that when we make sacrifices to the Creator with a desire to connect with the Creator, we avoid the worshipping of idols. Idol worship is more than just serving statues; it includes assigning power to things outside of ourselves and the Light. It also has to do with making decisions and acting out of purely selfish motives—out of pride, out of the need to impress people, and so on. All of our actions should be motivated by a desire to connect with the Creator, a desire that will then bring about that very connection. If the intention of connecting to the Creator does not underlie an action, that action constitutes idol worship.

FIRST READING - ABRAHAM - CHESED

6:1 **T**he Lord spoke to Moses, saying: 2 "Command Aaron and his sons, saying: This is the regulation for the burnt offering: The burnt offering is to remain on the altar hearth throughout the night, till morning, and the fire must be kept burning on the altar.

3 The priest shall then put on his linen clothes, with linen undergarments next to his body, and shall remove the ashes of the burnt offering that the fire has consumed on the altar and place them beside the altar.

4 Then he is to take off these clothes, and put on other clothing, and carry the ashes outside the camp to a place that is ceremonially clean.

5 The fire on the altar must be kept burning; it must not go out. Every morning the priest is to add firewood and arrange the burnt offering on the fire and burn the fat of the peace offerings on it.

6 The fire must be kept burning on the altar continuously; it must not go out.

FROM THE RAV

The word *tzav* means "commandment." The *Zohar* says very clearly that "commandment" is idol worship. But what is it that we do in a temple, if not follow the commandments? Are we to consider our presence in this temple ordered by God—as conditional and as idol worshipping? Idol worship has only one definition: It is the realm of chaos dictated, commanded, and dominated by Satan.

Everywhere we go, there's chaos. We can't escape this consciousness of the dominion of chaos in our human world. Yet here we are trying to retool our consciousness, to undo millennia of thinking, to change. This change requires a constant support system; it's not enough to just merely think about this physical reality of chaos as being illusionary. We need a support system, and that's why we come here every Shabbat. It is impossible to alter our consciousness without having this support, and yet the world continues on with this fabrication of a concept of what God is about.

I'm not only referring here to the Jewish religion, but to all religions—whether in the name of Allah, in the name of Jesus, or in the name of God—"because this is what God wants." And yet we have found, and we have learned according to the principles of Kabbalah originating with this *Zohar*, that God never commands. God merely furnishes us with the methodology, the technology, by which we can avoid the pitfalls of chaos. And thus we have an opportunity to understand that God didn't simply thrust us into this world of chaos without giving us a way to get out.

The *Zohar* and the kabbalists explain that the word "sacrifice" mentioned here in the Lesson of Tzav means to "sacrifice our chaos." The sacrifices are our way

FIRST READING - ABRAHAM - CHESED

וַיְדַבֵּר ראה יְהוָֹואֲדֹנֵיאֶהֱדֹוִנֶהֵי מהא, אל שדי אֶל־מֹשֶׁה לֵּאמֹר: 2 צַו פוי אֶת־ 1 6

אַהֲרֹן ע"ב ורבוע ע"ב וְאֶת־בָּנָיו לֵאמֹר זֹאת תּוֹרַת הָעֹלָה הִוא הָעֹלָה עַל

מוֹקְדָה עַל־הַמִּזְבֵּחַ ז, נגד כָּל־ ילי הַלַּיְלָה מלה עַד־הַבֹּקֶר וְאֵשׁ אלהים דיודין ע"ה

הַמִּזְבֵּחַ ז, נגד תּוּקַד בּוֹ: 3 וְלָבַשׁ הַכֹּהֵן מלה מִדּוֹ בַד וּמִכְנְסֵי־בַד יִלְבַּשׁ

עַל־בְּשָׂרוֹ וְהֵרִים אֶת־הַדֶּשֶׁן אֲשֶׁר תֹּאכַל הָאֵשׁ שאה אֶת־הָעֹלָה עַל־

הַמִּזְבֵּחַ ז, נגד וְשָׂמוֹ אֵצֶל הַמִּזְבֵּחַ ז, נגד: 4 וּפָשַׁט אֶת־בְּגָדָיו וְלָבַשׁ בְּגָדִים

אֲחֵרִים וְהוֹצִיא אֶת־הַדֶּשֶׁן אֶל־מִחוּץ לַמַּחֲנֶה אֶל־מָקוֹם יהוה ברבוע, ר"פ אל

טָהוֹר י"פ אכא: 5 וְהָאֵשׁ שאה עַל־הַמִּזְבֵּחַ ז, נגד תּוּקַד־בּוֹ לֹא תִכְבֶּה וּבִעֵר

עָלֶיהָ פהל הַכֹּהֵן מלה עֵצִים בַּבֹּקֶר בַּבֹּקֶר וְעָרַךְ עָלֶיהָ פהל הָעֹלָה

וְהִקְטִיר עָלֶיהָ פהל חֶלְבֵי הַשְּׁלָמִים: 6 אֵשׁ אלהים דיודין ע"ה תָּמִיד

---

to connect to and benefit from the power of the Light in our lives. Each sacrifice mentioned in this chapter corresponds to a different level of chaos. We need to understand that chaos comes in different levels, and in different intensities. The different sacrifices are our way of eliminating these different levels and types of chaos from our life.

A person making a sacrifice is given the opportunity and the ability to transcend time, space, and motion, and to repair the chaos that he or she has created in the universe. Sacrifices radiate an energy beyond our perception, and they have the power to instantly repair negative actions committed years before and long distances away.

הָעֹלָה

Leviticus 6:2 – The first offering mentioned in this chapter is the burnt offering, which symbolizes the destruction of our personal agendas. If we do things for personal gain, we will make mistakes and thereby suffer the consequences of our wrong decisions. On the other hand, if we "burn" our own agendas, relying solely on Divine guidance, then our decisions will be correct.

מוֹקְדָה

Leviticus 6:2 – A small *Mem* is found in the word *mokdah*, which means "stays on the flame." The numerical value of *Mem* is 40, a number that has many spiritual connotations: the number of days Moses spent on the mountain; the age at which one's soul becomes elevated; the number of years Moses lived in Egypt. The kabbalists teach that forty is also a reference to the bridge between the Upper and Lower Worlds, but it's a narrow bridge. We can cross it only when we realize that the Creator is the Source of everything; when we reach that point where we understand that we're always and forever getting help from Above.

7 These are the regulations for the meal offering; Aaron's sons are to bring it before the Lord, in front of the altar.

8 The priest is to take a handful of fine flour and oil, together with all the incense on the meal offering, and burn the memorial portion on the altar as an aroma pleasing to the Lord.

9 Aaron and his sons shall eat the rest of it, but it is to be eaten without yeast in a holy place; they are to eat it in the courtyard of the Tent of Meeting.

10 It must not be baked with yeast; I have given it as their share of the offerings made to me by fire. It is most holy, like the sin offering and the guilt offering.

11 Any male descendant of Aaron may eat it. It is his regular share of the offerings made to the Lord by fire for the generations to come. Whatever touches them will become holy."

SECOND READING - ISAAC - GEVURAH

12 The Lord spoke to Moses, saying:

13 "This is the offering Aaron and his sons are to bring to the Lord on the day he is anointed: a tenth of an ephah of fine flour as a regular meal offering, half of it in the morning and half in the evening.

14 Prepare it with oil on a griddle; bring it well-mixed and present the meal offering broken in pieces as an aroma pleasing to the Lord.

תּוֹרַת הַמִּנְחָה

Leviticus 6:7 – The meal offering allows us to tip the scales of justice in the world from negative to positive by helping us to transform those worlds from the Left to the Right. The Right Column represents the energy of mercy and sharing; the Left Column, the energy of judgment. When we act selfishly, we give power to the forces of the Left Column, of judgment. Moreover, every negative action on our part makes the universal Negative Side stronger. Luckily, this principle applies equally to positive actions, so that every positive action we do makes the universal Positive Side stronger.

The numerical value of the Aramaic word for "meal offering" (*Minchah*) is 130. According to the *Zohar*, there are 130 worlds that connect to the Left Column. The Ari wrote:

"We have explained that Minchah is 130 worlds on the left hand, and that this is the meaning of, "and took of that which came to his hand a present" (Genesis 32:14) – not in his 'hands' but to his 'hand', which are the Gevurot of his one hand, the secret of Minchah."
— *Writings of the Ari (Kitvei Ari), Torah Compilations 3, Vayishlach 3*

וְזֹאת 7 לֹא תִכְבֶּה: זן, גגד תּוּקַד עַל־הַמִּזְבֵּחַ ע"ה נתה, קס"א קנ"א קמ"ג

תּוֹרַת הַמִּנְחָה הַקְרֵב אֹתָהּ בְּנֵי־אַהֲרֹן ע"ב ורבוע ע"ב לִפְנֵי וחכמה בינה

יְהֹוָה אלהים־אהדונהי אֶל־פְּנֵי וחכמה בינה הַמִּזְבֵּחַ זן, גגד: 8 וְהֵרִים מִמֶּנּוּ בְּקֻמְצוֹ

מִסֹּלֶת הַמִּנְחָה ע"ה ב"פ בן וּמִשַּׁמְנָהּ וְאֵת כָּל יּלי ־הַלְּבֹנָה אֲשֶׁר עַל־

הַמִּנְחָה ע"ה ב"פ בן וְהִקְטִיר הַמִּזְבֵּחַ זן, גגד רֵיחַ נִיחֹחַ אַזְכָּרָתָהּ לַיהֹוָה אלהים־אהדונהי:

9 וְהַנּוֹתֶרֶת מִמֶּנָּה יֹאכְלוּ אַהֲרֹן ע"ב ורבוע ע"ב וּבָנָיו מַצּוֹת תֵּאָכֵל בְּמָקוֹם

קָדֹשׁ בַּחֲצַר אֹהֶל לאה ־מוֹעֵד יֹאכְלוּהָ: 10 לֹא תֵאָפֶה יהוה ברבוע, ר"פ אל

חָמֵץ חֶלְקָם נָתַתִּי אֹתָהּ מֵאִשָּׁי קֹדֶשׁ קָדָשִׁים הוּא כַּחַטָּאת וְכָאָשָׁם:

11 כָּל יּלי ־זָכָר בִּבְנֵי אַהֲרֹן ע"ב ורבוע ע"ב יֹאכְלֶנָּה חָק־עוֹלָם לְדֹרֹתֵיכֶם

מֵאִשֵּׁי יְהֹוָה אלהים־אהדונהי כֹּל יּלי אֲשֶׁר־יִגַּע בָּהֶם יִקְדָּשׁ:

SECOND READING - ISAAC - GEVURAH

12 וַיְדַבֵּר ראה יְהֹוָה אלהים־אהדונהי אֶל־מֹשֶׁה מהש, אל שדי לֵּאמֹר: 13 זֶה קָרְבַּן

אַהֲרֹן ע"ב ורבוע ע"ב וּבָנָיו אֲשֶׁר־יַקְרִיבוּ לַיהֹוָה אלהים־אהדונהי בְּיוֹם ע"ה = גגד, זן, מזבח

הִמָּשַׁח אֹתוֹ עֲשִׂירִת הָאֵפָה אלהים מִנְחָה ע"ה ב"פ בן תָּמִיד

מַחֲצִיתָהּ בַּבֹּקֶר וּמַחֲצִיתָהּ בָּעָרֶב רבוע יהוה ורבוע אלהים: ע"ה נתה, קס"א קנ"א קמ"ג

14 עַל־מַחֲבַת בַּשֶּׁמֶן י"פ טל, י"פ כוזו, ביט תֵּעָשֶׂה מֻרְבֶּכֶת תְּבִיאֶנָּה תֻּפִינֵי

קָרְבַּן

Leviticus 6:13 – The sacrifices performed by Aaron and his sons are described in this section. As mentioned previously, through sacrifice, we can purify ourselves. The reading of this section helps us to desire to connect to Right Column energy.

It is important to understand how much depends on our actions. In the time of the Temple, the priests performed sacrifices and other rituals on behalf of the people. Today, with no physical Temple, each one of us must bring about the same results through the strength of our own spiritual commitment, and through our decisions, our intentions, and our actions. It is necessary to make the decision to disconnect from our selfish desires and become more sharing beings, because we need to act as our own *"kohenim"* and perform the *Minchah* ourselves.

15 *The son who is to succeed him as anointed priest shall prepare it. It is the Lord's regular share and is to be burned completely.*

16 *Every meal offering of a priest shall be burned completely; it must not be eaten."*

17 *The Lord spoke to Moses, saying,* 18 *"Say to Aaron and his sons: These are the regulations for the sin offering: The sin offering is to be slaughtered before the Lord in the place the burnt offering is slaughtered; it is most holy.*

19 *The priest who offers it shall eat it; it is to be eaten in a holy place, in the courtyard of the Tent of Meeting.*

20 *Whatever touches any of the flesh will become holy, and if any of the blood is spattered on a garment, you must wash it in a holy place.*

21 *The clay pot the meat is cooked in must be broken; but if it is cooked in a bronze pot, the pot is to be scoured and rinsed with water.* 22 *Every male among priests may eat it; it is most holy.*

23 *But any sin offering whose blood is brought into the Tent of Meeting to make atonement in the Holy Place must not be eaten; it must be burned.*

7:1 *These are the regulations for the guilt offering; it is most holy:*

הַחַטָּאת

Leviticus 6:18 – Sin offerings help us to atone for any kind of misdeed and to cleanse the negativity we have inside us. We often lack the courage and strength to correct all of our flaws, choosing instead to see ourselves as blameless victims rather than as responsible beings, wholly accountable for the state of our own life.

The *Zohar* tells us that anyone who rises during the night, to study the Bible (spiritual wisdom) is informed by the Bible about his sins.

> *Whoever rises up at night to study the Torah, the Torah informs him of his sin. It is not by way of judgment, but as a mother who tells her child with soothing words. And he does not forget but repents before his Master.*
> — *The Zohar, Vayikra 61:405*

We see that the Bible does not act with harsh judgment, but instead reveals the man's error

to him as a loving parent would do, firmly but soothingly, and with mercy. This awakens the man's repentance so that he can begin to purify himself.

According to Kabbalah, a person can cleanse himself either through pain or through proactive transformation. When we experience poor health, if we lose our business or go broke, if our marriage breaks down or our children cause heartache, we are becoming spiritually cleansed, albeit painfully. But we can choose, instead, to use spiritual tools like this reading to correct our past iniquities so we need not experience pain to be purified.

הָאָשָׁם

Leviticus 7:1 – The guilt offering, referred to in this verse, has nothing to do with the traditional guilt trip—that uncomfortable feeling that follows some negative action we have done. The guilt offering is about true repentance. Connecting

מִנְחַת פִּתִּים תַּקְרִיב רֵיחַ־נִיחֹחַ לַיהוֹוָהיאהדונהי 15 וְהַכֹּהֵן מלה הַמָּשִׁיחַ

תַּחְתָּיו מִבָּנָיו יַעֲשֶׂה אֹתָהּ חָק־עוֹלָם לַיהוֹוָהיאהדונהי כָּלִיל תָּקְטָר:

16 וְכָל־ ילי ־מִנְחַת כֹּהֵן מלה כָּלִיל תִּהְיֶה לֹא תֵאָכֵל: 17 וַיְדַבֵּר ראה

יְהוֹוָהיאהדונהי אֶל־מֹשֶׁה מהש, אל שדי לֵּאמֹר: 18 דַּבֵּר ראה אֶל־אַהֲרֹן

וְאֶל־בָּנָיו לֵאמֹר זֹאת תּוֹרַת הַחַטָּאת בִּמְקוֹם

אֲשֶׁר תִּשָּׁחֵט הָעֹלָה תִּשָּׁחֵט הַחַטָּאת לִפְנֵי יְהוֹוָהיאהדונהי קֹדֶשׁ

קָדָשִׁים הִוא: 19 הַכֹּהֵן מלה הַמְחַטֵּא אֹתָהּ יֹאכְלֶנָּה בְּמָקוֹם

קָדֹשׁ תֵּאָכֵל בַּחֲצַר אֹהֶל מוֹעֵד: 20 כֹּל ילי אֲשֶׁר־יִגַּע בִּבְשָׂרָהּ

יִקְדָּשׁ וַאֲשֶׁר יִזֶּה מִדָּמָהּ עַל־הַבֶּגֶד אֲשֶׁר יִזֶּה עָלֶיהָ תְּכַבֵּס

בְּמָקוֹם קָדֹשׁ: 21 וּכְלִי־חֶרֶשׂ אֲשֶׁר תְּבֻשַּׁל־בּוֹ יִשָּׁבֵר

וְאִם־בִּכְלִי נְחֹשֶׁת בֻּשָּׁלָה וּמֹרַק וְשֻׁטַּף בַּמָּיִם: 22 כָּל ילי ־

זָכָר בַּכֹּהֲנִים מלה יֹאכַל אֹתָהּ קֹדֶשׁ קָדָשִׁים הִוא: 23 וְכָל ילי ־חַטָּאת

אֲשֶׁר יוּבָא מִדָּמָהּ אֶל־אֹהֶל מוֹעֵד לְכַפֵּר בַּקֹּדֶשׁ לֹא תֵאָכֵל

בָּאֵשׁ תִּשָּׂרֵף: 7 1 וְזֹאת תּוֹרַת הָאָשָׁם קֹדֶשׁ קָדָשִׁים

הוּא: 2 בִּמְקוֹם אֲשֶׁר יִשְׁחֲטוּ אֶת־הָעֹלָה יִשְׁחֲטוּ אֶת־

---

with this particular verse bestows upon us the same benefit as did the guilt offering presented in the Temple. The benefit of the guilt offering is the power it gives us to travel back to the precise moment prior to our infraction. We can then meditate with true remorse to remove the character flaw that motivated our negative action. The *Zohar* says:

. . . atonement comes through the words of Torah. Why? It is because words of Torah are superior to all sacrifices. As has been accepted, it is written: "This is the Torah of the burned offering, of the meal offering, and of the sin offering, and of the guilt offering." (Leviticus 7:37) THIS INDICATES THAT *the Torah is equal to all sacrifices in the world. He replied:*

This is surely so. For even if a penalty of Heaven is decreed against whoever toils in Torah, the penalty is canceled because the study of the Torah is better for him than all the sacrifices and offerings . . .
— The Zohar, Kedoshim 3:10-11

Kabbalah explains that there are no victims: The people who are injured by our actions deserve their injuries because of misdeeds they committed in the past. However, it is vital to understand that our own repentance depends on our empathy for their pain. Only through our empathy and sincere repentance can we be cleansed of the consequences of our own negative and hurtful actions. Connection with the guilt offering in this reading cleanses us and diminishes the dark side of our nature without the need for pain.

² The guilt offering is to be slaughtered in the place where the burnt offering is slaughtered, and its blood is to be sprinkled against the altar on all sides.

³ All its fat shall be offered: the fat tail and the fat that covers the inner parts, ⁴ both kidneys with the fat on them near the loins, and the covering of the liver, which is to be removed with the kidneys.

⁵ The priest shall burn them on the altar as an offering made to the Lord by fire. It is a guilt offering.

⁶ Every male among the priests may eat it, but it must be eaten in a holy place; it is most holy. ⁷ The same law applies to both the sin offering and the guilt offering: They belong to the priest who makes atonement with them.

⁸ The priest who offers a burnt offering for anyone may keep its hide for himself. ⁹ Every meal offering baked in an oven or cooked in a pan or on a griddle belongs to the priest who offers it,

¹⁰ and every meal offering, whether mixed with oil or dry, belongs equally to all the sons of Aaron.

THIRD READING - JACOB - TIFERET

¹¹ These are the regulations for the peace offering a person may present to the Lord:

¹² If he offers it as an expression of thanksgiving, then along with this thanksgiving offering he is to offer cakes of unleavened bread and mixed with oil, wafers made without yeast and spread with oil, and cakes of fine flour well-kneaded and mixed with oil.

¹³ Along with his peace offering of thanksgiving, he is to present an offering with cakes of bread made with yeast.

בַּכֹּהֲנִים

Leviticus 7:6 – At the time of the Temple, gifts were given to the *kohenim* as a way of tithing. The priests were like electrical cords that helped the people plug into the Light. Lacking that kind of intermediary now, we must act as our own *kohenim*, finding our own ways to share and

tithe. We must find people to whom we can give and with whom we can share.

זֶבַח הַשְּׁלָמִים

Leviticus 7:11 – An olive branch was presented as a peace offering. On a physical level, everyone

הָאָשָׁ֑ם וְאֶת־דָּמ֛וֹ יִזְרֹ֥ק עַל־הַמִּזְבֵּ֖חַ זֶּ נגד סָבִֽיב׃ 3 וְאֵ֤ת כָּל־יּלּי ־חֶלְבּוֹ֙ יַקְרִ֣יב מִמֶּ֔נּוּ אֵ֚ת הָ֣אַלְיָ֔ה וְאֶת־הַחֵ֖לֶב הַֽמְכַסֶּ֥ה אֶת־הַקֶּֽרֶב׃ 4 וְאֵת֙ שְׁתֵּ֣י הַכְּלָיֹ֔ת וְאֶת־הַחֵ֙לֶב֙ אֲשֶׁ֣ר עֲלֵיהֶ֔ן אֲשֶׁ֖ר עַל־הַכְּסָלִ֑ים וְאֶת־ הַיֹּתֶ֙רֶת֙ עַל־הַכָּבֵ֔ד עַל־הַכְּלָיֹ֖ת יְסִירֶֽנָּה׃ 5 וְהִקְטִ֨יר אֹתָ֤ם הַכֹּהֵן֙ מלה הַמִּזְבֵּ֔חָה אִשֶּׁ֖ה לַיהוה וָאֲדֹנָיﭏﬄﭏﬄ מלה אָשָׁ֥ם ה֖וּא׃ 6 כָּל־יּלּי ־זָכָ֥ר ⸤בַּכֹּהֲנִ֖ים⸥ יֹאכְלֶ֑נּוּ בְּמָק֤וֹם יהוה ברבוע, רפ אל קָדוֹשׁ֙ יֵֽאָכֵ֔ל קֹ֥דֶשׁ קָֽדָשִׁ֖ים הֽוּא׃ 7 כַּֽחַטָּאת֙ כָּֽאָשָׁ֔ם תּוֹרָ֥ה אַחַ֖ת לָהֶ֑ם הַכֹּהֵ֛ן מלה אֲשֶׁ֥ר יְכַפֶּר־בּ֖וֹ ל֥וֹ יִהְיֶֽה יּּי׃ 8 וְהַכֹּהֵ֗ן מלה הַמַּקְרִ֛יב אֶת־עֹלַ֥ת אבגית״ן, ושר, אהבת חנם אִ֖ישׁ עה קנ״א קס״א ע֑וֹר הָֽעֹלָ֛ה אֲשֶׁ֣ר הִקְרִ֑יב לַכֹּהֵ֛ן מלה ל֥וֹ יִהְיֶֽה יּּי׃ 9 וְכָל־יּלּי ־מִנְחָה֙ עה ב״פ ב״ן אֲשֶׁ֤ר תֵּֽאָפֶה֙ בַּתַּנּ֔וּר וְכָל־יּלּי ־נַעֲשָׂ֥ה בַמַּרְחֶ֖שֶׁת וְעַל־מַֽחֲבַ֑ת לַכֹּהֵ֛ן מלה הַמַּקְרִ֥יב אֹתָ֖הּ ל֥וֹ תִהְיֶֽה׃ 10 וְכָל־יּלּי ־מִנְחָ֥ה עה ב״פ ב״ן בְלוּלָֽה־בַשֶּׁ֖מֶן יּ״פ טל, י״פ כוז״ו, ביט וַֽחֲרֵבָ֑ה לְכָל־יה אדני ־בְּנֵ֥י אַֽהֲרֹ֛ן ע״ב ורבוע ע״ב תִֽהְיֶ֖ה אִ֥ישׁ כְּאָחִֽיו׃ ע״ה קנ״א קס״א

THIRD READING - JACOB - TIFERET

11 וְזֹ֥את תּוֹרַ֖ת ⸤זֶ֣בַח הַשְּׁלָמִ֑ים⸥ אֲשֶׁ֥ר יַקְרִ֖יב לַֽיהוה וָאֲדֹנָיﭏﬄﭏﬄ׃ 12 אִ֣ם יוהך, עה מ״ב עַל־תּוֹדָה֮ יַקְרִיבֶ֒נּוּ֒ וְהִקְרִ֣יב ׀ עַל־זֶ֣בַח הַתּוֹדָ֗ה חַלּ֤וֹת מַצּוֹת֙ בְּלוּלֹ֣ת בַּשֶּׁ֔מֶן יּ״פ טל, י״פ כוז״ו, ביט וּרְקִיקֵ֥י מַצּ֖וֹת מְשֻׁחִ֣ים בַּשָּׁ֑מֶן יּ״פ טל, י״פ כוז״ו, ביט וְסֹ֣לֶת מֻרְבֶּ֔כֶת חַלֹּ֖ת בְּלוּלֹ֥ת בַּשָּֽׁמֶן יּ״פ טל, י״פ כוז״ו, ביט׃ 13 עַל־חַלֹּת֙ לֶ֔חֶם

---

received a piece of this offering: God, the priest, and the person offering the sacrifice.

For peace to prevail, each party in a difficult relationship has to have their needs met.

When someone wants more than they deserve, problems ensue. If we remember this, it will help us to focus our attention on others instead of ourselves first, so that we can achieve peace on both a personal and global level.

¹⁴ He is to bring one of each kind as an offering, a contribution to the Lord; it belongs to the priest who sprinkles the blood of the peace offerings.

¹⁵ The meat of his peace offering of thanksgiving must be eaten on the day it is offered; he must leave none of it till morning.

¹⁶ If, however, his offering is the result of a vow or is a freewill offering, the sacrifice shall be eaten on the day he offers it, but anything left over may be eaten on the next day.

¹⁷ Any meat of the sacrifice left over till the third day must be burned up.

¹⁸ If any meat of the peace offering is eaten on the third day, it will not be accepted. It will not be credited to the one who offered it, for it is impure; the person who eats any of it will be held responsible.

¹⁹ Meat that touches anything ceremonially unclean must not be eaten; it must be burned up. As for other meat, anyone ceremonially clean may eat it.

²⁰ But if anyone who is unclean eats any meat of the peace offering belonging to the Lord, that person must be cut off from his people.

²¹ If anyone touches something unclean—whether human uncleanness or an unclean animal or any unclean, detestable thing—and then eats any of the meat of the peace offering belonging to the Lord, that person must be cut off from his people."

²² The Lord spoke to Moses, saying,

²³ "Say to the Children of Israel: Do not eat any of the fat of cattle, sheep or goats.

²⁴ The fat of an animal found dead or torn by wild animals may be used for any other purpose, but you must not eat it.

²⁵ Anyone who eats the fat of an animal from which an offering by fire may be made to the Lord must be cut off from his people.

²⁶ And wherever you live, you must not eat the blood of any bird or animal.

²⁷ If anyone eats blood, that person must be cut off from his people."

²⁸ The Lord spoke to Moses, saying, ²⁹ "Say to the Children of Israel: Anyone who brings a peace offering to the Lord is to bring part of it as his sacrifice to the Lord.

³⁰ With his own hands he is to bring the offering made to the Lord by fire; he is to bring

וּמִמֶּנּוּ יַקְרִיב קָרְבָּנוֹ עַל־זֶבַח תּוֹדַת שְׁלָמָיו 14 וְהִקְרִיב מִמֶּנּוּ
אֶחָד מִכָּל־קָרְבָּן תְּרוּמָה לַיהוה לַכֹּהֵן הַזֹּרֵק
אֶת־דַּם הַשְּׁלָמִים לוֹ יִהְיֶה 15 וּבְשַׂר זֶבַח תּוֹדַת שְׁלָמָיו
בְּיוֹם קָרְבָּנוֹ יֵאָכֵל לֹא־יַנִּיחַ מִמֶּנּוּ עַד־בֹּקֶר 16 וְאִם
נֶדֶר | אוֹ נְדָבָה זֶבַח קָרְבָּנוֹ בְּיוֹם הַקְרִיבוֹ
אֶת־זִבְחוֹ יֵאָכֵל וּמִמָּחֳרָת וְהַנּוֹתָר מִמֶּנּוּ יֵאָכֵל 17 וְהַנּוֹתָר מִבְּשַׂר
הַזָּבַח בַּיּוֹם הַשְּׁלִישִׁי בָּאֵשׁ יִשָּׂרֵף 18 וְאִם
הֵאָכֹל יֵאָכֵל מִבְּשַׂר־זֶבַח שְׁלָמָיו בַּיּוֹם הַשְּׁלִישִׁי
לֹא יֵרָצֶה הַמַּקְרִיב אֹתוֹ לֹא יֵחָשֵׁב לוֹ פִּגּוּל יִהְיֶה וְהַנֶּפֶשׁ
הָאֹכֶלֶת מִמֶּנּוּ עֲוֹנָהּ תִּשָּׂא 19 וְהַבָּשָׂר אֲשֶׁר־יִגַּע בְּכָל־
טָמֵא לֹא יֵאָכֵל בָּאֵשׁ יִשָּׂרֵף וְהַבָּשָׂר כָּל־טָהוֹר
יֹאכַל בָּשָׂר 20 וְהַנֶּפֶשׁ אֲשֶׁר־תֹּאכַל בָּשָׂר מִזֶּבַח הַשְּׁלָמִים
אֲשֶׁר לַיהוה וְטֻמְאָתוֹ עָלָיו וְנִכְרְתָה הַנֶּפֶשׁ הַהִוא
מֵעַמֶּיהָ 21 וְנֶפֶשׁ כִּי־תִגַּע בְּכָל־טָמֵא בְּטֻמְאַת
אָדָם אוֹ | בִּבְהֵמָה טְמֵאָה אוֹ בְּכָל־שֶׁקֶץ טָמֵא
וְאָכַל מִבְּשַׂר־זֶבַח הַשְּׁלָמִים אֲשֶׁר לַיהוה וְנִכְרְתָה הַנֶּפֶשׁ
הַהִוא מֵעַמֶּיהָ 22 וַיְדַבֵּר יהוה אֶל־מֹשֶׁה
לֵּאמֹר 23 דַּבֵּר אֶל־בְּנֵי יִשְׂרָאֵל לֵאמֹר כָּל־חֵלֶב שׁוֹר
וְכֶשֶׂב וָעֵז לֹא תֹאכֵלוּ 24 וְחֵלֶב נְבֵלָה
וְחֵלֶב טְרֵפָה יֵעָשֶׂה לְכָל־מְלָאכָה וְאָכֹל לֹא
תֹאכְלֻהוּ 25 כִּי כָּל־אֹכֵל חֵלֶב מִן־הַבְּהֵמָה אֲשֶׁר יַקְרִיב
מִמֶּנָּה אִשֶּׁה לַיהוה וְנִכְרְתָה הַנֶּפֶשׁ הָאֹכֶלֶת מֵעַמֶּיהָ
26 וְכָל־דָּם לֹא תֹאכְלוּ בְּכֹל מוֹשְׁבֹתֵיכֶם לָעוֹף
וְלַבְּהֵמָה 27 כָּל־נֶפֶשׁ אֲשֶׁר־תֹּאכַל

the fat on the breast, together with the breast, and wave it before the Lord as a wave offering.

31 The priest shall burn the fat on the altar, but the breast belongs to Aaron and his sons.

32 You are to give the right thigh of your peace offerings to the priest as a contribution.

33 The son of Aaron who offers the blood and the fat of the peace offering shall have the right thigh as his share.

34 I have taken the breast that is waved and the thigh that is presented from the peace offerings of the Children of Israel, and I have given them to Aaron the priest and his sons as their regular share from the Children of Israel."

35 This is the portion of the offerings made to the Lord by fire that were allotted to Aaron and his sons on the day they were presented to serve the Lord as priests.

36 On the day they were anointed, the Lord commanded that the Children of Israel give this to them as their regular share for the generations to come.

37 These, then, are the regulations for the burnt offering, the meal offering, the sin offering, the guilt offering, the ordination offering and the peace offering,

38 which the Lord commanded Moses on Mount Sinai, on the day He commanded the children of Israel to present their offerings to the Lord, in the wilderness of Sinai.

מִשְׁוֹת

Leviticus 7:35 – The *kohenim* were originally chosen from among the ordinary people and were given the awesome duty of channeling energy for everyone else. They were completely dedicated to the sacrifices and ceremonies that they performed. Their dedication serves as an inspiration to us as we go through the process of elevating and transforming ourselves. All of us have our mundane daily work to do; however, we need to remind ourselves that our "real" work in this world is to make our correction (*tikkun*) and that we have an obligation to elevate and transform ourselves. This section reminds us of the order and process of our correction. Our transformation takes place in a certain sequence, using particular issues as catalysts. We need to correct and change ourselves, and then as a result of this growth and understanding, we develop into more sharing and elevated beings.

כָּל יִלי ־דָּם רבוע אהיה וְנִכְרְתָה הַנֶּפֶשׁ רמ״ח ז וויֹת הַהִוא מֵעַמֶּיהָ: 28 וַיְדַבֵּר

ראה יְהֹוָﬡﬡדﬡﬥﬡﬡﬡﬡﬡ אֶל־מֹשֶׁה מהטֹ, אל שדי לֵאמֹר: 29 דַּבֵּר ראה אֶל־בְּנֵי

יִשְׂרָאֵל לֵאמֹר הַמַּקְרִיב אֶת־זֶבַח שְׁלָמָיו לַיהֹוָﬡﬡדﬡﬡﬡﬡﬡ יָבִיא אֶת־

קָרְבָּנוֹ לַיהֹוָﬡﬡדﬡﬡﬡﬡﬡ מִזֶּבַח שְׁלָמָיו: 30 יָדָיו תְּבִיאֶינָה אֵת אִשֵּׁי

יְהֹוָﬡﬡדﬡﬡﬡﬡﬡ אֶת־הַחֵלֶב עַל־הֶחָזֶה יְבִיאֶנּוּ אֵת הֶחָזֶה לְהָנִיף אֹתוֹ

תְּנוּפָה לִפְנֵי וחכמה בינה יְהֹוָﬡﬡדﬡﬡﬡﬡﬡ: 31 וְהִקְטִיר הַכֹּהֵן מלה אֶת־הַחֵלֶב

הַמִּזְבֵּחָה וְהָיָה יהוה הֶחָזֶה לְאַהֲרֹן ע״ב ורבוע ע״ב וּלְבָנָיו: 32 וְאֵת שׁוֹק הַיָּמִין

תִּתְּנוּ תְרוּמָה לַכֹּהֵן מלה מִזִּבְחֵי שַׁלְמֵיכֶם: 33 הַמַּקְרִיב רבוע אהיה אֶת־דַּם

הַשְּׁלָמִים וְאֶת־הַחֵלֶב מִבְּנֵי אַהֲרֹן ע״ב ורבוע ע״ב לוֹ תִהְיֶה שׁוֹק הַיָּמִין

לְמָנָה ע״ה פי: 34 כִּי אֶת־חֲזֵה הַתְּנוּפָה וְאֵת | שׁוֹק הַתְּרוּמָה לָקַחְתִּי

מֵאֵת בְּנֵי־יִשְׂרָאֵל מִזִּבְחֵי שַׁלְמֵיהֶם וָאֶתֵּן אֹתָם לְאַהֲרֹן ע״ב ורבוע ע״ב

הַכֹּהֵן מלה וּלְבָנָיו לְחָק־עוֹלָם מֵאֵת בְּנֵי יִשְׂרָאֵל: 35 זֹאת מִשְׁחַת אַהֲרֹן

ע״ב ורבוע ע״ב וּמִשְׁחַת בָּנָיו מֵאִשֵּׁי יְהֹוָﬡﬡדﬡﬡﬡﬡﬡ ע״ה = גגר, זן, מזבח בְּיוֹם הַקְרִיב

אֹתָם לְכַהֵן לַיהֹוָﬡﬡדﬡﬡﬡﬡﬡ מלה: 36 אֲשֶׁר צִוָּה פי יְהֹוָﬡﬡדﬡﬡﬡﬡﬡ לָתֵת לָהֶם

בְּיוֹם ע״ה = גגר, זן, מזבח מָשְׁחוֹ אֹתָם מֵאֵת בְּנֵי יִשְׂרָאֵל חֻקַּת עוֹלָם לְדֹרֹתָם:

37 זֹאת הַתּוֹרָה לָעֹלָה לַמִּנְחָה ע״ה ב״פ בן וְלַחַטָּאת וְלָאָשָׁם וְלַמִּלּוּאִים

וּלְזֶבַח הַשְּׁלָמִים: 38 אֲשֶׁר צִוָּה פי יְהֹוָﬡﬡדﬡﬡﬡﬡﬡ אֶת־מֹשֶׁה מהטֹ, אל שדי

בְּהַר אור, רז, אין סוף סִינָי נגמם, ה״פ יהוה בְּיוֹם ע״ה = גגר, זן, מזבח צַוֺּתוֹ אֶת־בְּנֵי יִשְׂרָאֵל

לְהַקְרִיב אֶת־קָרְבְּנֵיהֶם לַיהֹוָﬡﬡדﬡﬡﬡﬡﬡ בְּמִדְבַּר רמ״ח, ו״פ אל סִינָי

נגמם, ה״פ יהוה:

FOURTH READING - MOSES - NETZACH

8:¹ The Lord spoke to Moses, saying, ² "Bring Aaron and his sons, the garments, the anointing oil, the bull for the sin offering, the two rams and the basket containing unleavened bread,

³ and gather the entire assembly at the entrance to the Tent of Meeting." ⁴ Moses did as the Lord commanded him and the assembly gathered at the entrance to the Tent of Meeting.

⁵ Moses said to the assembly, "This is what the Lord has commanded to be done."

⁶ Then Moses brought Aaron and his sons forward and washed them with water.

⁷ He put the tunic on Aaron, tied the sash around him, clothed him with the robe and put the ephod on him. He also tied the ephod to him by its skillfully woven waistband; so it was fastened on him.

⁸ He placed the breastplate on him and put the Urim and Thumim in the breastplate.

⁹ Then he placed the mitre (turban) on Aaron's head and set the gold plate, the sacred diadem, on the front of the mitre, as the Lord commanded Moses.

¹⁰ Then Moses took the anointing oil and anointed the Tabernacle and everything in it, and so consecrated them.

¹¹ He sprinkled some of the oil on the altar seven times, anointing the altar and all its utensils and the basin with its stand, to consecrate them.

¹² He poured some of the anointing oil on Aaron's head and anointed him to consecrate him. ¹³ Then he brought Aaron's sons forward, put tunics on them, tied sashes around them and put headbands on them, as the Lord commanded Moses.

Leviticus 8:7 – With the word *bo* (in it), we reach the middle of the Torah Scroll in verses. Wherever there is two halves of anything, there is an opportunity to connect to Central Column energy. Before we can do this, however, we need resistance to reveal the Light. Just as a light bulb cannot create light without the simultaneous resistance of the filament through which the electricity is passed, so too do we need to resist our selfish desires before we can reveal the Light in our lives. Furthermore, we need to understand the meaning of the Left and Right Column energies before we can utilize Central Column energy. Left Column energy is one of judgment and receiving, Right Column energy is one of mercy and sharing, and the balance between these energies, the Central Column, is the level the *Desire to Receive for the Sake of Sharing*.

FOURTH READING - MOSES - NETZACH

וַיְדַבֵּר ראה יְהֹוָאֲדֹנִי אֶל־מֹשֶׁה מהע, אל שדי לֵאמֹר: 2 קַח אֶת־ 8 1

אַהֲרֹן ע"ב ורבוע ע"ב וְאֶת־בָּנָיו אִתּוֹ וְאֵת הַבְּגָדִים וְאֵת שֶׁמֶן י"פ טל, י"פ כוזו, ביט

הַמִּשְׁחָה וְאֵת | פַּר סמזוזר, ערי, סנדלפון הַחַטָּאת וְאֵת שְׁנֵי הָאֵילִים וְאֵת סַל

הַמַּצּוֹת: 3 וְאֵת כָּל־ יל־ הָעֵדָה הַקְהֵל ע"ב ס"ג אֶל־פֶּתַח אֹהֶל לאה מוֹעֵד:

4 וַיַּעַשׂ מֹשֶׁה מהע, אל שדי כַּאֲשֶׁר צִוָּה פוי יְהֹוָאֲדֹנִי אֹתוֹ וַתִּקָּהֵל הָעֵדָה

אֶל־פֶּתַח אֹהֶל לאה מוֹעֵד: 5 וַיֹּאמֶר מֹשֶׁה מהע, אל שדי אֶל־הָעֵדָה זֶה

הַדָּבָר ראה אֲשֶׁר־צִוָּה פוי יְהֹוָאֲדֹנִי לַעֲשׂוֹת: 6 וַיַּקְרֵב מֹשֶׁה מהע, אל שדי

אֶת־אַהֲרֹן ע"ב ורבוע ע"ב וְאֶת־בָּנָיו וַיִּרְחַץ אֹתָם בַּמָּיִם: 7 וַיִּתֵּן י"פ מלוי ע"ב עָלָיו

אֶת־הַכֻּתֹּנֶת וַיַּחְגֹּר אֹתוֹ בָּאַבְנֵט וַיַּלְבֵּשׁ אֹתוֹ אֶת־הַמְּעִיל וַיִּתֵּן עָלָיו

אֶת־הָאֵפֹד ע"ה אלהים וַיַּחְגֹּר אֹתוֹ בְּחֵשֶׁב הָאֵפֹד ע"ה אלהים וַיֶּאְפֹּד לוֹ בּוֹ :

8 וַיָּשֶׂם עָלָיו אֶת־הַחֹשֶׁן שדי ורבוע אהיה וַיִּתֵּן י"פ מלוי ע"ב אֶל־הַחֹשֶׁן שדי ורבוע אהיה

אֶת־הָאוּרִים וְאֶת־הַתֻּמִּים: 9 וַיָּשֶׂם אֶת־הַמִּצְנֶפֶת עַל־רֹאשׁוֹ וַיָּשֶׂם

עַל־הַמִּצְנֶפֶת אֶל־מוּל פָּנָיו אֵת צִיץ הַזָּהָב לתו נֵזֶר הַקֹּדֶשׁ כַּאֲשֶׁר צִוָּה

פוי יְהֹוָאֲדֹנִי אֶת־מֹשֶׁה מהע, אל שדי: 10 וַיִּקַּח וזלם מֹשֶׁה מהע, אל שדי אֶת־

שֶׁמֶן י"פ טל, י"פ כוזו, ביט הַמִּשְׁחָה וַיִּמְשַׁח אֶת־הַמִּשְׁכָּן ב"פ (רבוע אלהים ÷ ה) וְאֶת־

כָּל־ יל־ אֲשֶׁר־בּוֹ וַיְקַדֵּשׁ אֹתָם: 11 וַיַּז מִמֶּנּוּ עַל־הַמִּזְבֵּחַ זן, נגד שֶׁבַע

ע"ב ואלהים דיורין פְּעָמִים וַיִּמְשַׁח אֶת־הַמִּזְבֵּחַ זן, נגד וְאֶת־כָּל־ יל־ כֵּלָיו וְאֶת־

הַכִּיֹּר וְאֶת־כַּנּוֹ לְקַדְּשָׁם: 12 וַיִּצֹק מִשֶּׁמֶן י"פ טל, י"פ כוזו, ביט הַמִּשְׁחָה עַל

רֹאשׁ ריבוע אלהים ואלהים דיורין ע"ה אַהֲרֹן ע"ב ורבוע ע"ב וַיִּמְשַׁח אֹתוֹ לְקַדְּשׁוֹ:

13 וַיַּקְרֵב מֹשֶׁה מהע, אל שדי אֶת־בְּנֵי אַהֲרֹן ע"ב ורבוע ע"ב וַיַּלְבִּשֵׁם כֻּתֳּנֹת

וַיַּחְגֹּר אֹתָם אַבְנֵט וַיַּחֲבֹשׁ לָהֶם מִגְבָּעוֹת כַּאֲשֶׁר צִוָּה פוי יְהֹוָאֲדֹנִי

אֶת־מֹשֶׁה מהע, אל שדי:

FIFTH READING - AARON - HOD

14 He then presented the bull for the sin offering, and Aaron and his sons laid their hands on the head of the sin offering.

15 Moses slaughtered the bull and took some of the blood, and with his finger he put it on all the horns of the altar to purify the altar. He poured out the rest of the blood at the base of the altar. So he consecrated it to make atonement for it.

16 Moses also took all the fat around the inner parts, the covering of the liver, and both kidneys and their fat, and burned it on the altar.

17 But the bull with its hide and its flesh and its offal he burned up outside the camp, as the Lord commanded Moses. 18 He then presented the ram for the burnt offering, and Aaron and his sons laid their hands on its head.

19 Then Moses slaughtered the ram and sprinkled the blood against the altar on all sides. 20 He cut the ram into pieces and burned the head, the pieces and the fat.

21 He washed the inner parts and the legs with water and burned the whole ram on the altar as a burnt offering, a pleasing aroma, an offering made to the Lord by fire, as the Lord commanded Moses.

הַחַטָּאת

Leviticus 8:14 – Here, the sin offering is discussed. This was the first sacrifice in the transformation process of the *kohenim*. Because of the power they held, the priests had to reach and maintain a higher spiritual standard than most people. Even Aaron, who was exceedingly elevated, still had aspects of himself that he needed to cleanse. When we reach the higher spiritual levels, our task of self-purification becomes even more rigorous. On the lower levels, we could do many unenlightened things without apparent ill effects. But as we progress upward, performing those same kinds of actions becomes poisonous to us, making us fall back down to a lower spiritual level.

אַיִל

Leviticus 8:18 – This verse is about the ram, which kabbalists say represents the ego. The

more powerful a person becomes, the more ego he or she has invested in that power. Ego is the most dangerous and powerful enemy of an elevated person.

Rav Brandwein, in a letter to Rav Berg, wrote about Rav Ashlag and his relationship with his teacher:

"Since then, I started acquiring a little ego, and as my ego grew, so did my holy teacher of blessed memory keep his distance from me. I did not even take notice of that. This carried on for about three months till finally, in the last few days, I could never find him at home. I sought him, but I found him not. That is when I realized that he had actually alienated himself from me. I felt great sorrow and started improving my ways. And on the ninth day of Nissan, in the morning, I found him and repented for what I had done, and he accepted

FIFTH READING - AARON - HOD

14 וַיַּגֵּשׁ אֵת פַּר סזּ׳זׄךְ, ערי, סנדלפוֹן ‏ הַחַטָּאת ‏ וַיִּסְמֹךְ אַהֲרֹן ע״ב ורבוע ע״ב וּבָנָיו
אֶת־יְדֵיהֶם עַל־רֹאשׁ רבוע אלהים וואלהים דיודין ע״ה ‏ פַּר סזּ׳זׄךְ, ערי, סנדלפוֹן ‏ הַחַטָּאת:
15 וַיִּשְׁחָט וַיִּקַּח וֹעם מֹשֶׁה מהע׳ אל שׁדי אֶת־הַדָּם רבוע אהיה וַיִּתֵּן י״פ מלוי ע״ב עַל־
קַרְנוֹת הַמִּזְבֵּחַ ז׳, נגד סָבִיב בְּאֶצְבָּעוֹ וַיְחַטֵּא אֶת־הַמִּזְבֵּחַ ז׳, נגד וְאֶת־
הַדָּם רבוע אהיה יָצַק אֶל־יְסוֹד ההע הַמִּזְבֵּחַ ז׳, נגד וַיְקַדְּשֵׁהוּ מצפצ לְכַפֵּר עָלָיו:
16 וַיִּקַּח וֹעם אֶת־כָּל־ יל׳ הַחֵלֶב אֲשֶׁר עַל־הַקֶּרֶב וְאֵת יֹתֶרֶת הַכָּבֵד
וְאֶת־שְׁתֵּי הַכְּלָיֹת וְאֶת־חֶלְבְּהֶן וַיַּקְטֵר מֹשֶׁה מהע׳ אל שׁדי הַמִּזְבֵּחָה:
17 וְאֶת־הַפָּר סזּ׳זׄךְ, ערי, סנדלפוֹן וְאֶת־עֹרוֹ וְאֶת־בְּשָׂרוֹ וְאֶת־פִּרְשׁוֹ שָׂרַף
בָּאֵשׁ אלהים דיודין ע״ה מִחוּץ לַמַּחֲנֶה כַּאֲשֶׁר צִוָּה פי׳ יְהֹוָאֲדֹנָיההדי אֶת־מֹשֶׁה
מהע׳ אל שׁדי: 18 וַיַּקְרֵב אֵת ‏ אֵיל ‏ הָעֹלָה וַיִּסְמְכוּ אַהֲרֹן ע״ב ורבוע ע״ב וּבָנָיו
אֶת־יְדֵיהֶם עַל־רֹאשׁ רבוע אלהים וואלהים דיודין ע״ה 19 וַיִּשְׁחָט וַיִּזְרֹק הָאָיִל:
מֹשֶׁה מהע׳ אל שׁדי אֶת־הַדָּם רבוע אהיה עַל־הַמִּזְבֵּחַ ז׳, נגד סָבִיב: 20 וְאֶת־הָאַיִל
נִתַּח לִנְתָחָיו וַיַּקְטֵר מֹשֶׁה מהע׳ אל שׁדי אֶת־הָרֹאשׁ רבוע אלהים וואלהים דיודין ע״ה
וְאֶת־הַנְּתָחִים וְאֶת־הַפָּדֶר: 21 וְאֶת־הַקֶּרֶב וְאֶת־הַכְּרָעַיִם רָחַץ בַּמָּיִם
וַיַּקְטֵר מֹשֶׁה מהע׳ אל שׁדי אֶת־כָּל־ יל׳ הָאַיִל הַמִּזְבֵּחָה עֹלָה הוּא לְרֵיחַ
רמ״ח נִיחֹחַ אִשֶּׁה הוּא לַיְהֹוָהאדניאהדנהי כַּאֲשֶׁר צִוָּה פי׳ יְהֹוָאֲדֹנָיההדי אֶת־
מֹשֶׁה מהע׳ אל שׁדי:

---

me, in the same manner that he was previously."
— *Yedid Nafshi, Part III, Essay 1*

The following day, Rav Ashlag's beloved teacher died. It caused Rav Ashlag much grief to know that he had wasted so much precious time away from his teacher because of his own ego. Thus we can see that even highly spiritual people must struggle with their ego throughout their lives and must remain constantly aware of its pernicious influence on their actions.

SIXTH READING - JOSEPH - YESOD

22 He then presented the other ram, the ram for the ordination, and Aaron and his sons laid their hands on its head.

23 Moses slaughtered it and took some of its blood and put it on the lobe of Aaron's right ear, on the thumb of his right hand and on the big toe of his right foot.

24 Moses also brought Aaron's sons forward and put some of the blood on the lobes of their right ears, on the thumbs of their right hands and on the big toes of their right feet. Then he sprinkled blood against the altar on all sides.

25 He took the fat, the fat tail, all the fat around the inner parts, the covering of the liver, both kidneys and their fat and the right thigh.

26 Then from the basket of unleavened bread, which was before the Lord, he took one unleavened cake, and one made with oil, and a wafer; he put these on the fat portions and on the right thigh.

27 He put all these in the hands of Aaron and his sons and waved them before the Lord as a wave offering.

28 Then Moses took them from their hands and burned them on the altar on top of the burnt offering as an ordination offering, a pleasing aroma, an offering made to the Lord by fire.

29 He also took the breast and waved it before the Lord as a wave offering—this was Moses' share of the ordination ram—as the Lord commanded Moses.

SEVENTH READING - DAVID - MALCHUT

30 Then Moses took some of the anointing oil and some of the blood from the altar and sprinkled them on Aaron and his garments and on his sons and their garments. So he consecrated Aaron and his garments and his sons and their garments.

SIXTH READING - JOSEPH - YESOD

וַיַּקְרֵב֙ אֶת־הָאַ֣יִל הַשֵּׁנִ֔י אֵ֖יל הַמִּלֻּאִ֑ים וַֽיִּסְמְכ֧וּ אַהֲרֹ֛ן ע"ב ורבוע ע"ב 22

וּבָנָ֛יו אֶת־יְדֵיהֶ֖ם עַל־רֹ֣אשׁ רבוע אלהים ואלהים דיודין ע"ה הָאָ֑יִל | 23 וַיִּשְׁחָ֗ט

וַיִּקַּ֤ח וועם מֹשֶׁה֙ מהע׳ אל שדי מִדָּמ֔וֹ וַיִּתֵּ֛ן י"פ מלוי ע"ב עַל־תְּנ֥וּךְ אֹ֖זֶן יוד הי ואו הה

אַהֲרֹ֖ן ע"ב ורבוע ע"ה הַיְמָנִ֑ית וְעַל־בֹּ֤הֶן יָדוֹ֙ הַיְמָנִ֔ית וְעַל־בֹּ֖הֶן רַגְל֥וֹ הַיְמָנִֽית:

וַיַּקְרֵב֮ אֶת־בְּנֵ֣י אַהֲרֹן֒ ע"ב ורבוע ע"ב וַיִּתֵּ֨ן י"פ מלוי ע"ב מֹשֶׁ֤ה מהע׳ אל שדי מִן־ 24

הַדָּם֙ רבוע אהיה עַל־תְּנ֣וּךְ אׇזְנָ֣ם הַיְמָנִ֔ית וְעַל־בֹּ֤הֶן יָדָם֙ הַיְמָנִ֔ית וְעַל־בֹּ֖הֶן

רַגְלָ֣ם הַיְמָנִ֑ית וַיִּזְרֹ֨ק מֹשֶׁ֧ה מהע׳ אל שדי אֶת־הַדָּ֛ם רבוע אהיה עַל־הַמִּזְבֵּ֖חַ זן, נגד

סָבִֽיב: 25 וַיִּקַּ֣ח וועם אֶת־הַחֵ֣לֶב וְאֶת־הָֽאַלְיָ֗ה וְאֶֽת־כׇּל־ יל׳ הַחֵ֨לֶב֙ אֲשֶׁ֣ר

עַל־הַקֶּ֔רֶב וְאֵת֙ יֹתֶ֣רֶת הַכָּבֵ֔ד וְאֶת־שְׁתֵּ֥י הַכְּלָיֹ֖ת וְאֶֽת־חֶלְבְּהֶ֑ן וְאֵ֖ת

שׁ֥וֹק הַיָּמִֽין: 26 וּמִסַּ֨ל הַמַּצּ֜וֹת אֲשֶׁ֣ר | לִפְנֵ֣י וחכמה בינה יְהֹוָ֗הואהדונהי לָקַ֞ח

חַלַּ֨ת מַצָּ֤ה ע"ב ס"ג אַחַת֙ וְֽחַלַּ֨ת לֶ֥חֶם ג"פ יהוה שֶׁ֛מֶן י"פ טל, י"פ כוז"ו, ביט יהוה אהיה אדני

אַחַ֖ת וְרָקִ֣יק אֶחָ֑ד אהבה, דאגה וַיָּ֨שֶׂם֙ עַל־הַ֣חֲלָבִ֔ים וְעַ֖ל שׁ֥וֹק הַיָּמִֽין:

וַיִּתֵּ֣ן י"פ מלוי ע"ב אֶת־הַכֹּ֗ל יל׳ עַ֚ל כַּפֵּ֣י אַהֲרֹ֔ן ע"ב ורבוע ע"ב וְעַ֖ל כַּפֵּ֣י בָנָ֑יו וַיָּ֧נֶף 27

אֹתָ֛ם תְּנוּפָ֖ה לִפְנֵ֣י וחכמה בינה יְהֹוָֽהואהדונהי: 28 וַיִּקַּ֨ח וועם מֹשֶׁ֤ה מהע׳ אל שדי

אֹתָם֙ מֵעַ֣ל אלם כַּפֵּיהֶ֔ם וַיַּקְטֵ֥ר הַמִּזְבֵּ֖חָה עַל־הָעֹלָ֑ה מִלֻּאִ֥ים הֵם֙ לְרֵ֣יחַ

נִיחֹ֔חַ רמ"ח אִשֶּׁ֥ה ה֖וּא לַֽיהֹוָֽהואהדונהי: 29 וַיִּקַּ֤ח וועם מֹשֶׁה֙ מהע׳ אל שדי אֶת־

הֶ֣חָזֶ֔ה וַיְנִיפֵ֥הוּ תְנוּפָ֖ה לִפְנֵ֣י וחכמה בינה יְהֹוָ֑הואהדונהי מֵאֵ֣יל הַמִּלֻּאִ֗ים לְמֹשֶׁ֤ה

הָיָה֙ יהה לְמָנָ֔ה ע"ה פוי כַּאֲשֶׁ֛ר פוי צִוָּ֥ה יְהֹוָ֖הואהדונהי אֶת־מֹשֶֽׁה: מהע׳ אל שדי

SEVENTH READING - DAVID - MALCHUT

וַיִּקַּ֨ח וועם מֹשֶׁ֜ה מהע׳ אל שדי מִשֶּׁ֤מֶן י"פ טל, י"פ כוז"ו, ביט הַמִּשְׁחָה֙ וּמִן־הַדָּם֙ 30

אֲשֶׁ֣ר רבוע אהיה עַל־הַמִּזְבֵּ֔חַ זן, נגד וַיַּ֤ז וין עַֽל־אַהֲרֹן֙ ע"ב ורבוע ע"ב עַל־בְּגָדָ֔יו וְעַֽל־

³¹ *Moses then said to Aaron and his sons, "Cook the meat at the entrance to the Tent of Meeting and eat it there with the bread from the basket of ordination offerings, as I commanded, saying, 'Aaron and his sons are to eat it.'*

³² *Then burn up the rest of the meat and the bread.*

MAFTIR

³³ *Do not leave the entrance to the Tent of Meeting for seven days, until the days of your ordination are completed, for your ordination will last seven days.*

³⁴ *What has been done today the Lord commanded be done to make atonement for you.*

³⁵ *You must stay at the entrance to the Tent of Meeting day and night for seven days and do what the Lord requires, so you will not die; for that is what I have been commanded."*

³⁶ *So Aaron and his sons did everything the Lord commanded through Moses.*

וּבְמִפְתָּוּוֹ

Leviticus 8:33 – Aaron and his sons had to go into seclusion for seven days before becoming priests. Moses did this as well, and he ended up elevating to the highest level a human being has ever reached; he became a link between humanity and the Creator. We can tap into that link through dreams and visions. Through seclusion and dedication, we can link ourselves to the wisdom and presence of Moses, even today.

"And you shall not go out from the door of the Tent of Meeting for seven days... for seven days shall God consecrate you." (Leviticus 8:33). Those seven, WHICH ARE BINAH WITH THE SIX DAYS INCLUDED WITHIN, AS IT IS MENTIONED ABOVE, were perfected and adorned and anointed by the priests in everything. When they reached the Congregation of Israel, WHICH IS MALCHUT, being the eighth DAY, WHICH COMES AFTER THE SEVEN DAYS - BINAH, CHESED, GEVURAH, TIFERET, NETZACH, HOD AND YESOD - Aaron was ordered to offer a calf - which is the son of a cow, WHICH ALLUDES TO MALCHUT. This was to atone for the sin of that other 'calf' whom Aaron created, thereby sinning against the 'cow,' WHICH IS MALCHUT, and which is the eighth DAY OF THOSE SEVEN DAYS MENTIONED ABOVE, FOR SHE IS CALLED 'the peaceful and faithful in Israel.' THEN, the priest is considered complete in all, in the eight different vestments of glory, complete in all the Sefirot Above and Below.
— The Zohar, Shemini 4:26, 29

בָּנָיו וְעַל־בִּגְדֵי בָנָיו אִתּוֹ וַיְקַדֵּשׁ אֶת־אַהֲרֹן אֶת־בְּגָדָיו וְאֶת־בָּנָיו

וְאֶת־בִּגְדֵי בָנָיו אִתּוֹ: 31 וַיֹּאמֶר מֹשֶׁה מהע, אל שדי **אֶל־אַהֲרֹן** ע"ב ורביע ע"ב

וְאֶל־בָּנָיו בַּשְּׁלוּ אֶת־הַבָּשָׂר פֶּתַח אֹהֶל לאה מוֹעֵד וְשָׁם יהוה שדי תֹּאכְלוּ

אֹתוֹ וְאֶת־הַלֶּחֶם ג"פ יהוה אֲשֶׁר בְּסַל הַמִּלֻּאִים כַּאֲשֶׁר צִוֵּיתִי לֵאמֹר

אַהֲרֹן ע"ב ורביע ע"ב וּבָנָיו יֹאכְלֻהוּ: 32 וְהַנּוֹתָר בַּבָּשָׂר וּבַלָּחֶם ג"פ יהוה בָּאֵשׁ

אלהים דיודין ע"ה תִּשְׂרֹפוּ:

MAFTIR

33 וּמִפֶּתַח‬ אֹהֶל לאה מוֹעֵד לֹא תֵצְאוּ שִׁבְעַת יָמִים נלך עַד יוֹם

ע"ה = נגד, זן, מזבח מְלֹאת יְמֵי מִלֻּאֵיכֶם כִּי שִׁבְעַת יָמִים נלך יְמַלֵּא אֶת־

יֶדְכֶם: 34 כַּאֲשֶׁר עָשָׂה בַּיּוֹם ע"ה = נגד, זן, מזבח הַזֶּה וְהו צִוָּה פוי יהואדניאהדונהי

לַעֲשֹׂת מצפצ לְכַפֵּר עֲלֵיכֶם: 35 וּפֶתַח אֹהֶל לאה מוֹעֵד תֵּשְׁבוּ יוֹמָם וָלַיְלָה

מלה שִׁבְעַת יָמִים נלך וּשְׁמַרְתֶּם אֶת־מִשְׁמֶרֶת יְהוֹ‬אֲדֹנֵיאההדונהי וְלֹא תָמוּתוּ

כִּי־כֵן צֻוֵּיתִי: 36 וַיַּעַשׂ אַהֲרֹן ע"ב ורביע ע"ב וּבָנָיו אֵת כָּל־ ילי הַדְּבָרִים ראה

אֲשֶׁר־צִוָּה פוי יְהוֹ‬אֲדנֵיאיאההדונהי בְּיַד־מֹשֶׁה מהע, אל שדי :

HAFTARAH OF TZAV

In this Haftarah, Jeremiah foretells the dire events that would befall the Israelites if they did not change. This reminds us that to prevent calamity and bring goodness to our own future, it is necessary that we transform so we can draw the Light of the Creator into our lives.

Jeremiah 7:21-8:3; 9:22-23

7:²¹ Thus says the Lord of Hosts, the God of Israel: Add your burnt offerings to your sacrifices and eat your meat.

²² For I spoke not to your fathers nor commanded them on the day that I brought them out of the land of Egypt, about burnt offerings and sacrifices,

²³ but I gave them this command, saying: Hear My Voice, and I will be your God and you will be My people; and walk in all the ways that I command you, that it may go well with you.

²⁴ But they heard not nor inclined their ear, but followed their own counsels, even in the stubbornness of their evil hearts; and went backward and not forward,

²⁵ ever since the day your fathers came forth out of the land of Egypt until today, and even though I sent you all My Servants the Prophets, daily rising up early and sending them,

²⁶ yet they did not hear Me, nor incline their ear, but made their neck stiff, they did worse than their fathers.

²⁷ Therefore, you shall speak all these words to them, but they will not hear you; when you call to them, they will not answer you.

²⁸ But you shall say to them, 'This is the nation that does not obey the Voice of the Lord, their God, nor receives correction. Truth has perished and is cut off from their mouth.

²⁹ Cut off your hair, Jerusalem, and throw it away; and take up a lament on high places, for the Lord has rejected and forsaken the generation of His wrath.'

³⁰ For the children of Judah have done evil in My eyes, says the Lord. They have set up their abominations in the house that bears My Name to pollute it.

HAFTARAH OF TZAV

ירמיהו פרק ז

7 21 כֹּה אָמַר יְהוָה צְבָאוֹת אֱלֹהֵי יִשְׂרָאֵל עֹלוֹתֵיכֶם סְפוּ עַל־זִבְחֵיכֶם וְאִכְלוּ בָשָׂר: 22 כִּי לֹא־דִבַּרְתִּי אֶת־אֲבוֹתֵיכֶם וְלֹא צִוִּיתִים בְּיוֹם הוֹצִיאִי (כתיב: הוציא) אוֹתָם מֵאֶרֶץ מִצְרָיִם עַל־דִּבְרֵי עוֹלָה וָזָבַח: 23 כִּי אִם־אֶת־הַדָּבָר הַזֶּה צִוִּיתִי אוֹתָם לֵאמֹר שִׁמְעוּ בְקוֹלִי וְהָיִיתִי לָכֶם לֵאלֹהִים וְאַתֶּם תִּהְיוּ־לִי לְעָם וַהֲלַכְתֶּם בְּכָל־הַדֶּרֶךְ אֲשֶׁר אֲצַוֶּה אֶתְכֶם לְמַעַן יִיטַב לָכֶם: 24 וְלֹא שָׁמְעוּ וְלֹא־הִטּוּ אֶת־אָזְנָם וַיֵּלְכוּ בְּמֹעֵצוֹת בִּשְׁרִרוּת לִבָּם הָרָע וַיִּהְיוּ לְאָחוֹר וְלֹא לְפָנִים: 25 לְמִן־הַיּוֹם אֲשֶׁר יָצְאוּ אֲבוֹתֵיכֶם מֵאֶרֶץ מִצְרַיִם עַד הַיּוֹם הַזֶּה וָאֶשְׁלַח אֲלֵיכֶם אֶת־כָּל־עֲבָדַי הַנְּבִיאִים יוֹם הַשְׁכֵּם וְשָׁלֹחַ: 26 וְלוֹא שָׁמְעוּ אֵלַי וְלֹא הִטּוּ אֶת־אָזְנָם וַיַּקְשׁוּ אֶת־עָרְפָּם הֵרֵעוּ מֵאֲבוֹתָם: 27 וְדִבַּרְתָּ אֲלֵיהֶם אֶת־כָּל־הַדְּבָרִים הָאֵלֶּה וְלֹא יִשְׁמְעוּ אֵלֶיךָ וְקָרָאתָ אֲלֵיהֶם וְלֹא יַעֲנוּכָה: 28 וְאָמַרְתָּ אֲלֵיהֶם זֶה הַגּוֹי אֲשֶׁר לוֹא־שָׁמְעוּ בְּקוֹל יְהוָה אֱלֹהָיו וְלֹא לָקְחוּ מוּסָר אָבְדָה הָאֱמוּנָה וְנִכְרְתָה מִפִּיהֶם: 29 גָּזִּי נִזְרֵךְ וְהַשְׁלִיכִי וּשְׂאִי עַל־שְׁפָיִם קִינָה כִּי מָאַס יְהוָה וַיִּטֹּשׁ אֶת־דּוֹר עֶבְרָתוֹ: 30 כִּי־עָשׂוּ בְנֵי־יְהוּדָה הָרַע בְּעֵינַי נְאֻם־יְהוָה שָׂמוּ שִׁקּוּצֵיהֶם בַּבַּיִת אֲשֶׁר־נִקְרָא־שְׁמִי עָלָיו לְטַמְּאוֹ: 31 וּבָנוּ בָּמוֹת הַתֹּפֶת אֲשֶׁר בְּגֵיא בֶן־הִנֹּם לִשְׂרֹף אֶת־בְּנֵיהֶם

31 And they have built the high places of Tophet in the Valley of Ben Hinnom, to burn their sons and their daughters in the fire, which I commanded them not to do, nor did it enter My Heart.

32 Therefore behold, the days are coming, says the Lord, that it shall no longer be called Tophet, or the Valley of Ben Hinnom, but the Valley of Slaughter, for they will bury the dead in Tophet until there is no place.

33 And the carcasses of this people shall be meat for the birds of the heaven and the beasts of the earth, and none shall frighten them away.

34 Then I will bring an end from the cities of Judah and from the streets of Jerusalem, the voice of joy and the voice of gladness, the voice of bridegroom and the voice of bride, for the land shall be desolate.

8:1 At that time, says the Lord, they shall bring out the bones of the kings of Judah and the bones of his princes, and the bones of the priests and the bones of the prophets, and the bones of the inhabitants of Jerusalem out of their graves.

2 And they shall spread them before the sun and the moon and all the hosts of the heavens, which they have loved and which they have served and after which they have walked and in which they sought and in which they have worshiped. They shall not be gathered nor buried, they shall be for dung on the face of the earth.

3 And death shall be chosen rather than life by all the survivors that remain of this evil family, who remain in the places where I have driven them, says the Lord of Hosts.'

9:22 Thus says the Lord: "Let not the wise man glory in his wisdom, neither let the mighty man glory in his might; let not the rich man glory in his riches."

23 "But let him who glories glory in this:That he understands and knows Me, that I am the Lord, exercising loving kindness, judgment, and righteousness in the earth. For in these I delight," says the Lord.

וְאֶת־בְּנֹתֵיהֶם בָּאֵשׁ אלהים דיורין ע״ה אֲשֶׁר לֹא צִוִּיתִי וְלֹא עָלְתָה עַל־לִבִּי:

32 לָכֵן הִנֵּה מ״ה יה יָמִים בּלך בָּאִים נְאֻם־יְהֹוָהאדניאהדונהי וְלֹא־יֵאָמֵר עוֹד

הַתֹּפֶת וְגֵיא בֶן־הִנֹּם כִּי אִם יוהך, ע״ה מ״ב ־גֵּיא הַהֲרֵגָה וְקָבְרוּ בְתֹפֶת

מֵאֵין מָקוֹם יהוה ברביע: 33 וְהָיְתָה נִבְלַת הָעָם הַזֶּה והו לְמַאֲכָל אדני יהוה

לְעוֹף ג״ה ב״ן, יוסף, ציון הַשָּׁמַיִם י״פ טל, י״פ כוזו וּלְבֶהֱמַת הָאָרֶץ אלהים דההין ע״ה וְאֵין

מַחֲרִיד: 34 וְהִשְׁבַּתִּי | מֵעָרֵי עדי יְהוּדָה וּמֵחֻצוֹת יְרוּשָׁלַ͏ִם ריו ע״ע קוֹל

ע״ב ס״ג ע״ה שָׂשׂוֹן וְקוֹל ע״ב ס״ג ע״ה שִׂמְחָה קוֹל ע״ב ס״ג ע״ה וְתַן וְקוֹל ע״ב ס״ג ע״ה

כַּלָּה כִּי לְחָרְבָּה תִּהְיֶה הָאָרֶץ ע״ה אלהים דההין: 8 1 בָּעֵת י״פ אהיה י הויות הַהִיא

נְאֻם־יְהֹוָהאדניאהדונהי יוֹצִיאוּ (כתיב: ויציאו) אֶת־עַצְמוֹת מַלְכֵי־יְהוּדָה וְאֶת־

עַצְמוֹת־שָׂרָיו וְאֶת־עַצְמוֹת הַכֹּהֲנִים מלה וְאֵת | עַצְמוֹת הַנְּבִיאִים וְאֵת

עַצְמוֹת יוֹשְׁבֵי־יְרוּשָׁלָ͏ִם רי״ו ע״ע מִקִּבְרֵיהֶם: 2 וּשְׁטָחוּם לַשֶּׁמֶשׁ ב״פ ש״ך

וְלַיָּרֵחַ וּלְכֹל אדני | צְבָא הַשָּׁמַיִם י״פ טל, י״פ כוזו אֲשֶׁר אֲהֵבוּם וַאֲשֶׁר

עֲבָדוּם וַאֲשֶׁר הָלְכוּ מ״ה אַחֲרֵיהֶם וַאֲשֶׁר דְּרָשׁוּם וַאֲשֶׁר הִשְׁתַּחֲווּ

לָהֶם לֹא יֵאָסְפוּ וְלֹא יִקָּבֵרוּ לְדֹמֶן עַל־פְּנֵי חכמה בינה הָאֲדָמָה יִהְיוּ אלה:

3 וְנִבְחַר מָוֶת מֵחַיִּים אהיה אהיה יהוה, בינה ע״ה לְכֹל יה אדני הַשְּׁאֵרִית הַנִּשְׁאָרִים

מִן־הַמִּשְׁפָּחָה הָרָעָה רתע הַזֹּאת בְּכָל ב״ן, יבמ ־הַמְּקֹמוֹת הַנִּשְׁאָרִים

אֲשֶׁר הִדַּחְתִּים שָׁם יהוה שדי נְאֻם יְהֹוָהאדניאהדונהי צְבָאוֹת נתה ורביע אהיה:

9 22 כֹּה הי | אָמַר יְהֹוָהאדניאהדונהי אַל־יִתְהַלֵּל חָכָם בְּחָכְמָתוֹ בינה ע״ה

וְאַל־יִתְהַלֵּל הַגִּבּוֹר בִּגְבוּרָתוֹ אַל־יִתְהַלֵּל עָשִׁיר בְּעָשְׁרוֹ: 23 כִּי אִם

יוהך, ע״ה מ״ב ־בְּזֹאת יִתְהַלֵּל הַמִּתְהַלֵּל הַשְׂכֵּל וְיָדֹעַ אוֹתִי כִּי אֲנִי אני,

טרהד כוזו יְהֹוָהאדניאהדונהי עֹשֶׂה חֶסֶד ע״ב, ריבוע יהוה מִשְׁפָּט ע״ה ה״פ אלהים וּצְדָקָה

ע״ה ריבוע אלהים בָּאָרֶץ אלהים דאלפין כִּי־בְאֵלֶּה חָפַצְתִּי נְאֻם־יְהֹוָהאדניאהדונהי:

SHEMINI

LESSON OF SHEMINI
(Leviticus 9:1-11:47)

This chapter describes the death of Aaron's two sons, Nadav and Avihu. There are some similarities between this event and the story of Joseph as described in Genesis.

When Joseph was sold into slavery in Egypt by his brothers, they confessed and said, "We are guilty." Yet it is said that the brothers initially did not really understand the profound wickedness of what they had done. It became clear to them only after they came to Jacob, their father, and saw his terrible sorrow, as it is written· "Jacob tore his clothes and put sackcloth around his hips and grieved over his son many days...and he refused to be consoled." (*Genesis 37:34-35*) Indeed, Jacob wept and mourned for 22 years, and our sages teach us that Judah, one of Joseph's older brothers, was saddened because he was unable to find any way to console his father.

But Judah's sadness was focused on the grief that Jacob felt, and nothing else. Beyond that, there is nothing in the Bible or the *Midrash* or the *Zohar* to indicate that Judah and his brothers understood the scope of the terrible error they had made. They thought there was nothing sinful in what they had done, and moreover, they saw that the *Shechina* was still with them in spite of their misdeeds. We have evidence for this in the verse: "and his brothers went to take care of their father's sheep." (*Genesis 37:12*) The word *et* has two dots above the letters; these dots tell us that the *Shechina* was in their presence.

> *...all the letters which are included in the Shechina,* which is *M*ALCHUT CALLED *Et (A*LEF *- T*AV*) SINCE IT INCLUDES ALL THE 22 LETTERS FROM A*LEF *TO T*AV*, ORIGINATE from the aspects of the 22 letters of the Torah.*
>
> — *The Zohar, Hashmatot 7:43*

Although it took 22 years for them to recognize their mistake, there finally came a time when Joseph's brothers understood clearly the wrong they had done. But even when they began to feel the physical pain of hunger during the time of the great famine, they still did not realize that any sin or transgression on their part could have brought on such devastation. It is the power of our ego that clouds our perception of the true cause of the pain in our lives.

Any form of suffering, whether physical or emotional, is a mechanism to awaken us to the need to examine our life. If we look closely, with honesty and sincere motivation, we will be able to see where we have gone wrong.

When Aaron heard about the death of both his sons, he was silent. He knew their death came about because of his role in creating the Golden Calf. It was Aaron who had collected the gold from the people and formed it into a calf. And with this action, he transferred his spiritual Light—his energy—into this abominable creature so that it could come alive. The *Zohar* says:

> Aaron had to be purified more because, but for him, the calf would not have been made. Why? Aaron is the Right and the strength of the sun. Gold is from the sun, FOR THE SUN, WHICH IS TIFERET, IS COMPRISED OF RIGHT AND LEFT. HENCE GOLD COMES FROM THE LEFT, BUT THE STRENGTH AND RULING OF THE SUN IS RIGHT. The spirit of unholiness descended to be included IN THE GOLD, THAT MADE THE CALF, and so were the people of Israel defiled and so was he, AARON, until they became purified.
>
> — The Zohar, Pekudei 35:314

When something painful happens in our life, we immediately ask, "Why me? What have I done to deserve this? Why is God letting this happen to me?" Righteous individuals like Aaron understand the truth. It may require a long period of reflection, as it did for Joseph's brothers who required a period of 22 years. But the brothers eventually opened themselves to the truth and were able to say, "We made a mistake."

With the help of God, we will all be able to reach this level of consciousness in our own lives.

SYNOPSIS OF SHEMINI

Shemini in Aramaic means "the eighth." The number eight connects us to the *Sefira* of *Binah*, the eighth *Sefira*, counting upward from *Malchut*. The number eight is also the numerical value of the Aramaic word for circumcision (*brit*), which also has a direct spiritual connection to *Binah*. A connection to *Binah* helps us to internalize the information we constantly absorb during the day and convert it into knowledge that is understood with our heart, not just with our head. It is this kind of understanding that we need to achieve to be able to connect to the Light and to help others do so as well.

Binah in this chapter gives us the opportunity to connect with the Light directly, without the need for intermediaries. The Aramaic language itself allows us to make this direct connection as well, which is why the *Zohar* is written in Aramaic. Kabbalah teaches that even the angels don't understand Aramaic, so we bypass them and go directly to the Upper World of *Binah*. Like reading or scanning the *Zohar*, reading this chapter of the Bible helps us reach *Binah* directly.

FIRST READING - ABRAHAM - CHESED

9:1 O*n the eighth day, Moses called Aaron and his sons and the elders of Israel, 2 and he said to Aaron, "Take a bull calf for your sin offering and a ram for your burnt offering, both without defect, and present them before the Lord.*

3 Then say to the Children of Israel the following: 'Take a male goat for a sin offering, a calf and a lamb—both a year old and without defect—for a burnt offering,

4 and an ox and a ram for a peace offering to sacrifice before the Lord, together with a meal offering mixed with oil. For today the Lord will appear to you.'"

5 They brought that which Moses commanded to the front of the Tent of Meeting, and the entire congregation came near and stood before the Lord. 6 Then Moses said, "This is what the Lord has commanded you to do, so that the glory of the Lord may appear to you."

7 Moses said to Aaron, "Come to the altar and sacrifice your sin offering and your burnt offering and make atonement for yourself and the people; sacrifice the offering that is for the people and make atonement for them, as the Lord has commanded."

FROM THE RAV

Nadav and Avihu, the sons of Aaron, the High Priest, were consumed by fire; only their souls were left intact. We have to understand what happened here because Nadav and Avihu were *tzadikim* (righteous people), not drunks or lowlifes.

Despite what the world would say, these two sons—these two *tzadikim*—and their other two brothers did what they had to do, even knowing that it would leave them in shame. They did it anyway because they felt it would be an everlasting lesson that Israel would learn from.

When you feel something is right, you do it, and however the marbles fall, it will come out right at the end. For Nadav and Avihu, on the surface, it looks like it didn't turn out right because they died.

The big lesson here is that no matter what is at stake, you do the right thing. You do the right thing—even if your life depends on it—which Nadav and Avihu knew was a possibility.

We are always concerned about opinions—about what our friends might think of us, what our family will think of us. We are always inhibited by the opinions of others around us, which limits our actions and prevents us from doing things that we believe in.

I do not live by that code. If it's right, I'm going to do it. What the people might think about it around me, that's another matter entirely.

FIRST READING - ABRAHAM - CHESED

9 1 וַיְהִי אֵל בַּיּוֹם ע״ה = נגד, זן, מזבח הַשְּׁמִינִ֔י קָרָ֣א מֹשֶׁ֑ה מהע, אל שדי לְאַהֲרֹ֣ן

ע״ב ורבוע ע״ב וּלְבָנָ֔יו וּלְזִקְנֵ֖י יִשְׂרָאֵ֑ל ע״ב ורבוע ע״ב 2 וַיֹּ֣אמֶר אֶֽל־אַהֲרֹ֗ן קַֽח־לְךָ֣

עֵ֣גֶל בֶּן־בָּקָ֥ר לְחַטָּ֛את וְאַ֥יִל לְעֹלָ֖ה תְּמִימִ֑ם וְהַקְרֵ֖ב לִפְנֵ֥י חכמה בינה

יְהֹוָ֑הָדֹנָ֥יאהדונהי 3 וְאֶל־בְּנֵ֥י יִשְׂרָאֵ֖ל תְּדַבֵּ֣ר ראה לֵאמֹ֑ר קְח֤וּ שְׂעִיר־עִזִּ֨ים

לְחַטָּ֗את וְעֵ֧גֶל וָכֶ֛בֶשׂ ב״פ קס״א בְּנֵֽי־שָׁנָ֥ה תְּמִימִ֖ם לְעֹלָֽה׃ 4 וְשׁ֨וֹר

אבגיתץ, ושר, אהבת חנם וְאַ֜יִל לִשְׁלָמִ֗ים לִזְבֹּ֨חַ֙ לִפְנֵ֣י חכמה בינה יְהֹוָ֔הָדֹנָ֥יאהדונהי וּמִנְחָ֖ה

ע״ה ב״פ בן בְּלוּלָ֣ה בַשָּׁ֑מֶן י״פ טל, י״פ כוזו, ביט כִּ֣י הַיּ֔וֹם ע״ה = נגד, זן, מזבח יְהֹוָ֖הָדֹנָ֥יאהדונהי

נִרְאָ֥ה ע״ב ורבוע ע״ב אֲלֵיכֶֽם׃ 5 וַיִּקְח֗וּ חעם אֵ֣ת אֲשֶׁ֤ר צִוָּה֙ פוי מֹשֶׁ֔ה מהע, אל שדי

אֶל־פְּנֵ֖י חכמה בינה אֹ֣הֶל לאה מוֹעֵ֑ד וַיִּקְרְבוּ֙ כָּל־ ילי הָ֣עֵדָ֔ה וַיַּֽעַמְד֖וּ לִפְנֵ֥י

חכמה בינה יְהֹוָֽהָדֹנָ֥יאהדונהי 6 וַיֹּ֣אמֶר מֹשֶׁ֔ה מהע, אל שדי זֶ֧ה הַדָּבָ֛ר ראה אֲשֶׁר־

צִוָּ֥ה פוי יְהֹוָ֖הָדֹנָ֥יאהדונהי תַּעֲשׂ֑וּ וְיֵרָ֥א אלף למד יהוה אֲלֵיכֶ֖ם כְּב֥וֹד יְהֹוָֽהָדֹנָ֥יאהדונהי׃

7 וַיֹּ֤אמֶר מֹשֶׁה֙ מהע, אל שדי אֶֽל־אַהֲרֹ֔ן ע״ב ורבוע ע״ב קְרַ֥ב אֶל־הַמִּזְבֵּ֖חַ֙ זן, נגד

וַיְהִי

Leviticus 9:1 – The month of Aries, the first sign the zodiac, controls all 12 signs. The nature of all Vessels is the *Desire to Receive*. Desire in and of itself is not negative. It's what we do with it—whether we share or whether we're selfish—that matters. The constellation of Aries, which represents the month of *Nissan*, can easily activate our *Desire to Receive for the Self Alone*. We need to be aware, however, that even acts of sharing can come out of selfishness. This is why it is so important to reflect constantly on our motives when sharing with others.

קַח־לְךָ

Leviticus 9:2 – The discussion of the sacrifices here teaches us that personal sacrifices are needed to connect to the power of the Light. We have to give up momentary pleasures to gain eternal fulfillment.

[8] *So Aaron came to the altar and slaughtered the calf as a sin offering for himself.*

[9] *His sons brought the blood to him, and he dipped his finger into the blood and put it on the horns of the altar; the rest of the blood he poured out at the base of the altar.*

[10] *He burned the fat, the kidneys and the covering of the liver from the sin offering on the altar, as the Lord commanded Moses;* [11] *the flesh and the hide he burned up outside the camp.*

[12] *Then he slaughtered the burnt offering. His sons handed him the blood, and he sprinkled it against the altar on all sides.*

[13] *They handed him the burnt offering piece by piece, including the head, and he burned them on the altar.*

[14] *He washed the inner parts and the legs and burned them on top of the burnt offering on the altar.*

[15] *Aaron then brought the offering that was for the people. He took the goat for the people's sin offering and slaughtered it and offered it for a sin offering as he did with the first one.*

[16] *He brought the burnt offering and offered it in the prescribed way.*

SECOND READING - ISAAC - GEVURAH

[17] *He also brought the meal offering, took a handful of it and burned it on the altar in addition to the morning's burnt offering.*

וְעָשָׂה

Leviticus 9:7 – Whenever Aaron performed the sacrifices, he focused on the needs of the people. As *Kohen HaGadol* (High Priest), his spiritual work was to draw down the Light for others, a job for which he had been chosen by God. Likewise, when we do our own spiritual work, our focus should be on sharing. When we receive Light, we have to share it. At every moment of our spiritual work, we should be thinking of others.

On all occasions Above, some kind of act must be manifested BELOW. Therefore, a ceremony was performed with Aaron Below, MEANING THAT HE DID NOT LEAVE THE TABERNACLE FOR SEVEN DAYS AND HE OFFERED THE SACRIFICE

וַיַּעֲשֶׂה אֶת־חַטָּאתְךָ וְאֶת־עֹלָתֶךָ וְכִפֶּר מצפצ בַּעַדְךָ וּבְעַד הָעָם

וַעֲשֵׂה אֶת־קָרְבַּן הָעָם וְכִפֶּר מצפצ בַּעֲדָם כַּאֲשֶׁר צִוָּה פו יְהֹוָאדֹנָיאהדונהי:

8 וַיִּקְרַב אַהֲרֹן ע״ב ורבוע ע״ב אֶל־הַמִּזְבֵּחַ זה, נגד וַיִּשְׁחַט אֶת־עֵגֶל הַחַטָּאת

אֲשֶׁר־לוֹ: 9 וַיַּקְרִבוּ בְּנֵי אַהֲרֹן ע״ב ורבוע ע״ב אֶת־הַדָּם רבוע אהיה אֵלָיו וַיִּטְבֹּל

אֶצְבָּעוֹ בַּדָּם רבוע אהיה וַיִּתֵּן י״פ מלוי ע״ב עַל־קַרְנוֹת הַמִּזְבֵּחַ זה, נגד וְאֶת־הַדָּם

רבוע אהיה יָצַק אֶל־יְסוֹד הטע הַמִּזְבֵּחַ זה, נגד 10: וְאֶת־הַחֵלֶב וְאֶת־הַכְּלָיֹת

וְאֶת־הַיֹּתֶרֶת מִן־הַכָּבֵד מִן־הַחַטָּאת הִקְטִיר הַמִּזְבֵּחָה כַּאֲשֶׁר צִוָּה פו

יְהֹוָאדֹנָיאהדונהי אֶת־מֹשֶׁה מהטע, אל שדי 11: וְאֶת־הַבָּשָׂר וְאֶת־הָעוֹר שָׂרַף

בָּאֵשׁ אלהים דיודין ע״ה מִחוּץ לַמַּחֲנֶה 12: וַיִּשְׁחַט אֶת־הָעֹלָה וַיַּמְצִאוּ בְּנֵי

אַהֲרֹן ע״ב ורבוע ע״ב אֵלָיו אֶת־הַדָּם רבוע אהיה וַיִּזְרְקֵהוּ עַל־הַמִּזְבֵּחַ זה, נגד סָבִיב:

13 וְאֶת־הָעֹלָה הִמְצִיאוּ אֵלָיו לִנְתָחֶיהָ וְאֶת־הָרֹאשׁ ריבוע אלהים ואלהים דיודין ע״ה

וַיַּקְטֵר עַל־הַמִּזְבֵּחַ 14: וַיִּרְחַץ אֶת־הַקֶּרֶב וְאֶת־הַכְּרָעָיִם וַיַּקְטֵר עַל־

הָעֹלָה הַמִּזְבֵּחָה 15: וַיַּקְרֵב אֵת קָרְבַּן הָעָם וַיִּקַּח חום אֶת־שְׂעִיר

הַחַטָּאת אֲשֶׁר לָעָם עלב וַיִּשְׁחָטֵהוּ וַיְחַטְּאֵהוּ כָּרִאשׁוֹן 16: וַיַּקְרֵב אֶת־

הָעֹלָה וַיַּעֲשֶׂהָ כַּמִּשְׁפָּט ע״ה ה״פ אלהים:

SECOND READING - ISAAC - GEVURAH

17 וַיַּקְרֵב אֶת־הַמִּנְחָה ע״ה ב״פ ב״ן וַיְמַלֵּא כַפּוֹ מִמֶּנָּה וַיַּקְטֵר עַל־

הַמִּזְבֵּחַ זה, נגד מִלְּבַד עֹלַת אבגית״ץ, ושר, אהבת חנם הַבֹּקֶר 18: וַיִּשְׁחַט אֶת־

ON THE EIGHTH DAY. By that act, he elicited a reaction Above and, in this way, all becomes one and all the worlds are blessed through the priest. By this act, the priest was made complete, with all PERFECTION, as he should be. Come and behold: the Congregation of Israel is blessed by the priest, and Israel are blessed by the priest, and the priest is blessed by the Supernal Priest, WHO IS CHESED OF ZEIR ANPIN, as is written: "And they shall put my Name upon the children of Israel and I will bless them." (Numbers 6:27)

— The Zohar, Shemini 4:30,41

¹⁸ He slaughtered the ox and the ram as the peace offering for the people. His sons handed him the blood, and he sprinkled it against the altar on all sides.

¹⁹ But the fat portions of the ox and the ram—the fat tail, the layer of fat, the kidneys and the covering of the liver – ²⁰ these they laid on the breasts, and then Aaron burned the fat on the altar.

²¹ Aaron waved the breasts and the right thigh before the Lord as a wave offering, as Moses commanded.

²² Then Aaron lifted his hands toward the people and blessed them. And having sacrificed the sin offering, the burnt offering and the peace offering, he stepped down.

²³ Moses and Aaron then went into the Tent of Meeting. When they came out, they blessed the people; and the glory of the Lord appeared to all the people.

THIRD READING - JACOB - TIFERET

²⁴ Fire came out from the presence of the Lord and consumed the burnt offering and the fat portions on the altar. And when all the people saw it, they shouted for joy and fell facedown.

10:¹ Aaron's sons Nadav and Avihu took their censers, put fire in them and added incense; and they offered unauthorized fire before the Lord, contrary to his command. ² So fire came out from the presence of the Lord and consumed them, and they died

---

וַיְבָרְכֵם

Leviticus 9:22 – After Aaron blessed the people, the Divine Presence—the *Shechina*— entered the Tabernacle. That was the first time there was ever a place in this physical world for the Creator to be present in a physical sense. The Tabernacle was a Vessel for the Light. This is what we want to connect to when we need Light. More importantly, we need to be Vessels for the Light so that the Light can dwell within us.

וַיִּקְחוּ

Leviticus 10:1 – This verse relates to the death of the sons of Aaron, Nadav and Avihu. Although they were among the highest souls in the nation,

they could still be affected by Satan, which demonstrates that regardless of our spiritual level, we are always vulnerable to our Opponent. Aaron's sons thought that because the Light had entered this world, it meant that humanity had reached the critical mass necessary to defeat Satan forever and that the battle between good and evil was over. But although the people were in the presence of the Light, they had not yet been completely imbued with Light—a vital requirement for the complete and final obliteration of Satan. The *Zohar* says:

This was until the hour arrived when Nadav and Avihu rose up and spoiled the general joy, so that wrath descended on the world, as it is written: "And the glory of

הַשּׁוֹר אבֹגיתֹץ, ושׁר, אהבת חום וְאֶת־הָאַיִל זֶבַח הַשְּׁלָמִים אֲשֶׁר לָעָם עלם
וַיַּמְצִאוּ בְּנֵי אַהֲרֹן ע״ב ורבוע ע״ב אֶת־הַדָּם רבוע אהיה אֵלָיו וַיִּזְרְקֵהוּ עַל־
הַמִּזְבֵּחַ זֹן, גגֹר סָבִיב: 19 וְאֶת־הַחֲלָבִים מִן־הַשּׁוֹר אבֹגיתֹץ, ושׁר, אהבת חום וּמִן־
הָאַיִל הָאַלְיָה וְהַמְכַסֶּה וְהַכְּלָיֹת וְיֹתֶרֶת הַכָּבֵד: 20 וַיָּשִׂימוּ אֶת־
הַחֲלָבִים עַל־הֶחָזוֹת וַיַּקְטֵר הַחֲלָבִים הַמִּזְבֵּחָה: 21 וְאֵת הֶחָזוֹת וְאֵת
שׁוֹק הַיָּמִין הֵנִיף אַהֲרֹן ע״ב ורבוע ע״ב תְּנוּפָה לִפְנֵי וחכמה בינה יְהֹוָהאדניאהדונהי
כַּאֲשֶׁר צִוָּה פֹּרִי מֹשֶׁה מהשׁ, אל שׁדי: 22 וַיִּשָּׂא אַהֲרֹן ע״ב ורבוע ע״ב אֶת־יָדוֹ אֶל־
הָעָם וַיְבָרְכֵם וַיֵּרֶד רִיי מֵעֲשֹׂת הַחַטָּאת וְהָעֹלָה וְהַשְּׁלָמִים: 23 וַיָּבֹא
מֹשֶׁה מהשׁ, אל שׁדי וְאַהֲרֹן ע״ב ורבוע ע״ב אֶל־אֹהֶל לאה מוֹעֵד וַיֵּצְאוּ וַיְבָרְכוּ
אֶת־הָעָם וַיֵּרָא אלף למד יהוה כְּבוֹד־יְהֹוָהאדניאהדונהי אֶל־כָּל־ ילי הָעָם:

THIRD READING - JACOB - TIFERET

24 וַתֵּצֵא אֵשׁ אלהים דיודין ע״ה מִלִּפְנֵי וחכמה בינה יְהֹוָהאדניאהדונהי וַתֹּאכַל עַל־
הַמִּזְבֵּחַ זֹן, גגֹר אֶת־הָעֹלָה וְאֶת־הַחֲלָבִים וַיַּרְא אלף למד יהוה כָּל־ ילי הָעָם
וַיָּרֹנּוּ וַיִּפְּלוּ עַל־פְּנֵיהֶם: 10 1 וַיִּקְחוּ חום בְנֵי־אַהֲרֹן ע״ב ורבוע ע״ב נָדָב
ע״ה אהיה בוכֹו וַאֲבִיהוּא אִישׁ ע״ה קנֹ״א קסֹ״א מַחְתָּתוֹ וַיִּתְּנוּ בָהֵן אֵשׁ אלהים דיודין ע״ה

God appeared to all the people." (Leviticus 9:23) Then at once, "the sons of Aaron took each of them his censer." (Leviticus 10:1) In many ways, they spoiled the joy of the Congregation of Israel. They did not marry a woman, for they were not worthy of an offering and the worlds were not blessed by them. Also, the time was not proper FOR OFFERING THE INCENSE, FOR IT WAS NOT IN THE TIME OF LIGHTING THE CANDLES; and they also hurried the time OF INHERITING THE PRIESTHOOD WHILE THEIR FATHER WAS STILL ALIVE. Even before THEY OFFERED THE INCENSE, they were

doomed, AS IS WRITTEN: "And offered strange fire before God." (Leviticus 10:1) Another thing, MEANING THE OTHER SIDE, was linked up by that tie, and they left the Congregation of Israel, WHICH IS MALCHUT, outside.

— The Zohar, Shemini 4:36, 38a

The death of his sons served as a cleansing for Aaron because of his involvement in the creation of the Golden Calf. Because he understood this, Aaron remained silent when they died, rather than crying out to God in protest.

before the Lord. *3 Moses then said to Aaron, "This is what the Lord spoke of when he said: 'Among those who approach me I will show myself holy; in the sight of all the people, I will be honored.'" Aaron remained silent.*

4 Moses summoned Mishael and Elzaphan, sons of Aaron's uncle Uziel, and said to them, "Come here; carry your cousins away from the front of the sanctuary, outside the camp." 5 So they came and carried them, still in their tunics, outside the camp, as Moses ordered.

6 Then Moses said to Aaron and his sons Eleazar and Ithamar, "Do not let your hair become unkempt, and do not tear your clothes or you will die and the Lord will be angry with the whole community. But your relatives, all the house of Israel, may mourn for those the Lord has destroyed by fire.

7 Do not leave the entrance to the Tent of Meeting or you will die, because the Lord's anointing oil is on you." So they did as Moses said.

8 Then the Lord spoke to Aaron, saying, 9 "You and your sons are not to drink wine or other fermented drink whenever you go into the Tent of Meeting, or you will die. This is a lasting ordinance for the generations to come. 10 You must distinguish between the holy and the common, between the unclean and the clean,

11 and you must teach the Children of Israel all the decrees the Lord has given them through Moses."

אַל־תֵּשְׁתְּ

Leviticus 10:9 – God commanded Aaron and his two remaining sons, Elazar and Ithamar, not to work in the Tabernacle when they were intoxicated with wine, thus reminding us that we should not be intoxicated by any substance when we connect with the Light. The Light is the only force that elevates us. This doesn't mean it's wrong to drink at other times; what counts is our consciousness.

Therefore, when a priest enters the Sanctuary to perform a Divine service, he is not allowed to drink wine, for all his actions are performed in silence. He concentrates ON THE UNISONS in silence, joins whom he should join, NAMELY MALE AND FEMALE, and he obtains blessings for all the worlds. And everything is done in silence, for all his actions are done in secret. THEREFORE, HE IS FORBIDDEN TO DRINK wine because it reveals a secret, FOR "WHEN WINE COMES IN, A SECRET GOES OUT," and it encourages the raising of the voice.
— *The Zohar, Shemini 6:66*

The *Zohar* offers a beautiful explanation of the inner meaning of wine: "Wine satiates all." Rav Ashlag's interpretation is that "this is the illumination of *Chochmah*, which is called wine."

Come and behold: oil, THE SECRET OF THE RIGHT, is for the priests, and wine, THE SECRET OF THE LEFT, is for the Levites. This is not because they must DRINK wine, but because it comes AND ISSUES from the preserved wine, WHICH

וַיָּשִׂימוּ עָלֶיהָ פהל קְטֹרֶת י"א אדני וַיַּקְרִיבוּ לִפְנֵי יְהֹוָ‍ֹאדנילאהדונהי וחכמה בינה אֵשׁ

זָרָה אשר אלהים דיודין ע"ה אֲשֶׁר לֹא צִוָּה פוי אֹתָם: 2 וַתֵּצֵא אֵשׁ אלהים דיודין ע"ה מִלִּפְנֵי

יְהֹוָ‍ֹאדנילאהדונהי וַתֹּאכַל אוֹתָם וַיָּמֻתוּ לִפְנֵי יְהֹוָ‍ֹאדנילאהדונהי וחכמה בינה: 3 וַיֹּאמֶר

מֹשֶׁה מהע, אל שדי אֶל־אַהֲרֹן ע"ב ורבוע ע"ב הוּא אֲשֶׁר־דִּבֶּר ראה יְהֹוָ‍ֹאדנילאהדונהי |

לֵאמֹר בִּקְרֹבַי שדי אֶקָּדֵשׁ וְעַל־פְּנֵי וחכמה בינה כָל־יל־הָעָם אֶכָּבֵד וַיִּדֹּם

אַהֲרֹן ע"ב ורבוע ע"ב: 4 וַיִּקְרָא ב"ן ב"פ קס"א + ה' אותיות מֹשֶׁה מהע, אל שדי אֶל־מִישָׁאֵל

וְאֶל אֶלְצָפָן בְּנֵי עֻזִּיאֵל דֹּד אַהֲרֹן ע"ב ורבוע ע"ב וַיֹּאמֶר אֲלֵהֶם קִרְבוּ שְׂאוּ

אֶת־אֲחֵיכֶם מֵאֵת פְּנֵי וחכמה בינה הַקֹּדֶשׁ אֶל־מִחוּץ לַמַּחֲנֶה: 5 וַיִּקְרְבוּ

וַיִּשָּׂאֻם בְּכֻתֳּנֹתָם אֶל־מִחוּץ לַמַּחֲנֶה כַּאֲשֶׁר דִּבֶּר ראה מֹשֶׁה מהע, אל שדי:

6 וַיֹּאמֶר מֹשֶׁה מהע, אל שדי אֶל־אַהֲרֹן ע"ב ורבוע ע"ב וּלְאֶלְעָזָר וּלְאִיתָמָר | בָּנָיו

רָאשֵׁיכֶם אַל־תִּפְרָעוּ | וּבִגְדֵיכֶם לֹא־תִפְרֹמוּ וְלֹא תָמֻתוּ וְעַל כָּל־יל־

הָעֵדָה יִקְצֹף וַאֲחֵיכֶם כָּל־יל־בֵּית ב"פ ראה יִשְׂרָאֵל יִבְכּוּ אֶת־הַשְּׂרֵפָה

אֲשֶׁר שָׂרַף יְהֹוָ‍ֹאדנילאהדונהי: 7 וּמִפֶּתַח אֹהֶל לאה מוֹעֵד לֹא תֵצְאוּ פֶּן־

תָּמֻתוּ כִּי־שֶׁמֶן י"פ טל, י"פ כוזו, ביט מִשְׁחַת יְהֹוָ‍ֹאדנילאהדונהי עֲלֵיכֶם וַיַּעֲשׂוּ

כִּדְבַר ראה מֹשֶׁה מהע, אל שדי: 8 וַיְדַבֵּר ראה יְהֹוָ‍ֹאדנילאהדונהי אֶל־אַהֲרֹן ע"ב ורבוע ע"ב

לֵאמֹר: 9 יַיִן מיכ, י"פ האא וְשֵׁכָר י"פ ב"ן אַל־תֵּשְׁתְּ אַתָּה | וּבָנֶיךָ אִתָּךְ

בְּבֹאֲכֶם אֶל־אֹהֶל לאה מוֹעֵד וְלֹא תָמֻתוּ חֻקַּת עוֹלָם לְדֹרֹתֵיכֶם:

10 וּלֲהַבְדִּיל בֵּין הַקֹּדֶשׁ וּבֵין הַחֹל וּבֵין הַטָּמֵא וּבֵין הַטָּהוֹר י"פ אכא:

11 וּלְהוֹרֹת אֶת־בְּנֵי יִשְׂרָאֵל אֵת כָּל־יל־הַחֻקִּים אֲשֶׁר דִּבֶּר ראה

יְהֹוָ‍ֹאדנילאהדונהי אֲלֵיהֶם בְּיַד־מֹשֶׁה מהע, אל שדי:

IS THE ABUNDANCE OF CHOCHMAH, OF THE LEFT COLUMN OF BINAH. It comes to them, AS IS MENTIONED ABOVE, in order to unite the worlds and cheer them all, so that Right and Left will be completely incorporated, the one within the other, and all friendship and the love of the faithful will be with them. FOR WHEN RIGHT AND LEFT ARE INCORPORATED, THE ONE WITHIN THE OTHER, ALL THE GRADES BECOME COMPLETE.

— The Zohar, Shemini 11:91

FOURTH READING - MOSES - NETZACH

12 Moses said to Aaron and his remaining sons, Eleazar and Ithamar, "Take the meal offering left over from the offerings made to the Lord by fire and eat it prepared without yeast beside the altar, for it is most holy. 13 Eat it in a holy place, because it is your share and your sons' share of the offerings made to the Lord by fire; for so I have been commanded.

14 But you and your sons and your daughters may eat the breast that was waved and the thigh that was presented. Eat them in a ceremonially clean place; they have been given to you and your children as your share of the Children of Israel's peace offerings.

15 The thigh that was presented and the breast that was waved must be brought with the fat portions of the offerings made by fire, to be waved before the Lord as a wave offering. This will be the regular share for you and your children, as the Lord has commanded."

FIFTH READING - AARON - HOD

16 When Moses inquired about the goat of the sin offering and found that it had been burned up, he was angry with Elazar and Ithamar, Aaron's remaining sons, and asked,

17 "Why didn't you eat the sin offering in the sanctuary area? It is most holy; it was given to you to take away the guilt of the community by making atonement for them before the Lord.

קוֹזוֹ

Leviticus 10:12 – Moses told Aaron that even though he was in mourning for his sons, Aaron needed to continue to perform his job as *Kohen HaGadol*. This teaches us that no matter how despondent we become, we cannot forget about our work, our daily prayers, and the connections we need.

Leviticus 10:16 – According to Kabbalah, anything that is in the middle of something

connects us with Central Column energy and balance. Central Column energy helps us to reactivate our immune system in the areas where we have shut it down. There are different ways to indicate the middle of the Torah: it can be either in the number of letters, words or verses. There is also a general "middle" of the Torah.

Here, with the word *darosh* (inquired), we reach the middle of the Torah in terms of the number of words. Another interesting point is that the actual Aramaic word for "word" is *tieva*, which also means "protection" or "Ark," as in Noah's

FOURTH READING - MOSES - NETZACH

וַיְדַבֵּר רֵאה מֹשֶׁה מהע, אל שׁדי אֶל־אַהֲרֹן ע"ב ורבוע ע"ב וְאֶל אֶלְעָזָר וְאֶל־ 12
אִיתָמָר | בָּנָיו הַנּוֹתָרִים קְחוּ אֶת־הַמִּנְחָה ע"ה ב"פ ב"ן הַנּוֹתֶרֶת מֵאִשֵּׁי
יְהֹוָאדֹנָיאהדונהי וְאִכְלוּהָ מַצּוֹת אֵצֶל הַמִּזְבֵּחַ זוֹ, נגד כִּי קֹדֶשׁ קָדָשִׁים הִוא:
וַאֲכַלְתֶּם אֹתָהּ בְּמָקוֹם יהוה ברבוע, ר"פ אל קָדֹשׁ כִּי חׇקְךָ וְחׇק־בָּנֶיךָ הִוא 13
מֵאִשֵּׁי יְהֹוָאדֹנָיאהדונהי כִּי־כֵן צֻוֵּיתִי: 14 וְאֵת חֲזֵה הַתְּנוּפָה וְאֵת | שׁוֹק
הַתְּרוּמָה תֹּאכְלוּ בְּמָקוֹם יהוה ברבוע, ר"פ אל טָהוֹר י"פ אכא אַתָּה וּבָנֶיךָ וּבְנֹתֶיךָ
אִתָּךְ כִּי־חׇקְךָ וְחׇק־בָּנֶיךָ נִתְּנוּ מִזִּבְחֵי שַׁלְמֵי בְּנֵי יִשְׂרָאֵל: 15 שׁוֹק
הַתְּרוּמָה וַחֲזֵה הַתְּנוּפָה עַל אִשֵּׁי הַחֲלָבִים יָבִיאוּ לְהָנִיף תְּנוּפָה לִפְנֵי
יְהֹוָאדֹנָיאהדונהי וחכמה בינה וְהָיָה יהוה לְךָ וּלְבָנֶיךָ אִתְּךָ לְחׇק־עוֹלָם כַּאֲשֶׁר
צִוָּה פרי יְהֹוָאדֹנָיאהדונהי:

FIFTH READING - AARON - HOD

וְאֵת | שְׂעִיר הַחַטָּאת דָּרֹשׁ דָּרַשׁ מֹשֶׁה מהע, אל שׁדי וְהִנֵּה מ"ה יה שֹׂרָף 16
וַיִּקְצֹף עַל־אֶלְעָזָר וְעַל־אִיתָמָר בְּנֵי אַהֲרֹן ע"ב ורבוע ע"ב הַנּוֹתָרִם לֵאמֹר:
מַדּוּעַ לֹא־אֲכַלְתֶּם אֶת־הַחַטָּאת בְּמָקוֹם יהוה ברבוע, ר"פ אל הַקֹּדֶשׁ כִּי 17

Ark. So when we connect to the word *darosh*, we not only do we receive the energy of balance and reactivation of our immune system, we also receive protection.

וַיִּקְצֹף

Leviticus 10:16 – There's a dispute in this section between Moses and Aaron's remaining sons, Elazar and Ithamar, regarding the sacrifices. Although all three were dedicated to God's work, they did not agree on the best way to do it. It is important in our own disputes to recognize that the other person may be dedicated to the same ends as we are, although he or she has an alternate viewpoint about how best to carry out the work. By respecting the knowledge and input of others, as well as treating them with human dignity, we can arrive at peaceful solutions to our disputes. All too often when we argue with someone, we tend to see that person only in terms of what we dislike about them. We should restrict our argument to the specific issue at hand and not allow it to be blown out of proportion by any other long-standing difficulties with that person.

18 Since its blood was not taken into the Holy Place, you should have eaten it in the sanctuary area, as I commanded."

19 Aaron replied to Moses, "Today they sacrificed their sin offering and their burnt offering before the Lord, but such things as this have happened to me. Would the Lord have been pleased if I had eaten the sin offering today?"

20 When Moses heard this, he was satisfied.

SIXTH READING - JOSEPH - YESOD

11:1 The Lord spoke to Moses and Aaron, saying,

2 "Say to the Children of Israel: Of all the animals that live on land, these are the ones you may eat:

3 You may eat any animal that has a split hoof completely divided and that chews the cud.

4 From those that only chew the cud or only have a split hoof, these are the ones you must not eat, the camel, though it chews the cud, does not have a split hoof; it is ceremonially unclean for you.

5 The rock badger, though it chews the cud, does not have a split hoof; it is unclean for you.

תֹּאכֵלוּ

Leviticus 11:2 – This next section deals with the laws of *kashrut* (kosher, or foods that may be eaten). The spiritual reasoning behind why certain foods can or can't be eaten is really all about reincarnation. When souls reincarnate as animals, their purpose for that lifetime is to become elevated by serving as food for people. But this is true only of foods identified as kosher. If souls reincarnate into foods that are not kosher, they are meant to be elevated in other ways. Identifying an animal as kosher gives us the assurance that the particular meat contains a soul that needs to be elevated through being eaten, thus allowing us to meditate on the soul and not just eat the physical piece of food. Since

food is the fuel used for performing actions, we want to be fueled by the positive action of elevating a soul.

Rabbi Elazar said: "These are the animals from among all the living creatures... that you shall eat," MEANS that you are allowed to eat from all of those that belong to the side OF PURITY, but you are not allowed to eat from those which do not belong to this side. There are beasts which come from the side OF PURITY and others from the other, unclean side. This is derived from the verse: "Whatever cleaves the hoof and is cloven footed." (Leviticus 11:3) We have learned that they are all marked and the scripture

קֹדֶשׁ קָדָשִׁים הִוא וְאַתָּה | נָתַן לָכֶם לָשֵׂאת אֶת־עֲוֺן

הָעֵדָה לְכַפֵּר עֲלֵיהֶם לִפְנֵי יְהוָֹה‏: 18 הֵן לֹא־הוּבָא

אֶת־דָּמָהּ אֶל־הַקֹּדֶשׁ פְּנִימָה אָכוֹל תֹּאכְלוּ אֹתָהּ בַּקֹּדֶשׁ כַּאֲשֶׁר

צִוֵּיתִי‏: 19 וַיְדַבֵּר אַהֲרֹן אֶל־מֹשֶׁה הֵן הַיּוֹם

הִקְרִיבוּ אֶת־חַטָּאתָם וְאֶת־עֹלָתָם לִפְנֵי

יְהוָֹה וַתִּקְרֶאנָה אֹתִי כָּאֵלֶּה וְאָכַלְתִּי חַטָּאת הַיּוֹם

הַיִּיטַב בְּעֵינֵי יְהוָֹה‏: 20 וַיִּשְׁמַע מֹשֶׁה וַיִּיטַב

בְּעֵינָיו‏:

SIXTH READING - JOSEPH - YESOD

11 1 וַיְדַבֵּר יְהוָֹה אֶל־מֹשֶׁה וְאֶל־אַהֲרֹן

לֵאמֹר אֲלֵהֶם‏: 2 דַּבְּרוּ אֶל־בְּנֵי יִשְׂרָאֵל לֵאמֹר זֹאת הַחַיָּה אֲשֶׁר

תֹּאכְלוּ מִכֹּל־הַבְּהֵמָה אֲשֶׁר עַל־הָאָרֶץ‏: 3 כֹּל

| מַפְרֶסֶת פַּרְסָה וְשֹׁסַעַת שֶׁסַע פְּרָסֹת מַעֲלַת גֵּרָה

בַּבְּהֵמָה אֹתָהּ תֹּאכֵלוּ‏: 4 אַךְ אֶת־זֶה לֹא תֹאכְלוּ מִמַּעֲלֵי

הַגֵּרָה וּמִמַּפְרִסֵי הַפַּרְסָה אֶת־הַגָּמָל כִּי־מַעֲלֵה גֵרָה

הוּא וּפַרְסָה אֵינֶנּוּ מַפְרִיס טָמֵא הוּא לָכֶם‏: 5 וְאֶת־הַשָּׁפָן

---

specifies them all. Therefore, he who eats from those which come from the unclean side defiles himself and defiles his soul, which issues from the clean side.

In cattle, living creatures, birds and fish are seen signs of Right or Left. We may eat whichever comes from the Right, but we may not eat whichever comes from the Left, because all of them are in the grade of uncleanness and all of them are unclean. An unclean spirit dwells in them. Therefore, the Holy Spirit of Israel must neither be mixed up with them nor be defiled by them, in order that ISRAEL may remain holy and be recognized as such Above and Below.
     — The Zohar, Shemini 14:105-109

⁶ The rabbit, though it chews the cud, does not have a split hoof; it is unclean for you.

⁷ And the pig, though it has a split hoof completely divided, does not chew the cud; it is unclean for you.

⁸ You must not eat their meat or touch their carcasses; they are unclean for you.

⁹ You may eat of all the creatures living in the water that have fins and scales and live in oceans or streams.

¹⁰ But all creatures in the seas or streams that do not have fins and scales—whether among all the swarming things or among all the other living creatures in the water—they are detestable to you.

¹¹ And since they are detestable to you, you must not eat their meat and you must detest their carcasses.

¹² Anything living in the water that does not have fins and scales is to be detestable to you.

¹³ These are the birds you are to detest and not eat because they are detestable: the eagle, the vulture, the black vulture, ¹⁴ the red kite, any kind of black kite, ¹⁵ any kind of raven, ¹⁶ the horned owl, the screech owl, the gull, any kind of hawk, ¹⁷ the little owl, the cormorant, the great owl, ¹⁸ the white owl, the desert owl, the osprey, ¹⁹ the stork, any kind of heron, the hoopoe and the bat.

²⁰ All flying insects that walk on all fours are to be detestable to you.

²¹ Of those winged creatures that walk on all fours these are the ones you may eat: those that have jointed legs for hopping on the ground.

²² Of these, you may eat any kind of locust, any kind of katydid, any kind of cricket or any kind of grasshopper.

²³ But all other winged creatures that have four legs are detestable to you.

²⁴ You will make yourselves unclean by these; whoever touches their carcasses will be unclean till evening.

²⁵ Whoever picks up one of their carcasses must wash his clothes, and he will be unclean till evening.

כִּי־מַעֲלֵה גֵרָה ד״פ ב״ן הוּא וּפַרְסָה ₪זזד״ך אדני לֹא יַפְרִיס טָמֵא הוּא לָכֶם:

6 וְאֶת־הָאַרְנֶבֶת כִּי־מַעֲלַת גֵּרָה ד״פ ב״ן הוּא וּפַרְסָה ₪זזד״ך אדני לֹא הִפְרִיסָה טְמֵאָה הִוא לָכֶם: 7 וְאֶת־הַחֲזִיר כִּי־מַפְרִיס פַּרְסָה ₪זזד״ך אדני הוּא וְשֹׁסַע שֶׁסַע פַּרְסָה ₪זזד״ך אדני וְהוּא גֵּרָה ד״פ ב״ן לֹא־יִגָּר טָמֵא הוּא לָכֶם:

8 מִבְּשָׂרָם לֹא תֹאכֵלוּ וּבְנִבְלָתָם לֹא תִגָּעוּ טְמֵאִים הֵם לָכֶם: 9 אֶת־זֶה תֹּאכְלוּ מִכֹּל יּלי אֲשֶׁר בַּמָּיִם כֹּל יּלי אֲשֶׁר־לוֹ סְנַפִּיר וְקַשְׂקֶשֶׂת בַּמַּיִם בַּיַּמִּים גלך וּבַנְּחָלִים אֹתָם תֹּאכֵלוּ: 10 וְכֹל יּלי אֲשֶׁר אֵין־לוֹ סְנַפִּיר וְקַשְׂקֶשֶׂת בַּיַּמִּים גלך וּבַנְּחָלִים מִכֹּל יּלי שֶׁרֶץ הַמַּיִם וּמִכֹּל יּלי נֶפֶשׁ רמ״ח - ז וויות הַחַיָּה אֲשֶׁר בַּמָּיִם שֶׁקֶץ הֵם לָכֶם: 11 וְשֶׁקֶץ יִהְיוּ אל לָכֶם מִבְּשָׂרָם לֹא תֹאכֵלוּ וְאֶת־נִבְלָתָם תְּשַׁקֵּצוּ: 12 כֹּל יּלי אֲשֶׁר אֵין־לוֹ סְנַפִּיר וְקַשְׂקֶשֶׂת בַּמָּיִם שֶׁקֶץ הוּא לָכֶם: 13 וְאֶת־אֵלֶּה תְּשַׁקְּצוּ מִן־הָעוֹף ג״פ ב״ן, יוסף, ציון לֹא יֵאָכְלוּ שֶׁקֶץ הֵם אֶת־הַנֶּשֶׁר וְאֶת־הַפֶּרֶס וְאֵת הָעָזְנִיָּה: 14 וְאֶת־הַדָּאָה וְאֶת־הָאַיָּה לְמִינָהּ: 15 אֵת כָּל יּלי ־עֹרֵב לְמִינוֹ: 16 וְאֵת בַּת הַיַּעֲנָה וְאֶת־הַתַּחְמָס וְאֶת־הַשַּׁחַף וְאֶת־הַנֵּץ לְמִינֵהוּ: 17 וְאֶת־הַכּוֹס מום, אלהים, אהיה אדני וְאֶת־הַשָּׁלָךְ וְאֶת־הַיַּנְשׁוּף: 18 וְאֶת־הַתִּנְשֶׁמֶת וְאֶת־הַקָּאָת וְאֶת־הָרָחָם אברהם, וו״ה אל, רמ״ח: 19 וְאֵת הַחֲסִידָה הָאֲנָפָה לְמִינָהּ וְאֶת־הַדּוּכִיפַת וְאֶת־הָעֲטַלֵּף: 20 כֹּל יּלי שֶׁרֶץ הָעוֹף ג״פ ב״ן, יוסף, ציון הַהֹלֵךְ מיה עַל־אַרְבַּע שֶׁקֶץ הוּא לָכֶם: 21 אַךְ אהיה אֶת־זֶה תֹּאכְלוּ מִכֹּל יּלי שֶׁרֶץ הָעוֹף ג״פ ב״ן, יוסף, ציון הַהֹלֵךְ מיה עַל־אַרְבַּע אֲשֶׁר־לוֹ (כתיב: לֹא) כְרָעַיִם מִמַּעַל עלם לְרַגְלָיו לְנַתֵּר בָּהֵן עַל־הָאָרֶץ אלהים דההין ע״ה: 22 אֶת־אֵלֶּה מֵהֶם תֹּאכֵלוּ אֶת־הָאַרְבֶּה יצחק, ד״פ ב״ן לְמִינוֹ וְאֶת־הַסָּלְעָם לְמִינֵהוּ וְאֶת־הַחַרְגֹּל לְמִינֵהוּ וְאֶת־הֶחָגָב לְמִינֵהוּ: 23 וְכֹל יּלי שֶׁרֶץ הָעוֹף ג״פ ב״ן, יוסף, ציון אֲשֶׁר־לוֹ אַרְבַּע רַגְלָיִם שֶׁקֶץ הוּא לָכֶם: 24 וּלְאֵלֶּה תִּטַּמָּאוּ כָּל יּלי ־הַנֹּגֵעַ בְּנִבְלָתָם יִטְמָא עַד־הָעָרֶב רבוע יהוה ורבוע אלהים:

26 Every animal that has a split hoof not completely divided or that does not chew the cud is unclean for you; whoever touches them will be unclean.

27 Of all the animals that walk on all fours, those that walk on their paws are unclean for you; whoever touches their carcasses will be unclean till evening.

28 Anyone who picks up their carcasses must wash his clothes, and he will be unclean till evening. They are unclean for you.

29 Of the animals that move about on the ground, these are unclean for you: the weasel, the rat, any kind of great lizard, 30 the gecko, the monitor lizard, the wall lizard, the skink and the chameleon.

31 Of all those that move along the ground, these are unclean for you. Whoever touches them when they are dead will be unclean till evening.

32 When one of them dies and falls on something, that article, whatever its use, will be unclean, whether it is made of wood, cloth, hide or sackcloth. Put it in water; it will be unclean till evening, and then it will be clean.

SEVENTH READING - DAVID - MALCHUT

33 If one of them falls into a clay pot, everything in it will be unclean, and you must break the pot.

34 Any food that could be eaten but has water on it from such a pot is unclean, and any liquid that could be drunk from it is unclean.

35 Anything that one of their carcasses falls on becomes unclean; an oven or cooking pot must be broken up. They are unclean, and you are to regard them as unclean.

יִפֵּל

Leviticus 11:32 – We learn that spiritual Vessels can become contaminated through negative actions such as, for example, touching a corpse. If Vessels become contaminated, the negativity can be cleansed by washing.

Of that, it is written: "Neither shall you make yourselves (Heb. venitmatem)

unclean with them," (Leviticus 11:43) without the Alef, TO SHOW that there is no remedy for his uncleanness and that he can never recover from his defilement. Rav Elazar was once sitting before his father, Rav Shimon, and he said to him: We have learned that the Holy One, blessed be He, will one day purify Israel. With what WILL HE PURIFY THEM? He replied: With that which is

25 וְכָל־ יל׳ ־הַנֹּשֵׂא מִנִּבְלָתָם יְכַבֵּס בְּגָדָיו וְטָמֵא עַד־הָעָרֶב

רבוע יהוה ורבוע אלהים: 26 לְכָל־ יה אדני ־הַבְּהֵמָה ב״ן, לכב, יבם אֲשֶׁר הִוא מַפְרֶסֶת

פַּרְסָה זו׳זּזּ׳ך אדני וְשֶׁסַע | אֵינֶנָּה שֹׁסַעַת וְגֵרָה דּ״פ ב״ן אֵינֶנָּה מַעֲלָה טְמֵאִים

הֵם לָכֶם כָּל־ יל׳ ־הַנֹּגֵעַ בָּהֶם יִטְמָא: 27 וְכֹל׀ יל׳ ־הוֹלֵךְ עַל־כַּפָּיו בְּכָל־

ב״ן, לכב, יבם ־הַחַיָּה הַהֹלֶכֶת עַל־אַרְבַּע טְמֵאִים הֵם לָכֶם כָּל־ יל׳ ־הַנֹּגֵעַ

בְּנִבְלָתָם יִטְמָא עַד־הָעָרֶב רבוע יהוה ורבוע אלהים: 28 וְהַנֹּשֵׂא אֶת־נִבְלָתָם

יְכַבֵּס בְּגָדָיו וְטָמֵא עַד־הָעָרֶב רבוע יהוה ורבוע אלהים ־טְמֵאִים הֵמָּה לָכֶם:

29 וְזֶה לָכֶם הַטָּמֵא בַּשֶּׁרֶץ הַשֹּׁרֵץ עַל־הָאָרֶץ אלהים דההין ע״ה ־הַחֹלֶד

וְהָעַכְבָּר וְהַצָּב לְמִינֵהוּ: 30 וְהָאֲנָקָה וְהַכֹּחַ וְהַלְּטָאָה וְהַחֹמֶט

וְהַתִּנְשָׁמֶת: 31 אֵלֶּה הַטְּמֵאִים לָכֶם בְּכָל־ ב״ן, לכב, יבם ־הַשָּׁרֶץ כָּל־ יל׳ ־

הַנֹּגֵעַ בָּהֶם בְּמֹתָם יִטְמָא עַד־הָעָרֶב רבוע יהוה ורבוע אלהים: 32 וְכֹל יל׳ אֲשֶׁר־

יִפֹּל־עָלָיו מֵהֶם | בְּמֹתָם יִטְמָא מִכָּל־ יל׳ ־כְּלִי כלי ־עֵץ ע״ה קס״א אוֹ בֶגֶד

אוֹ־עוֹר אוֹ שָׂק כָּל־ יל׳ ־כְּלִי כלי אֲשֶׁר־יֵעָשֶׂה מְלָאכָה אל אדני בָּהֶם

בַּמַּיִם יוּבָא וְטָמֵא עַד־הָעָרֶב רבוע יהוה ורבוע אלהים וְטָהֵר י״פ אכא:

SEVENTH READING - DAVID - MALCHUT

33 וְכָל־ יל׳ ־כְּלִי כלי ־חֶרֶשׂ אֲשֶׁר־יִפֹּל מֵהֶם אֶל־תּוֹכוֹ כֹּל יל׳ אֲשֶׁר

בְּתוֹכוֹ יִטְמָא וְאֹתוֹ תִשְׁבֹּרוּ: 34 מִכָּל־ יל׳ ־הָאֹכֶל אֲשֶׁר יֵאָכֵל אֲשֶׁר

יָבוֹא עָלָיו מַיִם יִטְמָא וְכָל־ יל׳ ־מַשְׁקֶה אֲשֶׁר יִשָּׁתֶה בְּכָל־ ב״ן, לכב, יבם

---

written in the verse: "Then will I sprinkle clean water upon you, and you shall be clean." (Ezekiel 36:25)
— The Zohar, 15:112 & 117

All of our actions create either positive entities, from which we can derive great good, or negative entities, which can cause us to suffer physical or spiritual harm; this is true whether the entities have been created by us or by others. When we take positive actions, the Light protects us from this potential harm.

36 A spring, however, or a cistern for collecting water will remain clean, but anyone who touches one of these carcasses is unclean.

37 If a carcass falls on any seeds that are to be planted, they remain clean. 38 But if water has been put on the seed and a carcass falls on it, it is unclean for you.

39 If an animal that you are allowed to eat dies, anyone who touches the carcass will be unclean till evening.

40 Anyone who eats some of the carcass must wash his clothes, and he will be unclean till evening. Anyone who picks up the carcass must wash his clothes, and he will be unclean till evening.

41 Every creature that moves about on the ground is detestable; it is not to be eaten.

42 You are not to eat any creature that moves about on the ground, whether it moves on its belly or walks on all fours or on many feet; it is detestable.

43 Do not defile yourselves by any of these creatures. Do not make yourselves unclean by means of them or be made unclean by them.

44 For I am the Lord, your God; consecrate yourselves and be holy, because I am holy. Do not make yourselves unclean by any creature that moves about on the ground.

MAFTIR

45 For I am the Lord who brought you up out of Egypt to be your God; therefore be holy, because I am holy.

יִטְמָא

Leviticus 11:39 – If an animal that was meant to be eaten has not fulfilled the purpose for which it was created, then those animals become empty. We can become contaminated by the bodies of dead animals because they are empty Vessels. We should avoid any Vessel that is empty. Totally selfish people are empty Vessels; human beings who are negative or who do not share are empty beings.

Leviticus 11:42 – The large letter *Vav* in the word *gachon* (belly) is at the middle of the Bible

כְּלִי כל 35 וְכֹל יל אֲשֶׁר־יִפֹּל מִנִּבְלָתָם | עָלָיו יִטְמָא תַּנּוּר יִטְמָא:

וְכִירַיִם יֻתָּץ טְמֵאִים הֵם וּטְמֵאִים יִהְיוּ אל לָכֶם: 36 אַךְ מַעְיָן וּבוֹר

מִקְוֵה־מַיִם יִהְיֶה טָהוֹר וְנֹגֵעַ בְּנִבְלָתָם יִטְמָא:

37 וְכִי יִפֹּל מִנִּבְלָתָם עַל־כָּל־זֶרַע זֵרוּעַ אֲשֶׁר יִזָּרֵעַ טָהוֹר

הוּא: 38 וְכִי יֻתַּן־מַיִם עַל־זֶרַע וְנָפַל מִנִּבְלָתָם עָלָיו טָמֵא הוּא לָכֶם:

39 וְכִי יָמוּת מִן־הַבְּהֵמָה אֲשֶׁר־הִיא לָכֶם לְאָכְלָה הַנֹּגֵעַ

בְּנִבְלָתָהּ יִטְמָא עַד־הָעָרֶב: 40 וְהָאֹכֵל מִנִּבְלָתָהּ

יְכַבֵּס בְּגָדָיו וְטָמֵא עַד־הָעָרֶב וְהַנֹּשֵׂא אֶת־נִבְלָתָהּ

יְכַבֵּס בְּגָדָיו וְטָמֵא עַד־הָעָרֶב: 41 וְכָל־הַשֶּׁרֶץ

הַשֹּׁרֵץ עַל־הָאָרֶץ שֶׁקֶץ הוּא לֹא יֵאָכֵל: 42 כֹּל הוֹלֵךְ

עַל־גָּחוֹן וְכֹל | הוֹלֵךְ עַל־אַרְבַּע עַד כָּל־מַרְבֵּה רַגְלַיִם לְכָל

הַשֶּׁרֶץ הַשֹּׁרֵץ עַל־הָאָרֶץ לֹא תֹאכְלוּם כִּי־שֶׁקֶץ

הֵם: 43 אַל־תְּשַׁקְּצוּ אֶת־נַפְשֹׁתֵיכֶם בְּכָל־הַשֶּׁרֶץ הַשֹּׁרֵץ

וְלֹא תִטַּמְּאוּ בָּהֶם וְנִטְמֵתֶם בָּם: 44 כִּי אֲנִי יְהֹוָה

אֱלֹהֵיכֶם וְהִתְקַדִּשְׁתֶּם וִהְיִיתֶם קְדֹשִׁים כִּי קָדוֹשׁ אָנִי

וְלֹא תְטַמְּאוּ אֶת־נַפְשֹׁתֵיכֶם בְּכָל־הַשֶּׁרֶץ הָרֹמֵשׂ עַל־

הָאָרֶץ:

MAFTIR

45 כִּי | אֲנִי יְהֹוָה הַמַּעֲלֶה אֶתְכֶם מֵאֶרֶץ

מִצְרַיִם לִהְיֹת לָכֶם לֵאלֹהִים וִהְיִיתֶם קְדֹשִׁים כִּי

---

in terms of the number of letters in the Torah Scroll. The kabbalists teach that the letter *Vav*, in this Central Column position, reminds us that we have a responsibility to the Light of God within us. Because we contain Light, we must be responsible for everything we do.

⁴⁶ These are the regulations concerning animals, birds, every living thing that moves in the water and every creature that moves about on the ground.

⁴⁷ You must distinguish between the unclean and the clean, between living creatures that may be eaten and those that may not be eaten."

HAFTARAH OF SHEMINI

King David rescued the Ark of the Covenant after it had been taken in battle, thereby allowing the people of Israel to reconnect to it. Metaphorically, we sometimes do actions that send the Ark back

Samuel 2 6:1-19

6:¹ Again, David brought together the chosen men of Israel, thirty thousand in all.

² And David arose and set out with all the people who were with him from Baale Judah to bring up from there the Ark of God, whose Name is called by the Name of the Lord of Hosts, who sits between the cherubim.

³ And they set the Ark of God on a new cart and brought it out of the house of Abinadab that was on the hill, and Uzzah and Ahio, the sons of Abinadab, drove the new cart.

⁴ And they brought it out of the house of Abinadab that was on the hill, with the Ark of God, and Ahio went before the Ark.

⁵ And David and the whole house of Israel played before the Lord, with all manner of instruments made of cypress wood, and with harps, and with lyres, and tambourines, and with sistrums and with cymbals.

⁶ And when they came to the threshing floor of Nacon, Uzzah reached out his hand to the Ark of God and took hold of it, because the oxen stumbled.

⁷ And the anger of the Lord was kindled against Uzzah and God smote him there for his error and there he died by the Ark of God.

קָד֖וֹשׁ אָ֑נִי אני, טרה״ד כו״ו: 46 זֹ֣את תּוֹרַ֣ת הַבְּהֵמָ֔ה ב״ן, לכב, יבמ וְהָע֔וֹף ג״פ ב״ן, יוסף, ציון

וְכֹל֙ נֶ֣פֶשׁ רמ״ח ז הויות הַֽחַיָּ֔ה הָרֹמֶ֖שֶׂת בַּמָּ֑יִם וּלְכָל־יה אדני נֶ֕פֶשׁ רמ״ח ז הויות

הַשֹּׁרֶ֖צֶת עַל־הָאָֽרֶץ אלהים דההין ע״ה: 47 לְהַבְדִּ֕יל בֵּ֥ין הַטָּמֵ֖א וּבֵ֣ין הַטָּהֹ֑ר

י״פ אכא וּבֵ֛ין הַֽחַיָּ֥ה הַֽנֶּאֱכֶ֖לֶת וּבֵ֥ין הַֽחַיָּ֔ה אֲשֶׁ֖ר לֹ֥א תֵאָכֵֽל:

HAFTARAH OF SHEMINI

into captivity. This Haftarah helps us do the spiritual cleansing necessary before the Ark can be returned to us.

שמואל ב פרק ו

6   1 וַיֹּ֨סֶף ע֥וֹד דָּוִ֛ד אֶת־כָּל־בָּח֖וּר ילי ־בְּיִשְׂרָאֵ֑ל שְׁלֹשִׁ֖ים אָֽלֶף

אלף למד שין דלת יוד ע״ה: 2 וַיָּ֣קָם | וַיֵּ֣לֶךְ כלי דָּוִ֗ד וְכָל־הָעָם֙ אֲשֶׁ֣ר אִתּ֔וֹ

מִֽבַּעֲלֵ֖י יְהוּדָ֑ה לְהַעֲל֣וֹת מִשָּׁ֗ם יהוה שדי אֵ֚ת אֲר֣וֹן ע״ה ג״פ אלהים הָאֱלֹהִ֔ים

מום, אהיה אדני; ילה אֲשֶׁר־נִקְרָ֣א שֵׁ֣ם יהוה שדי שֵׁ֗ם יהוה שדי יְ֠הוָֹה צְבָא֛וֹת

נתה ורבוע אהיה יֹשֵׁ֥ב הַכְּרֻבִ֖ים עָלָֽיו: 3 וַיַּרְכִּ֜בוּ אֶת־אֲר֤וֹן ע״ה ג״פ אלהים הָֽאֱלֹהִים֙

מום, אהיה אדני; ילה אֶל־עֲגָלָ֣ה חֲדָשָׁ֔ה וַיִּשָּׂאֻ֔הוּ מִבֵּ֥ית ב״ן ראה אֲבִינָדָ֖ב אֲשֶׁ֣ר

בַּגִּבְעָ֑ה וְעֻזָּ֣א וְאַחְי֗וֹ בְּנֵי֙ אֲבִ֣ינָדָ֔ב נֹהֲגִ֖ים אֶת־הָעֲגָלָ֥ה חֲדָשָֽׁה:

4 וַיִּשָּׂאֻ֗הוּ מִבֵּ֤ית ב״ן ראה אֲבִֽינָדָב֙ אֲשֶׁ֣ר בַּגִּבְעָ֔ה עִ֖ם אֲר֣וֹן ע״ה ג״פ אלהים

הָאֱלֹהִ֑ים מום, אהיה אדני; ילה וְאַחְי֕וֹ הֹלֵ֖ךְ מיה לִפְנֵ֥י וחכמה בינה הָֽאָרֽוֹן ע״ה ג״פ אלהים:

5 וְדָוִ֣ד | וְכָל־יל״י ־בֵּ֣ית ב״ן ראה יִשְׂרָאֵ֗ל מְשַֽׂחֲקִים֙ לִפְנֵ֣י וחכמה בינה יְ֠הוָֹה

בְּכֹ֞ל ב״ן, לכב, יבמ עֲצֵ֣י בְרוֹשִׁ֗ים וּבְכִנֹּר֤וֹת וּבִנְבָלִים֙ וּבְתֻפִּ֔ים וּבִמְנַֽעַנְעִ֖ים

וּֽבְצֶלְצֶלִֽים: 6 וַיָּבֹ֖אוּ עַד־גֹּ֣רֶן נָכ֑וֹן וַיִּשְׁלַ֨ח עֻזָּ֜ה אֶל־אֲר֤וֹן ע״ה ג״פ אלהים

הָֽאֱלֹהִים֙ מום, אהיה אדני; ילה וַיֹּ֣אחֶז בּ֔וֹ כִּ֥י שָֽׁמְט֖וּ הַבָּקָֽר: 7 וַיִּֽחַר־אַ֤ף

יְ֠הוָֹה בְּעֻזָּ֣ה וַיַּכֵּ֥הוּ שָׁ֛ם יהוה שדי הָאֱלֹהִ֖ים מום, אהיה אדני; ילה עַל־הַשַּׁ֑ל

וַיָּ֤מָת שָׁם֙ יהוה שדי עִ֚ם אֲר֣וֹן ע״ה ג״פ אלהים הָֽאֱלֹהִֽים מום, אהיה אדני; ילה: 8 וַיִּ֣חַר

8 *And David was displeased, because the Lord had broken forth against Uzzah, and to this day that place is called Perez Uzzah.*

9 *And David was afraid of the Lord that day and said, "How can the Ark of the Lord come to me?"*

10 *So David would not remove the Ark of the Lord to be with him in the City of David, David carried it aside to the house of Obed-Edom the Gittite.*

11 *And the Ark of the Lord remained in the house of Obed-Edom the Gittite for three months, and the Lord blessed Obed-Edom and his entire house.*

12 *And it was told King David saying, "The Lord has blessed the house of Obed-Edom and everything he has, because of the Ark of God." And David went down and brought up the Ark of God from the house of Obed-Edom to the City of David with joy.*

13 *And it was so, that when they bore that the Ark of the Lord had taken six steps, he sacrificed a ox and a fattened calf.*

14 *And David, wearing a linen ephod, danced before the Lord with all his might.*

15 *So David and the entire house of Israel brought up the Ark of the Lord with shouting and the sound of the horn.*

16 *And it was so, as the Ark of the Lord came into the City of David, that Michal the daughter of Saul, watched from a window, and saw King David leaping and dancing before the Lord, and she despised him in her heart.*

17 *And they brought the Ark of the Lord and set it in its place inside the tent that David had pitched for it, and David offered burnt offerings and peace offerings before the Lord.*

18 *And when David finished offering the burnt offering and the peace offerings, he blessed the people in the Name of the Lord of Hosts.*

19 *And he gave among all the people, even among the whole multitude of Israel, both to men and women, a loaf of bread, and a cake made in a pan and a sweet cake. And all the people departed and went to their homes.*

לְדָוִד עַל אֲשֶׁר פָּרַץ יְהוָֹה פֶּרֶץ בְּעֻזָּה וַיִּקְרָא ב"פ קס"א ־ ה' אותיות

לַמָּקוֹם יהוה ברבוע, ו"פ אל הַהוּא פֶּרֶץ עֻזָּה עַד הַיּוֹם ע"ה = נגד, זן, מזבח הַזֶּה והו:

9 וַיִּרָא אלף למד יהוה דָוִד אֶת־יְהוָֹה בַּיּוֹם ע"ה = נגד, זן, מזבח הַהוּא וַיֹּאמֶר

אֵיךְ אל יָבוֹא אֵלַי אֲרוֹן ע"ה ג"פ אלהים יְהוָֹה 10 וְלֹא־אָבָה דָוִד

לְהָסִיר אֵלָיו אֶת־אֲרוֹן ע"ה ג"פ אלהים יְהוָֹה עַל־עִיר סז\חור, ערי, סנדלפון

דָוִד וַיַּטֵּהוּ דָוִד בֵּית ב"פ ראה עֹבֵד־אֱדֹם מ"ה הַגִּתִּי: 11 וַיֵּשֶׁב אֲרוֹן

ע"ה ג"פ אלהים יְהוָֹה בֵּית ב"פ ראה עֹבֵד אֱדֹם מ"ה הַגִּתִּי שְׁלֹשָׁה חֳדָשִׁים

וַיְבָרֶךְ עסמ"ב יְהוָֹה אֶת־עֹבֵד אֱדֹם מ"ה וְאֶת־כָּל יל־בֵּיתוֹ: 12 וַיֻּגַּד

לַמֶּלֶךְ דָוִד לֵאמֹר בֵּרַךְ יְהוָֹה אֶת־בֵּית ב"פ ראה עֹבֵד אֱדֹם מ"ה

וְאֶת־כָּל יל־אֲשֶׁר־לוֹ בַּעֲבוּר אֲרוֹן ע"ה ג"פ אלהים הָאֱלֹהִים מום, אהיה אדני; ילה

וַיֵּלֶךְ כלי דָוִד וַיַּעַל אֶת־אֲרוֹן ע"ה ג"פ אלהים הָאֱלֹהִים מום, אהיה אדני; ילה מִבֵּית

ב"פ ראה עֹבֵד אֱדֹם מ"ה עִיר סז\חור, ערי, סנדלפון דָוִד בְּשִׂמְחָה: 13 וַיְהִי אל כִּי

צָעֲדוּ נֹשְׂאֵי אֲרוֹן ע"ה ג"פ אלהים ־יְהוָֹה עָשָׂה צְעָדִים וַיִּזְבַּח שׁוֹר

אבגיתץ, ושׂר, אהבת חנם וּמְרִיא: 14 וְדָוִד מְכַרְכֵּר בְּכָל בן, לכב, יבמ ־עֹז אני יהוה לִפְנֵי

וחכמה בינה יְהוָֹה וְדָוִד וְחָגוּר אֵפוֹד יהוה אדני בָּד: 15 וְדָוִד וְכָל יל ־בֵּית

ב"פ ראה יִשְׂרָאֵל מַעֲלִים אֶת־אֲרוֹן ע"ה ג"פ אלהים יְהוָֹה בִּתְרוּעָה וּבְקוֹל

ע"ב ס"ג ע"ה שׁוֹפָר רבוע אלהים אלהים דיודין ואלהים: 16 וְהָיָה יהוה אֲרוֹן ע"ה ג"פ אלהים יְהוָֹה

בָּא עִיר סז\חור, ערי, סנדלפון דָוִד וּמִיכַל בַּת־שָׁאוּל נִשְׁקְפָה | בְּעַד הַחַלּוֹן מנד

וַתֵּרֶא אֶת־הַמֶּלֶךְ דָוִד מְפַזֵּז וּמְכַרְכֵּר לִפְנֵי וחכמה בינה יְהוָֹה וַתִּבֶז לוֹ

בְּלִבָּהּ: 17 וַיָּבִאוּ אֶת־הָאָרוֹן ע"ה ג"פ אלהים יְהוָֹה וַיַּצִּגוּ אֹתוֹ בִּמְקוֹמוֹ

בְּתוֹךְ הָאֹהֶל לאה אֲשֶׁר נָטָה־לוֹ דָוִד וַיַּעַל דָוִד עֹלוֹת לִפְנֵי וחכמה בינה

יְהוָֹה וּשְׁלָמִים: 18 וַיְכַל דָוִד מֵהַעֲלוֹת הָעוֹלָה וְהַשְּׁלָמִים וַיְבָרֶךְ

אֶת־הָעָם בְּשֵׁם יהוה עדי יְהוָֹה צְבָאוֹת נתה ורבוע אהיה: 19 וַיְחַלֵּק

לְכָל יה, אדני ־הָעָם לְכָל יה אדני הֲמוֹן יִשְׂרָאֵל לְמֵאִישׁ ע"ה קנ"א קס"א וְעַד־אִשָּׁה

לְאִישׁ ע"ה קנ"א קס"א חַלַּת לֶחֶם ג"פ יהוה אַחַת וְאֶשְׁפָּר אֶחָד אהבה, דאגה וַאֲשִׁישָׁה

אֶחָת וַיֵּלֶךְ כלי כָּל ילי ־הָעָם אִישׁ ע"ה קנ"א קס"א לְבֵיתוֹ:

TAZRIA

LESSON OF TAZRIA
(Leviticus 12:1-13:59)

Why do people have leprosy?

The chapter of Tazria describes afflictions of the skin and reveals the cause of these afflictions. Most people are very careful about what goes into their mouths, but how many are careful about what emerges from their mouths? What we say can be as negative and destructive as bad food is for our bodies. In Aramaic, the word for leprosy (*tzara'at*) correlates to verbal negativity, as in evil speech (*lashon hara*). But negativity in speech isn't limited to what we actually say; it can also relate to what we don't say, what we hear, and even what we don't hear. The fact is, most of the time we talk and talk and talk, but we don't listen to what other people are telling us.

> *Just as punishment is afflicted on man because of evil speech, so is he punished because he could have pronounced good words but did not. For he blemished that speaking spirit, which is composed so as to speak Above and speak Below, and everything is in holiness. It is even truer if the nation walks the crooked path and he can talk to them and reprove them yet he is silent and does not speak. As I said, IT IS SAID OF HIM, "I was dumb with silence, I held my peace, and had no comfort and my pain was stirred up," stirred up by plagues of impurity.*
> — The Zohar, Tazria 18:87

A rabbi was once invited to give a sermon before the Torah reading at a temple. He was very tired, however, and felt that he didn't have the strength to comply. Still, he didn't want to disappoint the people who had invited him, so he said to the congregation, "I have given many sermons over the years, but this time I would like to hear what you have to say."

The importance of listening to others is something that people on a high spiritual level have always understood. Regardless of whether people are right or wrong, we have a responsibility to listen to them. If we don't fulfill this responsibility, how can we expect others to listen to us?

There was a great sage who, at the end of his days, was so sick and weak that he could only whisper. Yet he continued to instruct his students, who sat very close to hear him. A local rabbi went to observe this. He saw the great teacher whispering, sometimes for hours on end, with the students leaning close to listen.

"I don't understand," the rabbi said to one of the students. "In my temple, if I speak for more than 30 minutes, they want to drag me away from the pulpit. You not only listen to your teacher for many hours, but you listen despite the fact that he can barely speak!"

"We listen so closely and so long," the student answered him, "because we know that if one of us had to speak with our teacher and we had to whisper, he would bend over to hear what we had to say for as long as necessary."

If we want to reach a level from which we can teach other people, we must also reach the level where we listen carefully to others. To be saved from spiritual leprosy, we must learn to hear and not just to speak.

Zalman Shazar was a member of the Knesset (Israeli parliament) before he became president of Israel. One day, he went to Tel Aviv from Jerusalem to meet Rav Ashlag. When Zalman Shazar arrived, Rav Ashlag said to him, "So what's new in the Knesset?" Shazar answered, "Forgive me, but I didn't come to hear what I have to say. I could have stayed in Jerusalem for that. I came to hear only what you have to say."

Yet it's not enough just to listen, either. We learn from Job that there are times when we have to speak up and say what needs to be said. Along with Bilaam and Jethro, Job was one of the three consultants to Pharaoh during the time of Moses. When Pharaoh asked them what he should do with the children of Israel, Bilaam recommended they be killed. Jethro objected and fled to Midian, and Job remained silent. It is written that everything that befell Job later in his life was because he failed to say what he should have said in defense of his people.

Often, it's not what we say but what we don't say that plants the seed of negativity. It is written in the Bible: "Do not hate your brother in your heart." (*Leviticus 19:17*) It doesn't just say "don't hate;" it adds "in your heart." If we have hate in our hearts, damage is done whether we speak or remain silent. So when the time comes to speak, we mustn't remain silent. Of course, this doesn't mean we should be reactive and blurt out the first thing that comes to mind. If we're angry, for example, it's often important to let some time pass before reacting. When we finally do speak, not only have we released our personal hurt, but more importantly, we are able to reveal the Light of the Creator. In this way, we can be like the Creator. We can be a Cause rather than an Effect and avoid doing actions that result from a reactive frame of mind.

The Creator's connection to us never changes because of the way we act. Everything that happens to us happens solely to help us on our spiritual journey. We may need some "jolts" to reach fulfillment, but everything the Creator does comes from an intention to help us and to make things better for us.

The secret in "...and be brought to the priest" (*Leviticus 13:2*)

It is written that if a person appeared to have leprosy, he had to go to the *Kohen HaGadol* (the High Priest), who would decide if he or she had leprosy or not.

> *Rav Yitzchak said, we learned that in "a plague of leprosy," plague MEANS harsh Judgment that rests over the world. Leprosy MEANS closing, as we learned,*

> *which is a closing of the Supernal Light, shutting the Supernal Goodness from descending into the world. It "is in a man"—man in general ALLUDES BOTH TO MAN ABOVE AND MAN BELOW—"he shall be brought to the priest," NAMELY the priest below, who is knowledgeable in opening that closing and kindling the lamps, WHICH ARE THE SEFIROT, so that through him there will be blessings Above and Below, and that plague shall be removed and gone, and the Light of Mercy will dwell on everything. For that reason, "he shall be brought to the priest."*
> — The Zohar, Tazria 25:137

But why doesn't the Bible simply state the diagnostic symptoms of leprosy instead of saying that the individual had to go see the priest? By contrast, if we want to know how much *tzedakah* (charity) to give, it is written very clearly that we must tithe ten percent. Usually, for whatever we want to know, we can go straight to the Bible and find the answer. Why is leprosy different?

In answer to this, the *Gemara* teaches that we cannot see our own afflictions, but only the afflictions of other people. That is why the *Kohen* must be consulted about leprosy. If we ourselves have to decide whether we're pure or not, it's in our nature to always decide in our own favor. Without a doubt, this principle applies to much more than leprosy. We always see what's wrong with others, but not what's wrong with ourselves. The Maggid of Mezritch, Rav Dov Ber, taught that any characteristics we notice in others are actually present in ourselves. This is why when the Creator shows us a problem in another person, it's not so we can point out that person's faults: It's so we can see the problem in our own life.

Even if we understand why we must go to another person to learn what's wrong with ourselves, why does that person need to be a *Kohen*? What special qualities does a priest have that others lack? A story by Rav Yehuda beautifully answers this question.

There was once a princess who loved the wisdom of Rav Yehuda very much despite the fact that he happened to have a terrible hunchback. One day, the princess asked him, "Why did the Creator give such great wisdom to such an ugly Vessel?" Rav Yehuda answered with the question: "Where does your father put his wine?" "In a clay bottle," she answered. "Poor people also put their wine in a clay bottle," said Rav Yehuda. "But your father has all the money in the world. Why doesn't he put his wine in gold bottles?"

The princess went home and told her servants to put the king's wine in gold bottles. And some time later when they served the wine at a state dinner, it had gone bad. The king was furious and wanted to know who had ruined his wine. When the princess confessed, the king asked her, "Don't you know that wine should always be kept in a clay bottle?"

What we see on the outside rarely mirrors a person's true inner nature. This is a very important insight, but the question still remains: Why is a priest the only one who can really see what a person is like?

Consider this: A very learned man once complained to his rabbi that people coming to the temple on Shabbat were full of pride and thought only about themselves. To his surprise, the rabbi answered him, "Perhaps you, too, are full of pride. It is said that in the Holy Temple, there was a mirror in which not only the physical person but also the spirituality of a person could be seen. In our day, since the Holy Temple doesn't exist, every person is a mirror for others. What we see in other people is really within us."

That is why it is written in the Torah that one must go to a *Kohen*. The *Kohen* who checked for leprosy used to check himself first. If he hadn't looked at himself with complete truth and detachment, he couldn't be truthful with others.

Spiritually, the *Kohen* represented the *Sefira of Chesed* (Lovingkindness), meaning the priest had the ability to go "outside of himself." He didn't concentrate on his own needs, but instead was concerned about the needs of others.

It was to serve the needs of others that Abraham the Patriarch—the very embodiment of *Chesed*—had a tent with four openings. He wanted people to be able to reach him as easily as possible and to come in through any entrance. Only someone who leaves behind his own sense of self-importance and his own needs and desires can see what's wrong with himself and not just what's wrong with others. That's why only a *Kohen* could decide who was pure and who wasn't.

SYNOPSIS OF TAZRIA

The number of verses (67) in this chapter is also the numerical value of the word *Binah*. *Binah* is a non-physical dimension of the Light and is the storehouse or container of energy for all that we need and desire in life. Today, cancer is a scourge that afflicts us the way that leprosy used to do for the generations of the Bible. The connection to *Binah* in this reading helps us elevate ourselves to a dimension where cancer does not exist.

FIRST READING - ABRAHAM - CHESED

12:1 The Lord spoke to Moses, saying, *2* "Speak to the Israelites saying: A woman who becomes pregnant and gives birth to a son will be ceremonially unclean for seven days, just as she is unclean during her monthly period.

3 On the eighth day, the flesh of his foreskin is to be circumcised. *4* Then she must wait thirty-three days to be purified from her bleeding. She must not touch anything sacred or go to the sanctuary until the days of her purification are over.

5 If she gives birth to a daughter, for two weeks the woman will be unclean, as during her period. Then she must wait sixty-six days to be purified from her bleeding.

6 When the days of her purification for a son or daughter are over, she is to bring a year-old lamb for a burnt offering and a young pigeon or a dove for a sin offering to the priest at the entrance to the Tent of Meeting.

7 He shall offer them before the Lord to make atonement for her, and then she will be ceremonially clean from her flow of blood. These are the regulations for the woman who gives birth to a boy or a girl.

FROM THE RAV

Leviticus 13:33 is specifically for healing all forms of brain cancer. There is a large *Gimel* in the word *vehitgalach* (to shave or cut off), which helps us connect to *Binah,* and the Flawless Universe. The *Gimel* also stands for the word gomel (the sharing, proactive nature of the Creator that is within each of us). The power of the *Kohen* (the priest) is what will allow us to cut off and overcome the intolerance and lack of dignity, which is the cause of all of our suffering. It's high time we take responsibility for at least removing the chaos from within us.

Do we all understand what the power of the Lightforce of God is and that we merit having the tools to connect to this Lightforce, tools recommended by Abraham the Patriarch some 4000 years ago? How seriously do we take it? How much is it in our consciousness? Yes, we feel something. But do we understand the extent? When I say the Lightforce of God can remove everything negative and chaotic, I'm not repeating some theory of mine; as a result of some investigation I performed.

We don't realize how desperately important it is to be conscious of the power of negativity on this planet. If we change our behavior from being grounded in selfishness to being grounded in caring and sharing, we are not doing anyone a favor. Why do we get such pleasure or feel so amazed when someone becomes more proactive? It's a matter of life and death.

FIRST READING - ABRAHAM - CHESED

דָּבֵּר ראה 2 לֵאמֹר: אֶל-מֹשֶׁה מהע, אל שדי יְהֹוָאדֹנָיֶאהדֹוֵנָהי ראה וַיְדַבֵּר 1 12

יָמִים שִׁבְעַת וְטָמְאָה זָכָר וְיָלְדָה תַזְרִיעַ כִּי אִשָּׁה לֵאמֹר יִשְׂרָאֵל אֶל-בְּנֵי

עָרְלָתוֹ: בְּשַׂר יִמּוֹל הַשְּׁמִינִי וּבַיּוֹם 3 תִּטְמָא: דְּוֹתָהּ נִדַּת כִּימֵי גלך יָמִים

בְּכֹל טָהֳרָה בִּדְמֵי תֵּשֵׁב גלך יָמִים וּשְׁלֹשֶׁת יוֹם וּשְׁלֹשִׁים ע״ה = נגד, זץ, מזבח 4

יְמֵי עַד-מְלֹאת תָבֹא לֹא וְאֶל-הַמִּקְדָּשׁ לֹא-תִגָּע בְּזִ, לכב, יבמ קֹדֶשׁ

וְשִׁשִּׁים שִׁבְעַיִם כְּנִדָּתָהּ וְטָמְאָה תֵלֵד נְקֵבָה ע״ה מ״ב יוהך, וְאִם 5 טָהֳרָהּ:

וּבִמְלֹאת 6 טָהֳרָה: עַל-דְּמֵי תֵּשֵׁב גלך יָמִים וְשֵׁשֶׁת ע״ה = נגד, זץ, מזבח יוֹם

וּבֶן- לְעֹלָה בֶּן-שְׁנָתוֹ כֶּבֶשׂ תָּבִיא לְבַת אוֹ לְבֵן טָהֳרָה יְמֵי

מלה: אֶל-הַכֹּהֵן לאה ־מוֹעֵד אֶל-פֶּתַח אֹהֶל לְחַטָּאת אוֹ-תֹר יוֹנָה כ״י מ״ה

וְטָהֲרָה זְ וְכִפֶּר מצפצ עָלֶיהָ פהל יְהֹוָאדֹנָיֶאהדֹוֵנָהי בינה וחכמה לִפְנֵי וְהִקְרִיבוֹ 7

ע״ה, מ״ב יוהך, וְאִם 8 לַנְּקֵבָה: אוֹ לַזָּכָר הַיֹּלֶדֶת תּוֹרַת וְזֹאת דָּמֶיהָ מִמְּקֹר

תַזְרִיעַ

Leviticus 12:2 – *Tazria* means "she becomes pregnant." Bringing life into this world is the ultimate deed of sharing. Through the power of Tazria, we have an opportunity to do extraordinary acts of sharing, particularly with someone with whom we've had a problem in the past or perhaps even with a stranger. This sharing allows us to change in a way that was not possible before.

Sharing brings so much Light, but sometimes after we connect to an enormous amount of Light, there is a terrible feeling of letdown. It is equally important to be just as strong after we have connected to the Light as we are when we make the connection, so that the letdown won't be too severe.

8 If she cannot afford a lamb, she is to bring two doves or two young pigeons, one for a burnt offering and the other for a sin offering. In this way, the priest will make atonement for her, and she will be clean."

13:1 The Lord spoke to Moses and Aaron, saying, 2 "When anyone has a swelling or a scab or a bright spot on his skin that may become the plague of leprosy, he is to be brought to Aaron the priest or to one of his sons who is a priest.

3 The priest is to examine the plague on his skin, and if the hair in the plague has turned white and the plague appears to be more than skin deep, it is the plague of leprosy. When the priest examines him, he shall pronounce him unclean.

4 If the spot on his skin is white but does not appear to be more than skin deep and the hair in it has not turned white, the priest is to put the person that has the plague in isolation for seven days. 5 On the seventh day, the priest is to examine him, and if he sees that the plague is unchanged and the plague has not spread in the skin, he is to keep him in isolation another seven days.

אָדָם

Leviticus 13:2 – Leprosy, in all its different forms, is the predominant theme of this particular Bible reading. At first, leprosy was diagnosed by the *Kohen*. According to Kabbalah, leprosy actually served as a spiritual cleansing agent and thus created protection for the sufferer. But it is much better to cleanse ourselves proactively than to be cleansed by processes outside our control. Reading this verse and going through spiritual transformation is a cleansing that we can choose proactively, but it's not a process that can happen overnight. The potential for many diseases exists inside us, and there are many ways to cleanse. Skin problems, for example, indicate an inner problem that we need to cleanse through our actions. Spiritual cleansing and transformation can not only cure disease, but can also prevent diseases from occurring in the first place and/or prevent them from re-appearing.

As mentioned previously, according to the *Zohar*, the word "plague" (from the phrase "a plague of leprosy") refers to the harsh judgments that hover over the world as a result of the collective negativity of humanity. In the Aramaic language of the *Zohar*, the word "leprosy" is defined as "closing."

This passage of the *Zohar* refers to the closing of the gates that guard the 99 Percent Realm of spiritual Light—the source of all joy, well-being, and lasting fulfillment. When these gates are closed, Light cannot enter our world—and darkness and judgment reign.

In truth, this darkness is the real plague of plagues, the fertile ground that gives rise to all other forms of plague, be they cancer, heart disease, exotic viruses, poverty, terrorism, depression, or any other individual or social ill.

וְהוּבָא

Leviticus 13:2 – "He shall be brought to the priest." The priest who examined a person for leprosy represented the Light that flows through the *Ten Sefirot*, the ten dimensions that lie between humanity and the Creator. The *Zohar* explains that the priest "kindles the lamps," which are the *Sefirot*, so that blessings will rain down upon us to heal our sickness.

The priest is commanded to arrange lamps in the Temple daily. We have explained this in relation to the candelabra. This secret is in the likeness of Above, since the Supernal Light in the anointing oil first runs over the head of the Supernal Priest, WHICH IS THE FIRST THREE SEFIROT OF ZEIR ANPIN. Then he kindles the lamps, NAMELY, THE SEFIROT OF MALCHUT, THE ILLUMINATIONS OF

לֹא־תִמְצָא יָדָהּ דֵּי שֶׂה וְלָקְחָה שְׁתֵּי־תֹרִים אוֹ שְׁנֵי בְּנֵי יוֹנָה

אֶחָד לְעֹלָה וְאֶחָד לְחַטָּאת וְכִפֶּר עָלֶיהָ הַכֹּהֵן

וְטָהֵרָה: 13 1 וַיְדַבֵּר יְהוָֹה אֶל־מֹשֶׁה לֵּאמֹר: 2 אָדָם כִּי־יִהְיֶה בְעוֹר־בְּשָׂרוֹ שְׂאֵת

אוֹ־סַפַּחַת אוֹ בַהֶרֶת וְהָיָה בְעוֹר־

בְּשָׂרוֹ לְנֶגַע צָרַעַת וְהוּבָא אֶל־אַהֲרֹן הַכֹּהֵן

אוֹ אֶל־אַחַד מִבָּנָיו הַכֹּהֲנִים: 3 וְרָאָה הַכֹּהֵן אֶת־

הַנֶּגַע בְּעוֹר־הַבָּשָׂר וְשֵׂעָר בַּנֶּגַע הָפַךְ

לָבָן וּמַרְאֵה הַנֶּגַע עָמֹק מֵעוֹר בְּשָׂרוֹ נֶגַע

צָרַעַת הוּא וְרָאָהוּ הַכֹּהֵן וְטִמֵּא אֹתוֹ: 4 וְאִם־בַּהֶרֶת

לְבָנָה הִוא בְּעוֹר בְּשָׂרוֹ וְעָמֹק אֵין־מַרְאֶהָ מִן־הָעוֹר וּשְׂעָרָה

לֹא־הָפַךְ לָבָן וְהִסְגִּיר הַכֹּהֵן אֶת־הַנֶּגַע שִׁבְעַת

יָמִים: 5 וְרָאָהוּ הַכֹּהֵן בַּיּוֹם הַשְּׁבִיעִי וְהִנֵּה

הַנֶּגַע עָמַד בְּעֵינָיו לֹא־פָשָׂה הַנֶּגַע

בָּעוֹר וְהִסְגִּירוֹ הַכֹּהֵן שִׁבְעַת יָמִים שֵׁנִית:

FIRE, and makes them illuminate, as it is written: "It is like the precious ointment upon the head," (Psalms 133:2) and "the anointing oil of his Elohim is upon him." (Leviticus 21:12)

Each of us is a priest in our own right. Through our actions, we ourselves kindle the lamps—the *Sefirot*—to stimulate the revelation of blessings and Light. This Divine Energy immediately heals us and the world of all disease and sickness.

וְהִסְגִּיר

Leviticus 13:4 – The concept of "closing" also refers to the way our own ego closes us off from our soul. Instinctively, we are close-minded toward kabbalistic truths that often challenge our conventional thinking. When we open

ourselves to the wisdom of Kabbalah and to the idea of change and personal transformation, we open up the gates to our soul and to the Upper World. Light is then free to flow to us and fulfill us, and thus banish darkness and judgment and eradicate all plagues. As we connect to this verse with an open mind and a receptive heart, the gates to the Upper World open wide.

The Bible describes some of the ways leprosy can manifest itself. Each of these ailments stems from a deep, concealed spiritual cause. For instance, inflammation of the skin can be caused by an inflated ego. Ailments associated with the head may relate to the state of our consciousness: If we are in a negative space, mentally or emotionally, this can be expressed through diseases of or in the head. Ailments of the face can be caused by our own evil eye—the

ON A LEAP YEAR: SECOND READING - ISAAC - GEVURAH

⁶ And again on the seventh day, the priest is to examine him and if the plague has faded and the plague has not spread in the skin, the priest shall pronounce him clean; it is a scab and the man must wash his clothes, and he will be clean.

⁷ But if the scab does spread in the skin, after he has shown himself to the priest to be pronounced clean, he must appear before the priest again.

⁸ The priest is to examine him, and if the scab has spread in the skin, then the priest shall pronounce him unclean; it is leprosy.

⁹ When the plague of leprosy is in a man, he is to be brought to the priest.

¹⁰ The priest is to examine him, and if there is a white swelling in the skin that has turned the hair white and if there is raw flesh in the swelling,

¹¹ it is an old leprosy in the skin of his flesh and the priest shall pronounce him unclean; he will not put him in isolation, because he is already unclean.

---

envious or vengeful glances we direct towards others. Afflictions of the mouth can occur when we engage in evil speech and gossip. Burns on the skin can be related to the anger and rage that burns in our hearts. Every form of physical ailment has its root in a spiritual flaw that governs our behavior and our actions toward other people.

Each of us can be a plague carrier, spiritually speaking, if we speak evil about friends or foes, if we consort with others who commit egocentric deeds, if we display intolerance, or if we bear hatred in our heart for others. But the Light that is found here in the words that discuss the various forms of leprosy can expel hatred and intolerance from our heart, enabling us to protect ourselves both from disease and from being a carrier of plagues. This Light abolishes plagues and disease from our planet and inspires gladness, compassion, and unconditional love in the hearts of all mankind.

When we allow our carnal desires to dictate our behavior, we contaminate the body, empower the ego, and weaken the influence of the soul. When

there is a danger of tipping the scales permanently to the dark side of ego, disease occurs to weaken and destroy the negative influences of the body. In this sense, disease is purification.

This purification is the purpose behind both illness and plagues. According to Kabbalah, when a person becomes ill, it is a wake-up call that begins a process of cleansing. Illness and plagues need not be permanent. The body is a physical reflection of the soul: When the body becomes diseased, it is because part of our soul needs our attention and spiritual work. Once we begin our self-transformation, the illness is no longer necessary as a tool to awaken change, so it is removed.

You may ask, from where do these diseases that come upon them, come from? Come and see: It is written, "But it pleases God to crush him by disease." (Isaiah 53:10) "It pleases God to crush him," meaning that God desires to strike him and cause him illnesses, to grant him merits in the World to Come. But they do not come from the Other Side. They are

ON A LEAP YEAR: SECOND READING - ISAAC - GEVURAH

6 וְרָאָה הַכֹּהֵן מלה אֹתוֹ בַּיּוֹם ע"ה = נגד, זן, מזבח הַשְּׁבִיעִי שֵׁנִית וְהִנֵּה מ"ה יה

כֵּהָה הַנֶּגַע מלוי אהיה דאלפין ע"ה וְלֹא־פָשָׂה הַנֶּגַע מלוי אהיה דאלפין ע"ה בָּעוֹר וְטִהֲרוֹ

הַכֹּהֵן מִסְפַּחַת מלה אתב"ש ארני ע"ה הִוא וְכִבֶּס בְּגָדָיו וְטָהֵר י"פ אכא: 7 וְאִם

פָּשֹׂה תִפְשֶׂה הַמִּסְפַּחַת בָּעוֹר אַחֲרֵי הֵרָאֹתוֹ אֶל־הַכֹּהֵן יוהך, ע"ה מ"ב

לְטָהֳרָתוֹ וְנִרְאָה שֵׁנִית אֶל־הַכֹּהֵן ע"ב ורבוע ע"ב: 8 וְרָאָה הַכֹּהֵן מלה

וְהִנֵּה פָּשְׂתָה הַמִּסְפַּחַת בָּעוֹר וְטִמְּאוֹ הַכֹּהֵן מלה צָרַעַת הִוא: מלה

9 נֶגַע מלוי אהיה דאלפין ע"ה ‏boxed[צָרַעַת] כִּי תִהְיֶה בְּאָדָם מ"ה וְהוּבָא אֶל־הַכֹּהֵן: מלה

10 וְרָאָה הַכֹּהֵן מלה וְהִנֵּה מ"ה יה שְׂאֵת אל וארני מלא ‏־לְבָנָה בָּעוֹר וְהִיא הָפְכָה

שֵׂעָר לָבָן וּמִחְיַת בָּשָׂר חַי בַּשְׂאֵת אל וארני מלא: 11 צָרַעַת נוֹשֶׁנֶת הִוא

בְּעוֹר בְּשָׂרוֹ וְטִמְּאוֹ הַכֹּהֵן מלה לֹא יַסְגִּרֶנּוּ כִּי טָמֵא הוּא: 12 וְאִם

---

called 'sufferings of love.' It amounts to one weight unit of holiness.
— The Zohar, Pikudei 44:468

There are several sure-fire ways to perpetuate good health in the body. The first is to restrict the ego, the voice inside that wants us to blame or control others so that we can feel good or valuable. This voice causes us to judge others because we believe that what we see is all there is. It is also the voice of that part of us that feels entitled to become angry because things are not going our way—as if our way was so successful before! The second way of achieving wellness is through purification, one form of which is pain and suffering. A third way is to use the tools and technology of Kabbalah, which include listening to this reading on Shabbat, scanning the *Zohar*, meditating and reciting the *Ana Beko'ach*, and meditating on the 72 Names of God. These are the tools that give us the energy to proactively create spiritual transformation. The greatest gift the Creator has given us is the instrument of the Torah Scroll—and notably this chapter—that allows us to overcome the demands of the ego and cleanse ourselves proactively—without

suffering—through the purifying Light cast by these verses.

Through the wisdom of Kabbalah, we can now use these spiritual tools to demolish our ego instead of having diseases devastate our body. The actual words that speak of plagues and leprosy become the antidotes and spiritual cleansing agents that free us forever from judgment and sickness.

נֶגַע צָרַעַת

Leviticus 13:9 – This section discusses the many different forms of leprosy. When the Torah describes a condition of any kind, the description itself acts as an antidote for the condition, in much the same way that the injection of snake venom is the only cure for a lethal snakebite. Leprosy is the only plague described in such detail in the Bible, but it represents many different kinds of maladies that infect our lives. Cancer, for example, is the plague of our own generation; by making a connection to this reading, we can eliminate any traces of disease as well as protect ourselves from potential infection.

12 If the leprosy breaks out all over his skin and, so far as the priest can see, the leprosy covers all the skin of the plagued person from head to foot,

13 the priest is to examine him, and see if the leprosy has covered his whole body, he shall pronounce that person clean since it has all turned white, he is clean.

14 But whenever raw flesh appears on him, he will be unclean. 15 And when the priest sees the raw flesh, he shall pronounce him unclean; the raw flesh is unclean; it is leprosy.

16 Should the raw flesh change and turn white, the he must go to the priest,

17 and the priest is to examine him, and see if the plague has turned white, then the priest shall pronounce the person with the plague clean; then he will be clean.

ON A LEAP YEAR: THIRD READING - JACOB - TIFERET

18 When the flesh has a boil on the skin and it heals, 19 and in the place where the boil was, a white swelling or bright spot, reddish-white appears, he must present himself to the priest.

20 The priest is to examine it, and if it appears to be more than skin deep and the hair in it has turned white, the priest shall pronounce him unclean; it is the plague of leprosy that has broken out where the boil was.

21 But if, when the priest examines it, there is no white hair in it and it is not more than skin deep and has faded, then the priest is to put him in isolation for seven days. 22 If it is spreading in the skin, the priest shall pronounce him unclean; it is a plague.

23 But if the bright spot is unchanged and has not spread, it is only a scar from the boil, and the priest shall pronounce him clean.

לְבָנָה אֲדַמְדֶּמֶת

Leviticus 13:19 – The Bible explains how the colors red and white correspond to uncleanness and purification, respectively. The *Zohar* explains that red refers to the force of Judgment, while white pertains to the energy of Mercy:

Just as the lily among the thorns is tinged with red and white, so is the Community of Israel affected by the qualities of Judgment and Mercy.
— *The Zohar, Introduction 1:1*

The sacred words of this verse now remove Judgment (red) from this world by imparting sweet Mercy (white), which will heal all of humanity. Moreover, our own inclination to judge others harshly is negated, while compassion and mercy—which we often block off—are allowed to flow from our heart.

יוהך, ע״ה מ״ב ‎־פָּרוֹחַ תִּפְרַח‎ הַצָּרַעַת בָּעוֹר וְכִסְּתָה הַצָּרַעַת אֵת כָּל‎ ילי

עוֹר הַנֶּגַע מלוי אהיה דאלפין ע״ה מֵרֹאשׁוֹ וְעַד־רַגְלָיו לְכָל‎ אדני ‎יה ‎־לְמַרְאֵה עֵינֵי

ריבוע מ״ה הַכֹּהֵן מלה: 13 וְרָאָה הַכֹּהֵן מלה וְהִנֵּה מ״ה יה כִּסְּתָה הַצָּרַעַת אֶת־כָּל

ילי ‎־בְּשָׂרוֹ וְטִהַר יי״פ אכא אֶת־הַנֶּגַע מלוי אהיה דאלפין ע״ה כֻּלּוֹ הָפַךְ לָבָן טָהוֹר

יי״פ אכא הוּא: 14 וּבְיוֹם הֵרָאוֹת בּוֹ בָּשָׂר חַי יִטְמָא: 15 וְרָאָה הַכֹּהֵן מלה

אֶת־הַבָּשָׂר הַחַי וְטִמְּאוֹ הַבָּשָׂר הַחַי טָמֵא הוּא צָרַעַת הוּא: 16 אוֹ כִי

יָשׁוּב הַבָּשָׂר הַחַי וְנֶהְפַּךְ לְלָבָן וּבָא אֶל־הַכֹּהֵן מלה: 17 וְרָאָהוּ הַכֹּהֵן

מלה וְהִנֵּה מ״ה יה נֶהְפַּךְ הַנֶּגַע מלוי אהיה דאלפין ע״ה לְלָבָן וְטִהַר יי״פ אכא הַכֹּהֵן מלה

אֶת־הַנֶּגַע מלוי אהיה דאלפין ע״ה טָהוֹר יי״פ אכא הוּא:

ON A LEAP YEAR: THIRD READING - JACOB - TIFERET

18 וּבָשָׂר כִּי־יִהְיֶה יי בוֹ־בְעֹרוֹ שְׁחִין וְנִרְפָּא: 19 וְהָיָה יהוה בִּמְקוֹם

יהוה ברבוע, ו״פ אל הַשְּׁחִין שְׂאֵת אל ואדני מלא לְבָנָה אוֹ בַהֶרֶת מלוי אדני ע״ה

לְבָנָה אֲדַמְדָּמֶת וְנִרְאָה ע״ב ורבוע ע״ב אֶל־הַכֹּהֵן מלה: 20 וְרָאָה הַכֹּהֵן מלה

וְהִנֵּה מ״ה יה מַרְאֶהָ שָׁפָל מִן־הָעוֹר וּשְׂעָרָהּ הָפַךְ לָבָן וְטִמְּאוֹ הַכֹּהֵן

מלה נֶגַע מלוי אהיה דאלפין ע״ה צָרַעַת הִוא בַּשְּׁחִין פָּרָחָה: 21 וְאִם יוהך, ע״ה מ״ב

יִרְאֶנָּה הַכֹּהֵן מלה וְהִנֵּה מ״ה יה אֵין־בָּהּ שֵׂעָר לָבָן וּשְׁפָלָה אֵינֶנָּה מִן‎-

הָעוֹר וְהִיא כֵהָה וְהִסְגִּירוֹ הַכֹּהֵן מלה שִׁבְעַת יָמִים נלך: 22 וְאִם יוהך, ע״ה מ״ב

‎־פָּשֹׂה תִפְשֶׂה בָּעוֹר וְטִמֵּא הַכֹּהֵן מלה אֹתוֹ נֶגַע מלוי אהיה דאלפין ע״ה הוּא:

23 וְאִם יוהך, ע״ה מ״ב ‎־תַּחְתֶּיהָ תַּעֲמֹד הַבַּהֶרֶת מלוי אדני ע״ה לֹא פָשָׂתָה צָרֶבֶת

הַשְּׁחִין הִוא וְטִהֲרוֹ הַכֹּהֵן מלה:

ON A LEAP YEAR: FOURTH READING - MOSES - NETZACH
WHEN CONNECTED: SECOND READING - ISAAC - GEVURAH

24 When someone has a burn on his skin and a bright reddish-white spot or white spot appears in the raw flesh of the burn, 25 then the priest is to examine the spot, and see if the hair in the bright spot has turned white, and it appears to be more than skin deep, it is leprosy that has broken out in the burn, and the priest shall pronounce him unclean; it is the plague of leprosy.

26 But if the priest examines it and sees there is no white hair in the bright spot and if it is not below the skin but has faded, then the priest is to put him in isolation for seven days. 27 On the seventh day, the priest is to examine him, and if it is spreading in the skin, the priest shall pronounce him unclean; it is the plague of leprosy.

28 And if the spot is unchanged and has not spread in the skin but has faded, it is a swelling from the burn, and the priest shall pronounce him clean; it is only a scar from the burn.

ON A LEAP YEAR: FIFTH READING - AARON - HOD

29 If a man or woman has a plague on the head or on the beard, 30 then the priest is to examine the plague, and see if it appears to be more than skin deep and the hair in it is yellow and thin, then the priest shall pronounce that person unclean; it is a scaly eruption, it is a leprosy of the head or of the beard.

מִכְוַת-אֵשׁ

Leviticus 13:24 – In this verse, the Bible discusses burns and scars. The kabbalists explain that burns on the skin are indicative of "fire" in the stomach, liver, and intestines. Every part of the body takes on an aspect of our correction. Fire or heat in the stomach, liver, or intestines is a physical manifestation of anger. This verse heals the effects of our anger on our internal organs. However, we must take responsibility for our emotions and make a commitment to change, or the restoration will only be temporary.

And this is why boils and leprosy and skin sores of all the limbs are to be found in the liver, deriving from the filth that remains there. From the heart comes health for all the limbs, for that is how it is: Since the heart took all that is pure, clean, and bright, the liver takes what is left over there of the dirt and the filth and distributes it to all the other limbs, which are the other idol worshipping nations, against their will.
— The Zohar, Pinchas 61:375

And since the anger awakens from it, FROM THE GALL, towards the liver, the sages taught in the Mishnah: Anyone who is angry is as though he worshipped idols. And furthermore, any burning up and heat that comes with any of the illnesses of the parts of the body is only

ON A LEAP YEAR: FOURTH READING - MOSES - NETZACH
WHEN CONNECTED: SECOND READING - ISAAC - GEVURAH

כד אוֹ בָשָׂר כִּי־יִהְיֶה ייי אלהים דיודין ע"ה בְעֹרוֹ מִכְוַת־אֵשׁ וְהָיְתָה מִחְיַת

הַמִּכְוָה בַּהֶרֶת מלוי אדני ע"ה לְבָנָה אֲדַמְדֶּמֶת אוֹ לְבָנָה: כה וְרָאָה אֹתָהּ

הַכֹּהֵן מלה וְהִנֵּה מ"ה יה נֶהְפַּךְ שֵׂעָר לָבָן בַּבַּהֶרֶת מלוי אדני ע"ה וּמַרְאֶהָ עָמֹק

מִן־הָעוֹר צָרַעַת הִוא בַּמִּכְוָה פָּרָחָה וְטִמֵּא אֹתוֹ הַכֹּהֵן מלה נֶגַע

מלוי אהיה דאלפין ע"ה צָרַעַת הִוא: כו וְאִם יוהך, ע"ה מ"ב | יִרְאֶנָּה הַכֹּהֵן מלה וְהִנֵּה

מ"ה יה אֵין־בַּבַּהֶרֶת מלוי אדני ע"ה שֵׂעָר לָבָן וּשְׁפָלָה אֵינֶנָּה מִן־הָעוֹר וְהִוא

כֵהָה וְהִסְגִּירוֹ הַכֹּהֵן מלה שִׁבְעַת יָמִים גלך: כז וְרָאָהוּ הַכֹּהֵן מלה בַּיּוֹם

ע"ה = נגד, זן, מזבח הַשְּׁבִיעִי אִם יוהך, ע"ה מ"ב ־פָּשֹׂה תִפְשֶׂה בָעוֹר וְטִמֵּא הַכֹּהֵן

מלה אֹתוֹ נֶגַע מלוי אהיה דאלפין ע"ה צָרַעַת הִוא: כח וְאִם יוהך, ע"ה מ"ב ־הַבַּהֶרֶת

תַּעֲמֹד הַבַּהֶרֶת מלוי אדני ע"ה לֹא־פָשְׂתָה בָעוֹר וְהִוא כֵהָה שְׂאֵת אל ואדני מלא

הַמִּכְוָה הִוא וְטִהֲרוֹ הַכֹּהֵן מלה כִּי־צָרֶבֶת הַמִּכְוָה הִוא:

ON A LEAP YEAR: FIFTH READING - AARON - HOD

כט וְאִישׁ ע"ה קנ"א קס"א אוֹ אִשָּׁה כִּי־יִהְיֶה ייי בוֹ נָגַע מלוי אהיה דאלפין ע"ה בְּרֹאשׁ

ריבוע אלהים ואלהים דיודין ע"ה אוֹ בְזָקָן קנאה, ציון, יוסף: ל וְרָאָה הַכֹּהֵן מלה אֶת־

---

from the gall, FOR, AT THE TIME OF ILLNESS, it engulfs the arteries of the liver in flames and wishes to burn up the whole body. It is like a storm in the sea and its waves reach up to the skies and want to break out of their limits and destroy the world. And this would indeed happen were it not for the Shechina, which is for a sick person like the sand to the sea, surrounding it so that it should not break out. So, too, is the Shechina enwrapping the body and assisting it, as

it is written: "God strengthens him upon the bed of sickness." (Psalms 41:4)
— The Zohar, Pinchas 68:413

בְּרֹאשׁ

Leviticus 13:29 – Here the Torah discusses aspects of the head and brain. According to Kabbalah, the physical brain is only a receiver of information. There are two "broadcasting stations" that send out continuous signals: the

31 And if, when the priest examines the plague of the scaly eruption, it does not seem to be more than skin deep and there is no black hair in it, then the priest is to put the person with the scaly eruption in isolation for seven days.

32 On the seventh day, the priest is to examine the plague, and if the scaly eruption has not spread and there is no yellow hair in it and the scaly eruption does not appear to be more than skin deep,

33 he must be shaved except for the scaly eruption area, and the priest is to keep him in isolation another seven days.

34 On the seventh day, the priest is to examine the scaly eruption, and see if the scaly eruption has not spread in the skin and appears to be no more than skin deep, then the priest shall pronounce him clean, and he must wash his clothes, and he will be clean.

35 But if the scaly eruption does spread in the skin after he is pronounced clean,

36 the priest is to examine him, and see if the scaly eruption has spread in the skin, the priest does not need to look for yellow hair; the person is unclean.

37 But if the scaly eruption it is unchanged and black hair has grown in it, the scaly eruption is healed; he is clean, and the priest shall pronounce him clean.

38 And if a man or woman has bright spots on the skin, or even white bright spots,

39 then the priest is to examine them, and see if the bright spots are dull white, it is a tetter that has broken out on the skin; that person is clean.

Light and the Negative Side. Our mind is the non-physical part of us that has the free will to choose which of the stations we want to listen to. Negative thoughts—such as uncertainty, worry, fear, and the terrible thoughts we have about people who push our buttons—are the clearer and louder thoughts that originate from the broadcasting station of the Negative Side.

Our predisposition to one station or the other comes not from our heads but from our hearts. It is a cold heart that creates the opening for an onslaught of harmful, unproductive, negative thoughts, whereas an open, warm heart seals those openings so that we can tune out the signal from the Negative Side and tune into the Light and the faint, gentle sound of our souls.

Leviticus 13:33 – The large letter *Gimel* in the word *vehitgalach*, meaning "he will shave himself," represents our opportunity to remove pride—one of the deadliest enemies of our soul. The Aramaic word for pride, *ga'ava*, begins with a letter *Gimel*. The *Gimel* is the only one of the 22 letters of the Aramaic alphabet that is not present in any of the 72 Names of God. The *Zohar* explains that the Light cannot reside in a Vessel that also holds pride. The profound Light of mind-over-matter that the 72 Names of God gives us cannot be accessed while pride exists within us. Pride is an effect of the ego: When ego sows the seeds, pride is the crop we reap. Pride

הַנֶּ֫גַע מלוי אהיה דאלפין ע"ה וְהִנֵּה מ"ה יה מַרְאֵ֫הוּ עָמֹק מִן־הָע֑וֹר וּב֥וֹ שֵׂעָ֖ר צָהֹ֑ב

דָּ֑ק וְטִמֵּ֧א אֹת֣וֹ הַכֹּהֵ֗ן מלה נֶ֣תֶק ה֔וּא צָרַ֧עַת הָרֹ֛אשׁ ריבוע אלהים ואלהים דיודין ע"ה

א֥וֹ הַזָּקָ֖ן הֽוּא: 31 וְכִֽי־יִרְאֶ֨ה רי"ו, גבורה הַכֹּהֵן֮ מלה אֶת־נֶ֣גַע

מלוי אהיה דאלפין ע"ה הַנֶּתֶק֒ וְהִנֵּה מ"ה יה אֵֽין־מַרְאֵ֨הוּ עָמֹ֣ק מִן־הָע֔וֹר וְשֵׂעָ֥ר

שָׁחֹ֖ר אֵ֣ין בּ֑וֹ וְהִסְגִּ֧יר אֶת־נֶ֥גַע מלה הַכֹּהֵ֛ן מלוי אהיה דאלפין ע"ה הַנֶּ֖תֶק

שִׁבְעַ֥ת יָמִֽים: גלך 32 וְרָאָ֨ה מלה הַכֹּהֵ֣ן ראה אֶת־הַנֶּגַע֮ מלוי אהיה דאלפין ע"ה בַּיּ֣וֹם

ע"ה = נגד, זן, מזבח הַשְּׁבִיעִי֒ וְהִנֵּה מ"ה יה לֹֽא־פָשָׂ֣ה הַנֶּ֔תֶק וְלֹא־הָ֥יָה ב֖וֹ שֵׂעָ֣ר

צָהֹ֑ב וּמַרְאֵ֤ה הַנֶּ֨תֶק֙ אֵ֣ין עָמֹ֣ק מִן־הָע֔וֹר: 33 [וְהִ֨תְגַּלָּ֔ח] וְאֶת־הַנֶּ֖תֶק לֹ֣א

יְגַלֵּ֑חַ וְהִסְגִּ֨יר הַכֹּהֵ֧ן מלה אֶת־הַנֶּ֛תֶק שִׁבְעַ֥ת יָמִ֖ים שֵׁנִֽית: גלך 34 וְרָאָה֩ ראה

הַכֹּהֵ֨ן מלה אֶת־הַנֶּ֜תֶק בַּיּ֣וֹם ע"ה = נגד הַשְּׁבִיעִ֗י וְהִנֵּ֤ה מ"ה יה לֹֽא־פָשָׂ֤ה

הַנֶּ֨תֶק֙ בָּע֔וֹר וּמַרְאֵ֕הוּ אֵינֶ֥נּוּ עָמֹ֖ק מִן־הָע֑וֹר וְטִהַ֤ר י"פ אכא אֹתוֹ֙ הַכֹּהֵ֔ן מלה

וְכִבֶּ֥ס בְּגָדָ֖יו וְטָהֵֽר י"פ אכא: 35 וְאִם־פָּשֹׂ֧ה ע"ה מ"ב יוהך, פָשָׂ֛ה הַנֶּ֖תֶק בָּע֑וֹר

אַחֲרֵ֖י טָהֳרָתֽוֹ: 36 וְרָאָ֨הוּ֙ הַכֹּהֵ֔ן מלה וְהִנֵּ֛ה מ"ה יה פָּשָׂ֥ה הַנֶּ֖תֶק בָּע֑וֹר לֹֽא־

יְבַקֵּ֧ר הַכֹּהֵ֛ן מלה לַשֵּׂעָ֥ר הַצָּהֹ֖ב טָמֵ֥א הֽוּא: 37 וְאִם־ ע"ה מ"ב יוהך, בְּעֵינָ֞יו

ריבוע מ"ה עָמַ֤ד הַנֶּ֨תֶק֙ וְשֵׂעָ֨ר שָׁחֹ֛ר צָ֥מַח יהוה אהיה יהוה אדני ־בּ֖וֹ נִרְפָּ֥א הַנֶּ֛תֶק

טָה֥וֹר י"פ אכא הֽוּא וְטִהֲר֖וֹ הַכֹּהֵֽן מלה: 38 וְאִישׁ֙ ע"ה קנ"א קס"א א֣וֹ־אִשָּׁ֔ה כִּֽי־

יִהְיֶ֥ה יֵ֛י בְעוֹר־בְּשָׂרָ֖ם בֶּהָרֹ֑ת מלוי אדני ע"ה בֶּהָרֹ֖ת מלוי אדני ע"ה לְבָנֹֽת: 39 וְרָאָ֣ה

הַכֹּהֵ֗ן מלה וְהִנֵּ֧ה מ"ה יה בְעוֹר־בְּשָׂרָ֛ם בֶּהָרֹ֖ת מלוי אדני ע"ה כֵּה֥וֹת לְבָנֹ֖ת בֹּ֣הַק

ה֥וּא פָּרַ֛ח רפ"ח בָּע֖וֹר טָה֥וֹר י"פ אכא הֽוּא:

---

is a flashing red light that gives us a clue that our ego is dominating us at the moment.

When ego is in control, we are unhappy because ego is the foundation of all our misery. Ego compels us to try to convince others that we are right. Ego gives us the illusion that we are free when, in reality, we are captive to its desires. By connecting to the *Gimel* in this section, we are, in fact, receiving an immunization against pride, and thus we are granted the greatest of all freedoms: the freedom from ego-based desires. In their place, we gain life's truest lasting gifts of family, friendship, and fulfillment.

ON A LEAP YEAR: SIXTH READING - JOSEPH – YESOD
WHEN CONNECTED: THIRD READING - JACOB - TIFERET

[40] *And if a man has lost his hair and is bald, he is clean.*[41] *If he has lost his hair from the front of his scalp and has a bald forehead, he is clean.*

[42] *But if he has a reddish-white sore on his bald head or forehead, it is a leprosy breaking out on his head or forehead.*

[43] *Then the priest is to examine him, and see if the swollen plague on his head or forehead is reddish-white like the appearance of leprosy on the skin,*

[44] *the man is leprous and is unclean, and the priest shall pronounce him unclean because the plague is in his head.*

[45] *And the leper, in whom the plague is, must wear torn clothes, let his hair be unkempt, cover the lower part of his face and cry out, 'Unclean, unclean.'*

[46] *As long as he has the plague, he remains unclean; he must live alone; he must live outside the camp.*

[47] *If any clothing is contaminated with leprosy, whether it be woolen or linen clothing,*

קָרֵחַ

Leviticus 13:40 – According to Kabbalah, sudden baldness actually prevents sudden death. When a man is terminally blocked by an over-abundance of karmic actions with negative consequences, death is decreed upon him. However, a sudden loss of hair acts as purification that saves him from death. Hair is an antenna, a cable connected to the Upper World, the Source of life. When a person goes suddenly bald, the hair dies in place of the person.

"And the man whose hair is fallen off his head, he is bald; yet is he clean." (Leviticus 13:40) Come and see, there is a hard spark upon the head of that man, and for that reason his skull is red as a rose and the hair is red within the redness OF THE SKULL. The lower Sefirot from below are suspended from him that rouses Judgments in the world.

Once the hair is removed from him and he is bald, everything is firmly established by means of supernal Chesed, SINCE THE ILLUMINATION OF CHOCHMAH IN HIM IS ESTABLISHED THROUGH SUPERNAL CHESED, and he is named pure after him.
— *The Zohar, Tazria 23:119-120*

בָּדָד יֵשֵׁב

Leviticus 13:46 – The isolation of the leper is discussed here, and the lesson and power we can receive from this verse pertains to the ego. Our ego is the reason for our seclusion and misery. If an individual cannot recognize his or her own ego in a situation, then the ego has blinded the person and placed him or her in solitary confinement. The way we can conquer ego is by proactively taking the time to think. In doing so, we loosen the hold our ego has on us and give our soul the opportunity to "speak up" so that we can figure out what we are doing.

ON A LEAP YEAR: SIXTH READING - JOSEPH – YESOD
WHEN CONNECTED: THIRD READING - JACOB - TIFERET

40 וְאִישׁ ע״ה קנ״א קס״א כִּי יִמָּרֵט רֹאשׁוֹ קֵרֵחַ הוּא טָהוֹר יי אכא הוּא: 41 וְאִם

יוהך, ע״ה מ״ב מִפְּאַת פָּנָיו יִמָּרֵט רֹאשׁוֹ גִּבֵּחַ הוּא טָהוֹר יי אכא הוּא: 42 וְכִי־

יִהְיֶה יי בַקָּרַחַת אוֹ בַגַּבַּחַת נֶגַע מלוי אהיה דאלפין ע״ה לָבָן אֲדַמְדָּם צָרַעַת

פֹּרַחַת הִוא בְּקָרַחְתּוֹ אוֹ בְגַבַּחְתּוֹ: 43 וְרָאָה אֹתוֹ הַכֹּהֵן מלה וְהִנֵּה

מ״ה יה שְׂאֵת אל ואדני מלא הַנֶּגַע מלוי אהיה דאלפין ע״ה לְבָנָה אֲדַמְדֶּמֶת בְּקָרַחְתּוֹ

אוֹ בְגַבַּחְתּוֹ כְּמַרְאֵה צָרַעַת עוֹר בָּשָׂר: 44 אִישׁ ע״ה קנ״א קס״א צָרוּעַ

הוּא טָמֵא הוּא טַמֵּא יְטַמְּאֶנּוּ הַכֹּהֵן מלה בְּרֹאשׁוֹ נִגְעוֹ: 45 וְהַצָּרוּעַ

אֲשֶׁר־בּוֹ הַנֶּגַע מלוי אהיה דאלפין ע״ה בְּגָדָיו יִהְיוּ אל פְרֻמִים וְרֹאשׁוֹ יִהְיֶה יי

פָרוּעַ וְעַל־שָׂפָם יַעְטֶה וְטָמֵא וְטָמֵא יִקְרָא: 46 כָּל ילי יְמֵי אֲשֶׁר

הַנֶּגַע מלוי אהיה דאלפין ע״ה בּוֹ יִטְמָא טָמֵא הוּא בָּדָד יֵשֵׁב מִחוּץ לַמַּחֲנֶה

מוֹשָׁבוֹ: 47 וְהַבֶּגֶד כִּי־יִהְיֶה יי בוֹ נֶגַע מלוי אהיה דאלפין ע״ה צָרָעַת בְּבֶגֶד

צֶמֶר מצר אוֹ בְּבֶגֶד פִּשְׁתִּים: 48 אוֹ בִשְׁתִי אוֹ בְעֵרֶב רבוע יהוה ורבוע אלהים

When we connect to this reading, we remove the ball-and-chain of the ego that is the true cause of our isolation.

In biblical times, dying people went through a process of isolation. This was not necessarily because they were infectious and had to be quarantined, but rather because they were supposed to accomplish some inner spiritual work. The physical isolation provided time for the afflicted person to reflect. When something manifests itself physically, we always have to think about what we did spiritually to bring it about.

וְהַבֶּגֶד

Leviticus 13:47 – In this section we are told about afflictions in garments. According to Kabbalah, our clothing represents our Surrounding Light,

as well as our environment. The *Zohar* explains that every aspect of the physical world, whether it is the inanimate kingdom, the vegetable kingdom, or the animal kingdom, was created to assist humankind in completing *Tikkun HaOlam*, the Correction of the World. Everything we do contributes to either the purification or to the contamination of our universe. If we share and care and extend ourselves beyond our selfish nature, then the universe will be in harmony. If we are busy creating garbage, then the universe becomes a gigantic dump. Right now, at this very moment, we can take responsibility for our thoughts and our efforts and make a commitment at the seed level—which is the level of our intentions—to clean up ourselves and thus the universe.

48 *any woven or knitted material of linen or wool, any leather or anything made of leather.*

49 *If the plague is greenish or reddish, whether in the clothing, or leather, or woven or knitted material, or any leather article, it is the plague of leprosy and must be shown to the priest.*

50 *And the priest is to examine the plague and isolate the affected article for seven days.*

51 *On the seventh day, he is to examine it, and if the plague has spread in the clothing, or the woven or knitted material, or the leather, whatever its use, it is a malignant leprosy; the article is unclean.*

52 *And he must burn up the clothing, or the woven or knitted material of wool or linen, or any leather article that has the plague of leprosy in it, because it is a malignant leprosy; the article must be burned up.*

53 *And if the priest examines it, and sees the plague has not spread in the clothing, or the woven or knitted material, or the leather article,*

54 *he shall command that the leprous article be washed, and then he is to isolate it for another seven days.*

ON A LEAP YEAR: SEVENTH READING - DAVID – MALCHUT
WHEN CONNECTED: FOURTH READING - MOSES - NETZACH

55 *After the plagued article has been washed, the priest is to examine it, and see if the plague has not changed its appearance, even though it has not spread, it is unclean and you must burn it with fire, it is a fret, whether the bareness is within or without.*

56 *And ff, when the priest examines it, the plague has faded after the article has been washed, he is to tear the contaminated part out of the clothing, or the leather, or the woven or knitted material.*

לַפְּשָׁתִים וְלַצֶּמֶר אוֹ בְעוֹר אוֹ בְּכָל ‏ב״ן, לכב, יבם ‏-מְלֶאכֶת עוֹר ‏49 וְהָיָה

הַנֶּגַע ‏מלוי אהיה דאלפין ע״ה יְרַקְרַק | אוֹ אֲדַמְדָּם בַּבֶּגֶד אוֹ בָעוֹר אוֹ‏-

בַשְּׁתִי אוֹ‏-בָעֵרֶב ‏רבוע יהוה ורבוע אלהים אוֹ בְכָל ‏ב״ן, לכב, יבם ‏-כְּלִי ‏כלי ‏-עוֹר נֶגַע

‏מלוי אהיה דאלפין ע״ה צָרַעַת הוּא וְהָרְאָה אֶת‏-הַכֹּהֵן ‏מלה ‏50 וְרָאָה ‏ראה הַכֹּהֵן

אֶת‏-הַנָּגַע ‏מלוי אהיה דאלפין ע״ה וְהִסְגִּיר אֶת‏-הַנֶּגַע ‏מלוי אהיה דאלפין ע״ה שִׁבְעַת

יָמִים ‏נלך: ‏51 וְרָאָה ‏ראה אֶת‏-הַנֶּגַע ‏מלוי אהיה דאלפין ע״ה בַּיּוֹם ‏ע״ה = נגד, זן, מזבח

הַשְּׁבִיעִי כִּי‏-פָשָׂה הַנֶּגַע ‏מלוי אהיה דאלפין ע״ה בַּבֶּגֶד אוֹ‏-בַשְּׁתִי אוֹ‏-בָעֵרֶב

אוֹ בָעוֹר לְכֹל ‏אדני אֲשֶׁר‏-יֵעָשֶׂה הָעוֹר לִמְלָאכָה ‏אל אדני

צָרַעַת מַמְאֶרֶת הַנֶּגַע ‏מלוי אהיה דאלפין ע״ה טָמֵא הוּא: ‏52 וְשָׂרַף אֶת‏-הַבֶּגֶד

אוֹ אֶת‏-הַשְּׁתִי | אוֹ אֶת‏-הָעֵרֶב ‏רבוע יהוה ורבוע אלהים בַּצֶּמֶר ‏מצר אוֹ בַפִּשְׁתִּים

אוֹ אֶת‏-כָּל ‏ילי ‏-כְּלִי ‏כלי הָעוֹר אֲשֶׁר‏-יִהְיֶה ‏יהוה בוֹ הַנֶּגַע ‏מלוי אהיה דאלפין ע״ה

כִּי‏-צָרַעַת מַמְאֶרֶת הוּא בָּאֵשׁ ‏אלהים דיודין ע״ה תִּשָּׂרֵף: ‏53 וְאִם ‏יוהך, ע״ה מ״ב

יִרְאֶה ‏רי״ו, גבורה הַכֹּהֵן ‏מלה וְהִנֵּה ‏מ״ה יה לֹא‏-פָשָׂה הַנֶּגַע ‏מלוי אהיה דאלפין ע״ה בַּבֶּגֶד

אוֹ בַשְּׁתִי אוֹ בָעֵרֶב ‏רבוע יהוה ורבוע אלהים אוֹ בְכָל ‏ב״ן, לכב, יבם ‏-כְּלִי ‏כלי ‏-עוֹר:

‏54 וְצִוָּה ‏פיי הַכֹּהֵן ‏מלה וְכִבְּסוּ אֵת אֲשֶׁר‏-בּוֹ הַנָּגַע ‏מלוי אהיה דאלפין ע״ה וְהִסְגִּירוֹ

שִׁבְעַת‏-יָמִים ‏נלך שֵׁנִית:

ON A LEAP YEAR: SEVENTH READING - DAVID – MALCHUT
WHEN CONNECTED: FOURTH READING - MOSES - NETZACH

‏55 וְרָאָה ‏ראה הַכֹּהֵן ‏מלה אַחֲרֵי | הֻכַּבֵּס אֶת‏-הַנֶּגַע ‏מלוי אהיה דאלפין ע״ה וְהִנֵּה

‏מ״ה יה לֹא‏-הָפַךְ הַנֶּגַע ‏מלוי אהיה דאלפין ע״ה אֶת‏-עֵינוֹ ‏ריבוע מ״ה וְהַנֶּגַע ‏מלוי אהיה דאלפין ע״ה

לֹא‏-פָשָׂה טָמֵא הוּא בָּאֵשׁ ‏אלהים דיודין ע״ה תִּשְׂרְפֶנּוּ פְּחֶתֶת הִוא בְּקָרַחְתּוֹ

אוֹ בְגַבַּחְתּוֹ: ‏56 וְאִם ‏יוהך, ע״ה מ״ב רָאָה ‏ראה הַכֹּהֵן ‏מלה וְהִנֵּה ‏מ״ה יה כֵּהָה הַנֶּגַע

‏מלוי אהיה דאלפין ע״ה אַחֲרֵי הֻכַּבֵּס אֹתוֹ וְקָרַע ‏ב״פ אלף למד, שי״ע אלף למד אֹתוֹ מִן‏-הַבֶּגֶד אוֹ

מִן‏-הָעוֹר אוֹ מִן‏-הַשְּׁתִי אוֹ מִן‏-הָעֵרֶב ‏רבוע יהוה ורבוע אלהים:

ON A LEAP YEAR: MAFTIR

57 And if it still appears in the clothing, or in the woven or knitted material, or in the leather article, it is spreading, and whatever has the plague must be burned with fire.

58 The clothing, or the woven or knitted material, or any leather article that has been washed and is rid of the plague, and if the plague leaves it must be washed again, and it will be clean."

59 This is the law of the plague of leprosy in woolen or linen clothing, woven or knitted material, or any leather article, for pronouncing them clean or pronouncing them unclean.

ON A LEAP YEAR: HAFTARAH OF TAZRIA

Na'aman, head of the army of the nation of Aram, came to Israel to be healed of his leprosy and was cured by the prophet Elisha. This act of healing by Elisha indicates that the Bible and Kabbalah are not meant only for Israelites, but for all humanity. First, the Torah on Mount Sinai was given in 70 languages for all mankind to hear. Second, Kabbalah itself predates all religion, and is, in fact, considered the source of all spiritual teachings—the bridge that unites all traditions.

Kings 2 4:42-5:19

4:42 And there came a man from Baal Shalishah, bringing the man of God bread of the first fruits, twenty loaves of barley bread along with full ears of corn in the husk. And he said, "Give the people, so that they may eat."

43 And his servant said, "How can I set this before a hundred men?" And he said again, "Give the people that they may eat, for this is what the Lord says: 'They will eat and have some left over.' "

44 So he set it before them and they ate and had some left over, according to the word of the Lord.

ON A LEAP YEAR: MAFTIR

57 וְאִם יוהך, ע״ה מ״ב תֵּרָאֶה עוֹד בַּבֶּגֶד אוֹ־בַשְּׁתִי אוֹ־בָעֵרֶב רבוע יהוה ורבוע אלהים אוֹ בְכָל בֵּ״ן, לכב, יבמ ־כְּלִי כלי ־עוֹר פְּרַחַת הִוא בָּאֵשׁ אלהים דיודין ע״ה תִּשְׂרְפֶנּוּ אֵת אֲשֶׁר־בּוֹ הַנָּגַע מלוי אהיה דאלפין: 58 וְהַבֶּגֶד אוֹ־ הַשְּׁתִי אוֹ־הָעֵרֶב רבוע יהוה ורבוע אלהים אוֹ־כָל ־כְּלִי ילי ־הָעוֹר כלי אֲשֶׁר תְּכַבֵּס וְסָר הויות י מֵהֶם הַנָּגַע מלוי אהיה דאלפין ע״ה וְכֻבַּס שֵׁנִית וְטָהֵר י״פ אכא: 59 זֹאת תּוֹרַת נֶגַע מלוי אהיה דאלפין ע״ה צָרַעַת בֶּגֶד הַצֶּמֶר מצר | אוֹ הַפִּשְׁתִּים אוֹ הַשְּׁתִי אוֹ הָעֵרֶב רבוע יהוה ורבוע אלהים אוֹ כָל ילי ־כְּלִי כלי ־עוֹר לְטַהֲרוֹ אוֹ לְטַמְּאוֹ:

ON A LEAP YEAR: HAFTARAH OF TAZRIA

Next, the Name, from the 72 Names of God, that provides the energy of building bridges is אום (*Alef, Vav, final Mem*), and is the origin of the "Om" mantra that is part of the spiritual systems of the East. And finally, according to the kabbalists, Jesus and Mohammed immersed themselves in the study of Kabbalah during their lifetimes.

מלכים ב פרק ד

42 וְאִישׁ ע״ה קנ״א קס״א בָּא מִבַּעַל שָׁלִשָׁה וַיָּבֵא לְאִישׁ ע״ה קנ״א קס״א הָאֱלֹהִים מום, אהיה אדני; ילה לֶחֶם ג״פ יהוה בִּכּוּרִים עֶשְׂרִים־לֶחֶם ג״פ יהוה שְׂעֹרִים כתר וְכַרְמֶל בְּצִקְלֹנוֹ וַיֹּאמֶר תֵּן לָעָם עלם וְיֹאכֵלוּ: 43 וַיֹּאמֶר מְשָׁרְתוֹ מ״ה מ״ה אֶתֵּן זֶה לִפְנֵי וחכמה בינה מֵאָה מלוי ע״ב דמב, אִישׁ ע״ה קנ״א קס״א וַיֹּאמֶר תֵּן לָעָם וְיֹאכֵלוּ כִּי כֹה הוי אָמַר יְהוָהֱאֲדֹנָהֲדֹנֻהֵי אָכֹל וְהוֹתֵר ייון: 44 וַיִּתֵּן י״פ מלוי ע״ב לִפְנֵיהֶם וַיֹּאכְלוּ

5:¹ Now Naaman Captain of the army of the king of Aram, was a great man before his master and honorable, because through him the Lord had given victory to Aram. He was a valiant soldier, but he had leprosy.

² And the Arameans had gone out and had taken captive a young maid from the land of Israel, and she served Naaman's wife.

³ And she said to her mistress, "If only my master would see the prophet who is in Samaria! For he will heal him of his leprosy."

⁴ And he went in and told his lord, saying: "The maid from the land of Israel has said such and such."

⁵ And the king of Aram said, "Go now, and I will send a letter to the king of Israel." So he left, taking with him ten talents of silver, and six thousand pieces of gold and ten changes of clothing.

⁶ And he brought the letter to the king of Israel, saying: "And now when this letter comes to you, I am sending Naaman, my servant to you so that you may heal him of his leprosy."

⁷ And it came to pass, when the king of Israel read the letter, he rent his clothes and said, "Am I God to kill and bring back to life that this man sends someone to me to be healed of his leprosy? But consider, I pray you, and see how he is trying to pick a quarrel with me!"

⁸ And so it was, when Elisha, the man of God, heard that the king of Israel had rent his clothes, he sent him this message: "Why have you rent your clothes? Have the man come to me and he will know that there is a prophet in Israel."

⁹ So Naaman went with his horses and with his chariot and stopped at the door of Elisha's house.

¹⁰ And Elisha sent a messenger to say to him, "Go, wash yourself seven times in the Jordan, and your flesh will be restored and you will be cleansed."

¹¹ But Naaman went away angry and said, "I thought that he would surely come out to me and stand and call on the Name of the Lord, his God, and strike his hand over the spot and cure the leper.

¹² Are not Abana and Pharpar, the rivers of Damascus, better than any of the waters of Israel? May I not wash in them and be clean?" So he turned and went off in a rage.

וַיּוֹתֵר כִּדְבַר יְהוָֹה ראה ׃ 1 5 וְנַעֲמָן שַׂר־
צְבָא מֶלֶךְ־אֲרָם הָיָה אִישׁ גָּדוֹל לִפְנֵי
אֲדֹנָיו וּנְשֻׂא פָנִים כִּי־בוֹ נָתַן יְהוָֹה תְּשׁוּעָה לַאֲרָם
וְהָאִישׁ הָיָה גִּבּוֹר חַיִל מְצֹרָע ׃ 2 וַאֲרָם יָצְאוּ גְדוּדִים וַיִּשְׁבּוּ
מֵאֶרֶץ יִשְׂרָאֵל נַעֲרָה קְטַנָּה וַתְּהִי לִפְנֵי
אֵשֶׁת נַעֲמָן ׃ 3 וַתֹּאמֶר אֶל־גְּבִרְתָּהּ אַחֲלֵי אֲדֹנִי לִפְנֵי הַנָּבִיא
אֲשֶׁר בְּשֹׁמְרוֹן אָז יֶאֱסֹף אֹתוֹ מִצָּרַעְתּוֹ ׃ 4 וַיָּבֹא וַיַּגֵּד לַאדֹנָיו לֵאמֹר
כָּזֹאת וְכָזֹאת דִּבְּרָה הַנַּעֲרָה ראה אֲשֶׁר מֵאֶרֶץ יִשְׂרָאֵל ׃
5 וַיֹּאמֶר מֶלֶךְ־אֲרָם לֶךְ־בֹּא וְאֶשְׁלְחָה סֵפֶר אֶל־מֶלֶךְ יִשְׂרָאֵל וַיֵּלֶךְ
וַיִּקַּח בְּיָדוֹ עֶשֶׂר כִּכְּרֵי־כֶסֶף וְשֵׁשֶׁת אֲלָפִים זָהָב וְעֶשֶׂר
חֲלִיפוֹת בְּגָדִים ׃ 6 וַיָּבֵא הַסֵּפֶר אֶל־מֶלֶךְ יִשְׂרָאֵל לֵאמֹר וְעַתָּה כְּבוֹא
הַסֵּפֶר הַזֶּה אֵלֶיךָ הִנֵּה שָׁלַחְתִּי אֵלֶיךָ אֶת־נַעֲמָן עַבְדִּי
וַאֲסַפְתּוֹ מִצָּרַעְתּוֹ ׃ 7 וַיְהִי כִּקְרֹא מֶלֶךְ־יִשְׂרָאֵל אֶת־הַסֵּפֶר וַיִּקְרַע
בְּגָדָיו וַיֹּאמֶר הַאֱלֹהִים אָנִי לְהָמִית וּלְהַחֲיוֹת
כִּי־זֶה שֹׁלֵחַ אֵלַי לֶאֱסֹף אִישׁ מִצָּרַעְתּוֹ כִּי אַךְ־דְּעוּ־נָא
וּרְאוּ כִּי־מִתְאַנֶּה הוּא לִי ׃ 8 וַיְהִי כִּשְׁמֹעַ אֱלִישָׁע אִישׁ־
הָאֱלֹהִים כִּי־קָרַע מֶלֶךְ־יִשְׂרָאֵל אֶת־בְּגָדָיו וַיִּשְׁלַח אֶל־
הַמֶּלֶךְ לֵאמֹר לָמָּה קָרַעְתָּ בְּגָדֶיךָ יָבֹא־נָא אֵלַי וְיֵדַע כִּי יֵשׁ נָבִיא
בְּיִשְׂרָאֵל ׃ 9 וַיָּבֹא נַעֲמָן בְּסוּסוֹ וּבְרִכְבּוֹ וַיַּעֲמֹד פֶּתַח־הַבַּיִת ב״פ ראה
לֶאֱלִישָׁע ׃ 10 וַיִּשְׁלַח אֵלָיו אֱלִישָׁע מַלְאָךְ לֵאמֹר הָלוֹךְ וְרָחַצְתָּ
שֶׁבַע־פְּעָמִים בַּיַּרְדֵּן וְיָשֹׁב בְּשָׂרְךָ לְךָ וּטְהָר ׃ 11 וַיִּקְצֹף
נַעֲמָן וַיֵּלַךְ וַיֹּאמֶר הִנֵּה אָמַרְתִּי אֵלַי יֵצֵא יָצוֹא וְעָמַד
וְקָרָא בְשֵׁם־יְהוָֹה אֱלֹהָיו וְהֵנִיף יָדוֹ אֶל־הַמָּקוֹם
וְאָסַף הַמְּצֹרָע ׃ 12 הֲלֹא טוֹב אֲמָנָה (כתיב: אבנה) וּפַרְפַּר

13 And his servants went near and spoke to him, saying, "My father, if the prophet had told you to do some great thing, would you not have done it? How much more, then, when he tells you, 'Wash and be clean?' "

14 Then he went down and dipped himself in the Jordan seven times, as the man of God had told him, and his flesh was restored like the flesh of a little child and he was clean.

15 And he returned to the man of God, he and all his company and came and stood before him and he said, "Behold, now I know that there is no God in all the earth, except in Israel. Now therefore, I pray you, take a blessing from your servant."

16 But he said, "As surely as the Lord lives, before whom I serve, I will receive nothing." And he urged him to take it, but he refused.

17 And Naaman said, "If you will not, I pray you, give your servant as much earth as a pair of mules can carry, for your servant will never again make burnt offerings and sacrifices to any other gods, but to the Lord.

18 In this thing, may the Lord pardon your servant: When my master enters the house of Rimmon to worship there and he is leaning on my arm and I bow myself in the house of Rimmon, when I bow down in the house of Rimmon, may the Lord pardon your servant for this."

19 And he said to him, "Go in peace." So he departed from him a little way.

נַהֲרוֹת דַּמֶּשֶׂק מִכֹּל יּי מֵימֵי יִשְׂרָאֵל הֲלֹא־אֶרְחַץ בָּהֶם וְטָהַרְתִּי וַיִּפֶן

וַיֵּלֶךְ בְּחֵמָה: 13 וַיִּגְּשׁוּ עֲבָדָיו וַיְדַבְּרוּ אֵלָיו וַיֹּאמְרוּ אָבִי דָּבָר

גָּדוֹל הַנָּבִיא דִּבֶּר אֵלֶיךָ הֲלוֹא תַעֲשֶׂה וְאַף כִּי־

אָמַר אֵלֶיךָ רְחַץ וּטְהָר: 14 וַיֵּרֶד וַיִּטְבֹּל בַּיַּרְדֵּן שֶׁבַע

פְּעָמִים כִּדְבַר אִישׁ הָאֱלֹהִים

וַיָּשָׁב בְּשָׂרוֹ כִּבְשַׂר נַעַר קָטֹן וַיִּטְהָר: 15 וַיָּשָׁב אֶל־אִישׁ

הָאֱלֹהִים הוּא וְכָל־מַחֲנֵהוּ וַיָּבֹא וַיַּעֲמֹד לְפָנָיו וַיֹּאמֶר

הִנֵּה־נָא יָדַעְתִּי כִּי אֵין אֱלֹהִים בְּכָל־

הָאָרֶץ כִּי אִם־בְּיִשְׂרָאֵל וְעַתָּה קַח־נָא בְרָכָה

מֵאֵת עַבְדֶּךָ: 16 וַיֹּאמֶר חַי־יְהוָֹה אֲשֶׁר־עָמַדְתִּי לְפָנָיו אִם־

אֶקָּח וַיִּפְצַר־בּוֹ לָקַחַת וַיְמָאֵן: 17 וַיֹּאמֶר נַעֲמָן וָלֹא יֻתַּן־נָא

לְעַבְדְּךָ מַשָּׂא צֶמֶד־פְּרָדִים אֲדָמָה כִּי לוֹא־יַעֲשֶׂה עוֹד עַבְדְּךָ

עֹלָה וָזֶבַח לֵאלֹהִים אֲחֵרִים כִּי אִם־לַיהוָֹה: 18 לַדָּבָר

הַזֶּה יִסְלַח יְהוָֹה לְעַבְדֶּךָ בְּבוֹא אֲדֹנִי בֵית־

רִמּוֹן לְהִשְׁתַּחֲוֹת שָׁמָּה וְהוּא | נִשְׁעָן עַל־יָדִי וְהִשְׁתַּחֲוֵיתִי

בֵּית רִמֹּן בְּהִשְׁתַּחֲוָיָתִי בֵּית רִמֹּן יִסְלַח (כְּתִיב וְלֹא קְרִי׃ נָא)

יְהוָֹה לְעַבְדְּךָ בַּדָּבָר הַזֶּה: 19 וַיֹּאמֶר לוֹ לֵךְ לְשָׁלוֹם

וַיֵּלֶךְ מֵאִתּוֹ כִּבְרַת־אָרֶץ:

METZORA

LESSON OF METZORA
(Leviticus 14:1-15:33)

The Leper

We learn from the *Zohar* and from the *Gemara* (*Arachin* 15b) that leprosy is a punishment for *lashon hara* (evil speech). The *Zohar* explains that *metzora*, the Aramaic word for leprosy, is a variation of motzi ra, meaning "to invent rumors." A leper, therefore, was someone infected with a tendency toward rumor-mongering and gossip. The consequence of leprosy was enforced seclusion, since this was the only way to deal with an individual's "addiction" to evil speech. Therefore, all lepers had to be isolated from the people.

Rav Yisrael of Kozhnitz, in his book *Avodat Yisrael*, explains that purification from evil speech can occur only when the leper allows his soul to return to its true Source within the Creator. There, he will find the mercy and healing that makes a cure on the physical level possible. In other words, leprosy can only be healed when the leper first understands the nature of his impurity and how the physical action of his speech has corrupted his soul. Only when he starts to see the consequences of his words can he begin to heal

This issue of evil speech is extremely important, making it is necessary for us all be aware of our tendency to speak without thought, and guard against it. Such speech all too often turns to gossip; it's simply our nature. Because of this, the teachings regarding leprosy deserve to be looked at very closely.

The Creator made arteries that transport the blood throughout the body, carrying oxygen to the brain and to every organ. If one of the major arteries should become blocked, we might be unable to survive. There are other organs in the body whose true purpose is mysterious but whose importance and function is explained in *Kitvei Ha'Ari*, the Writings of Rav Isaac Luria (the Ari):

> *Beyond the body's physical needs, it also has needs on a spiritual level, and the organs of the body serve both kinds of needs. For example, the brain executes the life functions of the body. If there is a miscommunication between the brain and the nerves, physical paralysis can result. Similarly, spiritual paralysis can occur when we lose our connection with the Light of the Creator. That is why people come to pray with the tzaddikim (righteous people) or to ask their blessings, so that the tzaddikim can bring them Light and request the Creator's help in allowing their whole being to function properly, both physically and spiritually.*

The interconnectedness of physicality and spirituality is very clear in the case of a leper. The leper must seclude himself to quiet the barrage of impulses from his brain that caused him to sin. The problem must be dealt with at the seed level, which is the only way to purify the physical body of the consequences evil speech. As that purification takes place, the leper can beseech a *tzaddik* to pray for his body to function correctly again. Through his spiritual correction—turning back to the Creator with all his heart and promising never to sin again—the leper will see his spirit renewed and will become worthy of purification.

The issue of leprosy is an amazing demonstration of how negative actions influence our physical bodies:

> *Come and behold: the Holy One, blessed be He, grants pardons for all the sins of the world, save the evil tongue, for this man speaks evil of another, as it is written: "This shall be the Torah of the leper (Heb. metzora)." (Leviticus 14:2) THAT IS, he speaks evil of his friend, SINCE "METZORA" IS SPELLED WITH THE SAME LETTERS AS THE WORDS, MOTZI RA (LIT. 'SPREADS EVIL'). Rav Chiya said, "If someone spreads an evil name, all his limbs become defiled and he should be shut out, for his evil speech rises aloft and calls down an unclean spirit on him, and he is defiled. He who intends to defile is defiled; by the deed below another one is roused."*
> — *The Zohar, Metzora 4:14*

The spiritual laws dictate that there is a *mitzvah* (precept) for each part of the body: 248 positive commandments for the 248 parts of the body and 365 negative commandments for the body's 365 sinews. Connecting with this biblical chapter gives us the power not only to purify ourselves of leprosy but also to cleanse our *Desire to Receive for the Self Alone*. If we can truly understand what brings negative situations upon us both physically and spiritually, we will see that we ourselves are actually creating these blockages.

There is a special connection between the biblical chapter of Metzora and *Shabbat HaGadol* (the Shabbat prior to the cosmic event of *Pesach*). Without the *Desire to Receive for the Self Alone*, we would be able to achieve absolute certainty that nothing bad could happen to us—neither ill health nor misfortune in any other area of our lives. On the other hand, if we are not connected to the Light that is given to us by the Creator, we cannot enjoy any kind of fulfillment. On *Shabbat HaGadol*, we disconnect from our *Desire to Receive for the Self Alone*, thus allowing us to draw Light to the parts of our bodies that are lacking it.

Earlier, there was reference to a vital lesson regarding our speech. This is especially important with regard to speech that contains a reprimand or criticism because anything negative that comes out of our mouth is considered *motzi ra*. It is written in the Bible: "You shall not hate your brother in your heart: you shall certainly rebuke your neighbor..." (*Leviticus 19:17*) The *Zohar* explains:

> *"You shall not hate your brother in your heart: you shall certainly rebuke your neighbor..." (Leviticus 19:17). This precept is to rebuke one who has sinned and to show him that he loves that person, in order that THE REBUKER should not be punished. With regard to the Holy One, blessed be He, it is written, "for God reproves him whom He loves." (Proverbs 3:12) Just as the Holy One,*

> *blessed be He, does in rebuking those whom He loves, so should man learn*
> *from this practice and rebuke his neighbor WHOM HE LOVES. With what does*
> *the Holy One, blessed be He, rebuke man? He rebukes him with love, in secret.*
> *If he accepts HIS REBUKE, it is well. If not, He rebukes him openly among his*
> *friends. If he accepts that, then all is well. If not, He rebukes him publicly, before*
> *all. If he accepts, all is well. If not, He deserts him and does not rebuke him*
> *ANYMORE; He leaves him to go and do as he pleases.*
> — *The Zohar, Kedoshim 17:100*

It is very difficult to offer criticism with love. Every day, we are faced with situations, whether at work or at home with family, where we have to tell someone that something they are doing is not acceptable. But it's not easy. If our child is doing something that is not right, it is our responsibility to correct him, as we learn from the example of Absalom's father, King David. King David never spoke a word of criticism to his son in his entire life, yet eventually Absalom led a rebellion against his father. At work, too, when someone is not fulfilling their responsibilities, we are obligated to say something to them, realizing at the same time that we must not hurt our co-worker and thus create more negativity.

So what do we do? Considering an answer, one thinks of the *Ohev Yisrael* (Lover of Israel), Rav Avraham Yehoshua Heschel of Apta, also known as the Apta Rebbe. His nickname refers to the fact that he loved each and every person, and everyone loved him. He never told anyone what to do. Similarly, Rav Zusha told the story about his teacher, the Maggid of Mezritch, who blessed him so that he saw only the good in others. These *tzaddikim* (righteous people) never reprimanded anyone. Pious people in general believe in *ahavat Yisrael*, or love for one's fellow man, and the tzaddikim had ways of telling people what was wrong with their behavior without actually reprimanding them. There are always ways of saying things without letting people feel that they are being lectured to. Rav Elimelech and his brother Rav Zusha most certainly shared with others what they were doing wrong, but they did it in a special way and only when they truly cared about the person.

The same approach applies to correcting evil speech. If we truly care about a person, there is no way we could speak badly of him or her. The *tzaddikim* reprimanded wrongdoers, but no one felt hurt; they felt only the concern and the caring of the *tzaddik*. The cause of leprosy is a lack of caring between people, who, at some point, fall to speaking badly about one another. If we want to reach a level where we don't speak *lashon hara* about others, we need to start by being more sensitive to the people around us.

It is said that leprosy first begins with a blemish on the walls of a person's home. If the person does not get the message, a white spot appears on his clothes. Only after he misses these first two signs does the leprosy actually erupt on his body. In every aspect of life, the Creator tries to give us hints about ways we can change. We must ask ourselves what these messages mean. For example, why did we see a car accident on the road but were not a part of that accident, which took place mere seconds before we drove by? If we do not understand the message, then those "warning" events will come closer and closer to us. If we do not change, they will come so close that they could affect our bodies physically. All this happens because we do not pay attention to the clues that the Creator, with great mercy, gives us through our environment.

This lesson also applies to our discussion about reprimanding others. We must emulate the Creator, giving all the clues we can until the person accepts that what they are doing is wrong. If they still do not see their error, we must be more direct. Only if they completely miss the point can we come out and say it directly, but even then only if we truly care for the other person—and only if we think they will respond positively to that caring and accept our advice and use it.

There is a story about the process of reprimanding that was told by Rav Yechezkel Halevi, the son of Rav Yisrael, the Maggid of Kozhnitz. He said, "Two people came to me to testify against a villager, claiming they saw him doing a detestable transgression. I immediately announced that everyone in the adjacent villages should come to Shabbat to hear my sermon that week."

"The villagers came and I began my sermon, filling it with messages and lessons through which I spoke about this villager and his transgression, but without mentioning his name. I noticed that many other villagers were moved by my words to repent and there was hardly a dry eye in the house. I constantly looked at the villager in question, seeing that he was the only one unmoved and unaffected by my words. I could not contain myself a moment longer, so I called the man over and said to him, 'You could at least thank me for the sermon I just gave, since it was all for you. A few of your friends came by and mentioned to me what you've been up to.'"

"The villager replied, 'I committed no sin.' I reiterated my message, but he continued to deny his guilt, so I told the villagers that the next day I would show them how to punish the man. But that night as I slept, my father came to me in a dream and said, 'Son, what have you done? You have caused tremendous embarrassment to one of the greatest *tzaddikim* of your generation, one of the hidden *tzaddikim* upon whom the world stands. You must immediately visit him and take back your actions, so no one should know the harm you've done, as it is written:

$$\text{״וְהַצְנֵעַ לֶכֶת עִם ה' אֱלֹהֶיךָ״}$$

Micah 6:8: "and to walk humbly with your God"

"When I awoke, I knew I could not punish the man as I had intended. My father came to me again the following night, as well as the night after that. Finally, I rented a cart and traveled to the man's home, but he was nowhere to be found. I asked his wife where he was, and she said he had just left the house. I waited for him, but he did not return that day or that week or even that entire month. I made the journey to his house many times, but still did not merit seeing him. Finally, I understood that as long as I felt the pain of embarrassing him, I am protected from Above. Therefore, with his own power of prophecy, he is able to see me each time I attempt to visit him to make amends for my actions, and he disappears."

We see how our words can influence our lives, both for better and for worse. So often, as it is written: "Life and death are in the power of the tongue." (*Proverbs 18:21*) May we all merit life, especially during *Pesach*, at "the hands of our mouths."

SYNOPSIS OF METZORA

Metzora (leprosy) is often thought to be a result of evil speech. Connecting with this chapter helps us have the strength to overcome our desire to gossip, whether what we say is truthful or not.

ON A LEAP YEAR: FIRST READING - ABRAHAM - CHESED

14:1 The Lord spoke to Moses, saying, 2 "This is the law of the leper at the time of his cleansing, when he is brought to the priest:

3 And the priest is to go outside the camp and the priest is to examine and see if the plague of leprosy is healed in the leper.

4 Then the priest shall command that two live clean birds and some cedar wood, scarlet yarn and hyssop be brought for the one to be cleansed.

5 Then the priest shall command that one of the birds be killed over running water in a clay pot.

6 He is then to take the live bird and dip it, together with the cedar wood, the scarlet yarn and the hyssop, into the blood of the bird that was killed over the running water.

7 And he shall sprinkle the one to be cleansed of the leprosy seven times and pronounce him clean and then he is to release the live bird in the open fields.

FROM THE RAV

At The Kabbalah Centre, we are way ahead of our time—or Kabbalah is way ahead of its time and already into 25th century science. This may sound egotistical, I'm sorry to say, my friends, but everything that is contained in this chapter of Metzora is 25th century physics.

Do you know that trees suffer heart attacks? We have a very serious problem: This entire planet is being threatened like never before. The trees are suffering from every form of illness; bricks are suffering from the same illnesses, too. We are drinking dead water. We have no protection—it's as if we haven't drunk any water at all. At the subatomic level, too, the same kind of deterioration is happening everywhere. All diseases that exist in this world have one derivation—it ultimately all comes down to a breakdown of the immune system. And how are diseases transferred? How do they move in an airborne way? Rav Shimon bar Yochai says by leprosy. What is leprosy?

Psoriasis is the modem-day version of leprosy. Why are rashes and skin conditions of a similar nature so prevalent? The first and most important reason, Rav Shimon says, is that leprosy is caused by the speaking of evil tongue. Mankind is the culprit. Metzora says we had better stay away from the "evil tongue business" because otherwise we can become infected with these various airborne diseases. Walls, homes, people—all can get infected.

Strengthening our immune system is what the inner message of Metzora is all about. About the impurity, the Torah, in *Leviticus 15:31*, says: "you

ON A LEAP YEAR: FIRST READING - ABRAHAM - CHESED

14 1 וַיְדַבֵּר ראה יְהוָֹה‌אֲדֹנָ‌י‌אֱהֹוִ‌הָ‌‌‌אֲדֹנָֹי אֶל־מֹשֶׁה מהֹע, אל שדי לֵאמֹר: 2 זֹאת תִּהְיֶה

תּוֹרַת הַמְּצֹרָע ע‌ה = נגד, ז‌ן, מזבח בְּיוֹם טָהֳרָתוֹ וְהוּבָא אֶל־הַכֹּהֵן מלה:

3 וְיָצָא הַכֹּהֵן מלה אֶל־מִחוּץ מלה לַמַּחֲנֶה וְרָאָה הַכֹּהֵן מלה וְהִנֵּה מ‌ה‌יה נִרְפָּא

נֶגַע מלוי אהיה דאלפין ע‌ה ־הַצָּרַעַת מִן־הַצָּרוּעַ: 4 וְצִוָּה פוי הַכֹּהֵן מלה וְלָקַח

יהוה יהוה אדני לַמִּטַּהֵר שְׁתֵּי־צִפֳּרִים חַיּוֹת טְהֹרוֹת וְעֵץ קס‌א ע‌ה אֶרֶז ד‌פ ב‌ן

וּשְׁנִי תוֹלַעַת עקוצ‌ית וְאֵזֹב: 5 וְצִוָּה פוי הַכֹּהֵן מלה וְשָׁחַט אֶת־הַצִּפּוֹר הָאֶחָת

אֶל־כְּלִי כלי ־חֶרֶשׂ עַל־מַיִם חַיִּים בינה ע‌ה: 6 אֶת־הַצִּפֹּר ש‌ע הַחַיָּה יִקַּח חוֹם

אֹתָהּ וְאֶת־עֵץ ע‌ה קס‌א הָאֶרֶז ד‌פ ב‌ן וְאֶת־שְׁנִי הַתּוֹלַעַת עקוצ‌ית וְאֶת־הָאֵזֹב

וְטָבַל אוֹתָם וְאֵת | הַצִּפֹּר ש‌ע הַחַיָּה ש‌ע רבוע אהיה בְּדַם בְּדַם הַצִּפֹּר ש‌ע הַשְּׁחֻטָה

עַל הַמַּיִם הַחַיִּים בינה ע‌ה: 7 וְהִזָּה והו עַל הַמִּטַּהֵר מִן־הַצָּרַעַת שֶׁבַע

ע‌ב ואלהים דיודן פְּעָמִים וְטִהֲרוֹ וְשִׁלַּח אֶת־הַצִּפֹּר ש‌ע הַחַיָּה עַל־פְּנֵי חכמה בינה

---

must separate"—that is, cause the impurity to disappear. According to modern science, however, this is a physical impossibility. You cannot cause something to disappear, but you can transform it into another physical state. Water, for instance, becomes a gas, forms clouds, and becomes water again and so continues recycling physical matter. There is no annihilation. So when we separate, we create purification. We can separate the toxic material from the life-giving properties of a substance, as we do with distilled water. But we are still left with the sediment that accumulates, as well as the chemicals used in the distilling process: In this section of the *Zohar*, and through this reading, we have the ability to turn everything into Light, changing the molecular structure of even poisonous material into Light.

תּוֹרַת הַמְּצֹרָע

Leviticus 14:2 – Just as there are three stages for the purification of anything we want to cleanse, so, too, did the purification of the leper have three stages: looking within, making a clean break, and then starting over with a commitment to doing things differently in the future. The first stage—introspection—was sometimes enough to cause the external ailment to disappear. In the next stage—making a clean break—the leper shaved his own head. This shaving was symbolic of three things: the disconnection from negative energy, the embarking on a process of starting over physically and spiritually, and the removal of any connection to the leper's previous life. The final stage—making the commitment to reform—required that the leper offer a sacrifice and promise to transform those thoughts or actions that brought about the leprosy in the first place.

8 The person to be cleansed must wash his clothes and shave off all his hair and bathe himself in water; and he will be clean. After this, he may come into the camp, but he must stay outside his tent for seven days.

9 On the seventh day, he must shave off all his hair; he must shave his head, his beard, his eyebrows and the rest of his hair. He must wash his clothes and bathe himself with water, and he will be clean.

10 And on the eighth day he must bring two male lambs without blemish and one ewe lamb a year old without blemish, along with three-tenths of an ephah of fine flour mixed with oil for a grain offering, and one log of oil.

11 The priest who cleansed him shall present both the one to be cleansed and his offerings before the Lord at the entrance to the Tent of Meeting.

12 Then the priest is to take one of the male lambs and offer it as a guilt offering, along with the log of oil; he shall wave them before the Lord as a wave offering.

ON A LEAP YEAR: SECOND READING - ISAAC - GEVURAH

13 He is to slaughter the lamb in the holy place where the sin offering and the burnt offering are slaughtered. Like the sin offering, the guilt offering belongs to the priest; it is most holy.

14 The priest is to take some of the blood of the guilt offering and put it on the lobe of the right ear of the one to be cleansed, on the thumb of his right hand and on the big toe of his right foot.

15 The priest shall then take some of the log of oil, pour it in the palm of his own left hand,

16 dip his right forefinger into the oil in his left palm, and with his finger sprinkle some of it before the Lord seven times.

17 The priest is to put some of the oil remaining in his palm on the lobe of the right ear of the one to be cleansed, on the thumb of his right hand and on the big toe of his right foot, on top of the blood of the guilt offering.

18 The rest of the oil in his palm the priest shall put on the head of the one to be cleansed and make atonement for him before the Lord.

הַשָּׂדֶה שדי: 8 וְכִבֶּס הַמִּטַּהֵר אֶת־בְּגָדָיו וְגִלַּח אֶת־כָּל־ יל־ שְׂעָרוֹ וְרָחַץ

בַּמַּיִם וְטָהֵר יפ אכא וְאַחַר יָבוֹא אֶל־הַמַּחֲנֶה וְיָשַׁב מִחוּץ לְאָהֳלוֹ

שִׁבְעַת יָמִים נכך: 9 וְהָיָה עה = נגד, זן, מזבח בַּיּוֹם יהוה הַשְּׁבִיעִי יְגַלַּח אֶת־כָּל־

יל־ שְׂעָרוֹ אֶת־רֹאשׁוֹ וְאֶת־זְקָנוֹ וְאֵת גַּבֹּת עֵינָיו ריבוע מה וְאֶת־כָּל־ יל־

שְׂעָרוֹ יְגַלֵּחַ וְכִבֶּס אֶת־בְּגָדָיו וְרָחַץ אֶת־בְּשָׂרוֹ בַּמַּיִם וְטָהֵר יפ אכא:

10 וּבַיּוֹם עה = נגד, זן, מזבח הַשְּׁמִינִי יִקַּח חום שְׁנֵי־כְבָשִׂים תְּמִימִם וְכַבְשָׂה

אַחַת בַּת־שְׁנָתָהּ תְּמִימָה וּשְׁלֹשָׁה עֶשְׂרֹנִים סֹלֶת מִנְחָה עה = בפ בן

בְּלוּלָה בַשֶּׁמֶן יפ טל, יפ כוזו, ביט וְלֹג אֶחָד אהבה, דאגה שֶׁמֶן יפ טל, יפ כוזו, ביט:

11 וְהֶעֱמִיד מלה הַכֹּהֵן הַמְטַהֵר אֵת הָאִישׁ אדם הַמִּטַּהֵר וְאֹתָם לִפְנֵי

וחכמה בינה יְהֹוָ֑ההדיאהדונהי פֶּתַח אֹהֶל לאה מוֹעֵד: 12 וְלָקַח יהוה אהיה יהוה אדני הַכֹּהֵן

מלה אֶת־הַכֶּבֶשׂ בפ קסא הָאֶחָד אהבה, דאגה וְהִקְרִיב אֹתוֹ לְאָשָׁם וְאֶת־לֹג

הַשֶּׁמֶן וְהֵנִיף אֹתָם תְּנוּפָה לִפְנֵי וחכמה בינה יְהֹוָ֑ההדיאהדונהי:

ON A LEAP YEAR: SECOND READING - ISAAC - GEVURAH

13 וְשָׁחַט אֶת־הַכֶּבֶשׂ בפ קסא בִּמְקוֹם יהוה ברבוע, רפ אל אֲשֶׁר יִשְׁחַט אֶת־

הַחַטָּאת וְאֶת־הָעֹלָה בִּמְקוֹם יהוה ברבוע, רפ אל הַקֹּדֶשׁ כִּי כַּחַטָּאת הָאָשָׁם

הוּא לַכֹּהֵן מלה קֹדֶשׁ קָדָשִׁים הוּא: 14 וְלָקַח יהוה אהיה יהוה אדני הַכֹּהֵן מלה

מִדַּם רבוע אהיה הָאָשָׁם וְנָתַן אבגית"ץ, ושר, אהבת חנם הַכֹּהֵן מלה עַל־תְּנוּךְ אֹזֶן

יוד הי ואו הה הַמִּטַּהֵר הַיְמָנִית וְעַל־בֹּהֶן יָדוֹ הַיְמָנִית וְעַל־בֹּהֶן רַגְלוֹ

הַיְמָנִית: 15 וְלָקַח יהוה אהיה יהוה אדני הַכֹּהֵן מלה אדני מִלֹּג הַשֶּׁמֶן יפ טל, יפ כוזו, ביט וְיָצַק

עַל־כַּף הַכֹּהֵן מלה הַשְּׂמָאלִית: 16 וְטָבַל הַכֹּהֵן מלה אֶת־אֶצְבָּעוֹ הַיְמָנִית

מִן־הַשֶּׁמֶן יפ טל, יפ כוזו, ביט אֲשֶׁר עַל־כַּפּוֹ הַשְּׂמָאלִית וְהִזָּה והו מִן־הַשֶּׁמֶן

יפ טל, יפ כוזו, ביט בְּאֶצְבָּעוֹ שֶׁבַע עב ואלהים דיודין פְּעָמִים לִפְנֵי וחכמה בינה

[19] *Then the priest is to sacrifice the sin offering and make atonement for the one to be cleansed from his uncleanness. After that, the priest shall slaughter the burnt offering*

[20] *and offer it on the altar, together with the grain offering, and the priest will make atonement for him, and he will be clean.*

ON A LEAP YEAR: THIRD READING - JACOB - TIFERET
WHEN CONNECTED: FIFTH READING - AARON - HOD

[21] *If, however, he is poor and cannot afford these, he must take one male lamb as a guilt offering to be waved to make atonement for him, together with a tenth of an ephah of fine flour mixed with oil for a grain offering, a log of oil,*

[22] *and two doves or two young pigeons, which he can afford, one for a sin offering and the other for a burnt offering.*

[23] *On the eighth day he must bring them for his cleansing to the priest at the entrance to the Tent of Meeting, before the Lord.*

[24] *The priest is to take the lamb for the guilt offering, together with the log of oil, and wave them before the Lord as a wave offering.*

[25] *He shall slaughter the lamb for the guilt offering and take some of its blood and put it on the lobe of the right ear of the one to be cleansed, on the thumb of his right hand and on the big toe of his right foot.*

[26] *The priest is to pour some of the oil into the palm of his own left hand,*

[27] *and with his right forefinger sprinkle some of the oil from his left palm seven times before the Lord.*

מִשֶּׁגֶת

Leviticus 14:21 – The leper sacrificed what he could afford relative to his means and circumstances. This is true for all of us today as well. Our spiritual and physical level determines what we need to sacrifice. The nature of our sacrifice is less important than the fact that it is being made from our current position on our spiritual path.

יְהֹוָֽאֲדֹנָֽיאהדונהי 17 וּמִיֶּ֨תֶר הַשֶּׁ֜מֶן יש טל, יפ כוזו, ביט אֲשֶׁ֣ר עַל־כַּפּ֗וֹ יִתֵּ֤ן הַכֹּהֵן֙

מלה עַל־תְּנ֜וּךְ אֹ֤זֶן יוד הי ואו הה הַמִּטַּהֵר֙ הַיְמָנִ֔ית וְעַל־בֹּ֤הֶן יָדוֹ֙ הַיְמָנִ֔ית

וְעַל־בֹּ֥הֶן רַגְל֖וֹ הַיְמָנִ֑ית עַ֚ל דַּ֣ם הָֽאָשָׁ֔ם רבוע אהיה 18 וְהַנּוֹתָ֗ר בַּשֶּׁ֙מֶן֙

יפ טל, יפ כוזו, ביט אֲשֶׁר֙ עַל־כַּ֣ף הַכֹּהֵ֔ן מלה יִתֵּ֖ן עַל־רֹ֣אשׁ ריבוע אלהים ואלהים דיודין עה

הַמִּטַּהֵ֑ר מצפצ וְכִפֶּ֥ר עָלָ֛יו הַכֹּהֵ֖ן מלה לִפְנֵ֥י חכמה בינה יְהֹוָֽאֲדֹנָֽיאהדונהי 19 וְעָשָׂה֙

הַכֹּהֵ֔ן מלה אֶת־הַ֣חַטָּ֔את מצפצ וְכִפֶּ֕ר עַל־הַמִּטַּהֵ֖ר מִטֻּמְאָת֑וֹ וְאַחַ֛ר יִשְׁחַ֥ט

אֶת־הָעֹלָֽה 20 וְהֶעֱלָ֧ה הַכֹּהֵ֛ן מלה אֶת־הָעֹלָ֥ה וְאֶת־הַמִּנְחָ֖ה עה בפ בן

הַמִּזְבֵּ֑חָה וְכִפֶּ֥ר מצפצ עָלָ֛יו הַכֹּהֵ֖ן מלה וְטָהֵֽר יפ אכא

ON A LEAP YEAR: THIRD READING - JACOB - TIFERET
WHEN CONNECTED: FIFTH READING - AARON - HOD

21 וְאִם־דַּ֣ל יוהך, עה מב בוכו ה֔וּא וְאֵ֣ין יָד֗וֹ מַשֶּׂ֒גֶת֒ וְ֠לָקַ֠ח יהוה אהיה יהוה אדני

כֶּ֣בֶשׂ בפ קסא אֶחָ֛ד אהבה, דאגה אָשָׁ֥ם לִתְנוּפָ֖ה לְכַפֵּ֣ר מצפצ עָלָ֑יו וְעִשָּׂר֨וֹן

סֹ֜לֶת אֶחָ֗ד אהבה, דאגה בָּל֥וּל בַּשֶּׁ֛מֶן יש טל, יפ כוזו, ביט לְמִנְחָ֖ה עה בפ בן וְלֹ֥ג שָֽׁמֶן

יפ טל, יפ כוזו, ביט 22 וּשְׁתֵּ֣י תֹרִ֗ים א֤וֹ שְׁנֵי֙ בְּנֵ֣י יוֹנָ֔ה כזו מה אֲשֶׁ֥ר תַּשִּׂ֖יג יָד֑וֹ

וְהָיָ֤ה יהוה אֶחָד֙ אהבה, דאגה חַטָּ֔את וְהָאֶחָ֖ד עֹלָֽה 23 וְהֵבִיא֣ אֹתָ֡ם בַּיּ֣וֹם

עה = גגר, זן, מזבח הַשְּׁמִינִ֣י לְטָהֳרָת֔וֹ אֶל־הַכֹּהֵ֑ן מלה אֶל־פֶּ֥תַח אֹֽהֶל־מוֹעֵ֖ד לאה

לִפְנֵ֥י חכמה בינה יְהֹוָֽאֲדֹנָֽיאהדונהי 24 וְלָקַ֧ח יהוה אהיה יהוה אדני הַכֹּהֵ֛ן מלה אֶת־כֶּ֥בֶשׂ

בפ קסא הָֽאָשָׁ֖ם וְאֶת־לֹ֣ג הַשָּׁ֑מֶן יש טל, יפ כוזו, ביט וְהֵנִ֨יף אֹתָ֧ם הַכֹּהֵ֛ן מלה

תְּנוּפָ֖ה לִפְנֵ֥י חכמה בינה יְהֹוָֽאֲדֹנָֽיאהדונהי 25 וְשָׁחַט֮ אֶת־כֶּ֣בֶשׂ בפ קסא הָֽאָשָׁם֒

וְלָקַ֤ח יהוה אהיה יהוה אדני הַכֹּהֵן֙ מלה מִדַּ֣ם רבוע אהיה הָֽאָשָׁ֔ם מלה וְנָתַ֛ן אבגית"ץ, ועור, אהבת חנם

עַל־תְּנ֥וּךְ אֹֽזֶן־ יוד הי ואו הה הַמִּטַּהֵ֖ר הַיְמָנִ֑ית וְעַל־בֹּ֤הֶן יָדוֹ֙ הַיְמָנִ֔ית וְעַל־

בֹּ֥הֶן רַגְל֖וֹ הַיְמָנִֽית 26 וּמִן־הַשֶּׁ֖מֶן יש טל, יפ כוזו, ביט יִצֹ֣ק הַכֹּהֵ֑ן מלה עַל־כַּ֥ף

הַכֹּהֵ֖ן מלה הַשְּׂמָאלִֽית 27 וְהִזָּ֤ה והו הַכֹּהֵן֙ מלה בְּאֶצְבָּע֣וֹ הַיְמָנִ֔ית מִן־

28 Some of the oil in his palm he is to put on the same places he put the blood of the guilt offering—on the lobe of the right ear of the one to be cleansed, on the thumb of his right hand and on the big toe of his right foot.

29 The rest of the oil in his palm the priest shall put on the head of the one to be cleansed, to make atonement for him before the Lord.

30 Then he shall sacrifice the doves or the young pigeons, which the person can afford,

31 one as a sin offering and the other as a burnt offering, together with the grain offering, which the person can afford. The priest will make atonement before the Lord on behalf of the one to be cleansed."

32 These are the regulations for anyone who has an infectious skin disease and who cannot afford the regular offerings for his cleansing.

ON A LEAP YEAR: FOURTH READING - MOSES – NETZACH
WHEN CONNECTED: SIXTH READING - JOSEPH - YESOD

33 The Lord spoke to Moses and Aaron, saying, 34 "When you enter the land of Canaan, which I am giving you as your possession, and I put the plague of leprosy in a house in that land, 35 the owner of the house must go and tell the priest, 'I have seen something that looks like a plague in my house.'

בְּבֵית

Leviticus 14:34 – In commenting on this verse, the *Zohar* explains that when a house is contaminated by plague, we must demolish the house. During the demolition, however, a person may fortuitously find a treasure that was hidden in the house.

> *Rav Shimon said: "The purpose of all these plagues in the houses was to sanctify the land and remove the spirit of defilement from Israel. In addition, when a person demolished a house, he would find a treasure in it sufficient to rebuild and re-fill his house, so he would not regret the house that was destroyed, and he would then dwell in a holy habitation."*
> *— The Zohar, Tazria 30:161*

The word "house" is a code, a metaphor for our physical body—the Vessel that houses our soul. When the body is contaminated with ego and ruled by its primal reactive desires, the contaminations are referred to as "plagues in the houses." When we tear down and demolish our ego and our reactive nature, we find the ultimate treasure—the soul, which is referred to as "Israel" and "holy habitation."

Our worst fear in the breaking down of ego is a fear of loss—the loss of the pleasure and immediate reward that is derived from ego gratification. This fear is understandable. But the *Zohar* tells us that even greater joy and pleasure awaits us when we demolish the ego's reactive Vessel. A man will find a "treasure that is sufficient to rebuild and re-fill his house, so he will not be sorry for the house that was demolished."

הַשֶּׁמֶן יפ טל, יפ כוז"ו, ביט אֲשֶׁר עַל־כַּפּוֹ הַשְּׂמָאלִית שֶׁבַע ע"ב ואלהים דיודין

פְּעָמִים לִפְנֵי וחכמה בינה יְהֹוָאדֹנָיאהדונהי אבגית"ץ, ועור, אהבת חנם הַכֹּהֵן מלה 28 וְנָתַן

מִן־הַשֶּׁמֶן יפ טל, יפ כוז"ו, ביט | אֲשֶׁר עַל־כַּפּוֹ עַל־תְּנוּךְ אֹזֶן יוד הי ואו הה הַמִּטַּהֵר

הַיְמָנִית וְעַל־בֹּהֶן יָדוֹ הַיְמָנִית וְעַל־בֹּהֶן רַגְלוֹ הַיְמָנִית עַל־מְקוֹם

יהוה ברבוע, ר"פ אל דַּם רבוע אהיה הָאָשָׁם: 29 וְהַנּוֹתָר מִן־הַשֶּׁמֶן יפ טל, יפ כוז"ו, ביט

אֲשֶׁר עַל־כַּף הַכֹּהֵן מלה יִתֵּן עַל־רֹאשׁ ריבוע אלהים ואלהים דיודין ע"ה הַמִּטַּהֵר

לְכַפֵּר מצפצ עָלָיו לִפְנֵי וחכמה בינה יְהֹוָאדֹנָיאהדונהי: 30 וְעָשָׂה אֶת־הָאֶחָד

מִן־הַתֹּרִים אהבה, דאגה אוֹ מִן־בְּנֵי הַיּוֹנָה כ"י מ"ה מֵאֲשֶׁר תַּשִּׂיג יָדוֹ: 31 אֵת

אֲשֶׁר־תַּשִּׂיג יָדוֹ אֶת־הָאֶחָד אהבה, דאגה וְחַטָּאת וְאֶת־הָאֶחָד אהבה, דאגה

עֹלָה עַל־הַמִּנְחָה ע"ה ב"פ בן וְכִפֶּר מצפצ הַכֹּהֵן מלה עַל הַמִּטַּהֵר לִפְנֵי וחכמה בינה

יְהֹוָאדֹנָיאהדונהי: 32 זֹאת תּוֹרַת אֲשֶׁר־בּוֹ נֶגַע מלוי אהיה דאלפין ע"ה צָרַעַת אֲשֶׁר

לֹא־תַשִּׂיג יָדוֹ בְּטָהֳרָתוֹ:

ON A LEAP YEAR: FOURTH READING - MOSES – NETZACH
WHEN CONNECTED: SIXTH READING - JOSEPH - YESOD

33 וַיְדַבֵּר ראה יְהֹוָאדֹנָיאהדונהי אֶל־מֹשֶׁה מהש, אל שדי וְאֶל־אַהֲרֹן ע"ב ורבוע ע"ב

לֵאמֹר: 34 כִּי תָבֹאוּ אֶל־אֶרֶץ אלהים דאלפין כְּנַעַן אֲשֶׁר אֲנִי אני, טדהד כוז"ו נֹתֵן

אבגית"ץ, ועור, אהבת חנם לָכֶם לַאֲחֻזָּה וְנָתַתִּי נֶגַע מלוי אהיה דאלפין ע"ה צָרַעַת בְּבַיִת

ב"פ ראה אֶרֶץ אלהים דאלפין אֲחֻזַּתְכֶם: 35 וּבָא אֲשֶׁר־לוֹ הַבַּיִת ב"פ ראה וְהִגִּיד

This is a profound and powerful statement. Our fear is the result of a bluff implanted within us by the Evil Inclination. Logically, the only way a man will not regret giving something up is by receiving something far better in exchange. This is what the *Zohar* promises. Some spiritual doctrines demand the denial of pleasure, but the desire of the Creator is to bestow infinite pleasure upon His creations. A kabbalist, therefore, will only "trade up," renouncing temporary pleasure for eternal joy and fulfillment. We must always be aware that we are never asked to give something up when following the kabbalistic path. Rather, we are shown how to achieve even greater joy that will permanently and deeply satisfy our every desire.

36 The priest is to order the house to be emptied before he goes in to examine the plague, so that nothing in the house will be pronounced unclean. After this, the priest is to go in and inspect the house.

37 He is to examine the plague and see if the plague is on the walls of house with greenish or reddish depressions that appear to be deeper than the surface of the wall, 38 then the priest shall go out the doorway of the house and close it up for seven days.

39 On the seventh day the priest shall return to inspect and see if the plague has spread on the walls of the house, 40 then the priest must command that the plagued stones be torn out and thrown into an unclean place outside the town.

41 And he must have all the inside walls of the house scraped and the material that is scraped off dumped into an unclean place outside the town.

42 Then they are to take other stones to replace these and take new clay and plaster the house.

43 If the plague reappears in the house after the stones have been torn out and the house scraped and plastered,

44 then the priest is to go and examine it and see if the plague has spread in the house, it is a malignant leprosy in the house; it is unclean.

45 And he must tear down the house—its stones, timbers and all the plaster, and take these out of the town to an unclean place.

46 Anyone who goes into the house while it is closed up will be unclean till evening.

47 Anyone who sleeps in the house must wash his clothes, and anyone who eats in the house must wash his clothes.

Leviticus 14:40 – When a house is infected by leprosy, the infection happens in three stages. First, the house itself is affected. Then, if the people within it don't change, the infection moves into the clothing that's present in the house. If there is still no change, the people finally become infected. We also go through stages when we are infected by disease, and there are always warnings before the infection fully manifests itself.

The method of purifying the house is related to the extent of the contamination. Sometimes, the disease is localized, being found only in one or two rooms, while at other times the whole house is infected and has to be destroyed completely. Conflict within a household might generate a small amount of negativity affecting only one room; on the other hand, someone committing suicide in a house might affect the entire building. There are various ways we can cleanse a house, ranging from using purifying herbs, such as sage, to taking more drastic measures.

לְכֹהֵן מלה לֵאמֹר כְּנֶגַע מלוי אהיה דאלפין ע"ה נִרְאָה ע"ב ורבוע ע"ב לִי בַּבָּיִת ב"פ ראה

36 וְצִוָּה פוי הַכֹּהֵן מלה וּפִנּוּ אֶת־הַבַּיִת ב"פ ראה בְּטֶרֶם רמ"ח ע"ה יָבֹא הַכֹּהֵן מלה

לִרְאוֹת אֶת־הַנֶּגַע מלוי אהיה דאלפין ע"ה וְלֹא יִטְמָא כָּל יִלי ־אֲשֶׁר בַּבָּיִת ב"פ ראה

וְאַחַר כֵּן יָבֹא הַכֹּהֵן מלה לִרְאוֹת אֶת־הַבָּיִת ב"פ ראה: 37 וְרָאָה אֶת־הַנֶּגַע

מלוי אהיה דאלפין ע"ה וְהִנֵּה מ"ה יה הַנֶּגַע מלוי אהיה דאלפין ע"ה בְּקִירֹת הַבַּיִת ב"פ ראה

שְׁקַעֲרוּרֹת יְרַקְרַקֹּת אוֹ אֲדַמְדַּמֹּת וּמַרְאֵיהֶן שָׁפָל מִן־הַקִּיר: 38 וְיָצָא

הַכֹּהֵן מלה מִן־הַבַּיִת ב"פ ראה אֶל־פֶּתַח הַבָּיִת ב"פ ראה וְהִסְגִּיר אֶת־הַבַּיִת

ב"פ ראה שִׁבְעַת יָמִים גלך: 39 וְשָׁב הַכֹּהֵן מלה בַּיּוֹם ע"ה = נגד, זן, מזבח הַשְּׁבִיעִי

וְרָאָה וְהִנֵּה מ"ה יה פָּשָׂה הַנֶּגַע מלוי אהיה דאלפין ע"ה בְּקִירֹת הַבָּיִת ב"פ ראה:

40 וְצִוָּה פוי הַכֹּהֵן מלה וְחִלְּצוּ אֶת־הָאֲבָנִים אֲשֶׁר בָּהֵן הַנֶּגַע

מלוי אהיה דאלפין ע"ה וְהִשְׁלִיכוּ אֶתְהֶן אֶל־מִחוּץ לָעִיר בזוזך, ערי, סנדלפון אֶל־

מָקוֹם יהוה ברבוע, ר"פ אל טָמֵא: 41 וְאֶת־הַבַּיִת ב"פ ראה יַקְצִעַ מִבַּיִת ב"פ ראה סָבִיב

וְשָׁפְכוּ אֶת־הֶעָפָר אֲשֶׁר הִקְצוּ אֶל־מִחוּץ לָעִיר בזוזך, ערי, סנדלפון אֶל־

מָקוֹם יהוה ברבוע, ר"פ אל טָמֵא: 42 וְלָקְחוּ אֲבָנִים אֲחֵרוֹת וְהֵבִיאוּ אֶל־תַּחַת

הָאֲבָנִים וְעָפָר אַחֵר יִקַּח חלם וְטָח אֶת־הַבָּיִת ב"פ ראה: 43 וְאִם יוהך, ע"ה מ"ב־

יָשׁוּב הַנֶּגַע מלוי אהיה דאלפין ע"ה וּפָרַח רפ"ח בַּבַּיִת ב"פ ראה אַחַר וְחִלֵּץ אֶת־

הָאֲבָנִים וְאַחֲרֵי הִקְצוֹת אֶת־הַבָּיִת ב"פ ראה וְאַחֲרֵי הִטּוֹחַ: 44 וּבָא הַכֹּהֵן

מלה וְרָאָה וְהִנֵּה מ"ה יה פָּשָׂה הַנֶּגַע מלוי אהיה דאלפין ע"ה בַּבָּיִת ב"פ ראה צָרַעַת

מַמְאֶרֶת הִוא בַּבַּיִת ב"פ ראה טָמֵא הוּא: 45 וְנָתַץ אֶת־הַבַּיִת ב"פ ראה אֶת־

אֲבָנָיו וְאֶת־עֵצָיו וְאֵת כָּל יִלי ־עֲפַר הַבָּיִת ב"פ ראה וְהוֹצִיא אֶל־מִחוּץ

לָעִיר בזוזך, ערי, סנדלפון אֶל־מָקוֹם יהוה ברבוע, ר"פ אל טָמֵא: 46 וְהַבָּא אֶל־הַבַּיִת

ב"פ ראה כָּל יִלי ־יְמֵי הִסְגִּיר אֹתוֹ יִטְמָא עַד־הָעָרֶב רבוע יהוה ורבוע אלהים:

47 וְהַשֹּׁכֵב בַּבַּיִת ב"פ ראה יְכַבֵּס אֶת־בְּגָדָיו וְהָאֹכֵל בַּבָּיִת ב"פ ראה יְכַבֵּס

אֶת־בְּגָדָיו: 48 וְאִם יוהך, ע"ה מ"ב ־בֹּא יָבֹא הַכֹּהֵן מלה וְרָאָה וְהִנֵּה מ"ה יה לֹא־

48 And if the priest comes to examine it and sees the plague has not spread after the house has been plastered, he shall pronounce the house clean, because the plague is healed.

49 To purify the house, he is to take two birds and some cedar wood, scarlet yarn and hyssop.

50 And he must kill one of the birds over running water in a clay pot.

51 Then he is to take the cedar wood, the hyssop, the scarlet yarn and the live bird, dip them into the blood of the dead bird and the running water, and sprinkle the house seven times.

52 He must purify the house with the bird's blood, the running water, the live bird, the cedar wood, the hyssop and the scarlet yarn.

53 Then he is to release the live bird in the open fields outside the town; in this way, he will make atonement for the house, and it will be clean."

ON A LEAP YEAR: FIFTH READING - AARON - HOD

54 This is the law for all the types of the plague of leprosy, for a scaly eruption, 55 and for leprosy in clothing or in a house, 56 and for a swelling, and for a scab and for a bright spot, 57 to determine when it is unclean and when it is clean. This is the law of leprosy.

15:1 The Lord spoke to Moses and Aaron, saying, 2 "Speak to the Israelites and say to them: When any man has a bodily discharge, the discharge is unclean.

3 Whether it continues flowing from his body or is blocked, it will make him unclean. This is how his discharge will bring about uncleanness:

זָב

Leviticus 15:2 –The term for the kind of cleansing referred to in this passage is *zav*. When there is an irregular discharge from a man and his semen is contaminated, it is an indication that not enough thought is being given to the process of creating life. Every part of our body has been designed as a refined instrument to reveal Light, and as our consciousness becomes more in line with that purpose, our bodies become powerful, sensitive vehicles to manifest the desire of the Creator. But if our consciousness is more in line with the *Desire to Receive for the Self Alone*, then our limbs and organs will lose their precision and can malfunction. This section can help activate the cleansing necessary to awaken the awe of being a channel for life so that the proper functioning of our bodies can be restored.

פָּשָׂה הַנֶּגַע מלוי אהיה דאלפין ע"ה בַּבַּיִת ב"פ ראה אַחֲרֵי הִטּוֹחַ אֶת־הַבַּיִת ב"פ ראה

וְטָהֵר י"פ אכא הַכֹּהֵן מלה אֶת־הַבַּיִת ב"פ ראה כִּי נִרְפָּא הַנָּגַע מלוי אהיה דאלפין ע"ה:

49 וְלָקַח יהוה אהיה יהוה אדני לְחַטֵּא אֶת־הַבַּיִת ב"פ ראה שְׁתֵּי צִפֳּרִים וְעֵץ ע"ה קס"א

אֶרֶז ד"פ בן וּשְׁנִי תוֹלַעַת שקוצי"ת וְאֵזֹב: 50 וְשָׁחַט אֶת־הַצִּפֹּר ש"ע הָאֶחָת

אֶל־כְּלִי כלי חֶרֶשׂ עַל־מַיִם חַיִּים אהיה אהיה יהוה, בינה ע"ה: 51 וְלָקַח יהוה אהיה יהוה אדני

אֶת־עֵץ ע"ה קס"א הָאֶרֶז ד"פ בן וְאֶת־הָאֵזֹב וְאֵת | שְׁנִי

הַתּוֹלַעַת שקוצי"ת וְאֵת הַצִּפֹּר ש"ע הַחַיָּה וְטָבַל אֹתָם בְּדַם רבוע אהיה ע"ה הַצִּפֹּר

ש"ע הַשְּׁחוּטָה וּבַמַּיִם הַחַיִּים אהיה אהיה יהוה, בינה ע"ה וְהִזָּה והו אֶל־הַבַּיִת ב"פ ראה

שֶׁבַע ע"ב ואלהים דיודין פְּעָמִים: 52 וְחִטֵּא אֶת־הַבַּיִת ב"פ ראה בְּדַם רבוע אהיה

הַצִּפּוֹר וּבַמַּיִם הַחַיִּים אהיה אהיה יהוה, בינה ע"ה וּבַצִּפֹּר הַחַיָּה וּבְעֵץ ע"ה קס"א

הָאֶרֶז ד"פ בן וּבָאֵזֹב וּבִשְׁנִי הַתּוֹלָעַת שקוצי"ת: 53 וְשִׁלַּח אֶת־הַצִּפֹּר ש"ע

הַחַיָּה אֶל־מִחוּץ לָעִיר מזוזך, ערי, סנדלפון אֶל־פְּנֵי וחכמה בינה הַשָּׂדֶה שדי וְכִפֶּר

מצפצ עַל־הַבַּיִת ב"פ ראה וְטָהֵר י"פ אכא:

ON A LEAP YEAR: FIFTH READING - AARON - HOD

54 זֹאת הַתּוֹרָה לְכָל יה אדני ־נֶגַע מלוי אהיה דאלפין ע"ה הַצָּרַעַת וְלַנָּתֶק:

55 וּלְצָרַעַת הַבֶּגֶד וְלַבָּיִת ב"פ ראה: 56 וְלַשְׂאֵת אל ואדני מלא וְלַסַּפַּחַת וְלַבֶּהָרֶת

מלוי אדני ע"ה: 57 לְהוֹרֹת בְּיוֹם ע"ה = נגד, זן, מזבח הַטָּמֵא וּבְיוֹם הַטָּהֹר י"פ אכא זֹאת

תּוֹרַת הַצָּרָעַת: 15 1 וַיְדַבֵּר ראה יהוה אהיה אדני יאהדונהי אֶל־מֹשֶׁה מהש, אל שדי וְאֶל־

אַהֲרֹן ע"ב ורבוע ע"ב לֵאמֹר: 2 דַּבְּרוּ ראה אֶל־בְּנֵי יִשְׂרָאֵל וַאֲמַרְתֶּם אֲלֵהֶם

אִישׁ ע"ה קנ"א קס"א אִישׁ ע"ה קנ"א קס"א כִּי יִהְיֶה ... זב מִבְּשָׂרוֹ זוֹבוֹ טָמֵא הוּא:

3 וְזֹאת תִּהְיֶה טֻמְאָתוֹ בְּזוֹבוֹ רָר בְּשָׂרוֹ אֶת־זוֹבוֹ אוֹ־הֶחְתִּים בְּשָׂרוֹ

מִזּוֹבוֹ טֻמְאָתוֹ הוּא: 4 כָּל ילי ־הַמִּשְׁכָּב אֲשֶׁר יִשְׁכַּב עָלָיו הַזָּב יִטְמָא

4 Any bed the man with a discharge lies on will be unclean, and anything he sits on will be unclean. 5 Anyone who touches his bed must wash his clothes and bathe with water, and he will be unclean till the evening.

6 Whoever sits on anything that the man with a discharge sat on must wash his clothes and bathe with water, and he will be unclean till the evening.

7 Whoever touches the man who has a discharge must wash his clothes and bathe with water, and he will be unclean till the evening.

8 If the man with the discharge spits on someone who is clean, that person must wash his clothes and bathe with water, and he will be unclean till the evening.

9 Everything the man sits on when riding will be unclean, 10 and whoever touches any of the things that were under him will be unclean till evening; whoever picks up those things must wash his clothes and bathe with water, and he will be unclean till the evening.

11 Anyone the man with a discharge touches without rinsing his hands with water must wash his clothes and bathe with water, and he will be unclean till evening.

12 A clay pot that the man touches must be broken, and any wooden article is to be rinsed in water. 13 When a man is cleansed from his discharge, he is to count off seven days for his cleansing; and he must wash his clothes and bathe himself with running water, and he will be clean.

14 On the eighth day, he must take two doves or two young pigeons and come before the Lord to the entrance to the Tent of Meeting and give them to the priest.

15 The priest is to sacrifice them, the one for a sin offering and the other for a burnt offering, and the priest will make atonement before the Lord for the man because of his discharge.

ON A LEAP YEAR: SIXTH READING - JOSEPH – YESOD
WHEN CONNECTED: SEVENTH READING - DAVID - MALCHUT

16 When a man has an emission of semen, he must bathe his whole body with water, and he will be unclean till evening.

17 Any clothing or leather that has semen on it must be washed with water, and it will be unclean till evening.

וְכָל ילי ־הַכְּלִי כלי אֲשֶׁר־יֵשֵׁב עָלָיו יִטְמָא: 5 וְאִישׁ עה קנ״א קס״א אֲשֶׁר יִגַּע

בְּמִשְׁכָּבוֹ יְכַבֵּס בְּגָדָיו וְרָחַץ בַּמַּיִם וְטָמֵא עַד־הָעָרֶב רבוע יהוה ורבוע אלהים:

6 וְהַיֹּשֵׁב עַל־הַכְּלִי כלי אֲשֶׁר־יֵשֵׁב עָלָיו הַזָּב יְכַבֵּס בְּגָדָיו וְרָחַץ בַּמַּיִם

וְטָמֵא עַד־הָעָרֶב רבוע יהוה ורבוע אלהים: 7 וְהַנֹּגֵעַ בִּבְשַׂר הַזָּב יְכַבֵּס בְּגָדָיו

וְרָחַץ בַּמַּיִם וְטָמֵא עַד־הָעָרֶב רבוע יהוה ורבוע אלהים: 8 וְכִי־יָרֹק הַזָּב בַּטָּהוֹר

י"פ אכא וְכִבֶּס בְּגָדָיו וְרָחַץ בַּמַּיִם וְטָמֵא עַד־הָעָרֶב רבוע יהוה ורבוע אלהים:

9 וְכָל ילי ־הַמֶּרְכָּב אֲשֶׁר יִרְכַּב עָלָיו הַזָּב יִטְמָא: 10 וְכָל ילי ־הַנֹּגֵעַ

בְּכֹל בן, לכב, יבם אֲשֶׁר יִהְיֶה תַּחְתָּיו יִטְמָא עַד־הָעָרֶב מלוי אהיה דאלפין עה

רבוע יהוה ורבוע אלהים וְהַנּוֹשֵׂא אוֹתָם יְכַבֵּס בְּגָדָיו וְרָחַץ בַּמַּיִם וְטָמֵא עַד־

הָעָרֶב רבוע יהוה ורבוע אלהים: 11 וְכֹל ילי אֲשֶׁר יִגַּע־בּוֹ הַזָּב וְיָדָיו לֹא־שָׁטַף

בַּמָּיִם וְכִבֶּס בְּגָדָיו וְרָחַץ בַּמַּיִם וְטָמֵא עַד־הָעָרֶב רבוע יהוה ורבוע אלהים:

12 וּכְלִי כלי ־חֶרֶשׂ אֲשֶׁר־יִגַּע־בּוֹ הַזָּב יִשָּׁבֵר וְכָל ילי ־כְּלִי כלי ־עֵץ עה קס״א

יִשָּׁטֵף בַּמָּיִם: 13 וְכִי־יִטְהַר י"פ אכא הַזָּב מִזּוֹבוֹ וְסָפַר לוֹ שִׁבְעַת יָמִים נלך

לְטָהֳרָתוֹ וְכִבֶּס בְּגָדָיו וְרָחַץ בְּשָׂרוֹ בְּמַיִם חַיִּים אהיה אהיה יהוה, בינה עה

וְטָהֵר י"פ אכא: 14 וּבַיּוֹם עה = נגד, זן, מזבח הַשְּׁמִינִי יִקַּח וזמ ־לוֹ שְׁתֵּי תֹרִים אוֹ

שְׁנֵי בְּנֵי יוֹנָה כ״י מ״ה וּבָא | לִפְנֵי חכמה בינה יְהֹוָה אדני אלהים לפני אלהים אל־פֶּתַח אֹהֶל לאה

מוֹעֵד וּנְתָנָם אֶל־הַכֹּהֵן מלה: 15 וְעָשָׂה אֹתָם הַכֹּהֵן מלה אֶחָד מלה אהבה, דאגה

חַטָּאת וְהָאֶחָד עֹלָה וְכִפֶּר מצפצ עָלָיו הַכֹּהֵן מלה לִפְנֵי חכמה בינה יְהֹוָה אדני אלהים

מִזּוֹבוֹ:

ON A LEAP YEAR: SIXTH READING - JOSEPH – YESOD
WHEN CONNECTED: SEVENTH READING - DAVID - MALCHUT

16 וְאִישׁ עה קנ״א קס״א כִּי־תֵצֵא מִמֶּנּוּ שִׁכְבַת־זָרַע וְרָחַץ בַּמַּיִם אֶת־כָּל ילי ־

בְּשָׂרוֹ וְטָמֵא עַד־הָעָרֶב רבוע יהוה ורבוע אלהים: 17 וְכָל ילי ־בֶּגֶד וְכָל ילי ־עוֹר

18 When a man lies with a woman and there is an emission of semen, both must bathe with water, and they will be unclean till the evening.

19 When a woman has her regular flow of blood, the impurity of her monthly period will last seven days, and anyone who touches her will be unclean till the evening.

20 Anything she lies on during her period will be unclean, and anything she sits on will be unclean.

21 Whoever touches her bed must wash his clothes and bathe with water, and he will be unclean till the evening.

22 Whoever touches anything she sits on must wash his clothes and bathe with water, and he will be unclean till the evening.

23 Whether it is the bed or anything she was sitting on, when anyone touches it, he will be unclean till the evening.

24 If a man lies with her and her monthly flow touches him, he will be unclean for seven days; any bed he lies on will be unclean.

25 When a woman has a discharge of blood for many days at a time other than her monthly period or has a discharge that continues beyond her period, she will be unclean as long as she has the discharge, just as in the days of her period.

26 Any bed she lies on while her discharge continues will be unclean, as is her bed during her monthly period, and anything she sits on will be unclean, as during her period.

27 Whoever touches them will be unclean; he must wash his clothes and bathe with water, and he will be unclean till the evening.

28 When she is cleansed from her discharge, she must count off seven days, and after that she will be clean.

וְזֹבָה

Leviticus 15:19 – There could also be a irregular discharge that comes from a woman, which also calls attention to the importance that is placed on the process of creating life. A woman is designed to be a Vessel that manifests life, and when the Vessel is not used for the purpose of receiving Light, then it can lose that potential. This reading helps to restore the intention and capacity of the Vessel.

אֲשֶׁר־יִהְיֶה ייי עָלָיו שִׁכְבַת־זָרַע וְכִבֶּס בַּמַּיִם וְטָמֵא עַד־הָעָרֶב

רבוע יהוה ורבוע אלהים: 18 וְאִשָּׁה אֲשֶׁר יִשְׁכַּב אִישׁ ע"ה קנ"א קס"א אֹתָהּ שִׁכְבַת־

זָרַע וְרָחֲצוּ בַמַּיִם וְטָמְאוּ עַד־הָעָרֶב רבוע יהוה ורבוע אלהים: 19 וְאִשָּׁה כִּי־

תִהְיֶה זָבָה דָם רבוע אהיה יֶהְיֶה ייי זֹבָהּ בִּבְשָׂרָהּ שִׁבְעַת יָמִים גלך תִּהְיֶה

בְנִדָּתָהּ וְכָל־ יל"י הַנֹּגֵעַ בָּהּ יִטְמָא עַד־הָעָרֶב רבוע יהוה ורבוע אלהים: 20 וְכֹל יל"י

אֲשֶׁר תִּשְׁכַּב עָלָיו בְּנִדָּתָהּ יִטְמָא וְכֹל יל"י אֲשֶׁר־תֵּשֵׁב עָלָיו יִטְמָא:

21 וְכָל־ יל"י הַנֹּגֵעַ בְּמִשְׁכָּבָהּ יְכַבֵּס בְּגָדָיו וְרָחַץ בַּמַּיִם וְטָמֵא עַד־

הָעָרֶב רבוע יהוה ורבוע אלהים: 22 וְכָל־ יל"י הַנֹּגֵעַ בְּכָל־ בן, לכב, יבמ כְּלִי כלי אֲשֶׁר־

תֵּשֵׁב עָלָיו יְכַבֵּס בְּגָדָיו וְרָחַץ בַּמַּיִם וְטָמֵא עַד־הָעָרֶב

רבוע יהוה ורבוע אלהים: 23 וְאִם ע"ה מ"ב יוהך, עַל־הַמִּשְׁכָּב הוּא אוֹ עַל־הַכְּלִי כלי

אֲשֶׁר־הִוא יֹשֶׁבֶת־עָלָיו בְּנָגְעוֹ־בוֹ יִטְמָא עַד־הָעָרֶב רבוע יהוה ורבוע אלהים:

24 וְאִם ע"ה מ"ב יוהך, שָׁכֹב יִשְׁכַּב אִישׁ ע"ה קנ"א קס"א אֹתָהּ וּתְהִי נִדָּתָהּ עָלָיו

וְטָמֵא שִׁבְעַת יָמִים גלך וְכָל־ יל"י הַמִּשְׁכָּב אֲשֶׁר־יִשְׁכַּב עָלָיו יִטְמָא:

25 וְאִשָּׁה כִּי־יָזוּב זוֹב דָּמָהּ יָמִים גלך רַבִּים בְּלֹא עֶת־ ד"פ אהיה י הויות נִדָּתָהּ

אוֹ כִי־תָזוּב עַל־נִדָּתָהּ כָּל־ יל"י יְמֵי זוֹב טֻמְאָתָהּ כִּימֵי נִדָּתָהּ תִּהְיֶה

טְמֵאָה הוּא: 26 כָּל־ יל"י הַמִּשְׁכָּב אֲשֶׁר־תִּשְׁכַּב עָלָיו כָּל־ יל"י יְמֵי זוֹבָהּ

כְּמִשְׁכַּב נִדָּתָהּ יִהְיֶה ייי לָּהּ וְכָל־ יל"י הַכְּלִי כלי אֲשֶׁר תֵּשֵׁב עָלָיו טָמֵא

יִהְיֶה ייי כְּטֻמְאַת נִדָּתָהּ: 27 וְכָל־ יל"י הַנּוֹגֵעַ בָּם מ"ב יִטְמָא וְכִבֶּס בְּגָדָיו

וְרָחַץ בַּמַּיִם וְטָמֵא עַד־הָעָרֶב רבוע יהוה ורבוע אלהים: 28 וְאִם ע"ה מ"ב יוהך,

טָהֲרָה מִזּוֹבָהּ וְסָפְרָה לָּהּ שִׁבְעַת יָמִים גלך וְאַחַר תִּטְהָר:

ON A LEAP YEAR: SEVENTH READING - DAVID - MALCHUT

29 On the eighth day, she must take two doves or two young pigeons and bring them to the priest at the entrance to the Tent of Meeting.

30 The priest is to sacrifice one for a sin offering and the other for a burnt offering, and the priest will make atonement for her before the Lord for the uncleanness of her discharge.

MAFTIR

31 You must keep the Israelites separate from things that make them unclean, so they will not die in their uncleanness for defiling my dwelling place, which is among them.

32 This the law for a man with a discharge, for anyone made unclean by an emission of semen, 33 for a woman in her monthly period, for a man or a woman with a discharge, and for a man who lies with a woman who is unclean.

HAFTARAH OF METZORA

God told Elisha the Prophet that there would be an abundance of food after a period of hunger. This was a miracle created for the lepers, and it shows that although people need to go through a process of purification or correction, it doesn't mean they are not connected to the Light. Miracles can still

Kings 2 7:3-20

7:3 And there were four men with leprosy at the entrance of the city gate. They said to each other, "Why stay here until we die?

4 If we say, 'We'll go into the city' then the famine is in the city and we will die; and if we sit here, we will die. So let's go over to the camp of the Arameans and surrender. If they spare us, we live; and if they kill us, then we die."

ON A LEAP YEAR: SEVENTH READING - DAVID - MALCHUT

29 וּבַיּוֹם הַשְּׁמִינִ֗י תִּקַּ֣ח רבוע אהיה דאלפין ־לָ֤הּ שְׁתֵּ֣י תֹרִ֔ים א֖וֹ עֲנֵ֣י בְנֵ֣י יוֹנָ֑ה
כ"ו מ"ה וְהֵבִ֨יאָה אוֹתָם֙ אֶל־הַכֹּהֵ֔ן מלה אֶל־פֶּ֖תַח אֹ֣הֶל לאה מוֹעֵֽד: 30 וְעָשָׂ֣ה
הַכֹּהֵ֗ן מלה אֶת־הָאֶחָ֤ד אהבה, דאגה חַטָּאת֙ וְאֶת־הָֽאֶחָ֣ד אהבה, דאגה עֹלָ֔ה וְכִפֶּ֧ר
מצפצ עָלֶ֛יהָ פהל הַכֹּהֵ֖ן מלה לִפְנֵ֣י וחכמה בינה יְה֑וָֹאדֹנָ֗יאהדונהי מִזּ֖וֹב טֻמְאָתָֽהּ:

MAFTIR

31 וְהִזַּרְתֶּ֥ם אֶת־בְּנֵֽי־יִשְׂרָאֵ֖ל מִטֻּמְאָתָ֑ם וְלֹ֤א יָמֻ֙תוּ֙ בְּטֻמְאָתָ֔ם
בְּטַמְּאָ֥ם אֶת־מִשְׁכָּנִ֖י אֲשֶׁ֥ר בְּתוֹכָֽם: 32 זֹ֥את תּוֹרַ֖ת הַזָּ֑ב וַאֲשֶׁ֤ר תֵּצֵ֤א
מִמֶּ֙נּוּ֙ שִׁכְבַת־זֶ֔רַע לְטָמְאָה־בָֽהּ: 33 וְהַדָּוָה֙ בְּנִדָּתָ֔הּ וְהַזָּב֙ אֶת־זוֹב֔וֹ
לַזָּכָ֖ר וְלַנְּקֵבָ֑ה וּלְאִ֕ישׁ אֲשֶׁ֥ר יִשְׁכַּ֖ב עִם־טְמֵאָֽה:

HAFTARAH OF METZORA

happen for them and because of them. In fact, sometimes it's the depth of the struggles we go through that makes miracles occur.

מלכים ב פרק ז

7 3 וְאַרְבָּעָ֣ה אֲנָשִׁ֗ים הָי֛וּ מְצֹרָעִ֖ים פֶּ֣תַח הַשָּׁ֑עַר וַיֹּֽאמְרוּ֙ אִ֣ישׁ
ע"ה קנ"א קס"א אֶל־רֵעֵ֔הוּ מ"ה מ"ה אֲנַ֗חְנוּ מילה יֹשְׁבִ֥ים פֹּ֛ה ע"ה אלהים, ע"ה מום עַד־
מָֽתְנוּ: 4 אִם־ יוהך, ע"ה מ"ב ־אָמַ֩רְנוּ֩ סזלפין, ערי, סנדלפון נָב֨וֹא הָעִ֜יר וְהָרָעָ֤ב
ע"ב ורבוע אלהים בָּעִיר֙ סזלפין, ערי, סנדלפון וָמַ֣תְנוּ שָׁ֔ם יהוה עדי וְאִם־ יוהך, ע"ה מ"ב ־יָשַׁ֙בְנוּ֙

5 At dusk they got up and went to the camp of the Arameans, and when they reached the edge of the Aramean camp, not a man was there,

6 for the Lord had caused the army of the Arameans to hear the sound of chariots and horses and a great army, so that they said to one another, "Look, the king of Israel has hired the kings of the Hittites and the kings of the Egyptian to attack us!"

7 So they got up and fled in the dusk and abandoned their tents and their horses and donkeys and left the camp as it was and ran for their lives.

8 And when these men who had leprosy reached the edge of the camp and entered one of the tents, they ate and drank, and carried away silver and gold and clothes, and went and hid them. And they returned and entered another tent and took some things from it and hid them also.

9 Then they said to one another, "We're not doing right. This day is a day of good news and we hold our peace. If we wait until daylight, some mischief will come upon us. Let's go at once and report this to the king's household."

10 So they went and called out to the gatekeepers of the city and told them, saying, "We went to the camp of the Arameans and behold, not a man was there; not a sound of anyone, but tethered horses and tethered donkeys, and the tents left just as they were."

11 And he called the gatekeepers and they told it to the king's house within.

12 And the king rose in the night and said to his servants, "I will now show you what the Arameans have done to us. They know we are hungry; so they have left the camp to hide themselves in the fields, saying, 'When they come out of the city, we shall catch them alive and get into the city.' "

13 And one of his servants answered and said, "Have some men, I pray you, take five of the horses that are left in the city, and behold, they are as the multitude of Israel that are left in it, behold, I say, they are even as all the multitude of the Israelites who are consumed and let us send and see."

14 They took, therefore, two chariots with their horses, and the king sent them after the Aramean army saying, "Go and see."

15 And they followed them as far as the Jordan, and all the way was strewn with clothing and vessels which the Arameans had thrown away in their haste. And the messengers returned and told the king.

פֹּה מילה, ע״ה אלהים, ע״ה מום **וּמַתְנוּ וְעַתָּה לְכוּ וְנִפְּלָה אֶל־מַחֲנֵה אֲרָם אִם**

יוחרך, ע״ה מ״ב **יְחַיֻּנוּ נִחְיֶה וְאִם** יוחרך, ע״ה מ״ב **יְמִיתֻנוּ וָמָתְנוּ: 5 וַיָּקֻמוּ בַנֶּשֶׁף**

לָבוֹא אֶל־מַחֲנֵה אֲרָם וַיָּבֹאוּ עַד־קְצֵה הי״פ טל, ג׳יפ אדני **מַחֲנֵה אֲרָם וְהִנֵּה**

מ״ה יה **אֵין־שָׁם** יהוה שדי **אִישׁ** ע״ה קנ״א קס״א **6 וַאדֹנָי** ללה **הִשְׁמִיעַ | אֶת־מַחֲנֵה**

אֲרָם קוֹל ע״ב ס״ג ע״ה **רֶכֶב קוֹל** ע״ב ס״ג ע״ה **סוּס** ע״ה ס״ג ע״ה **קוֹל** ע״ב ס״ג ע״ה ומב **חַיִל** ומ״ב

גָּדוֹל ללהו, מבה, יזל, אום **וַיֹּאמְרוּ אִישׁ** ע״ה קנ״א קס״א **אֶל־אָחִיו הִנֵּה** מ״ה יה **שָׂכַר** י״פ בן

עָלֵינוּ ריבוע ס״ג **מֶלֶךְ יִשְׂרָאֵל אֶת־מַלְכֵי הַחִתִּים וְאֶת־מַלְכֵי מִצְרַיִם** מצר

לָבוֹא עָלֵינוּ ריבוע ס״ג **7 וַיָּקוּמוּ וַיָּנוּסוּ בַנֶּשֶׁף וַיַּעַזְבוּ אֶת־אָהֳלֵיהֶם וְאֶת־**

סוּסֵיהֶם וְאֶת־חֲמֹרֵיהֶם הַמַּחֲנֶה כַּאֲשֶׁר־הִיא וַיָּנֻסוּ אֶל־נַפְשָׁם: 8 וַיָּבֹאוּ

הַמְצֹרָעִים הָאֵלֶּה עַד־קְצֵה הי״פ טל, ג׳יפ אדני **הַמַּחֲנֶה וַיָּבֹאוּ אֶל־אֹהֶל** לאה

אֶחָד אהבה, דאגה **וַיֹּאכְלוּ וַיִּשְׁתּוּ וַיִּשְׂאוּ מִשָּׁם** יהוה שדי **כֶּסֶף וְזָהָב וּבְגָדִים**

וַיֵּלְכוּ כלי **וַיַּטְמִנוּ וַיָּשֻׁבוּ וַיָּבֹאוּ אֶל־אֹהֶל** לאה **אַחֵר וַיִּשְׂאוּ מִשָּׁם** יהוה שדי

וַיֵּלְכוּ כלי **וַיַּטְמִנוּ: 9 וַיֹּאמְרוּ אִישׁ** ע״ה קנ״א קס״א **אֶל־רֵעֵהוּ לֹא־כֵן | אֲנַחְנוּ**

עֹשִׂים הַיּוֹם ע״ה = נגד, זן, מזבח **הַזֶּה** ע״ה **יוֹם** הו = נגד, זן, מזבח **בְּשֹׂרָה הוּא וְאֲנַחְנוּ**

מַחְשִׁים וְחִכִּינוּ עַד־אוֹר רז, אין סוף **הַבֹּקֶר וּמְצָאָנוּ עָווֹן וְעַתָּה לְכוּ וְנָבֹאָה**

וְנַגִּידָה בֵּית ב״פ ראה **הַמֶּלֶךְ: 10 וַיָּבֹאוּ וַיִּקְרְאוּ אֶל־שֹׁעֵר הָעִיר**

סנדלפון, ערי, סנדלפון **וַיַּגִּידוּ לָהֶם לֵאמֹר בָּאנוּ אֶל־מַחֲנֵה אֲרָם וְהִנֵּה** מ״ה יה

אֵין־שָׁם יהוה שדי **אִישׁ** ע״ה קנ״א קס״א **וְקוֹל** ע״ב ס״ג ע״ה **אָדָם** מ״ה **כִּי אִם־** ע״ה מ״ב

הַסּוּס ריבוע אדני, כוק **אָסוּר וְהַחֲמוֹר אָסוּר וְאֹהָלִים כַּאֲשֶׁר־הֵמָּה:**

11 וַיִּקְרָא ב״פ קס״א + ה׳ אותיות **הַשֹּׁעֲרִים** כתר **וַיַּגִּידוּ** יי **בֵּית** ב״פ ראה **הַמֶּלֶךְ פְּנִימָה:**

12 וַיָּקָם הַמֶּלֶךְ לַיְלָה מלה **וַיֹּאמֶר אֶל־עֲבָדָיו אַגִּידָה־נָּא לָכֶם אֵת**

אֲשֶׁר־עָשׂוּ לָנוּ מום, אלהים, אהיה אדני **אֲרָם** אדני **יָדְעוּ כִּי־רְעֵבִים אֲנַחְנוּ וַיֵּצְאוּ**

מִן־הַמַּחֲנֶה לְהֵחָבֵה בַשָּׂדֶה (כתיב: בהשדה) **לֵאמֹר כִּי־יֵצְאוּ מִן־הָעִיר**

סנדלפון, ערי, סנדלפון **וְנִתְפְּשֵׂם חַיִּים וְאֶל־הָעִיר** בינה ע״ה **נָבֹא: 13 וַיַּעַן**

16 And the people went out and plundered the camp of the Arameans. So a measure of flour was sold for a shekel, and two measure of barley sold for a shekel, according to the word of the Lord.

17 And the king appointed the captain on whose arm he leaned to have charge of the gate, and the people trampled on him in the gate; and he died, as the man of God had said when the king came down to him.

18 And it came to pass as the man of God had spoken to the king, saying: "Two measure of barley for a shekel, and one measure of flour for a shekel shall be tomorrow this time at the gate of Samaria."

19 And that captain answered the man of God, and said "Now look, if the Lord should make windows in heaven, might such a thing be?" and he said, "Look, you shall see it with your own eyes, but you will not eat any of it;"

20 it came to pass even so unto him, for the people trampled him in the gate, and he died.

אֹחֵז אהבה, דאגה מֵעֲבָדָיו וַיֹּאמֶר וְיִקְחוּ חיעם נָא וַחֲמִשָּׁה מִן־הַסּוּסִים הַנִּשְׁאָרִים אֲשֶׁר נִשְׁאֲרוּ־בָהּ הִנָּם כְּכָל־הֲמוֹן (כתיב: ההמון) יִשְׂרָאֵל אֲשֶׁר נִשְׁאֲרוּ־בָהּ הִנָּם כְּכָל־הֲמוֹן יִשְׂרָאֵל אֲשֶׁר־תָּמּוּ וְנִשְׁלְחָה וְנִרְאֶה: 14 וַיִּקְחוּ חיעם שְׁנֵי רֶכֶב סוּסִים וַיִּשְׁלַח הַמֶּלֶךְ אַחֲרֵי מַחֲנֵה־אֲרָם לֵאמֹר לְכוּ וּרְאוּ: 15 וַיֵּלְכוּ כלי אַחֲרֵיהֶם עַד־הַיַּרְדֵּן י"פ יהוה וד' אותיות וְהִנֵּה מ"ה יה כָל־הַדֶּרֶךְ בע"פ יב"ק מְלֵאָה בְגָדִים וְכֵלִים אֲשֶׁר־הִשְׁלִיכוּ אֲרָם בְּהֵחָפְזָם (כתיב: בהחופזם) וַיָּשֻׁבוּ הַמַּלְאָכִים וַיַּגִּדוּ לַמֶּלֶךְ: 16 וַיֵּצֵא הָעָם וַיָּבֹזּוּ אֵת מַחֲנֵה אֲרָם וַיְהִי אל סְאָה־סֹלֶת בְּשֶׁקֶל וְסָאתַיִם שְׂעֹרִים כתר בְּשֶׁקֶל כִּדְבַר ראה יְהֹוָ[ה]אדני: 17 וְהַמֶּלֶךְ הִפְקִיד אֶת־הַשָּׁלִישׁ אֲשֶׁר־נִשְׁעָן עַל־יָדוֹ עַל־הַשַּׁעַר וַיִּרְמְסֻהוּ הָעָם בַּשַּׁעַר וַיָּמֹת כַּאֲשֶׁר דִּבֶּר ראה אִישׁ ע"ה קנ"א קס"א הָאֱלֹהִים מום, אהיה אדני; ילה אֲשֶׁר דִּבֶּר ראה בְּרֶדֶת הַמֶּלֶךְ אֵלָיו: 18 וַיְהִי אל כְּדַבֵּר ראה אִישׁ ע"ה קנ"א קס"א הָאֱלֹהִים מום, אהיה אדני; ילה אֶל־הַמֶּלֶךְ לֵאמֹר סָאתַיִם שְׂעֹרִים בְּשֶׁקֶל וְסְאָה־סֹלֶת בְּשֶׁקֶל יִהְיֶה יי כָּעֵת מָחָר רמ"ח בְּשַׁעַר שֹׁמְרוֹן: 19 וַיַּעַן הַשָּׁלִישׁ אֶת־אִישׁ ע"ה קנ"א קס"א הָאֱלֹהִים מום, אהיה אדני; ילה וַיֹּאמַר וְהִנֵּה מ"ה יה יְהֹוָ[ה]אדני עֹשֶׂה אֲרֻבּוֹת בַּשָּׁמַיִם י"פ טל, י"פ כוזו הֲיִהְיֶה יי כַּדָּבָר ראה הַזֶּה הו וַיֹּאמֶר הִנְּךָ רֹאֶה ראה בְּעֵינֶיךָ ע"ה קס"א וּמִשָּׁם לֹא תֹאכֵל: 20 וַיְהִי אל לוֹ כֵן וַיִּרְמְסוּ אֹתוֹ הָעָם בַּשַּׁעַר וַיָּמֹת:

ACHAREI MOT

LESSON OF ACHAREI MOT
(Leviticus 16:1-18:30)

Regarding *Yom Kippur*

On *Yom Kippur*, we read the opening verses in the Chapter of Acharei Mot, which relate the events that took place after the death of Aaron's sons. Thus, during the reading of Acharei Mot on Shabbat, we have the opportunity to receive the power of *Yom Kippur*, and through this power, to cleanse every form of negativity within us. But as with everything, there are terms and conditions in spirituality: If we don't go halfway to connect with the light, the Light will not come halfway to meet us. It is written: "God is your shadow." (*Psalms 121:5*) The Light is our shadow, and as we go, so our shadow goes, too.

It's as if we were looking into a mirror. When we move towards or away from the glass, the reflection becomes larger or smaller—seemingly closer or farther away. If we move even slightly closer to the Creator, the Creator comes towards us the rest of the way—but we must always take the first step. During the High Holidays, we pray to the Creator: "You give Your Hand to those who are open for repentance." (*Vechol Ma'aminim*) God's Hand is always reaching for us, but to grasp it, we must extend our own hands toward God.

Achieving this connection with God is a combination of desire and action. If someone steals and then says that he desires oneness with the Creator, it's as if he entered the *mikveh* (immersion bath that cleanses us spiritually) holding something filthy in his hand. Before we can achieve a connection with the Creator, we must first remove the negative energy of ego from our being through positive thoughts, feelings, and actions.

The *Desire to Receive for the Self Alone* is in each of us, and recognizing this fact is where our work of inner transformation must begin. Rav Ashlag wrote that we need to confront whatever we find most difficult for us. That place of difficulty is where our *tikkun* (our unique spiritual correction), is and where we can start our transformation.

The garments of the *Kohen HaGadol*, the High Priest

Acherei Mot says that when the *Kohen HaGadol* presided over a service in the Tabernacle, he changed his clothes four times. There's a parable that explains why this was necessary.

There was once a poor beggar who dressed in rags because he had no money to buy clothes. A kind tailor decided to help him. The tailor took his measurements and told the beggar to come back in a couple of hours. When the beggar returned and tried on the clothes, he immediately began yelling angrily at the tailor, "Look what you've done! You just wanted to make fun of me! These clothes don't even fit!"

Patiently, the tailor told him to calm down. "The new clothes will certainly fit you, but first you have to take off your old ones!" For that same reason, the *Kohen HaGadol* had to repeatedly change his physical garments as he was preparing himself for his work in the Temple. From this, we learn that we, too, need to remove our old garments—our *Desire to Receive for the Self Alone*—otherwise, there is no chance for the Light of the Creator to enter us.

There is a new secret

At The Kabbalah Centre, we always call attention to the presence of a special letter at the beginning of a column in the Torah Scroll. Generally, there is a letter *Vav* at the head of the column, taken from the phrase "*vavei ha'amudim*" (which literally means "hooks on the pillars"). But there are six places in the Torah where a special letter and word are needed at the beginning of a column. In the Book of Genesis, for example, the Aramaic letter *Bet* in the word "*Beresheet*" needs to be at the head of the column; likewise, *Yud* for "*Yehuda*" in the Chapter of Vayechi, *Hei* for "*haba'im*" in the Chapter of Beshalach; *Shin* in "*shnei ha'seerim*" in this particular chapter; *Mem* for "*ma tovu ohalecha*" in the Chapter of Balak; and *Vav* for "*ve'aida bam*" in the Chapter of Ha'azinu. These six words/phrases and initial letters make up a special sequence, whose power is equivalent to *Mem, Hei, Shin*, the 72 Name of God for healing.

And the numerical value of this sequence is also equal to *Vav, Hei, Vav* another one of the 72 Names of God. Through these two sequences, we gain the power of healing, but not just healing in the conventional sense. This is healing from the seed level, as *Vav, Hei, Vav* comes from the phrase "*vayechulu ha'shamaim ve'ha'aretz*" (*Genesis 2:1*), meaning: "Thus the Heaven and the Earth were completed." As Rav Berg has said, "Illness doesn't begin when the doctor reveals it." A sickness may have been present for many years on the physical level—and for even longer in the spiritual dimension of our being.

Dreams for healing are of special importance. It's interesting that the prayer for dreams includes the phrase "to heal dreams," as if a dream were an illness. But how can a dream be healed? A physical illness takes place in the here-and-now. It's very tangible—we have a fever, we go to a doctor. But dreams operate in the spiritual realm. So what's the connection between healing and dreams?

In Kabbalah, nothing is considered to be in the future. Everything is here right now. At *Pesach*, for example, we recreate the first *Pesach Seder* (Passover meal) from more than 3000 years ago. Similarly, our dreams are on a higher level (in the Upper World), and are not in the future; they are part of the present.

Therefore, if we have a dream that seems negative or destructive, we might ask how we can change it, considering that it's already here in the present. The truth is, however, that we can't change the outcome of the dream and transform the judgment in it to mercy if we remain forever on the same spiritual level. It is necessary to elevate to another level. It's not a matter of just reversing or fast-forwarding "the movie" we're in; rather, we must enter an entirely new movie of our life.

Awareness of the fact that we need to change ourselves at this fundamental level is the first, all-important step toward actually making the change. With regard to illness, for example, we can certainly try to cure cancer or heart disease once they are established, but a better course is changing our movie to one where there is no cancer or heart disease or AIDS or any kind of sickness whatsoever in the first place.

Of course, we need a tool to help us change this movie, and this tool exists in the form of a unique formula:

Vav, Hei, Vav + *Mem, Hei, Shin* = healing from the seed level

We also have an opportunity to change our movie, when we meditate on the *Tikkun HaNefesh* (Correction of the Soul) sequence from the *Ana Beko'ach*. If something destructive is destined to happen to us, we can change that destiny. However, the bottom line is, if we don't take full responsibility for all our actions, we will never be able to change our destiny—no matter how many spiritual tools we use.

If we want to change something, it's vital to understand that doing so is up to us. If we don't understand this, nothing will change.

"Love your neighbor as yourself."

In the Story of Miketz (*Genesis 42:3*), Joseph's brothers went together to Egypt. The question arises, why did Jacob send all ten of his sons (except for the youngest, Benjamin), considering how dangerous the trip was?

The Ramban (Rav Moshe Ben Nachman, 1195–1270), in a discourse on the story of Miketz, explains that Jacob sent all ten sons because of the unity that they represented. He did not want his sons separated from each other, even for one hour. He wanted them to be "one in their love." From this, we learn the crucial importance of unity among ourselves, which enables us to face even the worst of perils together.

Today, few nations exist amid more danger than the nation of Israel, and many people in Israel assert their belief that Israel is a unified country. Loving the nation of Israel is a very important *mitzvah* (precept). But truthfully, while most of these people may love Israel in general, they don't love each and every person in the nation of Israel. The precept of loving Israel and the unity of Israel does not mean that we must love "the nation of Israel." The precept is to love "the people of Israel" and to feel love for every person as if he or she were our own relative or loved one.

Because "all of Israel" is like one human body and encompasses all people who are striving to become more spiritual in their lives irrespective of religion or race, judgment will only fall upon any person who acts against his countryman, since it will be as if he had taken negative action against himself. This explanation of "loving the nation of Israel" expresses the principle of recognizing all human beings as one body—even people who have hurt us and caused us grief. We must see those people, too, as part of "our body," and we need to "love our neighbors as we love ourselves."

Speaking about the precept of "love your neighbor as yourself," Rav Akiva said:

> *"This is the greatest law of the Bible. If you will keep the precept of loving your neighbor as yourself and if you will love all the people of Israel as if they were your own body, you will merit the completion of the precepts between man and man, and also between man and God."*

In short, love of Israel in this way—love for all the people of Israel and for all the people of the world—is the key that opens us to true joy and fulfillment in our lives.

SYNOPSIS OF ACHAREI MOT

Acharei Mot is read twice: once on *Yom Kippur* (which offers the highest possible connection during the year to the Light of the Creator), and once on a Shabbat in the month of *Iyar* (Taurus). Because of this, when we listen to or connect with the reading on Shabbat, we are also connecting with the Light of *Yom Kippur*. As it does on *Yom Kippur*, however, this gift carries the responsibility for us to do some deep introspection and to awaken a desire to spiritually cleanse ourselves.

FIRST READING - ABRAHAM - CHESED

16:1 **A**nd the Lord spoke to Moses, after the death of the two sons of Aaron who died when they approached the Lord.

2 And the Lord said to Moses: "Tell your brother Aaron not to come whenever he chooses into the Most Holy Place behind the curtain in front of the cover on the Ark, or else he will die, because I appear in the cloud over the Ark cover.

3 This is how Aaron is to enter the sanctuary area: with a young bull for a sin offering and a ram for a burnt offering.

4 He is to put on the sacred linen tunic, with linen undergarments next to his body; he is to tie the linen sash around him and put on the linen mitre; these are sacred garments; so he must bathe himself in water before he puts them on.

5 And from the congregation of the Children of Israel, he is to take two male goats for a sin offering and a ram for a burnt offering.

FROM THE RAV

Things are moving very quickly in our time, both on the positive and the negative end. Information concerning 25th century science has already begun to be released into this earthly universe. We are currently experiencing an ever - broadening understanding of what the Torah is really about—which is to protect humanity—but without the *Zohar*, we could not even begin to understand what the Torah is really all about.

The *Zohar* teaches us that when we can feel the pain of someone who lived 3400 years ago (notwithstanding that we haven't even begun to see all the pain that is around us right now), when we take ourselves out of the limitations that are thrust upon us and over-ride time, space, and motion—this brings us to the point where we are out of the playing field of Satan and there is nothing in this physical reality that can threaten us.

When we feel the pain of the loss of the souls who lived 3400 years ago as well as the lack for the knowledge they could reveal to us, this removes every aspect of negativity inside us.

Some people can feel another's pain, but how many of us truly feel the pain of loss of someone who lived and died 3400 years ago? When we take ourselves out of our current situation and feel the pain of another, it is not because we want to become better people. It is because we have to take ourselves out of this playing field of Satan, where we are the central figure. If we did, there would be nothing in this physical reality that could threaten us. If this sounds like I am preaching, then I have failed. This is a very serious game. We are talking about controlling the forces of physical nature—a reverse turn-around.

FIRST READING - ABRAHAM - CHESED

16 1 וַיְדַבֵּר יְהֹוָה אֶל־מֹשֶׁה אַחֲרֵי מוֹת שְׁנֵי בְּנֵי

אַהֲרֹן בְּקָרְבָתָם לִפְנֵי־יְהֹוָה וַיָּמֻתוּ: 2 וַיֹּאמֶר

יְהֹוָה אֶל־מֹשֶׁה דַּבֵּר אֶל־אַהֲרֹן אָחִיךָ

וְאַל־יָבֹא בְכָל־עֵת אֶל־הַקֹּדֶשׁ מִבֵּית

לַפָּרֹכֶת אֶל־פְּנֵי הַכַּפֹּרֶת אֲשֶׁר עַל־הָאָרֹן וְלֹא יָמוּת

כִּי בֶּעָנָן אֵרָאֶה עַל־הַכַּפֹּרֶת: 3 בְּזֹאת יָבֹא אַהֲרֹן אֶל־

הַקֹּדֶשׁ בְּפַר בֶּן־בָּקָר לְחַטָּאת וְאַיִל לְעֹלָה: 4 כְּתֹנֶת־

בַּד קֹדֶשׁ יִלְבָּשׁ וּמִכְנְסֵי־בַד יִהְיוּ עַל־בְּשָׂרוֹ וּבְאַבְנֵט בַּד יַחְגֹּר

וּבְמִצְנֶפֶת בַּד יִצְנֹף בִּגְדֵי־קֹדֶשׁ הֵם וְרָחַץ בַּמַּיִם אֶת־בְּשָׂרוֹ וּלְבֵשָׁם:

5 וּמֵאֵת עֲדַת בְּנֵי יִשְׂרָאֵל יִקַּח שְׁנֵי־שְׂעִירֵי עִזִּים לְחַטָּאת וְאַיִל

אֶחָד לְעֹלָה: 6 וְהִקְרִיב אַהֲרֹן אֶת־הַפָּר

אַחֲרֵי מוֹת

Leviticus 16:1 – Aaron's two sons, Nadav and Avihu, died because Aaron had participated in the building of the Golden Calf. Aaron had to suffer the pain of this bereavement because of his connection to idol worship. We go through similar types of cleansing in our lives, where we are required to experience pain because of our negative actions in this or past lifetimes. However, we can take control over how long the painful process lasts.

לְעֹלָה

Leviticus 16:3 – Part of the cleansing process is making sacrifices, and here we read that Aaron had to sacrifice two goats. One animal was a sacrifice for God (the positive goat), while the other was made to take on all the negativity of the people and be destroyed (the negative goat). In this way, good was separated from evil.

We have learned that: "And Aaron shall cast lots upon the two goats.... One lot for God, and the other lot for Azazel." (Leviticus 16:8) HE QUESTIONS: These two goats SYMBOLIZE JUDGMENTS, so why should one of them be for God? HE ANSWERS: The Holy One, blessed be He, said, "Let one GOAT stay with Me and let the other wander around in the world, for if both joined together, the world would not be able to bear it."
— The Zohar, Acharei Mot 19:116

Before we do any kind of cleansing, we must make a clear distinction between good and evil. If we don't have an understanding about the nature of good and evil, we won't be able to cleanse ourselves.

⁶ *And Aaron is to offer the bull for his own sin offering to make atonement for himself and for his household.*

⁷ *Then he is to take the two goats and present them before the Lord at the entrance to the Tent of Meeting.*

⁸ *And Aaron is to cast lots for the two goats—one lot for the Lord and the other lot for Azazel.*

⁹ *And Aaron shall bring the goat whose lot falls to the Lord and sacrifice it for a sin offering.* ¹⁰ *But the goat on which the lot fell to Azazel must be presented alive before the Lord to be used for making atonement by sending it into the wilderness for Azazel.*

¹¹ *And Aaron shall bring the bull for his own sin offering to make atonement for himself and for his household, and he is to slaughter the bull for his own sin offering.*

¹² *And he is to take a censer full of burning coals from the altar before the Lord and two handfuls of finely ground fragrant incense and take them behind the curtain.*

¹³ *And he is to put the incense on the fire before the Lord, and the smoke of the incense will conceal the atonement cover above the Testimony, so that he will not die.*

¹⁴ *And he is to take some of the bull's blood and with his finger sprinkle it on the front of the cover of the Ark; then he shall sprinkle some of it with his finger seven times before the cover of the Ark.*

¹⁵ *Then he must slaughter the goat for the sin offering for the people and take its blood behind the curtain and do with it as he did with the bull's blood, and sprinkle it on the cover of the Ark and in front of the cover of the Ark.*

שְׁנֵי

Leviticus 16:8 – In this verse, the letter *Shin* (the beginning of the word *shnei*, meaning "two") appears at the top of the column in the Torah Scroll. As mentioned previously, except for six places—one of which is here—the letter *Vav* appears at the top of every column of the Torah. According to the *Zohar*, at the moment of Creation, six of the Ten Dimensions (*Sefirot*) of the Tree of Life compressed into one dimension known as *Zeir Anpin*. These six locations in the Torah represent the six levels of *Zeir Anpin* (*Chesed, Gevurah, Tiferet, Netzach, Hod,* and *Yesod*).

קְטֹרֶת

Leviticus 16:12 – A service with incense was performed to remove the power of Satan thus reclaiming the Light that the people had given over to the Negative Side. A great deal of negativity comes to us because we gave—and continue to give—our Light to Satan by being reactive.

Because only a High Priest could handle the enormous amount of Light revealed in a service with incense, only Aaron was allowed to be in the Tabernacle during this ceremony.

At the time when the Holy One, blessed be He, gave the sweet incense to Aaron,

הַחַטָּאת אֲשֶׁר־לוֹ וְכִפֶּר בַּעֲדוֹ וּבְעַד בֵּיתוֹ: 7 וְלָקַח
אֶת־שְׁנֵי הַשְּׂעִירִם וְהֶעֱמִיד אֹתָם לִפְנֵי יְהוָה פֶּתַח
אֹהֶל מוֹעֵד: 8 וְנָתַן אַהֲרֹן עַל־שְׁנֵי
הַשְּׂעִירִם גֹּרָלוֹת גּוֹרָל אֶחָד לַיהוָה וְגוֹרָל אֶחָד
לַעֲזָאזֵל: 9 וְהִקְרִיב אַהֲרֹן אֶת־הַשָּׂעִיר אֲשֶׁר עָלָה
עָלָיו הַגּוֹרָל לַיהוָה וְעָשָׂהוּ חַטָּאת: 10 וְהַשָּׂעִיר אֲשֶׁר עָלָה
עָלָיו הַגּוֹרָל לַעֲזָאזֵל יָעֳמַד־חַי לִפְנֵי יְהוָה לְכַפֵּר
עָלָיו לְשַׁלַּח אֹתוֹ לַעֲזָאזֵל הַמִּדְבָּרָה: 11 וְהִקְרִיב אַהֲרֹן אֶת־
פַּר הַחַטָּאת אֲשֶׁר־לוֹ וְכִפֶּר בַּעֲדוֹ וּבְעַד בֵּיתוֹ
וְשָׁחַט אֶת־פַּר הַחַטָּאת אֲשֶׁר־לוֹ: 12 וְלָקַח
מְלֹא־הַמַּחְתָּה גַּחֲלֵי־אֵשׁ מֵעַל הַמִּזְבֵּחַ מִלִּפְנֵי
יְהוָה וּמְלֹא חָפְנָיו קְטֹרֶת סַמִּים
דַּקָּה וְהֵבִיא מִבֵּית לַפָּרֹכֶת: 13 וְנָתַן אֶת־
הַקְּטֹרֶת עַל־הָאֵשׁ לִפְנֵי יְהוָה וְכִסָּה | עֲנַן
הַקְּטֹרֶת אֶת־הַכַּפֹּרֶת אֲשֶׁר עַל־הָעֵדוּת וְלֹא יָמוּת: 14 וְלָקַח
מִדַּם הַפָּר וְהִזָּה בְאֶצְבָּעוֹ עַל־פְּנֵי
הַכַּפֹּרֶת קֵדְמָה וְלִפְנֵי הַכַּפֹּרֶת יַזֶּה שֶׁבַע פְּעָמִים
מִן־הַדָּם בְּאֶצְבָּעוֹ: 15 וְשָׁחַט אֶת־שְׂעִיר הַחַטָּאת אֲשֶׁר לָעָם

He wanted no one else to deal with this during his lifetime. For what reason? Because Aaron increased peace in the world. The Holy One, blessed be He, said to him, "Since you wish to increase peace in the world, peace will multiply above through you. The sweet incense will be transmitted to you from now on, AS INCENSE INCREASES PEACE ABOVE, and during your life, no one else will be permitted to deal with it."
— The Zohar, Acharei Mot 10:69

וְשָׁחַט

Leviticus 16:15 – Aaron's sacrifice of the positive goat paved a way for us to connect directly with the Light, with no one acting as intermediary and nothing intervening between us and the Light. Connecting with this verse gives us the opportunity to let the Lightforce of the Creator enter us and remain with us constantly. This Light can help cleanse us, heal us, and even allow us to bring about miracles.

[16] *In this way, he will make atonement for the Holy Place because of the uncleanness and rebellion of the Israelites, whatever their sins have been, and he is to do the same for the Tent of Meeting, which is among them in the midst of their uncleanness.*

[17] *No one is to be in the Tent of Meeting from the time Aaron goes in to make atonement in the Holy Place until he comes out, having made atonement for himself, for his household and for the whole community of Israel.*

ON A LEAP YEAR: SECOND READING - ISAAC - GEVURAH

[18] *And then he shall come out to the altar that is before the Lord and make atonement for it, and shall take some of the bull's blood and some of the goat's blood and put it around all the horns of the altar.*

[19] *And he shall sprinkle some of the blood on it with his finger seven times to cleanse it and to consecrate it from the uncleanness of the children of Israel.*

[20] *And when he has finished making atonement for the Holy Place, and the Tent of Meeting and the altar, he shall bring forward the live goat.*

[21] *And Aaron is to lay both hands on the head of the live goat and confess over it all the iniquities of the Children of Israel, and all their transgressions, even all their sins, and put them on the goat's head; and he shall send the goat away into the wilderness in the care of an appointed man.*

אִישׁ עִתִּי

Leviticus 16:21 – There are people chosen to remove negativity from the physical world and who nevertheless become contaminated by it and thus become impure. In other words, even though they were chosen to engage the negative energy, they were touched by it at the spiritual level. Azazel was the person chosen to take the scapegoat (the negative goat) into the wilderness. Azazel had an evil eye, meaning that everything he looked at was destroyed. He was chosen because he could take on all of the negativity and destroy it.

There is a man who is fit for curses to occur through him. Wherever he looks, there would be curses, anathemas and confusions. For example, Bilaam was called evil-eyed, as he was ready for every evil but not prepared for good. Even when he blessed, his blessing was no blessing and it was not fulfilled. But when he cursed, it prevailed; even in one instance IT WOULD COME TO BE. Therefore, it is written: "Whose eyes are open," (Numbers 24:3) every place his eye had seen was cursed.
— The Zohar, Acharei Mot 20:125

We, too, have the power of the evil eye, so it's important to be careful to control how it works in our lives. We cannot use it to envy others or to judge what they have.

עלם וְהֵבִיא אֶת־דָּמוֹ אֶל־מִבֵּית ב״פ ראה לַפָּרֹכֶת וְעָשָׂה אֶת־דָּמוֹ כַּאֲשֶׁר

עָשָׂה לְדַם רבוע אהיה הַפָּר סזוֹךְ, ערי, סנדלפוֹן וְהִזָּה וְהוּ אֹתוֹ עַל־הַכַּפֹּרֶת וְלִפְנֵי

וחכמה בינה הַכַּפֹּרֶת: 16 וְכִפֶּר מצפצ עַל־הַקֹּדֶשׁ מִטֻּמְאֹת בְּנֵי יִשְׂרָאֵל

וּמִפִּשְׁעֵיהֶם לְכָל־ יה אדני ־חַטֹּאתָם וְכֵן יַעֲשֶׂה לְאֹהֶל לאה מוֹעֵד הַשֹּׁכֵן

שׂ״ע אִתָּם בְּתוֹךְ טֻמְאֹתָם: 17 וְכָל־ ילי ־אָדָם מ״ה לֹא־יִהְיֶה יהה | בְּאֹהֶל לאה

מוֹעֵד בְּבֹאוֹ לְכַפֵּר מצפצ בַּקֹּדֶשׁ עַד־צֵאתוֹ וְכִפֶּר מצפצ בַּעֲדוֹ וּבְעַד

בֵּיתוֹ ב״פ ראה וּבְעַד כָּל־ ילי ־קְהַל ע״ב ס״ג יִשְׂרָאֵל:

ON A LEAP YEAR: SECOND READING - ISAAC - GEVURAH

18 וְיָצָא אֶל־הַמִּזְבֵּחַ זן, גגד אֲשֶׁר לִפְנֵי וחכמה בינה ־יְהֹוָאדֹנָהִדֹּנָהִי וְכִפֶּר מצפצ

עָלָיו וְלָקַח יהוה אהיה אהיה אדני מִדַּם רבוע אהיה יהוה אדני הַפָּר סזוֹךְ, ערי, סנדלפוֹן וּמִדַּם רבוע אהיה

הַשָּׂעִיר וְנָתַן אבגית״ץ, ושר, אהבת חנם עַל־קַרְנוֹת הַמִּזְבֵּחַ זן, גגד סָבִיב: 19 וְהִזָּה וְהוּ

עָלָיו מִן־הַדָּם רבוע אהיה בְּאֶצְבָּעוֹ שֶׁבַע ע״ב ואלהים דיודין פְּעָמִים וְטִהֲרוֹ

וְקִדְּשׁוֹ מִטֻּמְאֹת בְּנֵי יִשְׂרָאֵל: 20 וְכִלָּה מִכַּפֵּר מצפצ אֶת־הַקֹּדֶשׁ וְאֶת־

אֹהֶל לאה מוֹעֵד וְאֶת־הַמִּזְבֵּחַ זן, גגד וְהִקְרִיב אֶת־הַשָּׂעִיר הֶחָי: 21 וְסָמַךְ

אַהֲרֹן ע״ב ורבוע ע״ב אֶת־שְׁתֵּי ידו עַל רֹאשׁ ריבוע אלהים ואלהים דיודין ע״ה הַשָּׂעִיר

הַחַי וְהִתְוַדָּה עָלָיו אֶת־כָּל־ ילי ־עֲוֹנֹת בְּנֵי יִשְׂרָאֵל וְאֶת־כָּל־ ילי

־פִּשְׁעֵיהֶם לְכָל־ יה אדני ־חַטֹּאתָם וְנָתַן אבגית״ץ, ושר, אהבת חנם אֹתָם עַל־רֹאשׁ

ריבוע אלהים ואלהים דיודין ע״ה הַשָּׂעִיר וְשִׁלַּח בְּיַד־ ⟨אִישׁ⟩ ע״ה קנ״א קס״א עִתִּי

הַמִּדְבָּרָה: 22 וְנָשָׂא הַשָּׂעִיר עָלָיו אֶת־כָּל־ ילי ־עֲוֹנֹתָם אֶל־אֶרֶץ

Often, we become comfortable with our chaos and don't want to let go of the negativity that causes it. Just as the scapegoat was taken by Azazel into the wilderness, we, too, must release all our negativity—and let it be removed from us.

The two goats used as the sacrifices were physically alike, but one was negative and the other positive. We humans are all the same, and we, too, can become either negative or positive.

22 And the goat will bear on itself all their iniquities to a land that is cut off; and he shall release the goat into the wilderness.

23 And Aaron is to go into the Tent of Meeting and take off the linen garments he put on before he entered the Holy Place, and he is to leave them there.

24 And he shall bathe himself with water in a holy place and put on his regular garments, and come out and sacrifice the burnt offering for himself and the burnt offering of the people, to make atonement for himself and for the people.

ON A LEAP YEAR: THIRD READING - JACOB - TIFERET
WHEN CONNECTED: SECOND READING - ISAAC - GEVURAH

25 And he shall burn the fat of the sin offering on the altar. 26 And he, who releases the goat for Azazel must wash his clothes and bathe himself in water; and afterward he may come into the camp.

27 And the bull for the sin offering and the goat for the sin offering, whose blood was brought into the Holy Place to make atonement, must be taken outside the camp; and their hides, flesh and offal are to be burned up in fire.

28 And he who burns them must wash his clothes and bathe himself in water; and afterward he may come into the camp. 29 And it shall be an ever lasting statue for you: on the tenth day of the seventh month you must afflict your souls and not do any work, whether native-born or a stranger living among you.

30 Because on this day atonement will be made for you, to cleanse you for all your sins so that you will be clean before the Lord. 31 It is a Sabbath of rest for you, and you must afflict your souls; it is an ever lasting statute.

32 And the priest who is anointed and ordained to succeed his father is to make atonement, and shall put on the linen garments, even the holy garments,

---

בְּעֵשׂוֹר

Leviticus 16:29 – The ceremony that Aaron performed with the two goats was also performed on *Yom Kippur*. Aaron was the first person who came into this world to be a High Priest, and he did it to open the gates in the cosmos for all the High Priests who would come after him. We are often the first to do certain things, becoming the pioneers who break ground and create openings for those who follow. This responsibility that we impose on ourselves can make it easier for others to grow and transform.

23 וּבָא֩ גּוֹרָ֜ל וְשִׁלַּ֤ח אֶת־הַשָּׂעִיר֙ בַּמִּדְבָּ֔ר אלהים דאלפין אברהם, רמ״ח, וח״פ אל׃

אַהֲרֹן֙ אֶל־אֹ֣הֶל מוֹעֵ֔ד וּפָשַׁט֙ אֶת־בִּגְדֵ֣י הַבָּ֔ד אֲשֶׁ֤ר לָבַשׁ֙ ע״ב ורבוע ע״ב לאה

בְּבֹא֣וֹ אֶל־הַקֹּ֔דֶשׁ וְהִנִּיחָ֖ם שָׁ֑ם יהוה עד״י 24 וְרָחַ֨ץ אֶת־בְּשָׂר֤וֹ בַמַּ֙יִם֙

בְּמָק֣וֹם יהוה ברבוע, ר״פ אל קָד֔וֹשׁ וְלָבַ֖שׁ אֶת־בְּגָדָ֑יו וְיָצָ֗א וְעָשָׂ֤ה אֶת־עֹֽלָתוֹ֙

וְאֶת־עֹלַ֣ת אבגית״ץ, וטר, אהבת חום הָעָ֔ם וְכִפֶּ֥ר מצפצ בַּעֲד֖וֹ וּבְעַ֥ד הָעָֽם׃

ON A LEAP YEAR: THIRD READING - JACOB - TIFERET
WHEN CONNECTED: SECOND READING - ISAAC - GEVURAH

25 וְאֵ֛ת חֵ֥לֶב הַֽחַטָּ֖את יַקְטִ֣יר הַמִּזְבֵּֽחָה׃ 26 וְהַֽמְשַׁלֵּ֤חַ אֶת־הַשָּׂעִיר֙

לַֽעֲזָאזֵ֔ל יְכַבֵּ֣ס בְּגָדָ֔יו וְרָחַ֥ץ אֶת־בְּשָׂר֖וֹ בַּמָּ֑יִם וְאַחֲרֵי־כֵ֖ן יָב֥וֹא אֶל־

הַֽמַּחֲנֶֽה׃ 27 וְאֵת֩ פַּ֨ר מזוזר, ערי, סנדלפין הַֽחַטָּ֜את וְאֵ֣ת ׀ שְׂעִ֣יר הַֽחַטָּ֗את

אֲשֶׁ֨ר הוּבָ֤א אֶת־דָּמָם֙ לְכַפֵּ֣ר מצפצ בַּקֹּ֔דֶשׁ יוֹצִ֖יא אֶל־מִח֣וּץ לַֽמַּחֲנֶ֑ה

וְשָׂרְפ֣וּ בָאֵ֔שׁ אלהים דיודין ע״ה אֶת־עֹרֹתָ֥ם וְאֶת־בְּשָׂרָ֖ם וְאֶת־פִּרְשָֽׁם׃

28 וְהַשֹּׂרֵ֣ף אֹתָ֔ם יְכַבֵּ֣ס בְּגָדָ֔יו וְרָחַ֥ץ אֶת־בְּשָׂר֖וֹ בַּמָּ֑יִם וְאַחֲרֵי־כֵ֖ן

יָב֥וֹא אֶל־הַֽמַּחֲנֶֽה׃ 29 וְהָיְתָ֥ה לָכֶ֖ם לְחֻקַּ֣ת עוֹלָ֑ם בַּחֹ֣דֶשׁ הַשְּׁבִיעִ֣י י״ב הויות

בֶּֽעָשׂוֹר֩ לַחֹ֨דֶשׁ י״ב הויות תְּעַנּ֣וּ אֶת־נַפְשֹֽׁתֵיכֶ֗ם וְכָל־מְלָאכָה֙ אל אדני לֹ֣א

תַעֲשׂ֔וּ הָֽאֶזְרָ֔ח וְהַגֵּ֖ר ד״פ בן הגר ד״פ בן בְּתֽוֹכְכֶֽם׃ 30 כִּֽי־בַיּ֥וֹם ע״ה = נגד, זן, מזוח

הַזֶּ֛ה ו,הו יְכַפֵּ֥ר מצפצ עֲלֵיכֶ֖ם לְטַהֵ֣ר י״פ אכא אֶתְכֶ֑ם מִכֹּל֙ ילי חַטֹּ֣אתֵיכֶ֔ם לִפְנֵ֥י

יְהוָ֖ה בינה אהדונהיאהדונהי תִּטְהָֽרוּ׃ 31 שַׁבַּ֨ת שַׁבָּת֥וֹן הִיא֙ לָכֶ֔ם וְעִנִּיתֶ֖ם אֶת־

נַפְשֹֽׁתֵיכֶ֑ם חֻקַּ֖ת עוֹלָֽם׃ 32 וְכִפֶּ֨ר מצפצ הַכֹּהֵ֜ן מלה אֲשֶׁר־יִמְשַׁ֣ח אֹת֗וֹ

וַאֲשֶׁ֤ר יְמַלֵּא֙ אֶת־יָד֔וֹ לְכַהֵ֖ן מלה תַּ֣חַת אָבִ֑יו וְלָבַ֛שׁ אֶת־בִּגְדֵ֥י הַבָּ֖ד

בִּגְדֵ֥י הַקֹּֽדֶשׁ׃ 33 וְכִפֶּר֙ מצפצ אֶת־מִקְדַּ֣שׁ הַקֹּ֔דֶשׁ וְאֶת־אֹ֧הֶל לאה מוֹעֵ֛ד

וְאֶת־הַמִּזְבֵּ֖חַ זן, נגד יְכַפֵּ֑ר מצפצ וְעַ֧ל הַכֹּהֲנִ֛ים מלה וְעַל־כָּל־ ילי עַם־ הַקָּהָ֖ל

33 and he shall make atonement for the Most Holy Place, for the Tent of Meeting and for the altar, and he shall make atonement for the priests and all the people of the assembly.

34 And this is to be an ever lasting statute for you, to make atonement once a year for all the sins of the children of Israel." And he did as the Lord commanded Moses.

ON A LEAP YEAR: FOURTH READING - MOSES - NETZACH

17:1 The Lord spoke to Moses, saying, 2 "Speak to Aaron and to his sons and to all the children of Israel and say to them: This is what the Lord has commanded, saying:

3 Any man from the house of Israel who kills an ox, or lamb or goat in the camp or kills it outside the camp,

4 and who has not brought it to the entrance to the Tent of Meeting to present it as an offering to the Lord in front of the Tabernacle of the Lord, that man shall be considered guilty of bloodshed; he has shed blood and must be cut off from among his people.

5 This is so the children of Israel may bring to the Lord their sacrifices they are now making in the open fields, that they may bring them to the Lord at the entrance to the Tent of Meeting, to the priest and sacrifice them as fellowship offerings to the Lord.

6 And the priest is to sprinkle the blood against the altar of the Lord at the entrance to the Tent of Meeting and burn the fat as an aroma pleasing to the Lord.

7 They must no longer offer any of their sacrifices to the goat idols to whom they prostitute themselves. This is to be an ever lasting statute for them and for their generations to come.

לְחֻקֹּת

Leviticus 16:34 – The Tabernacle (and later the Temple) was a place where physical sacrifices were performed, and in those days, there was a time and a ritual for everything. Now we have sanctuaries that provide a time and a place for certain connections, but there are also other times, other places, and other situations when we can also connect to God. Connecting and meditating on this verse can ensure that our

choices are made at the right times and in the right places.

דָּם שָׁפָךְ

Leviticus 17:4 – Ingesting blood is forbidden because it connects us to the essence of an animal, which may be negative. Animals are incarnations of souls, and, as with human beings, there was something they were unable to accomplish in a past life that caused their souls

עֹ״ב ס״א יְכַפֵּר מצפצ׃ 34 וְהָיְתָה־זֹּאת לָכֶם לְכַפֵּר מצפצ עַל־ לְחֻקַּת עוֹלָם

בְּנֵי יִשְׂרָאֵל מִכָּל־ ילי יְחַטֹּאתָם אַחַת בַּשָּׁנָה וַיַּעַשׂ כַּאֲשֶׁר צִוָּה פוי

יְהֹוָאדֹנָיאהדונהי אֶת־מֹשֶׁה מהש, אל שדי ׃

ON A LEAP YEAR: FOURTH READING - MOSES - NETZACH

17 1 וַיְדַבֵּר ראה יְהֹוָאדֹניאהדונהי אֶל־מֹשֶׁה מהש, אל שדי לֵאמֹר׃ 2 דַּבֵּר ראה

אֶל־אַהֲרֹן ע״ב ורבוע ע״ב וְאֶל־בָּנָיו וְאֶל כָּל ־בְּנֵי ילי יִשְׂרָאֵל וְאָמַרְתָּ אֲלֵיהֶם

זֶה הַדָּבָר ראה אֲשֶׁר־צִוָּה פוי יְהֹוָאדֹניאהדונהי לֵאמֹר׃ 3 אִישׁ עֹה קנ״א קס״א אִישׁ

עֹה קנ״א קס״א מִבֵּית ב״פ ראה יִשְׂרָאֵל אֲשֶׁר יִשְׁחַט שׁוֹר אבגיתץ, ושׁר, אהבת חנם אוֹ־

כֶשֶׂב ב״פ קס״א אוֹ־עֵז אני יהוה בַּמַּחֲנֶה אוֹ אֲשֶׁר יִשְׁחַט מִחוּץ לַמַּחֲנֶה׃

4 וְאֶל־פֶּתַח אֹהֶל לאה מוֹעֵד לֹא הֱבִיאוֹ לְהַקְרִיב קָרְבָּן לַיהֹואדׄניאהדונהי

לִפְנֵי וחכמה בינה מִשְׁכַּן ב״פ (רבוע אלהים + ה׳) יְהֹוָאדׄניאהדונהי דָּם רבוע אהיה יֵחָשֵׁב

לָאִישׁ עֹה קנ״א קס״א הַהוּא דָּם רבוע אהיה שָׁפָךְ וְנִכְרַת הָאִישׁ ז״פ אדם הַהוּא

מִקֶּרֶב עַמּוֹ׃ 5 לְמַעַן אֲשֶׁר יָבִיאוּ בְּנֵי יִשְׂרָאֵל אֶת־זִבְחֵיהֶם אֲשֶׁר הֵם

זֹבְחִים עַל־פְּנֵי וחכמה בינה הַשָּׂדֶה שדי וֶהֱבִיאָם לַיהֹוׄאדניאהדונהי אֶל־פֶּתַח

אֹהֶל לאה מוֹעֵד אֶל־הַכֹּהֵן מלה וְזָבְחוּ זִבְחֵי שְׁלָמִים לַיהֹוׄאדׄניאהדונהי

אוֹתָם׃ 6 וְזָרַק הַכֹּהֵן מלה אֶת־הַדָּם רבוע אהיה עַל־מִזְבַּח זן, נגד יְהֹוׄאדׄניאהדונהי

פֶּתַח אֹהֶל לאה מוֹעֵד וְהִקְטִיר הַחֵלֶב לְרֵיחַ רמ״ח נִיחֹחַ לַיהֹוׄאדׄניאהדונהי׃

7 וְלֹא־יִזְבְּחוּ עוֹד אֶת־זִבְחֵיהֶם לַשְּׂעִירִם אֲשֶׁר הֵם זֹנִים אַחֲרֵיהֶם

חֻקַּת עוֹלָם תִּהְיֶה־זֹּאת לָהֶם לְדֹרֹתָם׃

---

to return as animals. The meat of an animal can fuel us so that when we do positive actions, we can elevate the animal's soul as well. But if we connect to the animal's blood, we connect to the animal's physicality, which prevents us from helping it elevate.

ON A LEAP YEAR: FIFTH READING - AARON – HOD
WHEN CONNECTED: THIRD READING - JACOB - TIFERET

8 And you will say to them: Any man from the house of Israel or any stranger living among them who offers a burnt offering or sacrifice

9 and does not bring it to the entrance to the Tent of Meeting to sacrifice it to the Lord, even that man shall be cut off from his people.

10 Any man from the house of Israel or any stranger living among them who eats any manner of blood, I will set my face against that soul who eats blood and will cut him off from his people.

11 For the life of the flesh is in the blood, and I have given it to you to make atonement for yourselves on the altar; it is the blood that makes atonement for one's life.

12 Therefore, I say to the children of Israel, "None of you may eat blood, nor may any stranger living among you eat blood.

13 Any Israelite or any stranger living among you who hunts any animal or bird that may be eaten must drain out the blood and cover it with earth,

14 because the life of every creature is its blood, therefore, I have said to the children of Israel, "You must not eat the blood of any creature, because the life of every creature is its blood; anyone who eats it must be cut off.

15 And every soul, whether native-born or alien, who eats anything found dead or torn by wild animals must wash his clothes and bathe himself in water, and be unclean till the evening; then he will be clean.

16 But if he does not wash his clothes and bathe himself, he will bear his iniquity."

18:1 And the Lord spoke to Moses, saying, 2 "Speak to the children of Israel and say to them: I am the Lord your God.

וַיְדַבֵּר

Leviticus 18:1-5 – This specific verse is read during the *Minchah* (afternoon) service on both *Yom Kippur* and Shabbat. In life, there are always many levels of cleansing and spiritual work that we need to be aware of. On *Yom Kippur*, the morning service is an initial cleansing, while the afternoon one is a cleansing on a deeper level. So when we make this connection on the afternoon of Shabbat, our higher purpose is about cleansing on a deeper level.

ON A LEAP YEAR: FIFTH READING - AARON – HOD
WHEN CONNECTED: THIRD READING - JACOB - TIFERET

8 וַאֲלֵהֶם תֹּאמַר אִישׁ עיה קנא קסא אִישׁ עיה קנא קסא מִבֵּית בּיפ ראה יִשְׂרָאֵל

וּמִן־הַגֵּר דיפ בן אֲשֶׁר־יָגוּר בְּתוֹכָם אֲשֶׁר־יַעֲלֶה עֹלָה אוֹ־זֶבַח: 9 וְאֶל־

פֶּתַח אֹהֶל לאה מוֹעֵד לֹא יְבִיאֶנּוּ לַעֲשׂוֹת אֹתוֹ לַיהוֹוָאֲדֹנָהִיאֱהֹדִוֹנָהִי וְנִכְרַת

הָאִישׁ זיפ אדם הַהוּא מֵעַמָּיו: 10 וְאִישׁ עיה קנא קסא אִישׁ עיה קנא קסא מִבֵּית

בּיפ ראה יִשְׂרָאֵל וּמִן־הַגֵּר דיפ בן הַגֵּר דיפ בן בְּתוֹכָם אֲשֶׁר יֹאכַל כָּל יליּ ־דָּם

רבוע אהיה וְנָתַתִּי פָנַי וחכמה בינה בַּנֶּפֶשׁ רמיח ־ זי הויות הָאֹכֶלֶת אֶת־הַדָּם רבוע אהיה

וְהִכְרַתִּי אֹתָהּ מִקֶּרֶב עַמָּהּ: 11 כִּי נֶפֶשׁ רמיח ־ זי הויות הַבָּשָׂר בַּדָּם רבוע אהיה

הוּא וַאֲנִי ביפ אהיה יהוה נְתַתִּיו לָכֶם עַל־הַמִּזְבֵּחַ זז, נגד לְכַפֵּר מצפצ עַל־

נַפְשֹׁתֵיכֶם כִּי־הַדָּם רבוע אהיה הוּא בַּנֶּפֶשׁ רמיח ־ זי הויות יְכַפֵּר מצפצ: 12 עַל־כֵּן

אָמַרְתִּי ייפ אדני עיה לִבְנֵי יִשְׂרָאֵל כָּל יליּ ־נֶפֶשׁ רמיח ־ זי הויות מִכֶּם לֹא־תֹאכַל

דָּם רבוע אהיה וְהַגֵּר דיפ בן הַגֵּר דיפ בן בְּתוֹכְכֶם לֹא־יֹאכַל דָּם רבוע אהיה: 13 וְאִישׁ עיה קנא קסא אִישׁ עיה קנא קסא מִבְּנֵי יִשְׂרָאֵל וּמִן־הַגֵּר דיפ בן הַגֵּר דיפ בן

בְּתוֹכָם אֲשֶׁר יָצוּד צֵיד בּיפ בן וָחַיָּה אוֹ־עוֹף גּיפ בן, יוסף, ציון אֲשֶׁר יֵאָכֵל

וְשָׁפַךְ אֶת־דָּמוֹ וְכִסָּהוּ בֶּעָפָר: 14 כִּי־נֶפֶשׁ רמיח ־ זי הויות כָּל יליּ ־בָּשָׂר דָּמוֹ

בְּנַפְשׁוֹ הוּא וָאֹמַר לִבְנֵי יִשְׂרָאֵל דַּם רבוע אהיה כָּל יליּ ־בָּשָׂר לֹא תֹאכֵלוּ

כִּי נֶפֶשׁ רמיח ־ זי הויות כָּל יליּ ־בָּשָׂר דָּמוֹ הוּא כָּל יליּ ־אֹכְלָיו יִכָּרֵת: 15 וְכָל

יליּ ־נֶפֶשׁ רמיח ־ זי הויות אֲשֶׁר תֹּאכַל נְבֵלָה בּיפ רבוע יהוה וּטְרֵפָה בָּאֶזְרָח וּבַגֵּר

דיפ בן וְכִבֶּס בְּגָדָיו וְרָחַץ בַּמַּיִם וְטָמֵא עַד־הָעֶרֶב רבוע יהוה ורבוע אלהים וְטָהֵר

יפ אכא: 16 וְאִם יוהך, עיה מיב לֹא יְכַבֵּס וּבְשָׂרוֹ לֹא יִרְחָץ וְנָשָׂא עֲוֹנוֹ: 1 וַיְדַבֵּר

ראה יְהוֹוָאֲדֹנָהִיאֱהֹדִוֹנָהִי אֶל־מֹשֶׁה מהש, אל שדי לֵּאמֹר: 2 דַּבֵּר ראה אֶל־בְּנֵי יִשְׂרָאֵל

וְאָמַרְתָּ אֲלֵהֶם אֲנִי אני, טדהד כוזו יְהוֹוָאֲדֹנָהִיאֱהֹדִוֹנָהִי אֱלֹהֵיכֶם ילה: 3 כְּמַעֲשֵׂה

3 And you must not do as they do in Egypt, where you used to live, and you must not do as they do in the land of Canaan, where I am bringing you; do not follow their practices.

4 My Ordinances you must and My Statutes you must keep and walk in. I am the Lord your God.

5 You shall therefore, keep My Statutes and My Ordinances, which if a man does, he will live by them: I am the Lord.

ON A LEAP YEAR: SIXTH READING - JOSEPH - YESOD

6 No one is to approach any close relative to uncover their nakedness: I am the Lord.
7 The nakedness of your father and the nakedness of your mother you shall not uncover, she is your mother; you shall not uncover her nakedness.

8 The nakedness of your father's wife you shall not uncover: it is your father's nakedness. 9 The nakedness of your sister, the daughter of your father, or the daughter of your mother, whether born at home, or born abroad, even their nakedness you shall not uncover. 10 The nakedness of your son's daughter, or of your daughter's daughter, even their nakedness you shall not uncover; for theirs is your own nakedness.

11 The nakedness of your father's wife's daughter, begotten of your father, she is your sister, you shall not uncover her nakedness.

12 You shall not uncover the nakedness of your father's sister: she is your father's near family. 13 You shall not uncover the nakedness of your mother's sister; for she is your mother's near family.

14 You shall not uncover the nakedness of your father's brother, you shall not approach his wife: she is your aunt. 15 You shall not uncover the nakedness of your daughter-in-law: she is your son's wife; you shall not uncover her nakedness.

16 You shall not uncover the nakedness of your brother's wife: it is your brother's nakedness.

אִישׁ

Leviticus 18:6 – The Bible gives us a map for finding our soul mate. There are prohibitions laid out, but they are only there to save us from looking for our partners in places where there is no Light. These prohibitions save us from making connections where we're not supposed to.

אֶרֶץ אלהים דאלפין ־מִצְרַיִם מצר אֲשֶׁר יְשַׁבְתֶּם־בָּהּ לֹא תַעֲשׂוּ וּכְמַעֲשֵׂה

אֶרֶץ אלהים דאלפין ־כְּנַעַן אֲשֶׁר אֲנִי אני, טדהד כוזו מֵבִיא אֶתְכֶם שָׁמָּה

מהטע, משה, אל שדי לֹא תַעֲשׂוּ וּבְחֻקֹּתֵיהֶם לֹא תֵלֵכוּ: 4 אֶת־מִשְׁפָּטַי תַּעֲשׂוּ

וְאֶת־חֻקֹּתַי תִּשְׁמְרוּ לָלֶכֶת בָּהֶם אֲנִי אני, טדהד כוזו יְהֹוָה אלהיכם אֱלֹהֵיכֶם

ילה: 5 וּשְׁמַרְתֶּם אֶת־חֻקֹּתַי וְאֶת־מִשְׁפָּטַי אֲשֶׁר יַעֲשֶׂה אֹתָם הָאָדָם מה

וָחַי בָּהֶם אֲנִי אני, טדהד כוזו יְהֹוָה:

ON A LEAP YEAR: SIXTH READING - JOSEPH - YESOD

6 אִישׁ עה קנא קסא אֶל־כָּל־ ילי ־שְׁאֵר ג: מווזן דאלהים דקטנות

בְּשָׂרוֹ לֹא תִקְרְבוּ לְגַלּוֹת עֶרְוָה אֲנִי אני, טדהד כוזו יְהֹוָה: 7 עֶרְוַת

אָבִיךָ וְעֶרְוַת אִמְּךָ לֹא תְגַלֵּה אִמְּךָ הִוא לֹא תְגַלֶּה עֶרְוָתָהּ: 8 עֶרְוַת

אֵשֶׁת־אָבִיךָ לֹא תְגַלֵּה עֶרְוַת אָבִיךָ הִוא: 9 עֶרְוַת אֲחוֹתְךָ בַת־אָבִיךָ

אוֹ בַת־אִמֶּךָ מוֹלֶדֶת בַּיִת בפ ראה אוֹ מוֹלֶדֶת חוּץ לֹא תְגַלֶּה עֶרְוָתָן:

10 עֶרְוַת בַּת־בִּנְךָ אוֹ בַת־בִּתְּךָ לֹא תְגַלֶּה עֶרְוָתָן כִּי עֶרְוָתְךָ הֵנָּה

מה יה: 11 עֶרְוַת בַּת־אֵשֶׁת אָבִיךָ מוֹלֶדֶת אָבִיךָ אֲחוֹתְךָ הִוא לֹא תְגַלֶּה

עֶרְוָתָהּ: 12 עֶרְוַת אֲחוֹת־אָבִיךָ לֹא תְגַלֵּה שְׁאֵר אָבִיךָ הִוא: 13 עֶרְוַת

אֲחוֹת־אִמְּךָ לֹא תְגַלֵּה כִּי־שְׁאֵר אִמְּךָ הִוא: 14 עֶרְוַת אֲחִי־אָבִיךָ לֹא

תְגַלֵּה אֶל־אִשְׁתּוֹ לֹא תִקְרָב דֹּדָתְךָ הִוא: 15 עֶרְוַת כַּלָּתְךָ לֹא תְגַלֵּה

אֵשֶׁת בִּנְךָ הִוא לֹא תְגַלֶּה עֶרְוָתָהּ: 16 עֶרְוַת אֵשֶׁת־אָחִיךָ לֹא תְגַלֵּה

עֶרְוַת אָחִיךָ הִוא: 17 עֶרְוַת אִשָּׁה וּבִתָּהּ לֹא תְגַלֵּה אֶת־בַּת־בְּנָהּ

וְאֶת־בַּת־בִּתָּהּ לֹא תִקַּח רבוע אהיה דאלפין לְגַלּוֹת עֶרְוָתָהּ שַׁאֲרָה הֵנָּה מה יה

17 You shall not uncover the nakedness of a woman and her daughter; you shall not take her son's daughter, or her daughter's daughter, and uncover her nakedness: they are near family to each other; it is lewdness.

18 And you shall not take your wife's sister, to be a rival to her, to uncover her nakedness while your wife is living.

19 Do not approach a woman to uncover her nakedness during the uncleanness of her monthly period.

20 And you shall not have sexual relations with your neighbor's wife and defile yourself with her.

21 And you shall not sacrifice any children of your seed to Molech, nor profane the name of your God. I am the Lord.

ON A LEAP YEAR: SEVENTH READING - DAVID – MALCHUT
WHEN CONNECTED: FOURTH READING - MOSES - NETZACH

22 Do not lie with a man as one lies with a woman; that is an abomination.

23 Do not lie with any beast and defile yourself with it; neither shall a woman stand before a beast to lie down with it; that is a perversion.

24 Do not defile yourselves in any of these ways, because this is how the nations that I am going to drive out before you became defiled.

25 Even the land was defiled; so I visited the iniquity of it on it, and the land vomited out her inhabitants.

26 You, therefore, must keep My Statutes and My Ordinances and shall not do any of these abominations, neither the native-born and the strangers living among you,

27 for all these abominations were done by the people who lived in the land before you, and the land is defiled.

וְזִמָּה הִוא: 18 וְאִשָּׁה אֶל־אֲחֹתָהּ לֹא תִקָּח לִצְרֹר לְגַלּוֹת עֶרְוָתָהּ עָלֶיהָ בְּחַיֶּיהָ: 19 וְאֶל־אִשָּׁה בְּנִדַּת טֻמְאָתָהּ לֹא תִקְרַב לְגַלּוֹת עֶרְוָתָהּ: 20 וְאֶל־אֵשֶׁת עֲמִיתְךָ לֹא־תִתֵּן שְׁכָבְתְּךָ לְזָרַע לְטָמְאָה־בָהּ: 21 וּמִזַּרְעֲךָ לֹא־תִתֵּן לְהַעֲבִיר לַמֹּלֶךְ וְלֹא תְחַלֵּל אֶת־שֵׁם אֱלֹהֶיךָ אֲנִי יְהוָה:

ON A LEAP YEAR: SEVENTH READING - DAVID – MALCHUT
WHEN CONNECTED: FOURTH READING - MOSES - NETZACH

22 וְאֶת־זָכָר לֹא תִשְׁכַּב מִשְׁכְּבֵי אִשָּׁה תּוֹעֵבָה הִוא: 23 וּבְכָל־בְּהֵמָה לֹא־תִתֵּן שְׁכָבְתְּךָ לְטָמְאָה־בָהּ וְאִשָּׁה לֹא־תַעֲמֹד לִפְנֵי בְהֵמָה לְרִבְעָהּ תֶּבֶל הוּא: 24 אַל־תִּטַּמְּאוּ בְּכָל־אֵלֶּה כִּי בְכָל־אֵלֶּה נִטְמְאוּ הַגּוֹיִם אֲשֶׁר־אֲנִי מְשַׁלֵּחַ מִפְּנֵיכֶם: 25 וַתִּטְמָא הָאָרֶץ וָאֶפְקֹד עֲוֹנָהּ עָלֶיהָ וַתָּקִא הָאָרֶץ אֶת־יֹשְׁבֶיהָ: 26 וּשְׁמַרְתֶּם אַתֶּם אֶת־חֻקֹּתַי וְאֶת־מִשְׁפָּטַי וְלֹא תַעֲשׂוּ מִכֹּל הַתּוֹעֵבֹת הָאֵלֶּה הָאֶזְרָח וְהַגֵּר הַגָּר בְּתוֹכְכֶם: 27 כִּי אֶת־כָּל־הַתּוֹעֵבֹת הָאֵל עָשׂוּ אַנְשֵׁי־הָאָרֶץ אֲשֶׁר לִפְנֵיכֶם וַתִּטְמָא הָאָרֶץ:

וַתִּטְמָא הָאָרֶץ

Leviticus 18:25 – The negative actions of the Israelites made the land negative as well. When we act in negative ways, we affect not only ourselves but our entire environment, too.

ON A LEAP YEAR: MAFTIR

²⁸ And if you defile the land, it will vomit you out, as it vomited out the nations that were before you.

²⁹ Anyone who does any of these abominations, even the souls that do them shall be cut off from their people.

³⁰ Therefore, keep My Charge and do not follow any of the abominable customs that were practiced before you came and do not defile yourselves with them. I am the Lord, your God."

ON A LEAP YEAR: HAFTARAH OF ACHAREI MOT

The sages teach that no negativity can come to a person until he judges others. If we could just learn to stop judging others, we could remove all negativity from our life.

Ezekiel 22:1-16

22:¹ Moreover, the word of the Lord came to me, saying:

² "Now, you, son of man, will you judge? Will you judge this city of bloodshed? Then cause her to know all of her abominations

³ and say: 'Thus says the Lord, God: city that sheds blood in the midst of it midst, that her time may come and make idols to herself to defile herself,

⁴ you have become guilty in your blood you have shed and have defiled yourself by your idols which you have made, and you have caused your days to draw near, and the end of your years has come. Therefore, I will make you a reproach to the heathen and a mocking to all the countries.

⁵ Those who are near and those that are far from you, will mock you, who are defiled of name and full of tumult.

⁶ See of the princes of Israel, each one according to his might, have been in you to shed blood.

ON A LEAP YEAR: MAFTIR

28 וְלֹא־תָקִיא הָאָ֫רֶץ אלהים דההין ע״ה אֶתְכֶם בְּטַמַּאֲכֶם אֹתָהּ כַּאֲשֶׁר
קָאָה אֶת־הַגּוֹי אֲשֶׁר לִפְנֵיכֶם: 29 כִּי כָּל יל ־אֲשֶׁר יַעֲשֶׂה מִכֹּל יל
הַתּוֹעֵבֹת הָאֵלֶּה וְנִכְרְתוּ הַנְּפָשׁוֹת הָעֹשֹׂת מִקֶּרֶב עַמָּם: 30 וּשְׁמַרְתֶּם
אֶת־מִשְׁמַרְתִּי לְבִלְתִּי עֲשׂוֹת מֵחֻקּוֹת הַתּוֹעֵבֹת אֲשֶׁר נַעֲשׂוּ לִפְנֵיכֶם
וְלֹא תִטַּמְּאוּ בָּהֶם אֲנִי אני, טדה״ד כוז״י יְהֹוָה אהדנ״יאהדונהי אֱלֹהֵיכֶם: ילה:

ON A LEAP YEAR: HAFTARAH OF ACHAREI MOT

יוחזקאל פרק כב

22 1 וַיְהִי אל דְבַר ראה ־יְהֹוָה אהדנ״יאהדונהי אֵלַי לֵאמֹר: 2 וְאַתָּה בֶן־אָדָם
מ״ה הֲתִשְׁפֹּט הֲתִשְׁפֹּט אֶת־עִיר בוזוךר, עֵרי, סנדלפו״ן הַדָּמִים וְהוֹדַעְתָּהּ אֵת
כָּל יל ־תּוֹעֲבוֹתֶיהָ: 3 וְאָמַרְתָּ כֹּה היי אָמַר אֲדֹנָי יְהֹוָה לבה אהדנ״יאהדונהי עִיר
בוזוךר, עֵרי, סנדלפו״ן שֹׁפֶכֶת דָּם רבוע אהיה בְּתוֹכָהּ לָבוֹא עִתָּהּ וְעָשְׂתָה גִלּוּלִים
עָלֶיהָ פהל לְטָמְאָה: 4 בְּדָמֵךְ אֲשֶׁר־שָׁפַכְתְּ אָשַׁמְתְּ וּבְגִלּוּלַיִךְ אֲשֶׁר־
עָשִׂית טָמֵאת וַתַּקְרִיבִי יָמַיִךְ וַתָּבוֹא עַד־שְׁנוֹתָיִךְ עַל־כֵּן נְתַתִּיךְ
חֶרְפָּה לַגּוֹיִם וְקַלָּסָה לְכָל־הָאֲרָצוֹת: אדני יה 5 הַקְּרֹבוֹת וְהָרְחֹקוֹת
מִמֵּךְ יִתְקַלְּסוּ־בָךְ טְמֵאַת הַשֵּׁם שדי יהוה רַבַּת הַמְּהוּמָה: 6 הִנֵּה מ״ה יה
נְשִׂיאֵי יִשְׂרָאֵל אִישׁ ע״ה קנ״א קס״א לִזְרֹעוֹ הָיוּ בָךְ לְמַעַן שְׁפָךְ־דָּם: רבוע אהיה
7 אָב וָאֵם יוהך, ע״ה מ״ב קנ״א ב״ן הֵקַלּוּ בָךְ לַגֵּר עָשׂוּ בַעֹשֶׁק בְּתוֹכֵךְ יָתוֹם יוסף

7 In you they have made light of father and mother; in the midst of you they have oppressed the stranger, in you they have wronged the fatherless and the widow.

8 You have despised My Holy Things and have profaned My Sabbaths.

9 In you are talebearers to shed blood; and in you they have eaten on the mountains and in the midst of you have committed lewd acts.

10 In you, they have uncovered their father's nakedness; in you they have humbled her that was unclean in her impurity.

11 And each has committed abomination with his neighbor's wife, and each has lewdly defiled his daughter-in-law, and each in you has humbled his sister, his father's daughter.

12 In you they have taken gifts to shed blood; you have taken interest and increase, and you have greedily gained from your neighbors by oppression, and have forgotten Me, says the Lord, God.

13 See, therefore, I have smitten My Hand at your dishonest gain which you have made, and at your blood you have shed in your midst.

14 Can your heart endure or can your hands be strong in the day I deal with you? I, the Lord, have spoken, and will do it.

15 And I will scatter you among the nations and disperse you through the countries; and I will consume to your filthiness out of you.

16 And you shall be profaned in yourself in the eyes of the nations, you shall know that I am the Lord.' "

וְאַלְמָנָ֖ה הוֹנ֥וּ בָֽךְ׃ 8 קָדָשַׁ֣י בָּזִ֔ית וְאֶת־שַׁבְּתֹתַ֖י חִלָּֽלְתְּ׃ 9 אַנְשֵׁ֣י רָכִ֗יל

הָ֤יוּ בָךְ֙ לְמַ֣עַן שְׁפָךְ־דָּ֔ם רבוע אהיה וְאֶל־הֶֽהָרִים֙ הַיִיה אָ֣כְלוּ בָ֔ךְ זִמָּ֖ה עָשׂ֥וּ

בְתוֹכֵֽךְ׃ 10 עֶרְוַת־אָ֖ב גִּלָּה־בָ֑ךְ טֻמְאַ֥ת הַנִּדָּ֖ה עִנּ֥וּ ג"פ מ"ב, רבוע אדני בָֽךְ׃

11 וְאִ֣ישׁ ע"ה קנ"א קס"א אֶת־אֵ֤שֶׁת רֵעֵ֙הוּ֙ עָשָׂ֣ה תּֽוֹעֵבָ֔ה וְאִ֗ישׁ ע"ה קנ"א קס"א

אֶת־כַּלָּת֛וֹ טִמֵּ֥א בְזִמָּ֑ה וְאִ֣ישׁ ע"ה קנ"א קס"א אֶת־אֲחֹת֧וֹ בַת־אָבִ֛יו עִנָּה־

בָֽךְ׃ 12 שֹׁ֣חַד לָֽקְחוּ־בָ֖ךְ לְמַ֣עַן שְׁפָךְ־דָּ֑ם רבוע אהיה נֶ֧שֶׁךְ וְתַרְבִּ֣ית לָקַ֗חַתְּ

וַתְּבַצְּעִ֤י רֵעַ֙יִךְ֙ בַּעֹ֔שֶׁק וְאֹתִ֥י שָׁכַ֖חַתְּ נְאֻ֥ם אֲדֹנָ֥י כלה יֱהֹוִ֖האהדונהי׃

13 וְהִנֵּה֙ מ"ה יה הִכֵּ֣יתִי כַפִּ֔י אֶל־בִּצְעֵ֖ךְ אֲשֶׁ֣ר עָשִׂ֑ית וְעַל־דָּמֵ֔ךְ אֲשֶׁ֥ר

הָי֖וּ בְתוֹכֵֽךְ׃ 14 הֲיַעֲמֹ֤ד לִבֵּךְ֙ אִם־ יוהך, ע"ה מ"ב תֶּחֱזַ֣קְנָה יָדַ֔יִךְ לַיָּמִ֕ים

נלך אֲשֶׁ֣ר אֲנִ֗י אני, טדהד כוז"ו עֹשֶׂ֣ה אוֹתָ֑ךְ אֲנִ֞י אני, טדהד כוז"ו יֱהֹוָ֧האהדונהי

דִּבַּ֖רְתִּי ראה וְעָשִֽׂיתִי׃ 15 וַהֲפִיצוֹתִ֤י אוֹתָךְ֙ בַּגּוֹיִ֔ם וְזֵרִיתִ֖יךְ בָּאֲרָצ֑וֹת

וַהֲתִמֹּתִ֥י טֻמְאָתֵ֖ךְ מִמֵּֽךְ׃ 16 וְנִחַ֥לְתְּ בָּ֖ךְ לְעֵינֵ֣י ריבוע מ"ה גוֹיִ֑ם וְיָדַ֖עַתְּ כִּֽי־

אֲנִ֣י אני, טדהד כוז"ו יֱהֹוָֽהאהדונהי׃

KEDOSHIM

LESSON OF KEDOSHIM
(Leviticus 19:1-20:27)

"You shall be holy" (*Leviticus 19:2*)

In most calendar years, the Chapter of Kedoshim, meaning "holy" in the plural, is generally read together with the previous Chapter of Acharei Mot, meaning "after death." If you join the two translations, they read: "After death, they are holy."

It has been said that people become holy only after they die. There's some truth to this. After all, who is thought to be holy in his or her own time? The Israelites even wanted to do away with Moses, who cried out to the Creator, "They're going to kill me any minute!" when they were literally at his throat. The Romans wanted to kill Rav Shimon bar Yochai, as did a number of Israelites. It is even written of Mordechai, who saved the lives of so many Persians and, in fact, saved the entire kingdom of Persia, that "he was loved by most of his brethren." In other words, there were still a certain number of people who did not particularly care for Mordechai.

Both Rav Isaac Luria (the Ari) and his disciple Rav Chaim Vital also had problems with their fellow rabbis, and there is no question that Rav Moshe Chaim Luzzato suffered until the day he left this world. From an early age, he was tormented by his adversaries, and his books were burned. In our own time, Rav Ashlag and Rav Brandwein were persecuted ostensibly in the name of Kabbalah. Even Rav and Karen Berg had to overcome great obstacles put before them by people who wanted to prevent Kabbalah from being made available to the layperson.

Often, it is only when people leave this world that we see them for who they really were and for what they had to give us. Herein lies a number of lessons that can elevate us, the first lesson being that we begin to appreciate what we have only when we start to lose it. How many of us pray for health only when our health is jeopardized, or for financial sustenance only when our bank accounts are low?

We will never lose the blessings in our life if we can learn to appreciate them. At one time, for example, there were many *tzaddikim* (righteous people) in the world, but no one paid attention to them. When the Ari was alive, not all of his fellow citizens of Safed came to hear him speak. But when he left this world, everyone thought, "He lived right here among us in our city, and we did not take the opportunity to connect to him!" This also happened with Rav Ashlag and Rav Brandwein, neither of whom had many students. Now they have far more students than they did when they were alive. Many people of their generation said that had they only known these great teachers existed, they would have connected to them. Only after we lose something do we appreciate what we had.

A second lesson arises when we shift the perspective we've gained from the first lesson. Just as we do not appreciate others, other people do not appreciate us. In response, we may do things just so people will notice us. Here, we must learn from the *tzaddikim*, who never wanted or expected anything in return for their labors on behalf of others. They knew that if they put their energy into getting the attention of the people around them, they would sacrifice their connection to the Light.

Many *tzaddikim* were not only unappreciated, they were also actually hated. Yet that hatred did not stop them from helping others. If we think about what we will get in return for our labors, we can never be holy. We must live in accordance with Acharei Mot–Kedoshim, even though we may not see the results in our lifetime. We should not do things expecting a payoff. The truth is that if we act from the heart when we help others, the payoff will come. It may not come today or tomorrow or even the day after, but it will come. And it may not happen in the way we expect. In fact, it will probably happen in a way we never dreamed of. But if we give and share, the good that we have done will come back to us.

The third lesson concerns the fact that we are the most important generation in all history. This is not because we are spiritually greater than those who came before us, but rather because we live in the time of Messiah. Therefore, we have a greater responsibility than other generations had: We must learn how to be immortal. *Tzaddikim* are the most alive after they have left this world. That is what we learn from Acharei Mot–Kedoshim. Everyone wanted to kill the *tzaddikim*; no one wanted to listen to what they had to say. Only when they left this world did they become holy, and that is what being immortal means: being like a *tzaddik*, being alive even after death.

The generations of 100 or 1000 years ago did not have the merit of living in the time of Messiah. Our merit is not only that we can rise above death when we leave this world, remaining alive even when our body lies in its grave, but also that we can actually overcome Satan and completely erase the power of the Angel of Death. We can bring the energy of life after death into our life before death and thereby achieve immortality.

We are taught that Rav Elimelech overcame death. It is written in the book *Ha'achim HaKedoshim* that during the Holocaust, the Germans invaded his hometown of Lizhensk. They brutally murdered many people there, and only a few managed to hide in Rav Elimelech's mausoleum, hoping to evade death by his merit.

The Nazis searched for money and jewelry in the townspeople's homes. When they didn't find much, they went to dig up the graves in the cemetery, hoping to find buried riches. Next to Rav Elimelech's grave, they found a few frightened people trying to hide. The Nazis commanded them to open the grave, but the town rabbi forbade them from doing so. Regardless of their fear of the soldiers, their respect was even greater for Rav Elimelech's holiness. The Nazis demanded again that the grave be opened, finally calling the groundskeeper to do it. But even this man would not execute their command. He had too much appreciation for the righteousness of Rav Elimelech.

Finally, the Nazis themselves opened the grave. They found Rav Elimelech's coffin intact, even though it had been more than 150 years since his passing. When they opened the coffin, they were amazed to find inside a body so beautiful and perfect. They were so shocked that they fled. The people who had been crouching in the cemetery then escaped to the forest where they were able to hide, and those who survived the war told how Rav Elimelech protected them even after he had left this world.

After the Holocaust, the people who returned to Lizhensk found it desolate. Even the cemetery had been destroyed. From their neighbors, the returning survivors heard another tale of what happened at Rav Elimelech's grave. There was a band of thieves in town who took anything that was left after the Nazis killed and plundered. They, too, had ventured to the cemetery to look for buried treasure. They thought that the people had hidden their belongings in the graves. But like the Nazis before them, they did not find a thing.

The leader of the thieves suggested that they dig up the great rabbi's grave. The townspeople used to leave notes with their prayers on the tombs of the righteous, and the tragedy and danger of the times had resulted in an unusually large number of notes. The bandits refused to comply with their leader's decision to open the grave because of the holiness of the *tzaddik*, which was obvious from all the messages that had been left. Only the leader was arrogant and foolish enough to dig up the grave. He was sure he would find a great deal of wealth, so without anyone's help, he desecrated Rav Elimelech's grave.

The bandit leader committed a double sin. Not only is it forbidden to desecrate the gravesite of a *tzaddik*, but it is also forbidden to steal or even to waste funds that have been designated for holy uses. This is why it is so important to take great care of the money designated for any organization whose purpose is to help others and that uses its funds for the purpose of revealing Light in the world and for producing spiritual tools that help people connect to the Light. We must pay close attention to even the smallest things we do. Rav Berg calls *tzedakah* (charity) "*mammon ha kodesh*" (holy wealth). We must never waste it, and more importantly, we must make sure that we are not holding on to money that is meant for *tzedakah*. We must never hold on to money that is not meant for us, and sacred funds especially cannot help us as individuals, no matter how well they're invested.

The story goes on to say that after a few days, the band of thieves celebrated their pillaging. They drank very heavily and began to fight with the leader. When the fight escalated, the thieves attacked and killed their leader, and then drank to their success. The story of the slaying spread among the remaining inhabitants of Lizhensk. They saw God's hand in the fight and the slaying, for there could be no other ending to the life of anyone who defiled Rav Elimelech's grave.

These stories show how very much alive Rav Elimelech of Lizhensk is. As with Rav Elimelech, anyone who overcomes his or her death is called holy. There are holy people whom we do not see, whose bodies have left this world but who have truly transcended death. The only reason why we cannot see Moses—for we know he did not die—is because we have yet to overcome death's power over our own lives. Moses is alive in the same way as Rav Elimelech. The same is written about Elijah the Prophet and about Enoch, who became the angel Metatron. Nevertheless, we cannot see any of them, although some people have the ability to commune with them. Those who rise above death can connect to those who left this world but did not die. Rav Shimon studied with Moses. How could he learn with Moses in this world if Moses was no longer part of it? The answer is that because Moses did not die, he was still present in Rav Shimon's world and is still present in ours. Only those who strive to overcome death can ever hope to connect to Moses. Only those who are holy—who are beyond death—can see and connect with Moses and Elijah. Elijah the Prophet was able to teach Rav Isaac Luria (the Ari), because the Ari lived beyond death's grasp.

We might ask why only Elijah the Prophet visits people in this world. When we hear about prophets appearing to human beings, we don't hear of any name other than Elijah. The reason that Elijah is the only biblical prophet still remaining in this world is because he did not die (*II Kings 2:1-17*). To merit Elijah's presence before us, we must first be holy. And what makes people holy is their ability to overcome death.

This brings to mind a story about Rav Menachem Mendel of Vitebsk (1730–1787). A *shofar* was once blown in the distance, and the townspeople asked Rav Menachem Mendel if the *Mashiach* (Messiah) was on his way, for it is written that when the *Mashiach* comes, a *shofar* will be blown upon the Mount of Olives. The rabbi came out of his house, sniffed the air, and answered, "No, the Mashiach is not coming. His smell is not in the air." His action, however, puzzled the townspeople. They asked why the Rav had to come outside in order to know, and he answered that the *Mashiach* was already in his house.

For Rav Menachem Mendel, it did not matter what took place in the outer world. His connection to the Light was already securely in place. For us, it should be likewise. We need to connect to our own personal Mashiach. Then we will be holy, beyond death, and worthy to stand in the presence of Elijah the Prophet and Moses.

SYNOPSIS OF KEDOSHIM

Sometimes it is only after the fact that we realize we were wrong about a certain situation because information was concealed from us. The Chapter of Kedoshim helps us access information when we need it so that we can see and understand clearly.

ON A LEAP YEAR: FIRST READING - ABRAHAM - CHESED

19:1 The Lord spoke to Moses, saying, 2 "Speak to the congregation of the children of Israel and say to them: Be holy because I, the Lord, your God, am Holy.

3 Each of you must honor his mother and father, and you must keep my Sabbaths. I am the Lord, your God.

4 Do not turn to idols or make gods of cast metal for yourselves. I am the Lord, your God. 5 And when you offer a sacrifice of a fellowship offering to the Lord, offer it in such a way that it will be accepted on your behalf.

6 It shall be eaten on the day you offer it and on the next day; anything left over until the third day must be burned up.

7 And if any of it is eaten on the third day, it is an abomination and will not be accepted.

FROM THE RAV

This week's reading contains a concept that, as I grew up, I didn't know existed in Judaism: "Love your neighbor as yourself." What does this mean? You mean love everybody as yourself? That idea seemed to be just one of those ideas in Torah, but it also seemed to have very little relevance to living. What about your family? Those close to you, OK, but who could think like that: Love everyone as you love yourself?

Frankly, from the point of view of Kabbalah, the word "religion" was created by a small sect of people, known as the *erev rav* (the evil ones)—evil ones who had nothing else on their minds but to express intolerance for their fellow man. Intolerance was the only reason behind the destruction of the First and Second Temples—not mighty empires, just intolerance of each other, nothing more. People at that time, abided by all the laws of religion except for the one

that states to love your neighbor; to have tolerance. In the *Zohar*, it is expressly stated that there is very little capability of removing chaos unless we can adopt this behavior of human dignity. It's not that we have to embrace our adversary; after all, even Moses asked God, "Look, get rid of these people, start over again," and Moses was a tolerant man.

The only reason Moses was chosen as the leader of the Israelites was because he was a tolerant man. He had love for his fellow man, but even he couldn't continue operating within this framework of tolerance and loving one's neighbor as oneself.

So what about us? Human dignity for your opponent, your enemy—can you treat him with anything less than human dignity? No! That is why, Kedoshim (all about loving your neighbor), isn't about morality.

Human dignity is the only possession, the only instrument that we have to remove

ON A LEAP YEAR: FIRST READING - ABRAHAM - CHESED

וַיְדַבֵּר ראה יְהֹוָהאאדניאהדונהי מהמ, אל שדי אֶל־מֹשֶׁה לֵּאמֹר: 2 דַּבֵּר ראה 19 1

אֶל־כָּל־ יִי ־עֲדַת בְּנֵי־יִשְׂרָאֵל יִיַּד וְאָמַרְתָּ אֲלֵהֶם קְדֹשִׁים תִּהְיוּ כִּי

קָדוֹשׁ אָנִי, טדהד כוזו יְהֹוָהאאדניאהדונהי אֱלֹהֵיכֶם ילה: 3 אִישׁ עה קנא קסא אִמּוֹ

וְאָבִיו תִּירָאוּ וְאֶת־שַׁבְּתֹתַי תִּשְׁמֹרוּ אֲנִי, טדהד כוזו יְהֹוָהאאדניאהדונהי

אֱלֹהֵיכֶם ילה: 4 אַל־תִּפְנוּ אֶל־הָאֱלִילִם וֵאלֹהֵי לכב, דמב, ילה מַסֵּכָה לֹא

תַעֲשׂוּ לָכֶם אֲנִי, טדהד כוזו יְהֹוָהאאדניאהדונהי אֱלֹהֵיכֶם ילה: 5 וְכִי תִזְבְּחוּ

זֶבַח שְׁלָמִים לַיהֹוָהאאדניאהדונהי לִרְצֹנְכֶם תִּזְבָּחֻהוּ: 6 בְּיוֹם עה = נגד, זן, מזבח

זִבְחֲכֶם יֵאָכֵל וּמִמָּחֳרָת וְהַנּוֹתָר עַד־יוֹם עה = נגד, זן, מזבח הַשְּׁלִישִׁי בָּאֵשׁ

אלהים דיורדין עה יִשָּׂרֵף: 7 וְאִם יוהך, עה מב הֵאָכֹל יֵאָכֵל בַּיּוֹם עה = נגד, זן, מזבח

הַשְּׁלִישִׁי פִּגּוּל הוּא לֹא יֵרָצֶה: 8 וְאֹכְלָיו עֲוֹנוֹ יִשָּׂא כִּי־אֶת־קֹדֶשׁ

קָדוֹשׁ

Leviticus 19:2 – Because God is holy and we have God inside us, we have to be holy ourselves. When we become aware of the Divine Spark in every person, we awaken the holiness in our hearts. What does it mean to be holy? It means that we are aware that the world is one complete whole and that we are all connected to each other through the spark of the Creator that exists within each of us. If we harm others, we are in essence harming ourselves. Mistreating another person is like sticking a finger into an electric socket. And because there are repercussions arising from our every word and deed, it is always in our best interest to share with others.

chaos from our lives. It's a lost cause to even try without it. Anything less than human dignity in this world makes it impossible to remove chaos. So we have Kedoshim, this very powerful lesson—a small section, but one relating to the essence of what we are doing here. This is the only way we can earn our bread.

However, the closer an individual comes to another individual, which is the basis for love, the greater the chance of abuse. We should love those closest to us, but it often becomes otherwise. How many stories do we hear about how difficult it is to love those nearest us? Satan knows this. Therefore, it's not a question of a moral issue—that's not why we come here, to The Kabbalah Centre on Shabbat. Rather, we come here to receive and connect to the energy that empowers us to restrict so that we do not react in a way that would result in anything less than human dignity.

⁸ *Whoever eats it will be held responsible because he has desecrated what is holy to the Lord; and that soul will be cut off from his people.*

⁹ *And when you reap the harvest of your land, do not reap to the very edges of your field or gather the gleanings of your harvest.*

¹⁰ *And do not go over your vineyard a second time or pick up the fruit of your vineyard that have fallen, you shall leave them for the poor and for the stranger. I am the Lord your God.*

¹¹ *You shall not steal; neither shall you deal falsely nor lie to one another.*

¹² *And you shall not swear falsely by My Name and so profane the Name of your God. I am the Lord.*

¹³ *You shall not oppress your neighbor or rob him, and not hold back the wages of a hired servant overnight.*

¹⁴ *Your shall not curse the deaf or put a stumbling block in front of the blind, but fear your God. I am the Lord.*

ON A LEAP YEAR: SECOND READING - ISAAC – GEVURAH
WHEN CONNECTED: FIFTH READING - AARON - HOD

¹⁵ *You shall not pervert justice; do not show partiality to the poor or favoritism to the great, but judge your neighbor fairly.*

¹⁶ *You shall not go about spreading slander among your people, nor shall you do anything that endangers your neighbor's life. I am the Lord.*

תַּעֲזֹב

Leviticus 19:10 – The people were told here that they should leave a little of the harvest for the poor to gather up. Something not shared is something not properly used at all; this is why it's important to give gifts to the poor. Some people have nothing in order to be Vessels for those who wish to share. The most powerful gift to share is the wisdom of Kabbalah. Darkness—the cause of all pain and suffering—can exist only in the absence of Light. Sharing wisdom is like lighting a candle in a darkened world. Knowledge itself is the substance of spiritual Light, immortality, and increasing joy.

לֹא תִּגְנֹבוּ

Leviticus 19:11 – To be connected with the Light of the Creator, we have to be honest with ourselves and with others. Rav Ashlag said that he found that even the smallest untruth can disconnect us from the Light.

יְהֹוָאדנִיאהדונהי　וְחֻלָּל　וחיים, בינה ע"ה　וְנִכְרְתָה　הַנֶּפֶשׁ　רמ"ח - ז' וזות　הַהִוא　מֵעַמֶּיהָ׃

9　וּבְקֻצְרְכֶם　אֶת־קְצִיר　אַרְצְכֶם　לֹא　תְכַלֶּה　נתה, קס"א קנ"א קמ"ג　פְּאַת　שָׂדְךָ

לִקְצֹר　וְלֶקֶט　קְצִירְךָ　לֹא　תְלַקֵּט׃　10　וְכַרְמְךָ　לֹא　תְעוֹלֵל　וּפֶרֶט　רפ"ח ע"ה

כַּרְמְךָ　לֹא　תְלַקֵּט　לֶעָנִי　רבוע מ"ה　וְלַגֵּר　תַעֲזֹב　אֹתָם　אֲנִי, טדה"ד כוז"ו　אֲנִי

יְהֹוָאדנִיאהדונהי　אֱלֹהֵיכֶם　ילה׃　11　לֹא　תִגְנֹבוּ　וְלֹא־תְכַחֲשׁוּ　וְלֹא־תְשַׁקְּרוּ

אִישׁ　ע"ה קנ"א קס"א　בַּעֲמִיתוֹ׃　12　וְלֹא־תִשָּׁבְעוּ　בִשְׁמִי　רבוע ע"ב ורבוע ס"ג　לַשָּׁקֶר

וְחִלַּלְתָּ　אֶת־שֵׁם　אֱלֹהֶיךָ　יהוה שדי　אֲנִי　ילה　אֲנִי, טדה"ד כוז"ו　יְהֹוָאדנִיאהדונהי׃　13　לֹא־

תַעֲשֹׁק　אֶת־רֵעֲךָ　וְלֹא　תִגְזֹל　לֹא־תָלִין　פְּעֻלַּת　שָׂכִיר　אִתְּךָ　עַד־בֹּקֶר׃

14　לֹא־תְקַלֵּל　חֵרֵשׁ　וְלִפְנֵי　וחכמה בינה　עִוֵּר　לֹא　תִתֵּן　ב"פ כהת　מִכְשֹׁל　וְיָרֵאתָ

מֵּאֱלֹהֶיךָ　ילה　אֲנִי　אֲנִי, טדה"ד כוז"ו　יְהֹוָאדנִיאהדונהי׃

ON A LEAP YEAR: SECOND READING - ISAAC – GEVURAH
WHEN CONNECTED: FIFTH READING - AARON - HOD

15　לֹא־תַעֲשׂוּ　עָוֶל　בַּמִּשְׁפָּט　ע"ה ה"פ אלהים　לֹא־תִשָּׂא　פְנֵי　וחכמה בינה　־דָל　בוכ"ו

וְלֹא　תֶהְדַּר　פְּנֵי　וחכמה בינה　גָדוֹל　להה, מבה, יזל, אום　בְּצֶדֶק　תִּשְׁפֹּט　עֲמִיתֶךָ׃

16　לֹא־תֵלֵךְ　רָכִיל　בְּעַמֶּיךָ　לֹא　תַעֲמֹד　עַל־דַּם　רבוע אהיה　רֵעֶךָ　אֲנִי

אֲנִי, טדה"ד כוז"ו　יְהֹוָאדנִיאהדונהי׃　17　לֹא־תִשְׂנָא　אֶת־אָחִיךָ　בִּלְבָבֶךָ　הוֹכֵחַ

וְלֹא־תְשַׁקְּרוּ

Leviticus 19:11 – Honesty in business is important because if we receive something dishonestly, it will be taken away from us. Moreover, we could end up losing even what we already had. There is a spiritual order governing what we're supposed to receive: If we receive something the "wrong" way (for example, by theft or fraud), we lose not only what we gained but also what we were supposed to receive in the future. In other words, if we get what we don't deserve, something else will be taken away.

לֹא־תִשְׂנָא

Leviticus 19:17 – It's important to talk directly to people and to express any feelings of anger—in a non-reactive and non-judgmental way, of course—rather than keep the anger inside. Anger that is stored in our heart distorts our judgment. When we bring something out into the open, we can deal with it; when we keep it inside, it festers.

17 You shall not hate your brother in your heart; you shall surely rebuke your neighbor frankly so you will not share in his guilt. 18 You shall not seek revenge or bear a grudge against one of your people, but you shall love your neighbor as yourself. I am the Lord.

19 You shall keep My Statutes. You shall not mate your cattle with different kinds of animals; you shall not sow your field with two kinds of seed; nor shall you wear clothing woven of two kinds of material mingled together.

20 And if a man sleeps with a woman who is a bondmaid promised to another man but who has not been redeemed or given her freedom, there shall be inquisition, yet they are not to be put to death, because she had not been freed.

21 And he must bring his forfeit to the Lord at the entrance to the Tent of Meeting, a ram for a guilt offering.

22 And the priest will make atonement for him with the ram of the guilt offering before the Lord for the sin he has committed, and he shall be forgiven for his sin which he has committed.

ON A LEAP YEAR: THIRD READING - JACOB - TIFERET

23 And when you will enter the land and plant all kinds of fruit trees for food, regard its fruit as forbidden; for three years, you are to consider it forbidden; it must not be eaten. 24 In the fourth year, all its fruit will be holy, an offering of praise to the Lord.

וְאָהַבְתָּ לְרֵעֲךָ כָּמוֹךָ

Leviticus 19:18 – The prerequisite to be able to "love your neighbor as yourself" is the ability to love ourselves. When we reach a place where we love ourselves, we can connect to the reason the whole world was created. It was created to give us the ability to be able to share with others and to give of ourselves as well. When we love ourselves, we gain the ability to bring others into our lives.

וְחֻקֹּתַי

Leviticus 19:19 – There are certain combinations and mixtures (for example, in foods, clothing, relationships, and so on) that are forbidden. We don't have to be in the presence of anyone who is

still overwhelmingly negative, as long as we have tried to deal with them lovingly and proactively.

הָאָרֶץ

Leviticus 19:23 – From this verse, we learn that we need to connect with the Light of the Creator to the greatest extent possible. To achieve that connection, however, there are certain restrictions that are important to follow. In Israel, for example, we don't eat fruit from a tree that is less than three years old because the tree is still developing. We don't cut a child's hair during his or her first three years of life, either, because according to Kabbalah, human hairs are spiritual antennae that draw spiritual Light into our lives; before the child is three, his spiritual potential is

תּוֹכִיחַ אֶת־עֲמִיתֶךָ וְלֹא־תִשָּׂא עָלָיו וֵזְטְא: 18 לֹא־תִקֹּם וְלֹא־תִטֹּר

אֶת־בְּנֵי עַמֶּךָ ה הויות, גמם וְאָהַבְתָּ ב"פ רז, ב"פ אור, ב"פ אין־סוף לְרֵעֲךָ כָּמוֹךָ אלהים, מום

אֲנִי אני, טדה"ד כו"ו יְהֹוָׂאהּדֹנהּי: 19 אֶת־חֻקֹּתַי תִּשְׁמֹרוּ בְּהֶמְתְּךָ לֹא־

תַרְבִּיעַ כִּלְאַיִם שָׂדְךָ לֹא־תִזְרַע כִּלְאָיִם וּבֶגֶד כִּלְאַיִם שַׁעַטְנֵז לֹא

יַעֲלֶה עָלֶיךָ רבוע מ"ה: 20 וְאִישׁ ע"ה קנ"א קס"א כִּי־יִשְׁכַּב אֶת־אִשָּׁה שִׁכְבַת־

זֶרַע וְהִוא שִׁפְחָה ע"ה ג' מלוי אהיה נֶחֱרֶפֶת לְאִישׁ ע"ה קנ"א קס"א וְהָפְדֵּה לֹא

נִפְדָּתָה אוֹ חֻפְשָׁה לֹא נִתַּן־לָהּ בִּקֹּרֶת תִּהְיֶה לֹא יוּמְתוּ כִּי־לֹא

חֻפָּשָׁה: 21 וְהֵבִיא אֶת־אֲשָׁמוֹ לַיהֹוָׂאהּדֹנהּי אֶל־פֶּתַח אֹהֶל לאה מוֹעֵד

אֵיל אָשָׁם: 22 וְכִפֶּר מצפצ עָלָיו הַכֹּהֵן מלה בְּאֵיל הָאָשָׁם לִפְנֵי חכמה בינה

יְהֹוָׂאהּדֹנהּי עַל־חַטָּאתוֹ אֲשֶׁר חָטָא וְנִסְלַח לוֹ מֵחַטָּאתוֹ אֲשֶׁר

חָטָא:

ON A LEAP YEAR: THIRD READING - JACOB - TIFERET

23 וְכִי־תָבֹאוּ אֶל־הָאָרֶץ אלהים דההין ע"ה וּנְטַעְתֶּם כָּל־יְיִ עֵץ ע"ה קס"א מַאֲכָל

יהוה אדני וַעֲרַלְתֶּם עָרְלָתוֹ אֶת־פִּרְיוֹ שָׁלֹשׁ שָׁנִים יִהְיֶה ייי לָכֶם עֲרֵלִים

לֹא יֵאָכֵל: 24 וּבַשָּׁנָה הָרְבִיעִת יִהְיֶה ייי כָּל־יְיִ פִּרְיוֹ קֹדֶשׁ הִלּוּלִים

---

not yet fully formed. We do not eat from a young tree or cut a young child's hair because the Light of the Creator has to be fully developed in the fruit and in the child before it can be absorbed. The *Zohar* explains:

> ... a tree, THE SECRET OF ZEIR ANPIN, produces fruits only in the soil, DENOTING MALCHUT. The earth brings them forth, and shows those fruits to the world. The earth produces fruits only from another force above it, MEANING FROM ZEIR ANPIN, just as every female produces fruits only as a result of the force of the male. And that fruit, THAT MALCHUT CALLED

'EARTH', PRODUCES and does not become completed in its fullness until three years, MEANING UNTIL MALCHUT RECEIVES THREE COLUMNS FROM ZEIR ANPIN. The force upon it does not get appointed Above until its completion. After completion, its force is then appointed upon it, and then the earth is established by it. Prior to three years, MEANING BEFORE RECEIVING ALL THREE COLUMNS, the earth is not yet established by it, WITH ZEIR ANPIN, and not completed with him. After MALCHUT is perfected and set together, then there is perfection.
> — The Zohar, Kedoshim 21:124

25 But in the fifth year you may eat its fruit, that your harvest will be increased. I am the Lord your God.

26 You shall not eat anything with blood in it; not shall you practice divination or sorcery.

27 You shall not cut the hair at the sides of your head or clip off the edges of your beard.

28 You shall not cut your bodies for the dead or put tattoo marks on yourselves. I am the Lord.

29 Do not profane your daughter by making her a prostitute, lest the land turn to prostitution and be filled with lewdness.

30 You shall keep My Sabbaths and have reverence for My Sanctuary. I am the Lord.

31 Do not turn to ghosts or seek out familiar spirits, to be defiled by them. I am the Lord your God.

32 You shall rise in the presence of the aged, and show honor for the elderly and you shall fear your God. I am the Lord.

ON A LEAP YEAR: FOURTH READING - MOSES – NETZACH
WHEN CONNECTED: SIXTH READING - JOSEPH - YESOD

33 And if a stranger lives with you in your land, you shall not mistreat him.

34 The stranger living with you must be treated as if he is a citizen, and you shall love him as you would yourself, for you used to be strangers in the land of Egypt. I am the Lord your God.

35 You shall not use dishonest standards when measuring length, weight or quantity.

שַׁבְּתֹתַי

Leviticus 19:30 – Shabbat is the time when our spiritual battery is recharged. The energy of Shabbat creates a very powerful connection to the Upper Worlds. If we don't take at least five minutes of our Saturday to connect to Shabbat, we can expect a week filled with less Light.

כַּיֹּהֹוָ֖אֲדֹנָי֑אֱלֹהִ֑ים֒: 25 וּבַשָּׁנָ֣ה הַ֣חֲמִישִׁ֗ת תֹּאכְלוּ֙ אֶת־פִּרְי֔וֹ לְהוֹסִ֥יף לָכֶ֖ם

תְּבוּאָת֑וֹ אֲנִ֛י יְהֹוָ֨אֲדֹנָי֑אֱלֹהִ֑ים֒ אֱלֹֽהֵיכֶֽם: 26 לֹ֥א תֹאכְל֖וּ עַל־

הַדָּ֑ם לֹ֥א תְנַֽחֲשׁ֖וּ וְלֹ֥א תְעוֹנֵֽנוּ: 27 לֹ֣א תַקִּ֔פוּ פְּאַ֖ת רֹֽאשְׁכֶ֑ם וְלֹ֣א

תַשְׁחִ֔ית אֵ֖ת פְּאַ֥ת זְקָנֶֽךָ: 28 וְשֶׂ֣רֶט לָנֶ֗פֶשׁ לֹ֤א תִתְּנוּ֙

בִּבְשַׂרְכֶ֔ם וּכְתֹ֣בֶת קַֽעֲקַ֔ע לֹ֥א תִתְּנ֖וּ בָּכֶ֑ם אֲנִ֖י

יְהֹוָ֨אֲדֹנָי֑אֱלֹהִ֑ים֒: 29 אַל־תְּחַלֵּ֥ל אֶת־בִּתְּךָ֖ לְהַזְנוֹתָ֑הּ וְלֹא־תִזְנֶ֣ה הָאָ֔רֶץ

וּמָלְאָ֥ה הָאָ֖רֶץ זִמָּֽה: 30 אֶת־שַׁבְּתֹתַ֣י תִּשְׁמֹ֗רוּ

וּמִקְדָּשִׁ֖י תִּירָ֑אוּ אֲנִ֖י יְהֹוָֽה: 31 אַל־תִּפְנ֤וּ אֶל־הָֽאֹבֹת֙

וְאֶל־הַיִּדְּעֹנִ֔ים אַל־תְּבַקְשׁ֖וּ לְטָמְאָ֣ה בָהֶ֑ם אֲנִ֛י יְהֹוָ֨אֲדֹנָי֑אֱלֹהִ֑ים֒

אֱלֹֽהֵיכֶֽם: 32 מִפְּנֵ֤י שֵׂיבָה֙ תָּק֔וּם וְהָדַרְתָּ֖ פְּנֵ֣י

זָקֵ֑ן וְיָרֵ֥אתָ מֵּאֱלֹהֶ֖יךָ אֲנִ֥י יְהֹוָֽאֲדֹנָי֑אֱלֹהִ֑ים֒:

ON A LEAP YEAR: FOURTH READING - MOSES – NETZACH
WHEN CONNECTED: SIXTH READING - JOSEPH - YESOD

33 וְכִֽי־יָג֧וּר אִתְּךָ֛ גֵּ֖ר בְּאַרְצְכֶ֑ם לֹ֥א תוֹנ֖וּ אֹתֽוֹ: 34 כְּאֶזְרָ֣ח מִכֶּ֗ם

יִהְיֶ֤ה לָכֶם֙ הַגֵּ֣ר ׀ הַגָּ֣ר אִתְּכֶ֔ם וְאָהַבְתָּ֥

ל֖וֹ כָּמ֑וֹךָ כִּֽי־גֵרִ֥ים הֱיִיתֶ֖ם בְּאֶ֣רֶץ מִצְרָ֑יִם אֲנִ֖י

אֲנִ֛י יְהֹוָ֨אֲדֹנָי֑אֱלֹהִ֑ים֒ אֱלֹֽהֵיכֶֽם: 35 לֹא־תַעֲשׂ֥וּ עָ֖וֶל בַּמִּשְׁפָּ֑ט

בַּמִּדָּ֕ה בַּמִּשְׁקָ֖ל וּבַמְּשׂוּרָֽה: 36 מֹ֣אזְנֵי צֶ֜דֶק אַבְנֵי־צֶ֗דֶק

אֵ֥יפַת צֶ֛דֶק וְהִ֥ין צֶ֖דֶק יִהְיֶ֣ה לָכֶ֑ם אֲנִ֖י יְהֹוָ֨אֲדֹנָי֑אֱלֹהִ֑ים֒

עָ֖וֶל

Leviticus 19:35 – It's very important to avoid being tempted by things that are not good for us. For example, if we know a married person is interested in us, we should try not to be around that person. Even flirting with him or her, with no intention of going any further, can be harmful.

36 Use honest scales and honest weights, an honest ephah and an honest hin. I am the Lord your God, who brought you out of Egypt.

37 And you shall observe all My Statutes and all My Ordinances and follow them. I am the Lord."

ON A LEAP YEAR: FIFTH READING - AARON - HOD

20:1 And the Lord spoke to Moses, saying,

2 "Say to the children of Israel: Any Israelite or any stranger living in Israel who gives any of his children to Molech must be put to death; the people of the land are to stone him with stones.

3 I will also set My Face against that man and I will cut him off from his people; for by giving his children to Molech, he has defiled My Sanctuary and profaned My Holy Name.

4 And if the people of the land close their eyes from that man when he gives one of his children to Molech and they fail to put him to death,

5 then I will set My Face against that man and against his family and will cut off him and all that follow after him, to go astray after Molech, from their people.

6 And the soul who turns to ghosts and to the familiar spirits to go astray by following them, I will set My Face against that soul and I will cut him off from his people.

7 Therefore, sanctify yourselves and be holy, because I am the Lord your God.

לַמֹּלֶךְ

Leviticus 20:2 – The reading here discusses the Creator's prohibition against any sacrifices of children to the "god" known as *Molech*. And on the subject of children, we know that parents have a great responsibility to protect their children from harm and to ensure that only good things happen to them.

אֱלֹהֵיכֶ֑ם ילה אֲשֶׁר־הוֹצֵ֤אתִי אֶתְכֶם֙ מֵאֶ֣רֶץ אלהים דאלפין מִצְרָ֑יִם מצר־

37 וּשְׁמַרְתֶּ֤ם אֶת־כָּל־ ילי חֻקֹּתַי֙ וְאֶת־כָּל־ ילי ־מִשְׁפָּטַ֔י וַעֲשִׂיתֶ֖ם אֹתָ֑ם

אֲנִ֖י אני, טרהד כוזו יְהֹוָֽה אדניאהדונהי׃

ON A LEAP YEAR: FIFTH READING - AARON - HOD

20 1 וַיְדַבֵּ֥ר ראה יְהֹוָ֖ה אדניאהדונהי אֶל־מֹשֶׁ֥ה מהע, אל שדי לֵּאמֹֽר׃ 2 וְאֶל־בְּנֵ֣י

יִשְׂרָאֵ֘ל תֹּאמַר֒ אִ֣ישׁ ע"ה קנ"א קס"א אִ֣ישׁ ע"ה קנ"א קס"א מִבְּנֵ֣י יִשְׂרָאֵ֗ל וּמִן־הַגֵּ֤ר

הַגָּר֙ בן קנ"א בְּיִשְׂרָאֵ֔ל אֲשֶׁ֨ר יִתֵּ֧ן מִזַּרְע֛וֹ לַמֹּ֖לֶךְ מ֣וֹת יוּמָ֑ת עַ֥ם

הָאָ֖רֶץ אלהים דההין ע"ה יִרְגְּמֻ֥הוּ בָאָֽבֶן יוד הה ואו הה 3 וַאֲנִ֞י ב"פ אהיה יהוה אֶתֵּ֤ן אֶת־

פָּנַי֙ וחכמה בינה בָּאִ֣ישׁ ע"ה קנ"א קס"א הַה֔וּא וְהִכְרַתִּ֥י אֹת֖וֹ מִקֶּ֣רֶב עַמּ֑וֹ כִּ֤י מִזַּרְעוֹ֙

נָתַ֣ן לַמֹּ֔לֶךְ לְמַ֗עַן טַמֵּא֙ אֶת־מִקְדָּשִׁ֔י וּלְחַלֵּ֖ל אֶת־שֵׁ֥ם יהוה שדי קָדְשִֽׁי׃

4 וְאִ֡ם יוהך, ע"ה מ"ב הַעְלֵ֣ם יַעְלִ֩ימוּ֩ עַ֨ם הָאָ֜רֶץ אלהים דההין ע"ה אֶת־עֵֽינֵיהֶם֙ ריבוע מ"ה

מִן־הָאִ֣ישׁ זו"ף אדם הַה֔וּא בְּתִתּ֥וֹ מִזַּרְע֖וֹ לַמֹּ֑לֶךְ לְבִלְתִּ֖י הָמִ֥ית אֹתֽוֹ׃

5 וְשַׂמְתִּ֨י אֲנִ֧י אני, טרהד כוזו אֶת־פָּנַ֛י וחכמה בינה בָּאִ֥ישׁ ע"ה קנ"א קס"א הַה֖וּא

וּבְמִשְׁפַּחְתּ֑וֹ וְהִכְרַתִּ֨י אֹת֜וֹ וְאֵ֣ת ׀ כָּל־ ילי ־הַזֹּנִ֤ים אַחֲרָיו֙ לִזְנ֣וֹת אַֽחֲרֵ֣י

הַמֹּ֔לֶךְ מִקֶּ֖רֶב עַמָּֽם׃ 6 וְהַנֶּ֗פֶשׁ רמ"ח + ד' ווית אֲשֶׁ֨ר תִּפְנֶ֤ה אֶל־הָֽאֹבֹת֙ וְאֶל־

הַיִּדְּעֹנִ֔ים לִזְנֹ֖ת אַחֲרֵיהֶ֑ם וְנָתַתִּ֤י אֶת־פָּנַי֙ וחכמה בינה בַּנֶּ֣פֶשׁ רמ"ח + ד' ווית הַהִ֔וא

וְהִכְרַתִּ֥י אֹת֖וֹ מִקֶּ֥רֶב עַמּֽוֹ׃ 7 וְהִ֨תְקַדִּשְׁתֶּ֔ם וִהְיִיתֶ֖ם קְדֹשִׁ֑ים כִּ֛י אֲנִ֥י

אני, טרהד כוזו יְהֹוָ֖ה אדניאהדונהי אֱלֹהֵיכֶֽם ילה׃

ON A LEAP YEAR: SIXTH READING - JOSEPH – YESOD
WHEN CONNECTED: SEVENTH READING - DAVID - MALCHUT

8 And keep My Statutes and follow them. I am the Lord, who sanctifies you.

9 If anyone curses his father or mother, he shall surely be put to death; he has cursed his father or his mother; his blood will be on his own head.

10 And if a man commits adultery with another man's wife, even he that commits adultery with the wife of his neighbor, both the adulterer and the adulteress shall surely be put to death.

11 And if a man sleeps with his father's wife, he has uncovered his father's nakedness, and both of them shall surely be put to death; their blood will be on their own heads.

12 And if a man sleeps with his daughter-in-law, both of them shall surely be put to death, they have wrought corruption; their blood will be on their own heads.

13 And if a man lies with a man as one lies with a woman, both of them have committed an abomination; they shall surely be put to death; their blood will be on their own heads.

14 And if a man takes with his wife also her mother, it is wicked, both and they shall be burned with fire, so that no wickedness will be among you.

15 And if a man lies with a beast, he shall surely be put to death, and you must kill the beast.

16 And if a woman approaches a beast to lie down with it, kill both the woman and the beast, they shall surely be put to death; their blood will be on their own heads.

17 And if a man shall take his sister, the daughter of his father or the daughter of his mother, and see her nakedness and she sees his nakedness, it is a shameful thing and they shall be cut off before the eyes of the children of their people; he has uncovered his sister's nakedness and will bear his iniquity.

כִּי־אִישׁ

Leviticus 20:9 – There are certain things that disconnect us from the Light of the Creator. Severe disconnection can lead to physical or spiritual death. Spiritual death is a disconnection from the Light of the Creator that can sometimes also result in physical death. Conversely, one can die physically and yet still be very much alive spiritually, as was true of the ancient kabbalists.

ON A LEAP YEAR: SIXTH READING - JOSEPH – YESOD
WHEN CONNECTED: SEVENTH READING - DAVID - MALCHUT

8 וּשְׁמַרְתֶּם אֶת־חֻקֹּתַי וַעֲשִׂיתֶם אֹתָם אֲנִי יְהֹוָה אני, טדהד כוזו מְקַדִּשְׁכֶם: 9 כִּי־אִישׁ אֲשֶׁר יְקַלֵּל אֶת־

אָבִיו וְאֶת־אִמּוֹ מוֹת יוּמָת אָבִיו וְאִמּוֹ קִלֵּל דָּמָיו בּוֹ: 10 וְאִישׁ

אֲשֶׁר יִנְאַף אֶת־אֵשֶׁת אִישׁ אֲשֶׁר יִנְאַף אֶת־אֵשֶׁת

רֵעֵהוּ מוֹת־יוּמַת הַנֹּאֵף וְהַנֹּאָפֶת: 11 וְאִישׁ אֲשֶׁר יִשְׁכַּב אֶת־

אֵשֶׁת אָבִיו עֶרְוַת אָבִיו גִּלָּה מוֹת־יוּמְתוּ שְׁנֵיהֶם דְּמֵיהֶם בָּם:

12 וְאִישׁ אֲשֶׁר יִשְׁכַּב אֶת־כַּלָּתוֹ מוֹת יוּמְתוּ שְׁנֵיהֶם תֶּבֶל

עָשׂוּ דְּמֵיהֶם בָּם: 13 וְאִישׁ אֲשֶׁר יִשְׁכַּב אֶת־

זָכָר מִשְׁכְּבֵי אִשָּׁה תּוֹעֵבָה עָשׂוּ שְׁנֵיהֶם מוֹת יוּמְתוּ דְּמֵיהֶם בָּם:

14 וְאִישׁ אֲשֶׁר יִקַּח אֶת־אִשָּׁה וְאֶת־אִמָּהּ זִמָּה

הִוא בָּאֵשׁ יִשְׂרְפוּ אֹתוֹ וְאֶתְהֶן וְלֹא־תִהְיֶה זִמָּה בְּתוֹכְכֶם:

15 וְאִישׁ אֲשֶׁר יִתֵּן שְׁכָבְתּוֹ בִּבְהֵמָה מוֹת יוּמָת

וְאֶת־הַבְּהֵמָה תַּהֲרֹגוּ: 16 וְאִשָּׁה אֲשֶׁר תִּקְרַב אֶל־כָּל־

בְּהֵמָה לְרִבְעָה אֹתָהּ וְהָרַגְתָּ אֶת־הָאִשָּׁה וְאֶת־הַבְּהֵמָה

מוֹת יוּמְתוּ דְּמֵיהֶם בָּם: 17 וְאִישׁ אֲשֶׁר־יִקַּח

אֶת־אֲחֹתוֹ בַּת־אָבִיו אוֹ בַת־אִמּוֹ וְרָאָה אֶת־עֶרְוָתָהּ וְהִיא־תִרְאֶה

אֶת־עֶרְוָתוֹ חֶסֶד הוּא וְנִכְרְתוּ לְעֵינֵי בְּנֵי עַמָּם עֶרְוַת

אֲחֹתוֹ גִּלָּה עֲוֹנוֹ יִשָּׂא: 18 וְאִישׁ אֲשֶׁר־יִשְׁכַּב אֶת־אִשָּׁה דָּוָה

The degree of our connection determines how alive we are in the Higher Realms.

The ancient consequences for all sorts of unacceptable sexual relationships—for example, with animals or between fathers and daughters—are described in this section.

¹⁸ And if a man lies with a woman during her monthly period and shall uncover her nakedness, he has exposed the source of her flow, and she has also uncovered the source of her flow, both of them must be cut off from their people.

¹⁹ And you shall not uncover the nakedness of your mother's sister or of your father's sister, for that would dishonor a close relative; they shall bear their iniquity.

²⁰ And if a man shall lie with his uncle's wife, he has dishonored his uncle, they shall bear their sin; they will die childless. ²¹ And if a man shall take his brother's wife, it is impurity; he has dishonored his brother, they will be childless.

²² You shall therefore, keep all My Statutes and all My Ordinances and follow them, so that the land where I am bringing you to live does not vomit you out.

ON A LEAP YEAR: SEVENTH READING - DAVID - MALCHUT

²³ And you must not live according to the customs of the nation I am going to drive out before you, for they did all these things, and I abhorred them. ²⁴ But have I said to you, 'You will inherit their land; I will give it to you to possess it, a land flowing with milk and honey.' I am the Lord your God, who has set you apart from the nations.

MAFTIR

²⁵ You must, therefore, make a distinction between clean and unclean animals and between unclean and clean birds, and do not defile yourselves by any animal or bird or anything that moves along the ground which I have set apart as unclean for you.

וְלֹא תֵלְכוּ

Leviticus 20:23 – The land of Israel holds a tremendous amount of spiritual Light and energy, which is why this little piece of land has been and still is so desired by so many, and why so many nations and empires have tried to conquer it and failed. It is written that no man or nation can conquer the land of Israel. To connect to the energy of the land of Israel, whether spiritually or physically, we must have the spiritual desire plus an acceptance of our responsibility to reveal the Light contained there.

. . . Rav Yehuda said: Fortunate is the portion of he who deserves during his lifetime to make his dwelling in the Holy Land. All who merit it will cause the dew of the Heaven above to continue to descend upon the Earth, so all who deserve the Holy Land in this lifetime will later deserve the higher Holy Land, MALCHUT.
— The Zohar, AchareiMot 48:291

וְגִלָּה אֶת־עֶרְוָתָהּ אֶת־מְקֹרָהּ הֶעֱרָה וְהִוא גִּלְּתָה אֶת־מְקוֹר דָּמֶיהָ

וְנִכְרְתוּ שְׁנֵיהֶם מִקֶּרֶב עַמָּם: 19 וְעֶרְוַת אֲחוֹת אִמְּךָ וַאֲחוֹת אָבִיךָ

לֹא תְגַלֵּה כִּי אֶת־שְׁאֵרוֹ הֶעֱרָה עֲוֹנָם יִשָּׂאוּ: 20 וְאִישׁ עֵ"ה קֹנ"א קס"א אֲשֶׁר

יִשְׁכַּב אֶת־דֹּדָתוֹ עֶרְוַת דֹּדוֹ גִּלָּה חֶטְאָם יִשָּׂאוּ עֲרִירִים יָמֻתוּ:

21 וְאִישׁ עֵ"ה קֹנ"א קס"א אֲשֶׁר יִקַּח וחלם אֶת־אֵשֶׁת אָחִיו נִדָּה הִוא עֶרְוַת אָחִיו

גִּלָּה עֲרִירִים יִהְיוּ אל: 22 וּשְׁמַרְתֶּם אֶת־כָּל־יֹלי חֻקֹּתַי וְאֶת־כָּל־יֹלי

מִשְׁפָּטַי וַעֲשִׂיתֶם אֹתָם וְלֹא־תָקִיא אֶתְכֶם הָאָרֶץ אלהים דההין עֵ"ה אֲשֶׁר

אֲנִי אֲני, טדהד כוזו מֵבִיא אֶתְכֶם שָׁמָּה מהטע, מהש, מצה, אל עדי לָשֶׁבֶת בָּהּ:

ON A LEAP YEAR: SEVENTH READING - DAVID - MALCHUT

23 וְלֹא תֵלְכוּ בְּחֻקֹּת הַגּוֹי אֲשֶׁר־אֲנִי אני, טדהד כוזו מְשַׁלֵּחַ מִפְּנֵיכֶם כִּי

אֶת־כָּל־יֹלי אֵלֶּה עָשׂוּ וָאָקֻץ בָּם מ"ב: 24 וָאֹמַר לָכֶם אַתֶּם תִּירְשׁוּ אֶת־

אַדְמָתָם וַאֲנִי ב"פ אהיה יהוה אֶתְּנֶנָּה לָכֶם לָרֶשֶׁת אֹתָהּ אֶרֶץ אלהים דאלפין זָבַת

חָלָב וּדְבָשׁ אֲנִי אני, טדהד כוזו יְהֹוָה אהדונהי אֱלֹהֵיכֶם ילה אֲשֶׁר־הִבְדַּלְתִּי

אֶתְכֶם מִן־הָעַמִּים עֵ"ה קס"א:

MAFTIR

25 וְהִבְדַּלְתֶּם בֵּין־הַבְּהֵמָה ב"ן, לכב, יבמ הַטְּהֹרָה לַטְּמֵאָה וּבֵין־הָעוֹף

הַטָּמֵא לַטָּהֹר י"פ אכא וְלֹא־תְשַׁקְּצוּ אֶת־נַפְשֹׁתֵיכֶם בַּבְּהֵמָה ג"פ ב"ן, יוסף, ציון

וְהִבְדַּלְתֶּם

Leviticus 20:25 – There are spiritual reasons why we eat only kosher foods. One of them concerns the types of souls that are embodied in kosher and non-kosher foods. The souls in kosher foods are the ones that are meant to be elevated, while souls that should not be elevated descend into non-kosher foods. This understanding gives us a strong reason and responsibility for eating kosher. Rav Isaac Luria (the Ari) wrote:

In the First Man, all the purifications were made of the souls that were back

26 And you shall be holy to me for I, the Lord am holy, and I have set you apart from the nations that you should be Mine.

27 A man or woman who divines by ghosts or familiar spirits shall surely be put to death, they shall stone them with stones; their blood will be on their own heads."

HAFTARAH OF KEDOSHIM

The Creator spoke to Ezekiel about how the Israelites were taken out of Egypt and left to roam the desert for 40 years to rid them of any remnant of the energy of Egypt. Even though the Israelites failed to break loose completely from the *Desire to Receive for the Self Alone*, they were still handled in a compassionate manner. The land of Israel is very different from the land of Egypt. In metaphorical

Ezekiel 20:2-20

20:2 And the word of the Lord came to me, saying:

3 "Son of man, speak to the elders of Israel and say to them, 'Thus says the Lord, God: Have you come to inquire of Me? As I live, says the Lord, God, I will not be inquire of by you.'

4 Will you judge them, son of man, will you judge them? Cause them to know the abominations of their fathers;

5 and say to them: 'Thus says the Lord, God: On the day I chose Israel, and I lifted My Hand to the seed of the house of Jacob and revealed Myself to them in the land of Egypt, when I lifted My Hand to them saying: 'I am the Lord, your God.'

---

to back, and those that were face to face were missing. All the cattle were purified except "the cattle upon a thousand hills," (Psalms 50:10) and the inanimate objects and plants that did not finish being purified, so they ate them to purify them. When the First Man and Woman sinned, the souls and the cattle also returned to the depths of the klipot. The souls rise

by means of Female Waters, and the kosher animals alone are refined by our eating them, as are inanimate objects and plants. In the future, "the cattle upon a thousand hills" will be refined and so will the non-kosher, as said in Ra'aya Mehemna (the Faithful Shepherd) in the chapter of Pinchas of the Zohar. Know thus what the animal soul in man

אֲשֶׁר תִּרְמֹשׂ הָאֲדָמָה   וּבְכֹל ב"ן, לכב, יבם, ציון   וּבָעוֹף ג"פ ב"ן, יוסף   ב"ן, לכב, יבם אֲשֶׁר־הִבְדַּלְתִּי לָכֶם לְטַמֵּא: 26 וִהְיִיתֶם לִי קְדֹשִׁים כִּי קָדוֹשׁ אֲנִי אֲנִי, טדה"ד כוז"ו יְהֹוָאֲדֹנִיֱאהֹדֹנֹהי וָאַבְדִּל אֶתְכֶם מִן־הָעַמִּים ע"ה קס"א לִהְיוֹת לִי: 27 וְאִישׁ ע"ה קנ"א קס"א אוֹ־אִשָּׁה כִּי־יִהְיֶה יי בָהֶם אוֹב אוֹ יִדְּעֹנִי מוֹת יוּמָתוּ בָּאֶבֶן יוד הה ואו הה יִרְגְּמוּ אֹתָם דְּמֵיהֶם בָּם מ"ב:

HAFTARAH OF KEDOSHIM

terms only, Egypt represents the selfish way most people live and may be synonymous with Hell, while Israel represents giving and sharing and is synonymous with Heaven. Our choice to be either sharing or not is what determines whether we live in Heaven or Hell.

יְחֶזְקֵאל פֶּרֶק כ

20 2 וַיְהִי אל דְבַר רֹאה יְהֹוָאֲדֹנִיֱאהֹדֹנֹהי אֵלַי לֵאמֹר: 3 בֶּן־אָדָם מ"ה דַּבֵּר רֹאה אֶת־זִקְנֵי יִשְׂרָאֵל וְאָמַרְתָּ אֲלֵהֶם כֹּה הי אָמַר אֲדֹנָי לכב יְהֹוָאֲדֹנִיֱאהֹדֹנֹהי הַלִדְרֹשׁ אֹתִי אַתֶּם בָּאִים חַי־אָנִי אני, טדה"ד כוז"ו אִם יוהך, ע"ה מ"ב ־אִדָּרֵשׁ לָכֶם נְאֻם אֲדֹנָי לכב יְהֹוָאֲדֹנִיֱאהֹדֹנֹהי: 4 הֲתִשְׁפֹּט אֹתָם הֲתִשְׁפּוֹט בֶּן־אָדָם מ"ה אֶת־תּוֹעֲבֹת אֲבוֹתָם הוֹדִיעֵם: 5 וְאָמַרְתָּ אֲלֵיהֶם כֹּה הי ־אָמַר אֲדֹנָי לכב יְהֹוָאֲדֹנִיֱאהֹדֹנֹהי בְּיוֹם ע"ה בָּחֳרִי בְּיִשְׂרָאֵל וָאֶשָּׂא יָדִי לְזֶרַע בֵּית ב"פ ראה יַעֲקֹב וָאִוָּדַע לָהֶם בְּאֶרֶץ מצר מִצְרַיִם וָאֶשָּׂא יָדִי

---

really is: it is the Good Inclination and the Evil Inclination in man. The souls of the wicked are of three klipot: a cloud and a wind and a fire flaring up, which are all evil. The cattle, animals and fowl are also impure. But the animal soul in Israel and the animal soul in kosher animals and fowl are all from Nogah (Eng. 'brightness'), and so from the chest downward there is clean fat and unclean fat, good and evil, corresponding to the female of brightness.
— Kitvei Ha'Ari (Writings of the Ari), Torah Compilations 4:10

⁶ On that day I lifted My Hand to them, to bring them forth out of Egypt into a land I had sought out for them, flowing with milk and honey, the most beautiful of all lands;

⁷ And I said to them, 'Cast you away every man the detestable things of his eyes, and do not defile yourselves with the idols of Egypt. I am the Lord your God.'

⁸ But they rebelled against Me and would not hearken unto Me; they did not, every man, get rid of the detestable things of their eyes, nor did they forsake the idols of Egypt, and then I said I would pour out My Fury on them and spend My Anger against them in midst of the land of Egypt.

⁹ But I wrought for My Name's Sake, that it should not be profaned in the sight of the nations among who they were, in whose sight I made Myself known to them, so as to bring them forth out of the land of Egypt.

¹⁰ So I caused them to go forth out of the land of Egypt and brought them into the wilderness.

¹¹ And I gave them My Statutes and taught them My Ordinances, which if a man do, he shall live by them.

¹² Moreover, also I gave them My Sabbaths to be a sign between Me and them, that they may know that I am the Lord that sanctifies them.

¹³ But the house of Israel rebelled against Me in the wilderness; they did not walk in My Statutes and they rejected My Ordinances, which if a the man does, he shall live by them; and My Sabbaths the greatly profaned; then I said I would pour out My Fury on them in the wilderness, to consume them.

¹⁴ But I wrought for My Name's Sake, that it should not be profaned in the sight of the nations, in whose sight I had brought them out.

¹⁵ Yet, also I lifted My Hand to them in the wilderness that I would not bring them into the land I had given them, flowing with milk and honey, most beautiful of all lands;

¹⁶ because they rejected My Ordinances and did not walk in My Statutes and profaned My Sabbaths—for their hearts were after their idols.

¹⁷ Nevertheless, Mine Eye spared them from destroying them, nor did I put an end to them in the desert.

¹⁸ And I said to their children in the desert, "Do not walk in the statutes of your fathers nor observe their ordinances or defile yourselves with their idols.

לָהֶם לֵאמֹר אֲנִי יְהֹוָה אֱלֹהֵיכֶם בַּיּוֹם 6

הַהוּא נָשָׂאתִי יָדִי לָהֶם לְהוֹצִיאָם מֵאֶרֶץ מִצְרַיִם אֶל־

אֶרֶץ אֲשֶׁר־תַּרְתִּי לָהֶם זָבַת חָלָב וּדְבַשׁ צְבִי הִיא לְכָל־

הָאֲרָצוֹת: 7 וָאֹמַר אֲלֵהֶם אִישׁ שִׁקּוּצֵי עֵינָיו

הַשְׁלִיכוּ וּבְגִלּוּלֵי מִצְרַיִם אַל־תִּטַּמָּאוּ אֲנִי יְהֹוָה

אֱלֹהֵיכֶם: 8 וַיַּמְרוּ־בִי וְלֹא אָבוּ לִשְׁמֹעַ אֵלַי אִישׁ אֶת־

שִׁקּוּצֵי עֵינֵיהֶם לֹא הִשְׁלִיכוּ וְאֶת־גִּלּוּלֵי מִצְרַיִם לֹא עָזָבוּ

וָאֹמַר לִשְׁפֹּךְ חֲמָתִי עֲלֵיהֶם לְכַלּוֹת אַפִּי בָּהֶם בְּתוֹךְ אֶרֶץ

מִצְרָיִם: 9 וָאַעַשׂ לְמַעַן שְׁמִי לְבִלְתִּי הֵחֵל לְעֵינֵי

הַגּוֹיִם אֲשֶׁר־הֵמָּה בְתוֹכָם אֲשֶׁר נוֹדַעְתִּי אֲלֵיהֶם לְעֵינֵיהֶם

לְהוֹצִיאָם מֵאֶרֶץ מִצְרָיִם: 10 וָאוֹצִיאֵם מֵאֶרֶץ

מִצְרַיִם וָאֲבִאֵם אֶל־הַמִּדְבָּר: 11 וָאֶתֵּן לָהֶם אֶת־חֻקּוֹתַי וְאֶת־

מִשְׁפָּטַי הוֹדַעְתִּי אוֹתָם אֲשֶׁר יַעֲשֶׂה אוֹתָם הָאָדָם וָחַי בָּהֶם:

12 וְגַם אֶת־שַׁבְּתוֹתַי נָתַתִּי לָהֶם לִהְיוֹת לְאוֹת בֵּינִי וּבֵינֵיהֶם לָדַעַת

כִּי אֲנִי יְהֹוָה מְקַדְּשָׁם: 13 וַיַּמְרוּ־בִי בֵית־

יִשְׂרָאֵל בַּמִּדְבָּר בְּחֻקּוֹתַי לֹא־הָלָכוּ וְאֶת־מִשְׁפָּטַי מָאָסוּ

אֲשֶׁר יַעֲשֶׂה אֹתָם הָאָדָם וָחַי בָּהֶם וְאֶת־שַׁבְּתֹתַי חִלְּלוּ מְאֹד

וָאֹמַר לִשְׁפֹּךְ חֲמָתִי עֲלֵיהֶם בַּמִּדְבָּר לְכַלּוֹתָם: 14 וָאֶעֱשֶׂה

לְמַעַן שְׁמִי לְבִלְתִּי הֵחֵל לְעֵינֵי הַגּוֹיִם אֲשֶׁר

הוֹצֵאתִים לְעֵינֵיהֶם: 15 וְגַם אֲנִי נָשָׂאתִי יָדִי לָהֶם

בַּמִּדְבָּר לְבִלְתִּי הָבִיא אוֹתָם אֶל־הָאָרֶץ אֲשֶׁר־

נָתַתִּי זָבַת חָלָב וּדְבַשׁ צְבִי הִיא לְכָל־הָאֲרָצוֹת: 16 יַעַן

בְּמִשְׁפָּטַי מָאָסוּ וְאֶת־חֻקּוֹתַי לֹא־הָלְכוּ בָהֶם וְאֶת־שַׁבְּתוֹתַי חִלֵּלוּ

כִּי אַחֲרֵי גִלּוּלֵיהֶם לִבָּם הֹלֵךְ: 17 וַתָּחָס עֵינִי עֲלֵיהֶם

¹⁹ *I am the Lord, your God; walk in My Statutes and keep My Ordinances and do them;*

²⁰ *and keep My Sabbaths holy, that they may be a sign between Me and you, that you may know that I am the Lord, your God.' "*

מִשְׁפָּטַי וְלֹא־עָשִׂיתִי אוֹתָם כָּלָה בַּמִּדְבָּר רמ"ח, וז"ח אל 18 וָאֹמַר אֶל־

בְּנֵיהֶם בַּמִּדְבָּר רמ"ח, וז"ח אל בְּחוּקֵּי אֲבוֹתֵיכֶם אַל־תֵּלֵכוּ וְאֶת־מִשְׁפְּטֵיהֶם

אַל־תִּשְׁמֹרוּ וּבְגִלּוּלֵיהֶם אַל־תִּטַּמָּאוּ אני 19 אֲנִי טדהד כוז"ו יְהֹוָ֯ה

אֱלֹהֵיכֶם ילה בְּחֻקּוֹתַי לֵכוּ וְאֶת־מִשְׁפָּטַי שִׁמְרוּ וַעֲשׂוּ אוֹתָם: 20 וְאֶת־

שַׁבְּתוֹתַי קַדֵּשׁוּ וְהָיוּ לְאוֹת בֵּינִי וּבֵינֵיכֶם לָדַעַת כִּי אֲנִי אני טדהד כוז"ו

יְהֹוָ֯ה אֱלֹהֵיכֶם ילה:

EMOR

LESSON OF EMOR
(Leviticus 21:1-24:23)

More about "Love your neighbor as yourself" (*Leviticus 19:18*)

Rav Akiva teaches us that the precept to "love your neighbor" is the founding principle of every holiday or cosmic event. The energy of all the holidays and cosmic events is contained in this biblical chapter, but the only way we can connect to this amazing energy that's now available to us is through giving and sharing.

There is a famous story about a student who asked the great sage Hillel if he could teach him the whole Torah while standing on one leg. Hillel replied that he could certainly do so, and then he spoke the following words: "If there is anything you would not like have done to you; do not do that thing to others. That is the whole Torah. The rest is just commentary. Now go and learn."

Strictly speaking, however, there is a difference between what Hillel said and what is written in the Bible. The Bible expresses the same principle in even fewer words and with a different, more positive phrasing: "Love your neighbor as yourself." Hillel, on the other hand, adopted a negative perspective: "If there is anything you would not like have done..." Hillel's instruction suggests that it's enough to avoid doing evil, but the Bible verse says we must love in a positive sense. It is not enough to simply refrain from doing evil.

Love does not happen easily—not even among friends or in a close-knit family. If our family members were not our brothers and sisters or our parents, would we still love them? Many people, if they were to answer honestly, would have to say "no." There's no doubt about it: Love can be hard work, especially, love for those closest to us.

Someone once remarked to Rav Berg that people are lucky if in the course of their entire life, they have five true friends whom they really love. Rav Berg replied, "No, you're wrong. People are lucky if they have even one real friend." Of course, a friend whom we love is not just someone who goes with us to a movie or a basketball game. It's someone who stays connected with us always, even if everyone else decides to abandon us. That's what love in friendship really means—a closeness that goes well beyond just feeling comfortable with that person.

As Rav Berg says, loving friendship is very rare, but it's also something we should strive to achieve. Not because real friendship is fun or interesting, but rather, because true friendship is a basic need. We need to reach a level of closeness with another person where "you" and "I" stop being two and begin to merge into one, called "we." To reach this level, we must go even further than what Hillel taught. If our desire is to do something negative or destructive, it's not enough to avoid that action because we wouldn't want someone to do it to us. Instead, we have to avoid even thinking about a wrongful deed. While it's virtually impossible to decide not to think about something in particular, our thoughts can eventually be brought under control by means of self-transformation. The best way to achieve that transformation is by giving and sharing with others.

It's especially important to think about this during the time of the Omer—the period of 49 days between *Pesach* (Passover) and *Shavuot.* It was at this time of year when 24,000 students of Rav Akiva died, not because they didn't love one another but simply because **they did not treat each other with respect**. If we feel anger toward someone, we must take responsibility for bringing that feeling to an end. The memory of Rav Akiva's students can help us accomplish this. Similarly, the Holy Temple was destroyed because of "hatred for no reason," and it can only be rebuilt with "love for no reason." The truth is, of course, that real love can only be "for no reason." If there is a reason or a hidden agenda, then it isn't real love.

There is a *Midrash* that says if two people hate each other, the whole world is too small for them, but if two people love each other, even the point of a sword is room enough. This is because the two have become one; they no longer need room for two, but only enough room for the single entity they have become.

Regarding the *Kohen HaGadol* (High Priest)

The Chapter of Emor includes the precepts pertaining to the *Kohen HaGadol*. We may find ourselves asking why it is important to know about priestly duties in the time of Moses, but its important to remember that everything in the Bible gives us some knowledge and understanding we can use in our daily lives. There is not one superfluous word or letter in the entire Bible.

Reading about the *Kohenim* (the priests) teaches us that the spiritual work of one person is not identical to that of another. The priests were doing work on behalf of the entire nation of Israel, but theirs was not the work that everyone was expected to undertake. Each of us has our own level of spiritual work, and the nature of this work is constantly changing. When we elevate to a higher level, what was good enough for us today may not be good enough for us tomorrow. Most of our spiritual work consists simply of finding out what our true work actually is. If we don't know where we're supposed to go, we will certainly never get there. In this sense, life is like an escalator. If we try to go up on the down escalator, we will not end up where we intended. In his Path of the Just (*Mesilat Yesharim*), the Ramchal (Rav Moshe Chaim Luzzato, 1707–1746) summed this up very simply: "Every person must know what his duties are in this world."

Even Rav Shimon bar Yochai had to learn this. It is said that when he emerged after 12 years in the cave where he had taken refuge from the Romans, he saw people working in the fields. He said to himself, "How could these people leave the Tree of Life, the Torah, to do farm work?" And wherever he looked, the fields burst into flames!

Then a Voice from the sky said, "Rav Shimon! Did you come out to destroy the world? Go back into the cave!"

After another year had passed, Rav Shimon came out again, at which time his response to the work of the world was very different. Previously, he had seen everyone according to his truth, which held that Bible study was the true meaning of life. But now he saw that his truth was not the same as everyone else's. What Rav Shimon had learned, in his 13th year in the cave, is that everyone is on a different level.

"And you made him holy because he sacrifices God's bread." (*Leviticus 21:8*)

Why does the Bible have to tell us that the *Kohen HaGadol* was pure when he sacrificed the bread? Wasn't it enough that he was a *Kohen*? Why do we need the precise details of what he did in the Tabernacle (and would do later in the Temple) and what his spiritual condition was when he did it?

Here, the Torah is teaching us that most of the time we don't see the effects of our actions. But the High Priest did see the effects of his actions whenever he performed the sacrifice, and by virtue of this, he was made holy. Of course, the teaching here does not apply only to the priests. Every time we perform a negative action, a negative angel is created, just as every positive action creates a good angel. Our task is to be aware of this and to act accordingly. It is important to always remember that even a small action can have great consequences. In fact, the whole reason we are in this world may be because we have come to perform one "small" action.

SYNOPSIS OF EMOR

The word *Emor* means "to speak," and this chapter concerns the things we should and shouldn't say. How we perform an action is often more important than the action itself, and the mouth is usually involved in this process. When we connect with this reading, we can use the power of *Emor* to help us speak the truth.

FIRST READING - ABRAHAM - CHESED

21:1 And the Lord said to Moses, "Speak to the priests, the sons of Aaron, and say to them: 'A priest must not defile himself for any of his people who die,

2 except for a close relative, for his mother and for his father, and for his son and for his daughter, and for his brother;

3 and for an unmarried sister who is dependent on him since she has no husband, for her he may defile himself.

FROM THE RAV

The reading of the Chapter of Emor usually falls sometime around the middle of the *Omer*, the 49 days between *Pesach* and *Shavuot*, during which there is a deprivation of Light. At this time, however, we can work to earn the abundance of Light—the Light of immortality— that appears on the night of *Shavuot*.

What is the significance of this? It is that during this period of the *Omer*, God in his infinite wisdom and mercy provides an added boost, through the Chapter of Emor, for us to earn the Light in case we had not caught the full amount or had short-circuited some of this energy that should have reached us at the time of *Rosh Hashanah*.

We have become acquainted in our lifetime with clinical death, when by all medical calculations, a person has died. We've all heard about the patient under anesthesia, who suddenly is without a pulse and not among the living, but who then, after a time, suddenly comes back to life. It took many millennia to understand the idea of clinical death and to support this new/old teaching of Kabbalah.

Today, scientists and doctors have recorded the experiences of people who have undergone clinical death. When such a person awakes—in effect, coming back to the living after having died—he can often recount many of the activities that had gone on while he appeared to be dead, like the conversation of the doctors. He was not conscious at the time, but he could later discuss what had gone on. As phenomenal as that idea sounds, the *Zohar* says it is *Mati velo Mati* (a death for a moment and then immediately restored), which provides us with an insight into immortality, an assurance that immortality can be a reality.

Once we speak of immortality, we are speaking of restoration—of mortality and immortality at the same time—for example, when Pinchas died and was immediately reborn. These concepts are difficult to understand—even clinical death is difficult to understand. Once we put a body in the earth, we say the person is gone. But he or she is not gone, by any stretch of the imagination. *Rosh Hashanah*, for instance, provides us with the opportunity to reach up to *Binah*, a dimension of the Flawless Universe. There is a change in the universe that permeates our lives—we don't see it or comprehend it; we find it outlandish. But immortality is not so outlandish: The ability to become immortal is out there in the cosmos, and now people are writing about it.

FIRST READING - ABRAHAM - CHESED

מלה וַיֹּאמֶר יְהֹוָה‎אלהים‎יאהדונהי אֶל־מֹשֶׁה מהש, אל שדי אֱמֹר אֶל־הַכֹּהֲנִים 21 1

בְּנֵי אַהֲרֹן ע״ב ורבוע ע״ב וְאָמַרְתָּ אֲלֵהֶם לְנֶפֶשׁ רמ״ח ־ ז׳ הויות לֹא־יִטַּמָּא בְּעַמָּיו:

2 כִּי אִם יוהך, ע״ה מ״ב ־לִשְׁאֵרוֹ הַקָּרֹב אֵלָיו לְאִמּוֹ וּלְאָבִיו וְלִבְנוֹ וּלְבִתּוֹ

וּלְאָחִיו: 3 וְלַאֲחֹתוֹ הַבְּתוּלָה הַקְּרוֹבָה אֵלָיו אֲשֶׁר לֹא־הָיְתָה לְאִישׁ

But, says the *Zohar*, there is a force known as the Force of Death, and that Force of Death is very complex, taking in all of life's activities and then determining when death will occur. We are not talking about heart attacks or other diseases; we are talking about an entity that eclipses all maladies. Once this entity has been eliminated, then there will be no heart attacks or cancer or other reasons to go to a hospital. If you didn't know, if you didn't pay attention to the *Zohar*, you've missed out on an opportunity. If it's not in your consciousness that we're embarking on something new; if you do not have it in your consciousness, if you don't know, immortality can't be achieved.

הַכֹּהֲנִים

Leviticus 21:1 –This section tells us what the High Priest needed to do to maintain a state of holiness. And at the same time, it also points out how anyone in a position of power has a greater responsibility. Those who have the ability to share a greater amount of Light have more responsibility—and more constraints, as well.

"Speak to the priests, the sons of Aaron." (Leviticus 21:1) HE ASKS, "What is the reason it is written here, 'the sons of Aaron?'" They are "the sons of Aaron" rather than "the sons of Levi," because Aaron is the first of all the priests. For it is Aaron that the Holy One, blessed be He, had chosen above everyone, so as to

make peace in the world, and because Aaron's practices have elevated him up to this. For Aaron strove throughout his life to increase peace in the world. Since these were his ways, the Holy One, blessed be He, raised him TO PRIESTHOOD, to introduce peace among the celestial retinue, FOR THROUGH HIS WORSHIP HE BRINGS ABOUT THE UNION OF THE HOLY ONE, BLESSED BE HE AND HIS SHECHINA, WHICH BRINGS PEACE THROUGHOUT THE WORLDS. Hence, "Speak to the priests, the sons of Aaron," and "performed for those who trust in You." (Ibid.) For when the world was created, this Light was shining from the beginning of the world to its end. When the Holy One, blessed be He, saw the wicked that will live in the world, He concealed that Light. This is the meaning of, "And from the wicked, their Light is withheld." (Job 38:15) THE HOLY ONE, BLESSED BE HE, will shine it upon the righteous in the World to Come, so, "which You have laid up for those who fear You, WHICH YOU HAVE PERFORMED FOR THOSE WHO TRUST IN YOU." "PERFORMED" ALLUDES TO THE ACTION OF CONCEALMENT. It is also written, "But to you who fear My Name the sun of righteousness shall arise with healing in its wings." (Malachi 3:20)
— The Zohar, Emor 1:2-4

⁴ He must defile himself for people related to him by marriage, and so profane himself.

⁵ They shall not make their heads bald or shave off the edges of their beards or make any cuttings in their flesh.

⁶ They must be holy to their God and not profane the Name of their God, for they offer the offerings of the Lord made by fire, the bread for their God, therefore, they are to be holy.

⁷ They shall not take a woman that is a harlot or profaned, they shall not take a woman divorced from her husband, for he is holy to his God.

⁸ You shall sanctify him, for he offers the bread of your God, he shall be holy to you, because I, the Lord who sanctify you, Am Holy.

⁹ And if a priest's daughter profanes herself by becoming a prostitute, she profanes her father; she shall be burned with fire.

¹⁰ And the High Priest, the one among his brothers who has had the anointing oil poured on his head, and who has been ordained to wear the priestly garments, must not let his hair become unkempt or tear his clothes,

¹¹ must not enter a place where there is a dead body, nor defile himself for his father or for his mother,

¹² nor shall he leave the sanctuary of his God or profane the sanctuary of his God, for the consecration of the anointing oil of his God is upon him. I am the Lord.

¹³ And the woman he marries must be a virgin.

¹⁴ He must not marry a widow, a divorced woman, or a profaned woman or a prostitute, but only a virgin from his own people,

¹⁵ so he will not profane his offspring among his people, for I am the Lord, who sanctifies him."

וְהַכֹּהֵן הַגָּדוֹל

Leviticus 21:10 – The laws pertaining to the High Priest teach us that the more elevated we are, the more responsibility we have. No matter where we are on the spiritual ladder—top, bottom, or somewhere in-between—we all have different responsibilities and restrictions. We can no longer do the same things when we're elevated that we used to do when we were at a lower level of consciousness.

לָהּ יִטַּמָּא: 4 לֹא יִטַּמָּא בַּעַל בְּעַמָּיו לְהֵחַלּוֹ: 5 לֹא-יִקְרְחוּ (כתיב : יקרחה)

קָרְחָה בְּרֹאשָׁם וּפְאַת זְקָנָם לֹא יְגַלֵּחוּ וּבִבְשָׂרָם לֹא יִשְׂרְטוּ שָׂרָטֶת:

6 קְדֹשִׁים יִהְיוּ אל לֵאלֹהֵיהֶם ילה וְלֹא יְחַלְּלוּ שֵׁם יהוה שדי אֱלֹהֵיהֶם ילה כִּי

אֶת-אִשֵּׁי יְהוָֹאהדונהי לֶחֶם ג״פ יהוה אֱלֹהֵיהֶם ילה הֵם מַקְרִיבִם וְהָיוּ

קֹדֶשׁ: 7 אִשָּׁה זֹנָה וַחֲלָלָה לֹא יִקָּחוּ וְאִשָּׁה גְּרוּשָׁה מֵאִישָׁהּ לֹא יִקָּחוּ

כִּי-קָדֹשׁ הוּא לֵאלֹהָיו ילה: 8 וְקִדַּשְׁתּוֹ כִּי-אֶת-לֶחֶם ג״פ יהוה אֱלֹהֶיךָ ילה

הוּא מַקְרִיב קָדֹשׁ יִהְיֶה ייי -לָךְ כִּי קָדוֹשׁ אֲנִי אני, טדהד כוז׳׳ו יְהוָֹאהדונהי

מְקַדִּשְׁכֶם: 9 וּבַת אִישׁ ע״ה קנ״א קס״א כֹּהֵן מלה כִּי תֵחֵל לִזְנוֹת אֶת-אָבִיהָ

הִיא מְחַלֶּלֶת בָּאֵשׁ אלהים דיודין ע״ה תִּשָּׂרֵף: 10 וְהַכֹּהֵן הַגָּדוֹל לההו, מבה, יזל, אום

מֵאֶחָיו אֲשֶׁר-יוּצַק עַל-רֹאשׁוֹ | שֶׁמֶן י״פ טל, י״פ כוז׳׳ו, ביט הַמִּשְׁחָה וּמִלֵּא

אֶת-יָדוֹ לִלְבֹּשׁ אֶת-הַבְּגָדִים אֶת-רֹאשׁוֹ לֹא יִפְרָע וּבְגָדָיו לֹא יִפְרֹם:

11 וְעַל כָּל ילי -נַפְשֹׁת מֵת י״פ רבוע אהיה לֹא יָבֹא לְאָבִיו וּלְאִמּוֹ לֹא יִטַּמָּא:

12 וּמִן-הַמִּקְדָּשׁ לֹא יֵצֵא וְלֹא יְחַלֵּל אֵת מִקְדַּשׁ אֱלֹהָיו ילה כִּי נֵזֶר

שֶׁמֶן י״פ טל, י״פ כוז׳׳ו, ביט מִשְׁחַת אֱלֹהָיו ילה עָלָיו אָנִי אני, טדהד כוז׳׳ו יְהוָֹאהדונהי:

13 וְהוּא אִשָּׁה בִבְתוּלֶיהָ יִקָּח: 14 אַלְמָנָה כוק, רבוע אדני וּגְרוּשָׁה וַחֲלָלָה

זֹנָה אֶת-אֵלֶּה לֹא יִקָּח חעם כִּי אִם יודך, ע״ה מ״ב -בְּתוּלָה מֵעַמָּיו יִקָּח חעם

אִשָּׁה: 15 וְלֹא-יְחַלֵּל זַרְעוֹ בְּעַמָּיו כִּי אֲנִי אני, טדהד כוז׳׳ו יְהוָֹאהדונהי

מְקַדְּשׁוֹ:

Come and see, the Supernal Priest, THE HIGH PRIEST, needs to be with a beautiful countenance, with a welcoming countenance, and more joyous than anyone. He must not look sad or angry, but in all in the likeness of Above. Happy is his portion, as it is written regarding him, "I am your portion and your inheritance," (Numbers 18:20) and "God is their inheritance." (Deuteronomy 18:2) Hence he must look whole in every respect, in his person, in his apparel, so as not to discredit himself whatsoever, as we have learned.

— The Zohar, Emor 8:28

SECOND READING - ISAAC - GEVURAH

[16] *And the Lord spoke to Moses, saying,* [17] *"Say to Aaron the following: For the generations to come none of your descendants who have a blemish may approach to offer the bread of his God.*

[18] *For the man who has any blemish may not approach: a blind man or a lame, or he who has anything maimed or anything too long;*

[19] *or a man with a crippled foot or a crippled hand,* [20] *or who is hunchbacked or a dwarf, or who has any eye defect, or who is scabbed or scurvy, or had damaged testicles;*

[21] *no man of the seed of Aaron, the priest, who has a blemish shall come near to offer the offerings of the Lord made by fire; he has a blemish; he shall not come near to offer the bread of his God.*

[22] *He may eat the bread of his God, both of the most holy food and of the holy;*

[23] *yet he must not go near the curtain or approach the altar, because he has a blemish lest he profane My Holy Places, for I am the Lord, who sanctifies them."*

[24] *So Moses spoke to Aaron and to his sons and to all the children of Israel.*

[22:1] *And the Lord spoke to Moses, saying,* [2] *"Speak to Aaron and to his sons that they separate themselves from the holy things of the children of Israel, which they hallow to Me, so they will not profane My Holy Name. I am the Lord.*

[3] *Say to them: Whoever is from your seed throughout your generations who approaches the holy things, which the children of Israel hallow to the Lord, with his uncleanness before him, that soul shall be cut off from My Presence. I am the Lord.*

בינה

Leviticus 21:17 – In this verse, we learn that there were certain physical blemishes that disqualified a person from service as a *Kohen*, as any physical blemish might have been a result of a spiritual one. Being a *Kohen* means being able to share in people's lives, or even being able to save their lives. If we don't use the gift we have for sharing and healing, we can lose it completely.

"Whoever is of your seed in their generations that has any blemish...." (Leviticus 21:17) Rav Yitzchak said THE REASON IS because he is blemished, and whoever is blemished is unfit to serve in the Holy Place. We explained that a blemished man has no faith, to which that blemish bears testimony. This is truer in a priest, who has to be whole and faithful more than the rest.
— The Zohar, Emor 13:41

SECOND READING - ISAAC - GEVURAH

16 וַיְדַבֵּר רَاه יְהוָֹוַאֲדֹנָיאַהדֹנֹהי מהשע, אל שדי אֶל־מֹשֶׁה לֵּאמֹר: 17 דַּבֵּר רَاه אֶל־

אַהֲרֹן ע״ב ורבוע ע״ב לֵאמֹר אִישׁ ע״ה קנ״א קס״א מִזַּרְעֲךָ לְדֹרֹתָם אֲשֶׁר יִהְיֶה ייי

בוֹ מוּם מום, אלהים, אהיה אדני לֹא יִקְרַב לְהַקְרִיב לֶחֶם ג״פ יהוה אֱלֹהָיו יל״ה:

18 כִּי כָל־ ילי אִישׁ ע״ה קנ״א קס״א אֲשֶׁר־בּוֹ מוּם מום, אלהים, אהיה אדני לֹא יִקְרָב

אִישׁ ע״ה קנ״א קס״א עִוֵּר אוֹ פִסֵּחַ אוֹ חָרֻם אוֹ שָׂרוּעַ: 19 אוֹ אִישׁ ע״ה קנ״א קס״א

אֲשֶׁר־יִהְיֶה ייי בוֹ שֶׁבֶר רֶגֶל עסמ״ב ע״ה, קס״א ע״ב אוֹ שֶׁבֶר יָד: 20 אוֹ־גִבֵּן אוֹ־

דַק אוֹ תְּבַלֻּל בְּעֵינוֹ ריבוע מ״ה אוֹ גָרָב אוֹ יַלֶּפֶת אוֹ מְרוֹחַ אָשֶׁךְ: 21 כָּל

אִישׁ ילי ע״ה קנ״א קס״א אֲשֶׁר־בּוֹ מוּם מום, אלהים, אהיה אדני מִזֶּרַע אַהֲרֹן ע״ב ורבוע ע״ב

הַכֹּהֵן מלה לֹא יִגַּשׁ לְהַקְרִיב אֶת־אִשֵּׁי יְהוָֹוַאֲדֹנָיאַהדֹנֹהי מום, אלהים, אהיה אדני

אֵת לֶחֶם ג״פ יהוה אֱלֹהָיו יל״ה לֹא יִגַּשׁ לְהַקְרִיב: 22 לֶחֶם ג״פ יהוה אֱלֹהָיו יל״ה

מִקָּדְשֵׁי הַקֳּדָשִׁים וּמִן־הַקֳּדָשִׁים יֹאכֵל: 23 אַךְ אהיה אֶל־הַפָּרֹכֶת לֹא

יָבֹא וְאֶל־הַמִּזְבֵּחַ זן, נגד לֹא יִגַּשׁ כִּי־מוּם מום, אלהים, אהיה אדני בּוֹ וְלֹא יְחַלֵּל

אֶת־מִקְדָּשַׁי כִּי אֲנִי אני, טדהד כוזו יְהוָֹוַאֲדֹנָיאַהדֹנֹהי מְקַדְּשָׁם: 24 וַיְדַבֵּר רَاه

מֹשֶׁה מהשע, אל שדי אֶל־אַהֲרֹן ע״ב ורבוע ע״ב וְאֶל־בָּנָיו וְאֶל־כָּל־ ילי בְּנֵי יִשְׂרָאֵל:

22 1 וַיְדַבֵּר רَاه יְהוָֹוַאֲדֹנָיאַהדֹנֹהי אֶל־מֹשֶׁה מהשע, אל שדי לֵּאמֹר: 2 דַּבֵּר רَاه

אֶל־אַהֲרֹן ע״ב ורבוע ע״ב וְאֶל־בָּנָיו וְיִנָּזְרוּ מִקָּדְשֵׁי בְנֵי־יִשְׂרָאֵל וְלֹא יְחַלְּלוּ

אֶת־שֵׁם יהוה שדי קָדְשִׁי אֲשֶׁר הֵם מְקַדְּשִׁים לִי אֲנִי אני, טדהד כוזו

יְהוָֹוַאֲדֹנָיאַהדֹנֹהי: 3 אֱמֹר אֲלֵהֶם לְדֹרֹתֵיכֶם כָּל־ ילי אִישׁ ע״ה קנ״א קס״א | אֲשֶׁר־

יְחַלְּלוּ

Leviticus 22:2 – The only people allowed to enter the Tabernacle were those who were pure. Even a priest couldn't enter the Tabernacle if he was impure. Today, too, for us to maintain our connection to the Light, we must be pure.

If we have anger in our hearts when we pray or meditate, we're connecting more to negativity than to positive energy. It is also true, however, that we should not let anger stop us from praying, as it is only through our continual efforts to connect to the Light that we can overcome our deep anger and replace it with compassion.

4 If a descendant of Aaron is a leper or has a bodily discharge, he may not eat of the holy offerings until he is cleansed. And he who touches anyone defiled by a corpse or anyone who has an emission of semen,

5 or he who touches any swarming thing that makes him unclean, or any person who makes him unclean, whatever the uncleanness may be, 6 the soul who touches any such thing will be unclean till the evening and shall not eat of the holy offerings unless he has bathed himself in water.

7 And when the sun goes down, he will be clean, and after that he may eat the holy offerings, for they are his bread.

8 He must not eat anything found dead or torn by wild animals, and so become unclean through it. I am the Lord. 9 They shall therefore keep My Charge so that they do not bear sin for it and die if they profane it. I am the Lord, who sanctifies holy.

10 No common man may eat of the holy offering, nor may the guest of a priest or a hired servant eat of the holy offering.

11 But if a priest buys a soul with money, or if a slave is born in his household, they may eat his bread. 12 And if a priest's daughter marries a common man, she may not eat of that which is set apart from the holy things.

13 But if a priest's daughter becomes a widow or is divorced, and has no children, and she returns to live in her father's house as in her youth, she may eat of her father's bread, but no common man shall eat thereof.

14 And if a man eats a holy offering by mistake, then he must give to the priest a fifth of the value of the holy offering. 15 And they shall not profane the holy offerings of the children of Israel, which they set apart to the Lord

16 and so cause them to bear the iniquity that brings guilt when they eat their holy offerings. I am the Lord, who sanctifies them."

וַיְכַלֵּד

Leviticus 22:11 – The family of a High Priest had access to certain higher connections than other families did. From this verse, we understand that when a person reaches a high spiritual level, he can share that energy with his family and friends. The same is true for a person who is negative; their negativity affects their friends and family, too. A person's entire family partakes of both good and bad on a spiritual level.

יִקְרַב מִכָּל יל״ ־זַרְעֲכֶם אֶל־הַקֳּדָשִׁים אֲשֶׁר יַקְדִּישׁוּ בְנֵי־יִשְׂרָאֵל

לַיהֹוָה‏אדנידאהדונהי וְטֻמְאָתוֹ עָלָיו וְנִכְרְתָה הַנֶּפֶשׁ רמ״ח ־ ד׳ הויות הַהִוא מִלְּפָנַי

אֲנִי אני, טדה״ד כו״ו יְהֹוָה‏אדנידאהדונהי׃ 4 אִישׁ ע״ה קנ״א קס״א אִישׁ ע״ה קנ״א קס״א מִזֶּרַע

אַהֲרֹן ע״ב ורבוע ע״ב וְהוּא צָרוּעַ אוֹ זָב בַּקֳּדָשִׁים לֹא יֹאכַל עַד אֲשֶׁר

יִטְהָר וְהַנֹּגֵעַ בְּכָל בֶּ״ן, לכב, יבמ ־טְמֵא־נֶפֶשׁ רמ״ח ־ ד׳ הויות אוֹ אִישׁ ע״ה קנ״א קס״א

אֲשֶׁר־תֵּצֵא מִמֶּנּוּ שִׁכְבַת־זָרַע׃ 5 אוֹ־אִישׁ ע״ה קנ״א קס״א אֲשֶׁר יִגַּע בְּכָל

בֶּ״ן, לכב, יבמ ־שֶׁרֶץ אֲשֶׁר יִטְמָא־לוֹ אוֹ בְאָדָם מ״ה אֲשֶׁר יִטְמָא־לוֹ לְכֹל

יה ־ אדני טֻמְאָתוֹ׃ 6 נֶפֶשׁ רמ״ח ־ ד׳ הויות אֲשֶׁר תִּגַּע־בּוֹ וְטָמְאָה עַד־הָעָרֶב

רבוע יהוה ורבוע אלהים וְלֹא יֹאכַל מִן־הַקֳּדָשִׁים כִּי אִם ־רָחַץ בְּשָׂרוֹ

בַּמָּיִם׃ 7 וּבָא הַשֶּׁמֶשׁ ב״פ ש״ך וְטָהֵר יפ אכא וְאַחַר יֹאכַל מִן־הַקֳּדָשִׁים כִּי

לַחְמוֹ הוּא׃ 8 נְבֵלָה ב״פ רבוע יהוה וּטְרֵפָה לֹא יֹאכַל לְטָמְאָה־בָהּ אֲנִי

אני, טדה״ד כו״ו יְהֹוָה‏אדנידאהדונהי׃ 9 וְשָׁמְרוּ אֶת־מִשְׁמַרְתִּי וְלֹא־יִשְׂאוּ עָלָיו

חֵטְא וּמֵתוּ בוֹ כִּי יְחַלְּלֻהוּ אֲנִי אני, טדה״ד כו״ו יְהֹוָה‏אדנידאהדונהי מְקַדְּשָׁם׃

10 וְכָל יל״ ־זָר אור, רז, אין סוף לֹא־יֹאכַל קֹדֶשׁ תּוֹשַׁב כֹּהֵן מלה וְשָׂכִיר לֹא־

יֹאכַל קֹדֶשׁ׃ 11 וְכֹהֵן מלה כִּי־יִקְנֶה נֶפֶשׁ רמ״ח ־ ד׳ הויות קִנְיַן כַּסְפּוֹ הוּא יֹאכַל

בּוֹ וִילִיד בֵּיתוֹ ב״פ ראה הֵם יֹאכְלוּ בְלַחְמוֹ׃ 12 וּבַת־כֹּהֵן מלה כִּי תִהְיֶה

לְאִישׁ ע״ה קנ״א קס״א זָר אור, רז, אין סוף הִוא בִּתְרוּמַת הַקֳּדָשִׁים לֹא תֹאכֵל׃

13 וּבַת־כֹּהֵן מלה כִּי תִהְיֶה אַלְמָנָה כוק, רבוע אדני וּגְרוּשָׁה וְזֶרַע אֵין לָהּ

וְשָׁבָה אֶל־בֵּית ב״פ ראה אָבִיהָ כִּנְעוּרֶיהָ מִלֶּחֶם ג״פ יהוה אָבִיהָ תֹּאכֵל וְכָל

יל״ ־זָר אור, רז, אין סוף לֹא־יֹאכַל בּוֹ׃ 14 וְאִישׁ ע״ה קנ״א קס״א כִּי־יֹאכַל קֹדֶשׁ

בִּשְׁגָגָה וְיָסַף חֲמִשִׁיתוֹ עָלָיו אבגית״ץ, ושר, אהבת חנם וְנָתַן לַכֹּהֵן מלה אֶת־

הַקֹּדֶשׁ׃ 15 וְלֹא יְחַלְּלוּ אֶת־קָדְשֵׁי בְּנֵי יִשְׂרָאֵל אֵת אֲשֶׁר־יָרִימוּ

לַיהֹוָה‏אדנידאהדונהי׃ 16 וְהִשִּׂיאוּ אוֹתָם עֲוֹן ג״פ מ״ב אַשְׁמָה בְּאָכְלָם אֶת־

קָדְשֵׁיהֶם כִּי אֲנִי אני, טדה״ד כו״ו יְהֹוָה‏אדנידאהדונהי מְקַדְּשָׁם׃

THIRD READING - JACOB - TIFERET

[17] And the Lord spoke to Moses, saying, [18] "Speak to Aaron and to his sons and to all the children of Israel and say to them: If any Israelite or any stranger living in Israel brings a gift for a burnt offering to the Lord, either to fulfill a vow or as a freewill offering,

[19] that it may be accepted on your behalf, you must present a male without blemish of the cattle, of the sheep or of the goats.

[20] Do not bring anything with a blemish, because it will not be accepted on your behalf.

[21] And whoever brings a peace offering to the Lord from the herd or flock to fulfill a special vow or as a freewill offering, it must be perfect to be accepted, there shall be no blemish on it.

[22] Blind, or injured or maimed, or anything with warts or scabbed or scurvy, you shall not offer these to the Lord, nor make an offering by fire of them on the altar to the Lord.

[23] You may, however, present—as a freewill offering—an ox or a sheep that has anything too short or too long, but it will not be accepted in fulfillment of a vow.

[24] An animal whose testicles are bruised, crushed, torn or cut, you may not bring for an offering to the Lord, nor shall you do this in your own land.

[25] And you must not accept such animals from the hand of a foreigner and offer them as the bread of your God, because their corruption is in them, there is a blemish in them and they shall not be accepted on your behalf."

[26] The Lord spoke to Moses, saying, [27] "When a calf, a lamb or a goat is born, it is to remain with its mother for seven days. From the eighth day on, it will be acceptable as an offering made to the Lord by fire.

קָרְבֵּנוּ

Leviticus 22:18 – Animals brought for offering had to be 100 percent pure—completely unblemished—or they were unfit for sacrifice. A physical defect shows that something is missing on the spiritual level. It's important to realize that we don't always recognize blemishes. If we want to know people on a deep level, we should try to get glimpses of their real selves through the small things they do. It's about always intercepting clues.

"Therefore everything dwells only in a wholesome place, and therefore, whatever man that has a blemish, he

THIRD READING - JACOB - TIFERET

17 וַיְדַבֵּר יְהֹוָאדֹנָיאהדונהי אֶל־מֹשֶׁה לֵּאמֹר: 18 דַּבֵּר אֶל־
אַהֲרֹן וְאֶל־בָּנָיו וְאֶל כָּל־בְּנֵי יִשְׂרָאֵל וְאָמַרְתָּ אֲלֵהֶם אִישׁ
אִישׁ מִבֵּית יִשְׂרָאֵל וּמִן־הַגֵּר בְּיִשְׂרָאֵל
אֲשֶׁר יַקְרִיב קָרְבָּנוֹ לְכָל־נִדְרֵיהֶם וּלְכָל־נִדְבוֹתָם
אֲשֶׁר־יַקְרִיבוּ לַיהֹוָאדֹנָיאהדונהי לְעֹלָה: 19 לִרְצֹנְכֶם תָּמִים זָכָר בַּבָּקָר
בַּכְּשָׂבִים וּבָעִזִּים: 20 כֹּל אֲשֶׁר־בּוֹ מוּם לֹא תַקְרִיבוּ
כִּי־לֹא לְרָצוֹן יִהְיֶה לָכֶם: 21 וְאִישׁ כִּי־יַקְרִיב
זֶבַח־שְׁלָמִים לַיהֹוָאדֹנָיאהדונהי לְפַלֵּא־נֶדֶר אוֹ לִנְדָבָה בַּבָּקָר
אוֹ בַצֹּאן תָּמִים יִהְיֶה לְרָצוֹן כָּל־מוּם
לֹא יִהְיֶה־בּוֹ: 22 עַוֶּרֶת אוֹ שָׁבוּר אוֹ־חָרוּץ אוֹ־
יַבֶּלֶת אוֹ גָרָב אוֹ יַלֶּפֶת לֹא־תַקְרִיבוּ אֵלֶּה לַיהֹוָאדֹנָיאהדונהי וְאִשֶּׁה לֹא־
תִתְּנוּ מֵהֶם עַל־הַמִּזְבֵּחַ לַיהֹוָאדֹנָיאהדונהי: 23 וְשׁוֹר
וָשֶׂה שָׂרוּעַ וְקָלוּט נְדָבָה תַּעֲשֶׂה אֹתוֹ וּלְנֵדֶר לֹא יֵרָצֶה: 24 וּמָעוּךְ
וְכָתוּת וְנָתוּק וְכָרוּת לֹא תַקְרִיבוּ לַיהֹוָאדֹנָיאהדונהי וּבְאַרְצְכֶם לֹא
תַעֲשׂוּ: 25 וּמִיַּד בֶּן־נֵכָר לֹא תַקְרִיבוּ אֶת־לֶחֶם אֱלֹהֵיכֶם מִכָּל־
אֵלֶּה כִּי מָשְׁחָתָם בָּהֶם מוּם בָּם לֹא יֵרָצוּ
לָכֶם: 26 וַיְדַבֵּר יְהֹוָאדֹנָיאהדונהי אֶל־מֹשֶׁה לֵּאמֹר: 27 שׁוֹר
אוֹ־כֶשֶׂב אוֹ־עֵז כִּי יִוָּלֵד וְהָיָה שִׁבְעַת

---

shall not approach." (Leviticus 21:18) Similarly, a blemished sacrifice shall not be offered, since it is written, "it shall not be acceptable for you." (Leviticus 22:20) You may say that God only dwells in a broken place, in a broken Vessel, as it is written, "yet with him also that is of a contrite and humble spirit." (Isaiah 57:15) HE ANSWERS, "Such a place is the most wholesome, because one humbles himself so as to allow the loftiest will to dwell on him—Supernal loftiness." Such a one is whole...

— The Zohar, Emor 11:46

28 And do not slaughter a cow or a sheep and its young on the same day.

29 And when you sacrifice a thanks offering to the Lord, sacrifice it in such a way that it will be accepted on your behalf.

30 It must be eaten that same day; leave none of it till morning. I am the Lord. 31 And you shall keep My Commandments and follow them. I am the Lord.

32 And you shall not profane My Holy Name, but I will be hallowed among the children of Israel. I am the Lord, who hallows you 33 Who brought you out of Egypt to be your God. I am the Lord."

FOURTH READING - MOSES - NETZACH

23:1 And the Lord spoke to Moses, saying, 2 "Speak to the children of Israel and say to them: The appointed seasons of the Lord which you are to proclaim to be holy convocations, even these are My Appointed Seasons.

3 Work may be done for six days, but the seventh day is a solemn Sabbath of rest, a holy convocation, you shall do no manner of work; wherever you live, it is a Sabbath to the Lord.

יֵרָצֶה

Leviticus 22:27 – God doesn't need anything from us, not even sacrifices, yet there are rules pertaining to desecrating and sanctifying God's Name. These rules actually deal with the Essence of God within each of us. We diminish the spark of Light within when we do negative things, and we allow it to shine when we perform positive actions. It's not for God's Sake that we shouldn't be negative or reactive—it's for our own.

###

Leviticus 23:3 – Every Shabbat and all the holidays are opportunities to withdraw from the physical world and move into the spiritual realm. If we didn't have these special days, the world would be too much for us to handle. These special connections give us the power to carve out a joyful, immortal destiny. *Pesach* is the only time of year that we get the key to unlock the

prison of our faulty belief systems—those robotic ways of our ego's thinking that prevent us from achieving our truest potential. *Pesach* is about breaking free from our slavery to the things, ideas, and people that hold us back. We receive all the Light we acquire during *Pesach* for free, and it is this Light that releases us from our slave mentality. According to the spiritual Universal Law, that which we do not earn, we cannot keep. To be the Cause of our own Light, we need to behave proactively to earn the Light we receive. Through the counting of the Omer (the 49 days between *Pesach* and *Shavuot*) and by meeting the challenges and opportunities this powerful period gives us, we cleanse ourselves, level by level. As a result of this cleansing, we can receive more of the Light of immortality—a continuing force of endless renewal.

If *Pesach* is about quality of life, *Rosh Hashanah* is about *quantity* of life. On *Rosh Hashanah*, we determine and seal our portion of life for the coming year, as well as establishing the amount

יָמִים גלך תַּחַת אִמּוֹ וּמִיּוֹם ע"ה = נגד, זן, מזבח הַשְּׁמִינִי וָהָלְאָה ⸢יֵרָצֶה⸣ לְקָרְבַּן

אִשֶּׁה לַיהוָֹאדניאהדונהי: 28 וְשׁוֹר אבגיתץ, ושר, אהבת חנם אוֹ־שֶׂה אֹתוֹ וְאֶת־בְּנוֹ

לֹא תִשְׁחֲטוּ בְּיוֹם ע"ה = נגד, זן, מזבח אֶחָד אהבה, דאגה: 29 וְכִי־תִזְבְּחוּ זֶבַח־

תּוֹדָה לַיהוָֹאדניאהדונהי לִרְצֹנְכֶם תִּזְבָּחֻהוּ 30 בַּיּוֹם ע"ה = נגד, זן, מזבח הַהוּא

יֵאָכֵל לֹא־תוֹתִירוּ מִמֶּנּוּ עַד־בֹּקֶר אֲנִי אני, טדה"ד כוז"ו יְהוָֹאדניאהדונהי:

31 וּשְׁמַרְתֶּם מִצְוֹתַי וַעֲשִׂיתֶם אֹתָם אֲנִי אני, טדה"ד כוז"ו אַתֶּם יְהוָֹאדניאהדונהי:

32 וְלֹא תְחַלְּלוּ אֶת־שֵׁם יהוה עדי קָדְשִׁי וְנִקְדַּשְׁתִּי בְּתוֹךְ בְּנֵי יִשְׂרָאֵל

אֲנִי אני, טדה"ד כוז"ו יְהוָֹאדניאהדונהי מְקַדִּשְׁכֶם: 33 הַמּוֹצִיא אֶתְכֶם מֵאֶרֶץ

אלהים דאלפין מִצְרַיִם מצר לִהְיוֹת לָכֶם לֵאלֹהִים מום, אהיה אדני ; ילה אֲנִי אני, טדה"ד כוז"ו

יְהוָֹאדניאהדונהי:

FOURTH READING - MOSES - NETZACH

23 1 וַיְדַבֵּר ראה יְהוָֹאדניאהדונהי מהע, אל שדי אֶל־מֹשֶׁה לֵּאמֹר: 2 דַּבֵּר ראה

אֶל־בְּנֵי יִשְׂרָאֵל וְאָמַרְתָּ אֲלֵהֶם מוֹעֲדֵי יְהוָֹאדניאהדונהי אֲשֶׁר־תִּקְרְאוּ

אֹתָם מִקְרָאֵי קֹדֶשׁ אֵלֶּה הֵם מוֹעֲדָי: 3 שֵׁשֶׁת יָמִים גלך ⸢תֵּעָשֶׂה⸣

מְלָאכָה אל אדני וּבַיּוֹם ע"ה = נגד, זן, מזבח הַשְּׁבִיעִי שַׁבַּת שַׁבָּתוֹן מִקְרָא

שם ע"ה, יהוה שדי ־קֹדֶשׁ כָּל ילי ־מְלָאכָה אל אדני לֹא תַעֲשׂוּ שַׁבָּת הוּא

---

of money we will earn and the number of children we will have. In this way, Rosh Hashanah allows us to control all aspects of what will happen in the year ahead. Falling in the second half of the secular calendar year, *Rosh Hashanah* is the two-day interval between the seeds we planted earlier at *Pesach* (in the first half of the year) and the manifestation of their effects at *Sukkot*. On *Rosh Hashanah*, we can go back in time and alter the root Cause of things so that, upon returning to the present, we are able to change their Effect.

Once we have made those changes, we are ready to plug into the generator that will give us the power to energize all of our initiatives.

Leviticus 23:27 tells us that *Yom Kippur*, the Day of Atonement, is a time when we reach levels of spiritual enlightenment greater than at any other time of year. On *Yom Kippur*, we touch the *Sefira* of *Binah*, the dimension of the Tree of Life that provides us with all the energy we need to actualize our greatest desires. By fasting and disconnecting ourselves from any aspect

4 These are the appointed seasons of the Lord, even holy convocations which you shall proclaim at their appointed season: 5 on the fourteenth day of the first month, at dusk, is the Lord's Passover.

6 On the fifteenth day of the same month, is the Feast of Unleavened Bread to the Lord; for seven days you shall eat unleavened bread.

7 On the first day you shall have a holy convocation and do no manner of regular work.

8 And you shall bring an offering made by fire to the Lord for seven days, and on the seventh day is a holy convocation, you shall do no manner of regular work."

9 And the Lord spoke to Moses, saying, 10 "Speak to the children of Israel and say to them: When you enter the land which I am going to give you and you shall reap the harvest, and bring to the priest a sheaf of the first fruits of your harvest.

11 And he shall wave the sheaf before the Lord so it will be accepted on your behalf; the priest is to wave it on the day after the Sabbath.

12 On the day you wave the sheaf, you must offer a year old male lamb without blemish as a burnt offering to the Lord.

13 And together with its meal offering of two-tenths of an ephah of fine flour mixed with oil—an offering made to the Lord by fire, a pleasing aroma—and the drink offering of a quarter of a hin of wine.

14 You must not eat any bread, or roasted corn or new grain, until the very day you bring this offering to your God; this is an ever lasting statute for the generations to come, wherever you live.

15 And you shall count from the day after the Sabbath, the day you brought the sheaf of the wave offering, seven full weeks.

16 Count off fifty days up to the day after the seventh Sabbath, and then present a new meal offering to the Lord.

---

of physicality, we can raise our consciousness higher and higher so that we may draw down all the treasures of life. If we were given a preview of Heaven for only one day, would we turn around for even a moment to watch something on television? On *Yom Kippur*, it is important to make every effort to absorb as much as Light as possible.

Leviticus 23:34 tells us that the festival of *Sukkot*, which activates the Light of Mercy, gives us the opportunity to surround ourselves with this Light as a protection and guidance so that we will always find ourselves in the right place at the right time. *Sukkot* gives us the ability to expand our Surrounding Light—our potential—

לַיהוָואדֹנָיאהדֹנָהי בְּכֹל בּ״ן, לכבב, יבמ מוֹשְׁבֹתֵיכֶם: 4 אֵלֶּה מוֹעֲדֵי יְהוָואדֹנָיאהדֹנָהי

מִקְרָאֵי קֹדֶשׁ אֲשֶׁר־תִּקְרְאוּ אֹתָם בְּמוֹעֲדָם: 5 בַּחֹדֶשׁ הָרִאשׁוֹן

בְּאַרְבָּעָה עָשָׂר לַחֹדֶשׁ בֵּין הָעַרְבָּיִם פֶּסַח לַיהוָואדֹנָיאהדֹנָהי:

6 וּבַחֲמִשָּׁה עָשָׂר יוֹם לַחֹדֶשׁ הַזֶּה והו וְחַג הַמַּצּוֹת

לַיהוָואדֹנָיאהדֹנָהי שִׁבְעַת יָמִים מַצּוֹת תֹּאכֵלוּ: 7 בַּיּוֹם

הָרִאשׁוֹן מִקְרָא־קֹדֶשׁ יִהְיֶה לָכֶם כָּל־מְלֶאכֶת עֲבֹדָה

לֹא תַעֲשׂוּ: 8 וְהִקְרַבְתֶּם אִשֶּׁה לַיהוָואדֹנָיאהדֹנָהי שִׁבְעַת יָמִים בַּיּוֹם

הַשְּׁבִיעִי מִקְרָא־קֹדֶשׁ כָּל־מְלֶאכֶת עֲבֹדָה

לֹא תַעֲשׂוּ: 9 וַיְדַבֵּר יְהוָואדֹנָיאהדֹנָהי אֶל־מֹשֶׁה לֵּאמֹר:

10 דַּבֵּר אֶל־בְּנֵי יִשְׂרָאֵל וְאָמַרְתָּ אֲלֵהֶם כִּי־תָבֹאוּ אֶל־הָאָרֶץ

אֲשֶׁר אֲנִי נֹתֵן לָכֶם וּקְצַרְתֶּם

אֶת־קְצִירָהּ וַהֲבֵאתֶם אֶת־עֹמֶר רֵאשִׁית קְצִירְכֶם אֶל־

הַכֹּהֵן: 11 וְהֵנִיף אֶת־הָעֹמֶר לִפְנֵי יְהוָואדֹנָיאהדֹנָהי

לִרְצֹנְכֶם מִמָּחֳרַת הַשַּׁבָּת יְנִיפֶנּוּ הַכֹּהֵן: 12 וַעֲשִׂיתֶם בְּיוֹם

הֲנִיפְכֶם אֶת־הָעֹמֶר כֶּבֶשׂ תָּמִים בֶּן־שְׁנָתוֹ

לְעֹלָה לַיהוָואדֹנָיאהדֹנָהי: 13 וּמִנְחָתוֹ שְׁנֵי עֶשְׂרֹנִים סֹלֶת בְּלוּלָה בַשֶּׁמֶן

אִשֶּׁה לַיהוָואדֹנָיאהדֹנָהי רֵיחַ נִיחֹחַ וְנִסְכֹּה יַיִן

רְבִיעִת הַהִין: 14 וְלֶחֶם וְקָלִי וְכַרְמֶל לֹא תֹאכְלוּ עַד־עֶצֶם הַיּוֹם

הַזֶּה והו עַד הֲבִיאֲכֶם אֶת־קָרְבַּן אֱלֹהֵיכֶם חֻקַּת עוֹלָם

לְדֹרֹתֵיכֶם בְּכֹל מֹשְׁבֹתֵיכֶם: 15 וּסְפַרְתֶּם לָכֶם מִמָּחֳרַת

הַשַּׁבָּת מִיּוֹם הֲבִיאֲכֶם אֶת־עֹמֶר הַתְּנוּפָה שֶׁבַע

---

incorporating this Light into our very being. Each year we participate in *Sukkot*, we expand our capacity to contain more Light. Then, providing we did our spiritual work, *Shemini Atzeret* and *Simchat Torah*, which fall at the end of *Sukkot*, take this inner work we have done during of all of the High Holidays and create from it one unified force that will ensure happiness for us, for the whole year.

17 From wherever you live, bring two loaves made of two-tenths of an ephah of fine flour, baked with yeast, as a wave offering of the first fruits to the Lord.

18 Present with this bread seven male lambs, each a year old and without blelmish, one young bull and two rams; they will be a burnt offering to the Lord, together with their meal offerings and drink offerings—an offering made by fire, a sweet aroma pleasing to the Lord.
19 Then sacrifice one male goat for a sin offering and two male lambs, each a year old, for a peace offering.

20 The priest is to wave the two lambs before the Lord as a wave offering; together with the bread of the first fruits they shall be holy to the Lord for the priest.

21 And on that same day, you are to proclaim a holy convocation and do no manner of regular work; this is an ever lasting statute for the generations to come, wherever you live.

22 And when you reap the harvest of your land, do not reap to the very edges of your field or gather the gleanings of your harvest; you shall leave them for the poor and for the stranger. I am the Lord your God."

FIFTH READING - AARON - HOD

23 And the Lord spoke to Moses, saying, 24 "Speak to the children of Israel saying: On the first day of the seventh month you are to have a solemn day of rest, a holy convocation commemorated with the blast of horns.

25 You shall do no manner of regular work, and you shall bring an offering made to the Lord by fire."

26 And the Lord spoke to Moses, saying,

27 "The tenth day of this seventh month is the Day of Atonement, you shall hold a holy convocation and you shall afflict your souls, and bring an offering made to the Lord by fire.

28 And you shall do no manner of work on that day, because it is the Day of Atonement, to make atonement for you before the Lord your God.

שַׁבָּתוֹת תְּמִימֹת תִּהְיֶינָה: 16 עַד מִמָּחֳרַת הַשַּׁבָּת ע"ב ואלהים דיודין

הַשְּׁבִיעִת תִּסְפְּרוּ חֲמִשִּׁים יוֹם ע"ה = נגר, זן, מזבח וְהִקְרַבְתֶּם מִנְחָה חֲדָשָׁה

לַיהוָֹה: 17 מִמּוֹשְׁבֹתֵיכֶם תָּבִיאוּ | לֶחֶם ג"פ יהוה תְּנוּפָה שְׁתַּיִם

שְׁנֵי עֶשְׂרֹנִים סֹלֶת תִּהְיֶינָה חָמֵץ תֵּאָפֶינָה בִּכּוּרִים לַיהוָֹה:

18 וְהִקְרַבְתֶּם עַל־הַלֶּחֶם ג"פ יהוה שִׁבְעַת כְּבָשִׂים תְּמִימִם בְּנֵי שָׁנָה וּפַר

בֶּן־בָּקָר אֶחָד אהבה, דאגה וְאֵילִם שְׁנָיִם יִהְיוּ אל עֹלָה מזוזך, ערי, סנדלפון

לַיהוָֹה וּמִנְחָתָם וְנִסְכֵּיהֶם אִשֵּׁה רֵיחַ־נִיחֹחַ לַיהוָֹה:

19 וַעֲשִׂיתֶם שְׂעִיר־עִזִּים אֶחָד אהבה, דאגה לְחַטָּאת וּשְׁנֵי כְבָשִׂים בְּנֵי

שָׁנָה לְזֶבַח שְׁלָמִים: 20 וְהֵנִיף הַכֹּהֵן מלה | אֹתָם עַל לֶחֶם ג"פ יהוה הַבִּכֻּרִים

תְּנוּפָה לִפְנֵי יְהוָֹה חכמה בינה עַל־שְׁנֵי כְּבָשִׂים קֹדֶשׁ יִהְיוּ אל

לַיהוָֹה לַכֹּהֵן מלה: 21 וּקְרָאתֶם בְּעֶצֶם הַיּוֹם ע"ה = נגר, זן, מזבח הַזֶּה והו

מִקְרָא יהוה שדי ע"ה ־קֹדֶשׁ יִהְיֶה יי לָכֶם כָּל ילי ־מְלֶאכֶת עֲבֹדָה לֹא תַעֲשׂוּ

חֻקַּת עוֹלָם בְּכָל ב"ן, לכב, יבמ ־מוֹשְׁבֹתֵיכֶם לְדֹרֹתֵיכֶם: 22 וּבְקֻצְרְכֶם

אֶת־קְצִיר אַרְצְכֶם לֹא־תְכַלֶּה נתה, קס"א קנ"א קמ"ג פְּאַת שָׂדְךָ בְּקֻצְרֶךָ

וְלֶקֶט קְצִירְךָ לֹא תְלַקֵּט לֶעָנִי ע"ה קס"א וְלַגֵּר תַּעֲזֹב אֹתָם אֲנִי אני, טדהד כוזו

יְהוָֹה אֱלֹהֵיכֶם: ילה:

FIFTH READING - AARON - HOD

23 וַיְדַבֵּר ראה יְהוָֹה מהע, אל שדי אֶל־מֹשֶׁה לֵּאמֹר: 24 דַּבֵּר ראה אֶל־

בְּנֵי יִשְׂרָאֵל לֵאמֹר בַּחֹדֶשׁ י"פ הוויות הַשְּׁבִיעִי בְּאֶחָד אהבה, דאגה לַחֹדֶשׁ

יִהְיֶה יי לָכֶם שַׁבָּתוֹן ע"ב קס"א מע"ב זִכְרוֹן תְּרוּעָה יהוה שדי ע"ה מִקְרָא י"ב הוויות

־קֹדֶשׁ: 25 כָּל ילי ־מְלֶאכֶת עֲבֹדָה לֹא תַעֲשׂוּ וְהִקְרַבְתֶּם אִשֶּׁה

לַיהוָֹה: 26 וַיְדַבֵּר ראה יְהוָֹה מהע, אל שדי אֶל־מֹשֶׁה לֵּאמֹר:

29 Anyone who shall not be afflicted on that day must be cut off from his people.

30 And anyone who does any manner work on that day, I will destroy that soul from among his people.

31 You shall do no manner of work at all; it is an ever lasting statute for the generations to come, wherever you live.

32 It shall be a Sabbath of solemn rest for you, and you shall afflict your souls; on the evening of the ninth day of the month, from evening until evening, you shall observe your Sabbath."

SIXTH READING - JOSEPH - YESOD

33 And the Lord spoke to Moses, saying,

34 "Speak to the children of Israel saying: On the fifteenth day of the seventh month is the Feast of Tabernacles for seven days to the Lord.

35 The first day shall be a holy convocation; you shall do no manner of regular work.

36 For seven days you shall bring an offering made by fire to the Lord, and the eighth day shall be a holy convocation to you and you shall bring an offering made by fire to the Lord; it is a day of solemn assembly; you shall do no manner of regular work.

37 These are the Lord's appointed seasons, which you are to proclaim to be holy convocations to bring an offering made by fire to the Lord; a burnt offering and a meal offering, a sacrifice and drink offerings each on its own day,

38 in addition to the Sabbaths of Lord, and besides your gifts, and besides all your vows and besides all your freewill offerings which you give to the Lord.

39 So beginning with the fifteenth day of the seventh month, after you have gathered the crops of the land, celebrate the festival to the Lord for seven days; the first day is a solemn day of rest, and the eighth day also is a solemn day of rest.

40 And on the first day, you shall take choice fruit from the trees, and palm fronds, boughs of thick trees and willows of the brook, and rejoice before the Lord your God for seven days.

27 אַ֠ךְ בֶּעָשׂ֨וֹר לַחֹ֜דֶשׁ הַשְּׁבִיעִ֤י הַזֶּה֙ י֣וֹם הַכִּפֻּרִ֣ים ה֗וּא מִֽקְרָא־קֹ֨דֶשׁ֙ יִהְיֶ֣ה לָכֶ֔ם וְעִנִּיתֶ֖ם אֶת־נַפְשֹׁתֵיכֶ֑ם וְהִקְרַבְתֶּ֥ם אִשֶּׁ֖ה לַֽיהֹוָֽה׃

28 וְכָל־מְלָאכָה֙ לֹ֣א תַעֲשׂ֔וּ בְּעֶ֖צֶם הַיּ֣וֹם הַזֶּ֑ה כִּ֣י י֤וֹם כִּפֻּרִים֙ ה֔וּא לְכַפֵּ֣ר עֲלֵיכֶ֔ם לִפְנֵ֖י יְהֹוָ֥ה אֱלֹהֵיכֶֽם׃

29 כִּ֤י כָל־הַנֶּ֙פֶשׁ֙ אֲשֶׁ֣ר לֹֽא־תְעֻנֶּ֔ה בְּעֶ֖צֶם הַיּ֣וֹם הַזֶּ֑ה וְנִכְרְתָ֖ה מֵֽעַמֶּֽיהָ׃

30 וְכָל־הַנֶּ֗פֶשׁ אֲשֶׁ֤ר תַּֽעֲשֶׂה֙ כָּל־מְלָאכָ֔ה בְּעֶ֖צֶם הַיּ֣וֹם הַזֶּ֑ה וְהַֽאֲבַדְתִּ֛י אֶת־הַנֶּ֥פֶשׁ הַהִ֖וא מִקֶּ֥רֶב עַמָּֽהּ׃

31 כָּל־מְלָאכָ֖ה לֹ֣א תַעֲשׂ֑וּ חֻקַּ֤ת עוֹלָם֙ לְדֹרֹ֣תֵיכֶ֔ם בְּכֹ֖ל מֹשְׁבֹֽתֵיכֶֽם׃

32 שַׁבַּ֨ת שַׁבָּת֥וֹן הוּא֙ לָכֶ֔ם וְעִנִּיתֶ֖ם אֶת־נַפְשֹׁתֵיכֶ֑ם בְּתִשְׁעָ֤ה לַחֹ֙דֶשׁ֙ בָּעֶ֔רֶב מֵעֶ֣רֶב עַד־עֶ֔רֶב תִּשְׁבְּת֖וּ שַׁבַּתְּכֶֽם׃

SIXTH READING - JOSEPH - YESOD

33 וַיְדַבֵּ֥ר יְהֹוָ֖ה אֶל־מֹשֶׁ֥ה לֵּאמֹֽר׃

34 דַּבֵּ֛ר אֶל־בְּנֵ֥י יִשְׂרָאֵ֖ל לֵאמֹ֑ר בַּחֲמִשָּׁ֨ה עָשָׂ֜ר י֗וֹם לַחֹ֤דֶשׁ הַשְּׁבִיעִי֙ הַזֶּ֔ה חַ֧ג הַסֻּכּ֛וֹת שִׁבְעַ֥ת יָמִ֖ים לַֽיהֹוָֽה׃

35 בַּיּ֥וֹם הָרִאשׁ֖וֹן מִקְרָא־קֹ֑דֶשׁ כָּל־מְלֶ֥אכֶת עֲבֹדָ֖ה לֹ֥א תַעֲשֽׂוּ׃

36 שִׁבְעַ֣ת יָמִ֔ים תַּקְרִ֥יבוּ אִשֶּׁ֖ה לַֽיהֹוָ֑ה בַּיּ֣וֹם הַשְּׁמִינִ֡י מִקְרָא־קֹדֶשׁ֩ יִהְיֶ֨ה לָכֶ֜ם וְהִקְרַבְתֶּ֨ם אִשֶּׁ֤ה לַֽיהֹוָה֙ עֲצֶ֣רֶת הִ֔וא כָּל־מְלֶ֥אכֶת עֲבֹדָ֖ה לֹ֥א תַעֲשֽׂוּ׃

37 אֵ֚לֶּה מֽוֹעֲדֵ֣י יְהֹוָ֔ה אֲשֶׁר־תִּקְרְא֥וּ אֹתָ֖ם מִקְרָאֵ֣י קֹ֑דֶשׁ

[41] Celebrate this as a festival to the Lord for seven days each year; it is an ever lasting statute for the generations to come; you shall keep it in the seventh month.

[42] You shall dwell in booths for seven days: all native-born Israelites shall dwell in booths;

[43] that your descendants will know that I made the children of Israel dwell in booths when I brought them out of the land of Egypt. I am the Lord your God."

[44] And Moses declared to the children of Israel the appointed seasons of the Lord.

SEVENTH READING - DAVID - MALCHUT

24:[1] And the Lord spoke to Moses, saying, [2] "Command the children of Israel to bring you pure oil of pressed olives for the light so that the lamps may be kept burning continually.

[3] Outside the curtain of the Testimony in the Tent of Meeting, Aaron is to tend the lamps before the Lord from evening till morning, continually; it shall be an ever lasting statute for the generations to come. [4] He shall tend the lamps on the pure gold lampstand before the Lord continually.

Leviticus 24:2 – Lighting the candles of the Menorah in the Tabernacle (later the Temple) was very important because it provided both physical and spiritual connections to the Light. Fire is a bridge to a higher level, representing the more potent fire of the Upper Worlds, so we use physical fire to bring down spiritual fire.

> The priest is commanded to arrange lamps in the Temple every day. We have explained this in relation to the candelabra. This secret is in the likeness of Above, since the Supernal Light in the anointing oil first runs over the head of the Supernal Priest, WHICH IS THE FIRST THREE SEFIROT OF ZEIR ANPIN. Then he kindles the lamps, NAMELY, THE SEFIROT

OF MALCHUT, THE ILLUMINATIONS OF FIRE, and makes them shine, as written, "It is like the precious ointment upon the head," (Psalms 133:2) and "the anointing oil of his Lord is upon him." (Leviticus 21:12) Thus only the priest is permitted to arrange the lamps and light them twice a day, to correspond to the illumination of unity THAT OCCURS twice a day, and the daily offering which is offered twice daily are all that is needed.

> The candles are shining everywhere through the efforts of the priest, Above and Below, so there will be rejoicing and that joy will abound in all directions, NAMELY RIGHT AND LEFT, with the lighting of the lamps.
> — The Zohar, Emor 2:14-15

לְהַקְרִיב אִשֶּׁה לַיהֹוָ֖הֵאלֹהִיאהדוני עֹלָ֥ה וּמִנְחָ֛ה ע״ה ב״פ ב״ן זֶ֥בַח וּנְסָכִ֖ים דְּבַר

רָאה יֽ֣וֹם ע״ה = נגד, זן, מזבח 38 בְּיוֹמֽוֹ: מִלְּבַ֖ד שַׁבְּתֹ֣ת יְהֹוָ֑הֵאלֹהִיאהדונהי וּמִלְּבַ֣ד

מַתְּנֽוֹתֵיכֶ֗ם וּמִלְּבַ֤ד כָּל יל״י ־נִדְרֵיכֶם֙ וּמִלְּבַד֙ כָּל יל״י ־נִדְבֽוֹתֵיכֶ֔ם אֲשֶׁ֥ר

תִּתְּנ֖וּ לַיהֹוָֽהֵאלֹהִיאהדונהי: 39 אַ֡ךְ אהיה בַּחֲמִשָּׁה֩ עָשָׂ֨ר יוֹם֙ ע״ה = נגד, זן, מזבח לַחֹ֣דֶשׁ

יב הויות הַשְּׁבִיעִ֗י בְּאָסְפְּכֶם֙ אֶת־תְּבוּאַ֣ת הָאָ֔רֶץ אלהים דההין ע״ה ההן תָּחֹ֥גּוּ אֶת־

חַג־יְהֹוָ֖הֵאלֹהיאהדונהי שִׁבְעַ֣ת יָמִ֑ים נלך בַּיּ֤וֹם ע״ה = נגד, זן, מזבח הָֽרִאשׁוֹן֙ שַׁבָּת֔וֹן

וּבַיּ֥וֹם הַשְּׁמִינִ֖י שַׁבָּתֽוֹן: 40 וּלְקַחְתֶּ֨ם לָכֶ֜ם בַּיּ֣וֹם ע״ה = נגד, זן, מזבח הָרִאשׁ֗וֹן

פְּרִי֙ ע״ה אלהים דאלפין עֵ֤ץ ע״ה קס״א הָדָר֙ ד״פ ב״ן ע״ה כַּפֹּ֣ת תְּמָרִ֔ים וַעֲנַ֥ף רבוע אלהים

עֵץ־ ע״ה קס״א עָבֹ֖ת וְעַרְבֵי־נָ֑חַל וּשְׂמַחְתֶּ֗ם לִפְנֵ֛י וחכמה בינה יְהֹוָ֥הֵאלֹהיאהדונהי

אֱלֹהֵיכֶ֖ם ילה שִׁבְעַ֥ת יָמִֽים נלך: 41 וְחַגֹּתֶ֤ם אֹתוֹ֙ חַ֣ג לַֽיהֹוָ֔הֵאלֹהיאהדונהי שִׁבְעַ֥ת

יָמִ֖ים נלך בַּשָּׁנָ֑ה חֻקַּ֤ת עוֹלָם֙ לְדֹרֹ֣תֵיכֶ֔ם בַּחֹ֥דֶשׁ יב הויות הַשְּׁבִיעִ֖י תָּחֹ֥גּוּ

אֹתֽוֹ: 42 בַּסֻּכֹּ֥ת סאל תֵּשְׁב֖וּ שִׁבְעַ֣ת יָמִ֑ים נלך כָּל יל״י ־הָֽאֶזְרָח֙ בְּיִשְׂרָאֵ֔ל

יֵשְׁב֖וּ בַּסֻּכֹּֽת סאל: 43 לְמַ֙עַן֙ יֵדְע֣וּ דֹרֹֽתֵיכֶ֔ם כִּ֣י בַסֻּכּ֗וֹת הוֹשַׁ֙בְתִּי֙ אֶת־

בְּנֵ֣י יִשְׂרָאֵ֔ל בְּהוֹצִיאִ֥י אוֹתָ֖ם מֵאֶ֣רֶץ אלהים דאלפין מִצְרָ֑יִם מצר אֲנִ֖י אני, טדהד כוזו

יְהֹוָ֥הֵאלֹהיאהדונהי אֱלֹהֵיכֶֽם ילה: 44 וַיְדַבֵּ֣ר רָאה מֹשֶׁ֔ה מהש, אל שדי אֶת־מֹעֲדֵ֖י

יְהֹוָ֑הֵאלֹהיאהדונהי אֶל־בְּנֵ֖י יִשְׂרָאֵֽל:

SEVENTH READING - DAVID - MALCHUT

24 1 וַיְדַבֵּ֥ר רָאה יְהֹוָ֖הֵאלֹהיאהדונהי אֶל־מֹשֶׁ֥ה מהש, אל שדי לֵּאמֹֽר: 2 צַ֞ו פוי אֶת־

בְּנֵ֣י יִשְׂרָאֵ֗ל וְיִקְח֨וּ וחם אֵלֶ֜יךָ שֶׁ֣מֶן אני זַ֥יִת י״פ טל, י״פ כוזו, ביט זַ֥יִת אלהים אל מצפ״צ זָ֛ךְ יו

כָּתִ֖ית לַמָּא֑וֹר לְהַעֲלֹ֥ת נֵ֖ר יהוה אהיה יהוה אלהים יהוה אדני תָּמִֽיד

ע״ה נתה, קס״א קנ״א קמ״ג: 3 מִח֞וּץ לְפָרֹ֣כֶת הָעֵדֻ֗ת בְּאֹ֣הֶל לאה מוֹעֵד֮ יַעֲרֹ֣ךְ אֹתוֹ֒

אַהֲרֹ֛ן ע״ב ורבוע ע״ב מֵעֶ֥רֶב רבוע יהוה ורבוע אלהים עַד־בֹּ֖קֶר לִפְנֵ֥י וחכמה בינה

⁵ And you shall take fine flour and bake twelve loaves of bread, using two-tenths of an ephah for each loaf.

⁶ And you shall set them in two rows, six in each row, on the pure table before the Lord.

⁷ And you shall put pure frankincense along each row that it may be to the bread as a memorial portion even an offering made by fire to the Lord.

⁸ Every Sabbath day this bread is to be set out before the Lord regularly, on behalf of the Israelites, an ever lasting covenant.

⁹ And it shall be for Aaron and his sons, and they shall eat it in a holy place, because it is a most holy part of their regular share of the offerings made by fire to the Lord."

¹⁰ And the son of an Israelite woman and an Egyptian father went out among the children of Israel, and the son of the Israelite woman and a man of Israel strove together in the camp.

¹¹ The son of the Israelite woman blasphemed the Name and cursed; so they brought him to Moses. And his mother's name was Shelomith, the daughter of Dibri of the tribe of Dan.

¹² And they put him in custody until the will of the Lord should be made clear to them.

¹³ Then the Lord spoke to Moses, saying: ¹⁴ "Take the person who cursed outside the camp, and let all those who heard him lay their hands on his head, and let the entire congregation stone him.

וְזֹלֹת

Leviticus 24:5 – The 12 loaves of bread (referred to as showbread) used in the Tabernacle (*Mishkan)* represent the 12 signs of the zodiac. These loaves stayed miraculously fresh, even though they remained a whole week in the Tabernacle. This is because they were used as spiritual tools rather than as physical bread. Today, we use bread on Shabbat for the same reason.

And how do we know that the showbread comes from the King's table? Because of what is written: "and He said to me: This (Heb.

zeh) is the table that is before God," (Ezekiel 41:22) AND THE NUMERICAL VALUE OF "this" (Heb. zeh) refers to the twelve countenances. Moreover, whoever can do so should arrange and establish on his table four loaves in each Shabbat meal, which at three meals MAKE TWELVE LOAVES, which are the twelve countenances.
   — The Zohar, Pinchas 91:618

Leviticus 24:10 – Moses killed the Egyptian man by using the Name from the 72 Names of God

עַל 4 וְזָקַת עוֹלָם לְדֹרֹתֵיכֶם: תָּמִיד ע״ה נתה, קס״א קנ״א קמ״ג יְהוָֹאדנִיאהדונהי

הַמְּנֹרָה הַטְּהֹרָה יַעֲרֹךְ אֶת־הַנֵּרוֹת לִפְנֵי חכמה בינה יְהוָֹאדנִיאהדונהי תָּמִיד

ע״ה נתה, קס״א קנ״א קמ״ג: 5 וְלָקַחְתָּ סֹלֶת וְאָפִיתָ אֹתָהּ שְׁתֵּים עֶשְׂרֵה וְחַלּוֹת

שְׁנֵי עֶשְׂרֹנִים יִהְיֶה ייי הַחַלָּה להו הָאֶחָת: 6 וְשַׂמְתָּ אוֹתָם שְׁתַּיִם

מַעֲרָכוֹת שֵׁשׁ הַמַּעֲרָכֶת עַל הַשֻּׁלְחָן הַטָּהֹר י״פ אכא לִפְנֵי חכמה בינה

יְהוָֹאדנִיאהדונהי: 7 וְנָתַתָּ עַל־הַמַּעֲרֶכֶת לְבֹנָה זַכָּה וְהָיְתָה לַלֶּחֶם ג״פ יהוה

לְאַזְכָּרָה אִשֶּׁה לַיהוָֹאדנִיאהדונהי ע״ה = נגד, זך, מזבח בַּיוֹם 8 בְּיוֹם הַשַּׁבָּת בְּיוֹם

ע״ה = נגד, זך, מזבח הַשַּׁבָּת יַעַרְכֶנּוּ לִפְנֵי חכמה בינה יְהוָֹאדנִיאהדונהי תָּמִיד

ע״ה נתה, קס״א קנ״א קמ״ג מֵאֵת בְּנֵי־יִשְׂרָאֵל בְּרִית עוֹלָם: 9 וְהָיְתָה לְאַהֲרֹן

ע״ב ורבוע ע״ב וּלְבָנָיו וַאֲכָלֻהוּ בְּמָקוֹם יהוה ברבוע, ר׳פ אל קָדֹשׁ כִּי קֹדֶשׁ קָדָשִׁים

הוּא לוֹ מֵאִשֵּׁי יְהוָֹאדנִיאהדונהי וְחָק־עוֹלָם: 10 וַיֵּצֵא בֶּן־אִשָּׁה יִשְׂרְאֵלִית

וְהוּא בֶּן ־אִישׁ ע״ה קנ״א קס״א מִצְרִי מצר בְּתוֹךְ בְּנֵי יִשְׂרָאֵל וַיִּנָּצוּ בַּמַּחֲנֶה

בֶּן הַיִּשְׂרְאֵלִית וְאִישׁ ע״ה קנ״א קס״א הַיִּשְׂרְאֵלִי: 11 וַיִּקֹּב בֶּן־הָאִשָּׁה

הַיִּשְׂרְאֵלִית אֶת־הַשֵּׁם יהוה שדי וַיְקַלֵּל וַיָּבִיאוּ אֹתוֹ אֶל־מֹשֶׁה מהט, אל שדי

וְשֵׁם יהוה שדי אִמּוֹ שְׁלֹמִית בַּת־דִּבְרִי ראה לְמַטֵּה־דָן: 12 וַיַּנִּיחֻהוּ בַּמִּשְׁמָר

לִפְרֹשׁ לָהֶם עַל־פִּי יְהוָֹאדנִיאהדונהי ראה: 13 וַיְדַבֵּר יְהוָֹאדנִיאהדונהי אֶל־מֹשֶׁה

מהט, אל שדי לֵּאמֹר: 14 הוֹצֵא אֶת־הַמְקַלֵּל אֶל־מִחוּץ לַמַּחֲנֶה וְסָמְכוּ כָל

---

that removes negativity (*Kaf, Hei, Tav*). Because the man consisted of pure negativity, once the Light of this Name removed all of his negativity, there was nothing else left of him and so he died. It was no surprise that the Egyptian's son was negative; negative parents affect their children adversely, since children contain a part of their parents' souls.

This passage is really about blasphemy, and the truth about blasphemy is that when we fight the Light of God within us, we have nothing left that is of any value. With our blasphemy, we are killing the very force that keeps us alive.

. . . Rav Chiya said, "Whoever curses his God" is said in general, without specifying. Such a man surely "shall bear his sin" AND NOT BE PUNISHED. But, "he that blasphemes the Name of God, shall surely be put to death," for this is the source for everybody's faith. He is allowed to plead nothing for himself. HE CANNOT CLAIM THAT HE REFERRED TO ANOTHER GOD.
— *The Zohar, Emor 43:322*

15 And you shall speak to the children of Israel saying: 'If anyone curses his God, he will bear his son.

16 And anyone who blasphemes the Name of the Lord, he shall surely be put to death, the entire congregation shall certainly stone him, whether a stranger or native-born, when he blasphemes the Name, he shall be put to death.

17 And anyone who takes the life of a human being shall surely be put to death.

18 And anyone who takes the life of an animal must make restitution—life for life.

19 And anyone who injures his neighbor, whatever he has done must be done to him:

20 breach for breach, eye for eye, tooth for tooth, as he has injured the other, so it shall be rendered to him.

MAFTIR

21 And anyone who kills a beast must make restitution, and whoever kills a man must be put to death.

22 You are to have the same law for the stranger as for the native-born, for I am the Lord, your God."

23 And Moses spoke to the children of Israel, and they brought the blasphemer outside the camp and stoned him with stones. And the children of Israel did as the Lord commanded Moses.

שֶׁבֶר תַּחַת שָׁבֶר

Leviticus 24:20 – The famous saying of "an eye for an eye" is in this section. The *Zohar* reveals that "an eye for an eye" is not about revenge or retribution. The cosmos takes care of justice; it is not our human responsibility. If a person has a pain of any sort in this lifetime, the pain is a direct result of what he has done in this life or in a previous one. There is always justice on a spiritual level, but it sometimes takes more than one lifetime to be meted out. That is the Universal Law of Cause and Effect.

הַשֹּׁמְעִים אֶת־יְדֵיהֶם עַל־רֹאשׁוֹ וְרָגְמוּ אֹתוֹ כָּל־הָעֵדָה:

15 וְאֶל־בְּנֵי יִשְׂרָאֵל תְּדַבֵּר לֵאמֹר אִישׁ אִישׁ כִּי־יְקַלֵּל אֱלֹהָיו וְנָשָׂא חֶטְאוֹ: 16 וְנֹקֵב שֵׁם־יְהוָה מוֹת יוּמָת רָגוֹם יִרְגְּמוּ־בוֹ כָּל־הָעֵדָה כַּגֵּר כָּאֶזְרָח בְּנָקְבוֹ־שֵׁם יוּמָת: 17 וְאִישׁ כִּי יַכֶּה כָּל־נֶפֶשׁ אָדָם מוֹת יוּמָת: 18 וּמַכֵּה נֶפֶשׁ־בְּהֵמָה יְשַׁלְּמֶנָּה נֶפֶשׁ תַּחַת נָפֶשׁ: 19 וְאִישׁ כִּי־יִתֵּן מוּם בַּעֲמִיתוֹ כַּאֲשֶׁר עָשָׂה כֵּן יֵעָשֶׂה לּוֹ:

20 שֶׁבֶר תַּחַת שֶׁבֶר עַיִן תַּחַת עַיִן שֵׁן תַּחַת שֵׁן כַּאֲשֶׁר יִתֵּן מוּם בָּאָדָם כֵּן יִנָּתֶן בּוֹ:

MAFTIR

21 וּמַכֵּה בְהֵמָה יְשַׁלְּמֶנָּה וּמַכֵּה אָדָם יוּמָת: 22 מִשְׁפַּט אֶחָד יִהְיֶה לָכֶם כַּגֵּר כָּאֶזְרָח יִהְיֶה כִּי אֲנִי יְהוָה אֱלֹהֵיכֶם: 23 וַיְדַבֵּר מֹשֶׁה אֶל־בְּנֵי יִשְׂרָאֵל וַיּוֹצִיאוּ אֶת־הַמְקַלֵּל אֶל־מִחוּץ לַמַּחֲנֶה וַיִּרְגְּמוּ אֹתוֹ אָבֶן וּבְנֵי־יִשְׂרָאֵל עָשׂוּ כַּאֲשֶׁר צִוָּה יְהוָה אֶת־מֹשֶׁה:

HAFTARAH OF EMOR

The Haftarah of Emor speaks about the linen clothing that the *Kohenim* wore to serve in the Tabernacle. We learn that before they joined the general public again, they needed to remove these clothes and put on other clothing. They wore linen because of its special power to protect

Ezekiel 44:15-31

44:15 "But the priests, the Levites, the sons of Zadok that kept the charge of My Sanctuary when the children of Israel went astray from Me, they shall come near to Me to minister before Me; and they shall stand before Me to offer to Me the fat and the blood, says the Lord, God;

16 They shall enter into My Sanctuary; and they shall come near to My Table to minister to Me and they shall keep My Charge.

17 And it shall be that when they enter in at the gates of the inner court, they shall be clothed with linen garments; and no wool shall come upon them, while they minister at the gates of the inner court and within.

18 They shall wear linen turbans on their heads and shall have linen breeches upon their loins; they shall not gird themselves with anything that causes sweat.

19 And when they go forth into the outer court, into the outer court to the people, they shall take off their garments they minister in and lay them in the holy chambers, and they shall put on other garments, that they not sanctify the people with their garments.

20 They must not shave their heads or let their hair grow long; they shall only trim the hair of their heads.

21 Neither shall any priest drink wine when they enter into the inner court.

22 Neither shall they take for their wives a widow or a divorced woman; but they shall take virgins of the seed of house of Israel, or a widow that is a widow of a priest.

23 And they shall teach My people the difference between the holy and the common and cause them to discern between the unclean and the clean.

24 And in a controversy, they shall stand to judge , according to My Ordinances, they shall judge it; and they are to keep My Laws and My Statutes in all My Appointed Seasons, and they shall hallow My Sabbaths.

HAFTARAH OF EMOR

them from negativity, including the evil eye. Today, on Shabbat, kabbalists wear linen to help protect them while they pray and while they are generating their energy for the coming week.

יוֹזְקָאל פֶּרֶק מד

15 44 וְהַכֹּהֲנִים הַלְוִיִּם בְּנֵי צָדוֹק אֲשֶׁר שָׁמְרוּ אֶת־מִשְׁמֶרֶת מִקְדָּשִׁי בִּתְעוֹת בְּנֵי־יִשְׂרָאֵל מֵעָלַי הֵמָּה יִקְרְבוּ אֵלַי לְשָׁרְתֵנִי וְעָמְדוּ לְפָנַי לְהַקְרִיב לִי חֵלֶב וָדָם נְאֻם אֲדֹנָי יֱהֹוִה:

16 הֵמָּה יָבֹאוּ אֶל־מִקְדָּשִׁי וְהֵמָּה יִקְרְבוּ אֶל־שֻׁלְחָנִי לְשָׁרְתֵנִי וְשָׁמְרוּ אֶת־מִשְׁמַרְתִּי: 17 וְהָיָה בְּבוֹאָם אֶל־שַׁעֲרֵי הֶחָצֵר הַפְּנִימִית בִּגְדֵי פִשְׁתִּים יִלְבָּשׁוּ וְלֹא־יַעֲלֶה עֲלֵיהֶם צֶמֶר בְּשָׁרְתָם בְּשַׁעֲרֵי הֶחָצֵר הַפְּנִימִית וָבָיְתָה: 18 פַּאֲרֵי פִשְׁתִּים יִהְיוּ עַל־רֹאשָׁם וּמִכְנְסֵי פִשְׁתִּים יִהְיוּ עַל־מָתְנֵיהֶם לֹא יַחְגְּרוּ בַּיָּזַע: 19 וּבְצֵאתָם אֶל־הֶחָצֵר הַחִיצוֹנָה אֶל־הֶחָצֵר הַחִיצוֹנָה אֶל־הָעָם יִפְשְׁטוּ אֶת־בִּגְדֵיהֶם אֲשֶׁר־הֵמָּה מְשָׁרְתִם בָּם וְהִנִּיחוּ אוֹתָם בְּלִשְׁכֹת הַקֹּדֶשׁ וְלָבְשׁוּ בְּגָדִים אֲחֵרִים וְלֹא־יְקַדְּשׁוּ אֶת־הָעָם בְּבִגְדֵיהֶם: 20 וְרֹאשָׁם לֹא יְגַלֵּחוּ וּפֶרַע לֹא יְשַׁלֵּחוּ כָּסוֹם יִכְסְמוּ אֶת־רָאשֵׁיהֶם: 21 וְיַיִן לֹא־יִשְׁתּוּ כָּל־כֹּהֵן בְּבוֹאָם אֶל־הֶחָצֵר הַפְּנִימִית: 22 וְאַלְמָנָה וּגְרוּשָׁה לֹא־יִקְחוּ לָהֶם לְנָשִׁים כִּי אִם־בְּתוּלֹת מִזֶּרַע בֵּית יִשְׂרָאֵל וְהָאַלְמָנָה אֲשֶׁר תִּהְיֶה אַלְמָנָה מִכֹּהֵן יִקָּחוּ: 23 וְאֶת־עַמִּי יוֹרוּ בֵּין קֹדֶשׁ לְחֹל וּבֵין־טָמֵא לְטָהוֹר יוֹדִעֻם: 24 וְעַל־רִיב הֵמָּה יַעַמְדוּ לְמִשְׁפָּט (כתיב: לשפט) בְּמִשְׁפָּטַי יִשְׁפְּטֻהוּ (כתיב: ושפטהו) וְאֶת־תּוֹרֹתַי וְאֶת־חֻקֹּתַי בְּכָל־מוֹעֲדַי

25 And they shall come near no dead person to defile themselves; but for father or for mother, of for son or for daughter, for brother or for sister that has no husband, they may defile themselves.

26 And after he is cleansed, they shall reckon unto him seven days.

27 And on the day that he goes into the Sanctuary, into the inner court, to minister in the Sanctuary, he shall offer his sin offering, says the Lord God.

28 And it shall be to them an inheritance: I am their inheritance and you shall give them no possession in Israel; I am their possession.

29 They will eat the meal offerings, the sin offerings and the guilt offerings; and every devoted thing in Israel shall be theirs.

30 And the first of all the first fruits of everything and every heave offering of everything of all your offerings shall be for the priests; you shall also give to the priest the first of your dough to cause a blessing to rest on your house.

31 The priests shall not eat anything that died by itself or is torn, whether it be bird or beast.

יִשְׁמֹרוּ וְאֶת־שַׁבְּתוֹתַי יְקַדֵּשׁוּ: 25 וְאֶל־מֵת י"פ רבוע אהיה אָדָם מ"ה לֹא

יָבוֹא לְטָמְאָה כִּי אִם ע"ה מ"ב יוהך, ־לְאָב וּלְאֵם וּלְבֵן וּלְבַת לְאָח וּלְאָחוֹת

אֲשֶׁר־לֹא־הָיְתָה לְאִישׁ ע"ה קנ"א קס"א יִטַּמָּאוּ: 26 וְאַחֲרֵי טָהֳרָתוֹ שִׁבְעַת

יָמִים גלך יִסְפְּרוּ־לוֹ: 27 וּבְיוֹם ע"ה = נגד, זן, מזבח בֹּאוֹ אֶל־הַקֹּדֶשׁ אֶל־הֶחָצֵר

הַפְּנִימִית לְשָׁרֵת בַּקֹּדֶשׁ יַקְרִיב וְחַטָּאתוֹ נְאֻם אֲדֹנָי ללה יְהֹוִה־אדנ־אהדנהי:אהדי

28 וְהָיְתָה לָהֶם לְנַחֲלָה אֲנִי אני נַחֲלָתָם וַאֲחֻזָּה לֹא־תִתְּנוּ לָהֶם בְּיִשְׂרָאֵל

אֲנִי אני אֲחֻזָּתָם: 29 הַמִּנְחָה ע"ה ב"פ בן וְהַחַטָּאת וְהָאָשָׁם הֵמָּה יֹאכְלוּם

וְכָל־ ילי ־חֵרֶם בְּיִשְׂרָאֵל לָהֶם יִהְיֶה ייי: 30 וְרֵאשִׁית כָּל־ ילי ־בִּכּוּרֵי כֹל ילי

וְכָל־ ילי ־תְּרוּמַת כֹּל ילי מִכֹּל ילי תְּרוּמוֹתֵיכֶם לַכֹּהֲנִים מלה יִהְיֶה ייי

וְרֵאשִׁית עֲרִסוֹתֵיכֶם תִּתְּנוּ לַכֹּהֵן מלה לְהָנִיחַ בְּרָכָה אֶל־בֵּיתֶךָ ב"פ ראה:

31 כָּל־ ילי ־נְבֵלָה ב"פ רבוע יהוה וּטְרֵפָה מִן־הָעוֹף ג"פ ב"ן, יוסף, ציון וּמִן־הַבְּהֵמָה

ב"ן, לכב, יבם לֹא יֹאכְלוּ הַכֹּהֲנִים מלה:

BEHAR

LESSON OF BEHAR
(Leviticus 25:1-26:2)

Before we can even begin to ask what we can do to ensure that we have only blessings and no curses in our lives, we must fully understand what blessings and curses actually are. We know that Satan's most powerful curse is sadness because it is a direct negation of the Essence of God, which is only joy. The difficulty is that everyone in this world thinks they know what happiness is. It seems so simple: *Anyone who can get what he wants in life is happy.* Because of this belief, we think that anyone with power or money or influence must be happy. We are forever hearing: "They have a lot of money... they vacation in faraway places in their private jet... what great lives they have... that is true happiness..." But if we look closely, we see among the wealthiest people those who are the most forlorn, the most bitter, and the most problem-ridden. Many probably never experience a moment of happiness all year long, except possibly when they are sleeping!

We now see how superficial our perspective on happiness is. If we want to find truly happy people, each one of us must seek within. We should not look to our friends or family for an answer. Just because a person has certain things does not mean he or she is happy. When we claim to know what happiness is, we are speaking about momentary, ephemeral happiness, when what we really want to know about is the happiness experienced by people whose faces glow all the time, who do not need physical things to bring them joy. Sure, these same people go to the movies and buy things for themselves, but that is not what brings them happiness.

Rav Berg has spoken about people who go to bars on Friday nights. They go to one bar, stay for a while, then go on to another bar, and then another and another; all night they must keep moving. If they aren't enjoying themselves, why do they keep going to yet another bar? We are people who enjoy things for a moment, but when the pleasure ends, we look for something else to give us pleasure, and then another thing, and another.

Just like the ending of a movie, the moment the entertainment is over, the pleasure is gone. The happiness does not stay with us, so tomorrow we'll need to see another movie. But what we are really looking for is true happiness, not the happiness that is here today and gone tomorrow. Almost every pleasure in this world is momentary and temporary.

The truth is this entire world is too fast-paced. Everything we desire must come to us immediately or we become irritable and angry. It seems impossible to find lasting happiness in such a world. Whenever something new comes up, everyone runs after it. When it's gone, something else takes its place, and we're off again, running after it. New computers, new programs, new games— everyone wants to be the first to get it, see it, use it. And then a week later, the craze is over. People think that these things will bring them happiness. But we know that's not true because we wouldn't run after the second thing if the first one had brought lasting happiness our way. And the same principle holds for food. The taste disappears almost immediately, and just as quickly, the body starts the elimination process. The issue is typified by the way we eat sunflower seeds: Before we've even finished chewing what's in our mouths, we're breaking open the next shell.

If we ask the rich—those who can throw money away without feeling any anxiety—about happiness, what would they say? "We are not happy and we haven't yet found what we are looking for in life." Thankfully, it's not that way for everyone, but most affluent individuals experience problems, no matter how much money they have.

If we ask the people who are moderately well-off—those who don't have all the money they want, but do not lack for anything either—we will often find very hard-working people who want more, even though they already have everything they really need. Usually these people are so busy trying to make money that at the end of the day, they don't even have time to enjoy the money they have made. What kind of happiness can that be?

And if we ask the working poor—those who barely make ends meet, and who hardly have enough to eat—if they were happy, what would they say? They work hard all day, sometimes all night, yet nonetheless find that they are at the bottom of the economic ladder, even though they work the hardest of everyone. They are certain that their rich employers are happy, while they, the workers, are the least happy of all the people in the world.

It looks as if no one in this world can find happiness. So we must ask ourselves how it can be that God seems to have created the world in such a way that no one would be happy and everyone would suffer. We know, however, that this is impossible because the Creator created this world only so that we and the rest of Creation would take pleasure in it. How can we correct all of this so that our sadness will be replaced with happiness? We must first understand that the Source of all happiness is the Creator. God designed the path for us to achieve happiness, but to truly understand this, its important to also understand the curse of Satan—the curse that puts limitations on our happiness and pleasure in this life. Where does the problem lie? It must lie within, for the Creator has no flaws and created the world perfectly; we are the ones who destroy the creation of this perfect world.

SYNOPSIS OF BEHAR

Behar means "on the mountain." In this chapter, "the mountain" refers to Mount Sinai, actually one of the smaller mountains of the world. The sages teach that because Mount Sinai is so small, it represents a spiritual lack of ego. When all the mountains were asked why they should be chosen for the immense revelation of Light that took place at the giving of the Ten Utterances, all the other mountains gave grandiose reasons about why they should be chosen. Mount Sinai, not having an ego, was willing to be chosen but didn't feel entitled to that honor—and was thus given the enormous grace of being the place of the Revelation. When we connect with this specific chapter, we have an opportunity to make a connection to Mount Sinai's energy by relinquishing our egos.

FIRST READING - ABRAHAM - CHESED

25:1 **A**nd the Lord spoke to Moses on Mount Sinai, saying, *2* "Speak to the children of Israel and say to them: When you enter the land I am going to give you, the land itself shall keep a Sabbath to the Lord.

3 For six years sow your fields, and for six years prune your vineyards and gather in the produce thereof. 4 But in the seventh year shall it be a Sabbath of solemn rest for the land, a Sabbath to the Lord; you shall neither sow your fields nor prune your vineyards.

5 You shall not reap what grows of itself or harvest the grapes of your untended vines; it shall be a year of solemn rest for the land.

6 Whatever the land yields during the Sabbath year will be food for you—for yourself, your servant and maidservant, and the hired servant and for the settlers who live among you, 7 as well as for your cattle and for the beasts in your land, whatever the land produces may be eaten.

8 And you shall count off seven Sabbaths of years—seven years seven times—so that the seven Sabbaths of years amount to a period of forty-nine years.

FROM THE RAV

The Torah teaches us that the world of chaos is *Malchut* (the 1 Percent Illusionary Reality) and the world of joy and happiness is *Zeir Anpin* (the 99 Percent Reality). The mind is unlimited, but the body is limited. When we look at chaos, it is always related to the physical reality. Poverty is not having money; illness is related to a sick body; a bad relationship has to do with another person.

The true lesson of Mount Sinai is the reality of mind over matter, not "Thou shall not steal" and the rest of the Ten Utterances. For thousands of years, we've been told "Thou shall not steal," so there's been no thievery, or "Thou shall not murder," so there's been no murder in the last ten years? No, Mount Sinai is about the power of mind over matter—that I can accomplish whatever I put my mind to, as long as I use the rules and work hard.

Uncertainty is the one main impediment to achieving mind over matter. If we aren't sure our health will be restored, our faulty relationship can be healed, and money can be earned, then our problems—our chaos—won't be fixed. But if we have the certainty that things can be restored, healed, cured, then certainty will cause mind over matter to manifest in the end—in spite of any apparent ups and downs in the process. All forms of chaos can change—that's what the Torah is about.

Religion and morals are not what Mount Sinai was about. It was about spirituality. And according to the *Zohar*, spirituality is one thing—*Zeir Anpin*, connecting to the 99 Percent Reality and not the illusion of the 1 Percent.

FIRST READING - ABRAHAM - CHESED

25 1 וַיְדַבֵּר רֵאה יְהוָֹוּ(אדנילאהדונהי אֶל־מֹשֶׁה מהטע, אל שׁדי בְּהַר אור, רז, אין סוף סִינַי

לֵאמֹר: 2 דַּבֵּר רֵאה אֶל־בְּנֵי יִשְׂרָאֵל וְאָמַרְתָּ אֲלֵהֶם כִּי תָבֹאוּ נגמם, ה״פ יהוה

אֶל־הָאָרֶץ אלהים דההין ע״ה אֲשֶׁר אֲנִי אני, טדהד כוזו נֹתֵן לָכֶם אבגית״ץ, וער, אהבת חום

וְשָׁבְתָה הָאָרֶץ אלהים דההין ע״ה שַׁבָּת לַיהוָֹו(אדנילאהדונהי: 3 שֵׁשׁ שָׁנִים תִּזְרַע

שָׂדֶךָ וְשֵׁשׁ שָׁנִים תִּזְמֹר כַּרְמֶךָ וְאָסַפְתָּ אֶת־תְּבוּאָתָהּ: 4 וּבַשָּׁנָה

הַשְּׁבִיעִת שַׁבַּת שַׁבָּתוֹן יִהְיֶה יהוה אלהים דאלפין לָאָרֶץ שַׁבָּת לַיהוָֹו(אדנילאהדונהי

שָׂדְךָ לֹא תִזְרָע וְכַרְמְךָ לֹא תִזְמֹר: 5 אֵת סְפִיחַ קְצִירְךָ לֹא תִקְצוֹר

וְאֶת־עִנְּבֵי נְזִירֶךָ לֹא תִבְצֹר שְׁנַת שַׁבָּתוֹן יִהְיֶה לָאָרֶץ יהוה אלהים דאלפין:

6 וְהָיְתָה שַׁבַּת הָאָרֶץ אלהים דההין ע״ה לָכֶם לְאָכְלָה לְךָ וּלְעַבְדְּךָ וְלַאֲמָתֶךָ

וְלִשְׂכִירְךָ וּלְתוֹשָׁבְךָ הַגָּרִים עִמָּךְ ה הויות, נגמם: 7 וְלִבְהֶמְתְּךָ וְלַחַיָּה אֲשֶׁר

בְּאַרְצֶךָ תִּהְיֶה כָל־תְּבוּאָתָהּ יכי לֶאֱכֹל: 8 וְסָפַרְתָּ לְךָ שֶׁבַע ע״ב ואלהים דיודין

שַׁבְּתֹת שָׁנִים שֶׁבַע ע״ב ואלהים דיודין שָׁנִים שֶׁבַע ע״ב ואלהים דיודין פְּעָמִים וְהָיוּ

שַׁבַּת שַׁבָּתוֹן

Leviticus 25:4 – There is a *shemitah*, or sabbatical, every seven years in Israel. Just as people "rest" from the toils of the work week on Shabbat, the seventh day, the land of Israel must disconnect from the world of *Malchut* (the physical world) every seventh year. So every seven years, the land in Israel cannot be worked. The *Zohar* explains that Israel is the heart of the body of the world.

> *. . . This must be so for the Holy One, blessed be He, made Israel the heart of the whole world, and the relationship of Israel to the other nations is as that of the heart to other parts of the body. And just as the other parts of the body have no existence, even for a moment, without the heart, so it is that none of the other peoples can exist in the world without*

Israel. Jerusalem, too, has the same relationship with the other countries, being as the heart to the parts of the body, which is why it is in the center of the whole world just as the heart is in the center of the limbs.
> — The Zohar, Pinchas 25:152

When Israel takes care of itself, this helps the rest of the world. For us, too, a constant connection to *Malchut* (physicality) will not work; we also need a connection to the 99 Percent Realm of spiritual Light. This is the greater reality that we cannot perceive from the limited point of view of our five earthly senses, which can comprehend only the 1 Percent Illusionary Reality, the physical world. Shabbat is our chance to disconnect from this physical world so that we can become elevated to the spiritual realm.

⁹ Then you shall proclaim with the blast of the horn sounded everywhere on the tenth day of the seventh month; on the Day of Atonement you shall make proclamation with the horn throughout your land.

¹⁰ And you shall hallow the fiftieth year and proclaim liberty throughout the land to all its inhabitants; it shall be a jubilee for you; and you shall return every man to his family property and you shall return every man to his family.

¹¹ The fiftieth year shall be a jubilee for you; you shall not sow, nor reap what grows of itself or gather the grapes of the untended vines.

¹² For it is a jubilee and is shall be holy to you; you shall eat only what is taken directly from the fields.

¹³ In this Year of Jubilee everyone is to return to his own property.

ON A LEAP YEAR: SECOND READING - ISAAC - GEVURAH

¹⁴ And if you sell land to one of your neighbors or buy of your neighbor's hand, do not wrong each other.

¹⁵ You are to buy from your neighbor according to the number of years since the Jubilee, and he shall sell to you according to the number of years left for harvesting crops.

¹⁶ According to the number of the years you are to increase the price, and when the years are few, you are to decrease the price, for what he is really selling you is the number of crops.

שְׁנַת הַחֲמִשִּׁים

Leviticus 25:10 – There is a *yovel*, or jubilee year, after every 49th year (that is, at the end of seven *shemitah* cycles, 7x7 = 49). Thus, every 50th year, the land of Israel cannot be worked. Disconnecting from *Malchut* every seven years is important, but the 50th year connection is even more vital, since it connects to *Binah*. In our personal lives, to connect to the energy and consciousness of *Binah*, it is necessary to disconnect from this world of physicality. Consequently, we have to make true sacrifices that transform and elevate us because this is

when and how we connect to the 99 Percent Realm.

"And you shall hallow the fiftieth year… it shall be a jubilee for you." (Leviticus 25:10) What is a jubilee? It accords with the words, "and that spreads out its roots by the river (Heb. yuval)." (Jeremiah 17:8) For jubilee means a river after the river, which is Ima that comes out, flows and emerges uninterruptedly to the garden, which is Malchut.
— The Zohar, Ha'azinu:86

לְךָ יְמֵי שֶׁבַע עּ״ב ו־אלהים דּיּוּדִין שַׁבְּתֹת הַשָּׁנִים תֵּשַׁע וְאַרְבָּעִים שָׁנָה:

9 וְהַעֲבַרְתָּ שׁוֹפַר תְּרוּעָה בַּחֹדֶשׁ י״ב הוויות הַשְּׁבִעִי בֶּעָשׂוֹר לַחֹדֶשׁ י״ב הוויות

בְּיוֹם עּ״ה = נגר, זך, מזבח הַכִּפֻּרִים תַּעֲבִירוּ שׁוֹפָר בְּכָל בּ״ן, לכב, יבמ אַרְצְכֶם:

10 וְקִדַּשְׁתֶּם אֵת ‏שְׁנַת הַחֲמִשִּׁים‏ שָׁנָה וּקְרָאתֶם דְּרוֹר ב״פ (רבוע אלהים + ה)

בָּאָרֶץ אלהים דאלפין לְכָל יה אדני יֹשְׁבֶיהָ יוֹבֵל הִוא תִּהְיֶה לָכֶם וְשַׁבְתֶּם

אִישׁ עּ״ה קנ״א קס״א אֶל־אֲחֻזָּתוֹ וְאִישׁ עּ״ה קנ״א קס״א אֶל־מִשְׁפַּחְתּוֹ ‏תָּשֻׁבוּ‏:

11 יוֹבֵל הִוא שְׁנַת הַחֲמִשִּׁים שָׁנָה תִּהְיֶה לָכֶם לֹא תִזְרָעוּ וְלֹא תִקְצְרוּ

אֶת־סְפִיחֶיהָ וְלֹא תִבְצְרוּ אֶת־נְזִרֶיהָ: 12 כִּי יוֹבֵל הִוא קֹדֶשׁ תִּהְיֶה

לָכֶם מִן־הַשָּׂדֶה שדי תֹּאכְלוּ אֶת־תְּבוּאָתָהּ: 13 בִּשְׁנַת הַיּוֹבֵל הַזֹּאת

תָּשֻׁבוּ אִישׁ עּ״ה קנ״א קס״א אֶל־אֲחֻזָּתוֹ:

ON A LEAP YEAR: SECOND READING - ISAAC - GEVURAH

14 וְכִי־תִמְכְּרוּ מִמְכָּר לַעֲמִיתֶךָ אוֹ קָנֹה עּ״ה = יוסף, ציון, ר״פ יהוה מִיַּד עֲמִיתֶךָ

אַל־תּוֹנוּ אִישׁ עּ״ה קנ״א קס״א אֶת־אָחִיו: 15 בְּמִסְפַּר שָׁנִים אַחַר הַיּוֹבֵל

תִּקְנֶה ג״פ אלף למד מֵאֵת עֲמִיתֶךָ בְּמִסְפַּר שְׁנֵי־תְבוּאֹת יִמְכָּר־לָךְ: 16 לְפִי |

רֹב עּ״ב ורבוע מ״ה הַשָּׁנִים תַּרְבֶּה מִקְנָתוֹ וּלְפִי מְעֹט הַשָּׁנִים תַּמְעִיט

מִקְנָתוֹ כִּי מִסְפַּר תְּבוּאֹת הוּא מֹכֵר לָךְ: 17 וְלֹא תוֹנוּ אִישׁ עּ״ה קנ״א קס״א

תָּשֻׁבוּ

Leviticus 25:10 – Every 50 years in Israel, land rights revert to the original owner. After the Israelites settled there, the land of Israel was divided into 12 pieces for the 12 tribes. No matter who bought land, there was no real transfer of property, since the property always reverted to the tribe. Metaphorically, land is not just a place where we live, but also a whole new incarnation. Every time we move into a new house or change the city we live in, we acquire part of the *tikkun*, or correction, of that land. When we move or make major changes in our lives, we should expect new and different things to happen.

¹⁷ And do not wrong each other, but you shall fear your God. I am the Lord your God.

¹⁸ You shall follow My Statutes and keep My Ordinances, and you will live safely in the land.

ON A LEAP YEAR: THIRD READING - JACOB - TIFERET
WHEN CONNECTED: SECOND READING - ISAAC - GEVURAH

¹⁹ And the land will yield its fruit, and you will eat your fill and live there in safety.

²⁰ And if you shall say, 'What will we eat in the seventh year if we do not plant or harvest our crops?'

²¹ then I will send you such a blessing in the sixth year that the land will yield enough for three years.

²² And you shall sow the eighth year, and eat from the produce, the old store, until the ninth year and will continue to eat from it until the harvest of the ninth year comes in.

²³ And the land shall not be sold in perpetuity, for the land is Mine and you are strangers and settlers with Me.

²⁴ And in all the land of your possession, you shall grant a redemption of the land.

ON A LEAP YEAR: FOURTH READING - MOSES - NETZACH

²⁵ If one of your countrymen becomes poor and sells some of his possession, then his nearest relative shall come and redeem that which his countryman has sold.

מַה־נֹּאכַל

Leviticus 25:20 – The people wondered what they would eat in the seventh year, when they were commanded not to work the land. There is an inverse relationship between the amount of energy we expend trying to retain control of everything and the amount of control we actually do manage to retain. This is because it's only through surrender—through giving up our control—that we acquire real control. The more we let go of our egotistic desires and agendas, the more we gain in all aspects of our life.

אֶת־עֲמִיתוֹ וְיָרֵאתָ מֵאֱלֹהֶיךָ יל״ה כִּי אֲנִי אני, טדה״ד כוז״ו יְהֹוָ֖ה אהדונהי
אֱלֹהֵיכֶם יל״ה: 18 וַעֲשִׂיתֶם אֶת־חֻקֹּתַי וְאֶת־מִשְׁפָּטַי תִּשְׁמְרוּ וַעֲשִׂיתֶם
אֹתָם וִישַׁבְתֶּם עַל־הָאָרֶץ אלהים דההין ע״ה לָבֶטַח:

ON A LEAP YEAR: THIRD READING - JACOB - TIFERET
WHEN CONNECTED: SECOND READING - ISAAC - GEVURAH

19 וְנָתְנָה הָאָרֶץ אלהים דההין ע״ה פִּרְיָהּ וַאֲכַלְתֶּם לָשֹׂבַע ע״ב ואלהים דיודין ויִשַׁבְתֶּם
לָבֶטַח עָלֶיהָ פהל: 20 וְכִי תֹאמְרוּ מַה־נֹּאכַל בַּשָּׁנָה הַשְּׁבִיעִת הֵן לֹא
נִזְרָע וְלֹא נֶאֱסֹף אֶת־תְּבוּאָתֵנוּ: 21 וְצִוִּיתִי אֶת־בִּרְכָתִי לָכֶם בַּשָּׁנָה
הַשִּׁשִּׁית וְעָשָׂת אֶת־הַתְּבוּאָה לִשְׁלֹשׁ הַשָּׁנִים: 22 וּזְרַעְתֶּם אֵת הַשָּׁנָה
הַשְּׁמִינִת וַאֲכַלְתֶּם מִן־הַתְּבוּאָה יָשָׁן עַד | הַשָּׁנָה הַתְּשִׁיעִת עַד־בּוֹא
תְּבוּאָתָהּ תֹּאכְלוּ יָשָׁן: 23 וְהָאָרֶץ אלהים דההין ע״ה לֹא תִמָּכֵר לִצְמִתֻת כִּי־
לִי הָאָרֶץ אלהים דההין ע״ה כִּי־גֵרִים וְתוֹשָׁבִים אַתֶּם עִמָּדִי: 24 וּבְכֹל
ב״ן, לכב, יבמ אֶרֶץ אלהים אלהים דאלפין אֲחֻזַּתְכֶם גְּאֻלָּה מ״ה תִּתְּנוּ לָאָרֶץ אלהים דאלפין:

ON A LEAP YEAR: FOURTH READING - MOSES - NETZACH

25 כִּי־יָמוּךְ אָחִיךָ וּמָכַר מֵאֲחֻזָּתוֹ וּבָא גֹאֲלוֹ הַקָּרֹב אֵלָיו וְגָאַל אֵת
מִמְכַּר אָחִיו: 26 וְאִישׁ ע״ה קנ״א קס״א כִּי לֹא יִהְיֶה ״״ לּוֹ גֹּאֵל וְהִשִּׂיגָה יָדוֹ

יָמוּךְ

Leviticus 25:25 – Here, the Bible says: "If your brother becomes poor...." It uses the word "brother" to remind us that we are all one, that the poverty of our brother is our own poverty. The *Zohar* says that we are all the same, and if one person feels pain, we should all feel pain. Rav Isaac Luria (the Ari) wrote:

The six positive precepts within the letter Vav are as follows: 1) "that your brother may live with you," (Leviticus 25:36) which is related to charity. It means that you should seek means for your brother to live with you and be able to sustain himself....
— Kitvei Ha'Ari, Writings of the Ari, Gate of Reincarnation, 17th Introduction:4

²⁶ And if a man has no one to redeem it for him but he himself prospers and acquires sufficient means to redeem it, ²⁷ he is to determine the value for the years since he sold it and refund the balance to the man to whom he sold it; and he can then go back to his own property.²⁸ But if he does not acquire the means to get it back for himself, then what he sold will remain in the possession of the buyer until the Year of Jubilee, and in the jubilee it will be returned, and he can then go back to his property.

ON A LEAP YEAR: FIFTH READING - AARON – HOD
WHEN CONNECTED: THIRD READING - JACOB - TIFERET

²⁹ And if a man sells a house in a walled city, then he retains the right of redemption a full year after its sale, during that time, he may redeem it. ³⁰ If it is not redeemed before a full year has passed, then the house in the walled city shall belong in perpetuity to the buyer and his descendants, it is not to be returned in the Jubilee.

³¹ But houses in villages without walls around them are to be considered with the fields of the country, they may be redeemed, and they shall be returned in the Jubilee. ³² But as for the cities of the Levites, the houses of the cities of their possessions, the Levites shall always have the right to redeem their houses.

³³ And if a man purchase of the Levite, then the house that was sold in the city of his possession, shall be returned in the Jubilee, because the houses in the towns of the Levites are their property among the children of Israel. ³⁴ But the pastureland about the cities belonging to their towns may not be sold; for it is their permanent possession.

וְעָרֵי הַלְוִיִּם

Leviticus 25:32 – In the time of the Temple, the Levites had no possessions. They were connected to God, almost as though they were living solely in the 99 Percent Spiritual Realm. Today, we have to live in the 1 Percent Illusionary World of our limited physical perception, but we can still connect to the 99 Percent. It's up to each of us, in the absence of the Temple, to be both a *Kohen* and a Levite so that we can connect to the Light ourselves, yet still be in balance with the physical world.

"Now, in this world, they eat from the fruits of the Tree of Life. And who is that, meaning, that area that is to be found by the poor? That is the secret of Malchut, which is called "poor," since she contains nothing of her own, except what Zeir Anpin provides her. And she, Malchut, is called the fruit of the tree that is within the Garden. And therefore they eat from that fruit, which is Malchut, in this world."
— The Zohar, Behar 3:12

וּמָצָא֙ כְּדֵ֣י גְאֻלָּת֔וֹ: 27 וְחִשַּׁב֙ אֶת־שְׁנֵ֣י מִמְכָּר֔וֹ וְהֵשִׁיב֙ אֶת־הָ֣עֹדֵ֔ף

לָאִ֕ישׁ אֲשֶׁ֥ר מָֽכַר־ל֖וֹ וְשָׁ֥ב לַאֲחֻזָּתֽוֹ: 28 וְאִ֨ם לֹא־

מָֽצְאָ֜ה יָד֗וֹ דֵּי֮ הָשִׁ֣יב לוֹ֒ וְהָיָ֣ה מִמְכָּר֗וֹ בְּיַד֙ הַקֹּנֶ֣ה

אֹת֔וֹ עַ֖ד שְׁנַ֣ת הַיּוֹבֵ֑ל וְיָצָא֙ בַּיֹּבֵ֔ל וְשָׁ֖ב לַאֲחֻזָּתֽוֹ:

ON A LEAP YEAR: FIFTH READING - AARON – HOD
WHEN CONNECTED: THIRD READING - JACOB - TIFERET

29 וְאִ֕ישׁ כִּֽי־יִמְכֹּ֥ר בֵּית־מוֹשַׁב֙ עִ֣יר

וְחוֹמָ֔ה וְהָיְתָה֙ גְּאֻלָּת֔וֹ עַד־תֹּ֖ם שְׁנַ֣ת מִמְכָּר֑וֹ יָמִ֖ים תִּהְיֶ֥ה

גְאֻלָּתֽוֹ: 30 וְאִ֣ם לֹֽא־יִגָּאֵ֗ל עַד־מְלֹ֤את לוֹ֙ שָׁנָ֣ה תְמִימָ֔ה וְ֠קָם

הַבַּ֨יִת אֲשֶׁר־בָּעִ֜יר אֲשֶׁר־ל֣וֹ (כתיב: לֹא) חֹמָ֗ה לַצְּמִיתֻ֧ת

לַקֹּנֶ֛ה אֹת֖וֹ לְדֹרֹתָ֑יו לֹ֥א יֵצֵ֖א בַּיֹּבֵֽל: 31 וּבָתֵּ֣י הַחֲצֵרִ֗ים

אֲשֶׁ֨ר אֵין־לָהֶ֤ם חֹמָה֙ סָבִ֔יב עַל־שְׂדֵ֥ה הָאָ֖רֶץ יֵחָשֵׁ֑ב גְּאֻלָּה֙

תִּֽהְיֶה־לּ֔וֹ וּבַיֹּבֵ֖ל יֵצֵֽא: 32 וְעָרֵי֙ הַלְוִיִּ֔ם בָּתֵּ֖י עָרֵ֣י אֲחֻזָּתָ֑ם גְּאֻלַּ֥ת

עוֹלָ֖ם תִּהְיֶ֥ה לַלְוִיִּֽם: 33 וַאֲשֶׁ֤ר יִגְאַל֙ מִן־הַלְוִיִּ֔ם וְיָצָ֧א מִמְכַּר־בַּ֛יִת

וְעִ֥יר אֲחֻזָּת֖וֹ בַּיֹּבֵ֑ל כִּ֣י בָתֵּ֞י עָרֵ֣י הַלְוִיִּ֗ם הִ֚וא אֲחֻזָּתָ֔ם

בְּת֖וֹךְ בְּנֵ֥י יִשְׂרָאֵֽל: 34 וּֽשְׂדֵ֛ה מִגְרַ֥שׁ עָרֵיהֶ֖ם לֹ֣א יִמָּכֵ֑ר כִּֽי־אֲחֻזַּ֥ת

עוֹלָ֛ם ה֖וּא לָהֶֽם: 35 וְכִֽי־יָמ֣וּךְ אָחִ֔יךָ וּמָ֥טָה יָד֖וֹ עִמָּ֑ךְ וְהֶחֱזַ֣קְתָּ

בּ֔וֹ גֵּ֧ר וְתוֹשָׁ֛ב וָחַ֖י עִמָּֽךְ: 36 אַל־תִּקַּ֤ח מֵֽאִתּוֹ֙

נֶ֣שֶׁךְ וְתַרְבִּ֔ית וְיָרֵ֖אתָ מֵֽאֱלֹהֶ֑יךָ וְחֵ֥י אָחִ֖יךָ עִמָּֽךְ:

נֶשֶׁךְ וְתַרְבִּית

Leviticus 25:36 – We learn here that we should never take advantage of someone in distress. We don't have to help everyone, but we should never use anyone's misfortune against them. As for ourselves, we are all "wanting" in some area of our lives, but if we speak enviously of what others have, we will end up with even less.

35 And if one of your brethren becomes poor and is unable to support himself among you, then you shall help him as a stranger and as a settler shall he live with you.

36 Do not take interest of any kind from him, but fear your God, so that your brethren may live with you. 37 You must not lend him money at interest or sell him food at a profit. 38 I am the Lord, your God, who brought you out of the land of Egypt to give you the land of Canaan; to be your God.

ON A LEAP YEAR: SIXTH READING - JOSEPH - YESOD
WHEN CONNECTED: FOURTH READING - MOSES - NETZACH

39 And if one of your brethren becomes poor among you and sells himself to you, do not make him work as a slave.

40 He is to be treated as a hired worker or a settler among you; he is to work for you until the Year of Jubilee.

41 Then he and his children are to be released, and he will go back to his own family and to the property of his forefathers.

42 For they are My servants, whom I brought out of land of Egypt, they shall not be sold as slaves.

43 You shall not rule over them ruthlessly, but fear your God. 44 And as for your male and female slaves whom you may have, from the nations around you; from them you may buy slaves.

45 Moreover of the children of the strangers that are living among you, you may buy and of the members of their family born in your land, and they may become your property.

46 You can will them to your children as inherited property and can make them slaves for ever, but you must not rule over your fellow Israelites ruthlessly.

וְנִמְכַּר־לָךְ

Leviticus 25:39 – The disposition of slaves is discussed in this verse, but we must never even contemplate having ownership of other people. If someone is working for us, we must not feel like his or her master. We are all independent, yet interdependent. There can never be a time when people are allowed to own one another, nor should parents feel a sense of ownership toward their children.

37 אֶת־כַּסְפְּךָ לֹא־תִתֵּן ב״פ כהת לוֹ בְּנֶשֶׁךְ יש״ע וּבְמַרְבִּית לֹא־תִתֵּן ב״פ כהת

אָכְלֶךָ: 38 אֲנִי אני, טדה״ד כו״י יְהוָֹהאדני ואהדנהי אֱלֹהֵיכֶם ילה אֲשֶׁר־הוֹצֵאתִי

אֶתְכֶם מֵאֶרֶץ אלהים דאלפין מִצְרַיִם מצר לָתֵת לָכֶם אֶת־אֶרֶץ אלהים דאלפין

כְּנַעַן לִהְיוֹת לָכֶם לֵאלֹהִים מום, אהיה אדני, ילה:

ON A LEAP YEAR: SIXTH READING - JOSEPH - YESOD
WHEN CONNECTED: FOURTH READING - MOSES - NETZACH

39 וְכִי־יָמוּךְ אָחִיךָ עִמָּךְ ה׳ הויות, נגמ וְנִמְכַּר־לָךְ לֹא־תַעֲבֹד בּוֹ עֲבֹדַת

עָבֶד: 40 כְּשָׂכִיר כְּתוֹשָׁב יִהְיֶה יי׳ עִמָּךְ ה׳ הויות, נגמ עַד־שְׁנַת הַיֹּבֵל יַעֲבֹד

עִמָּךְ ה׳ הויות, נגמ: 41 וְיָצָא מֵעִמָּךְ ה׳ הויות, נגמ הוּא וּבָנָיו עִמּוֹ וְשָׁב אֶל־

מִשְׁפַּחְתּוֹ וְאֶל־אֲחֻזַּת אֲבֹתָיו יָשׁוּב: 42 כִּי־עֲבָדַי הֵם אֲשֶׁר־הוֹצֵאתִי

אֹתָם מֵאֶרֶץ אלהים דאלפין מִצְרַיִם מצר לֹא יִמָּכְרוּ מִמְכֶּרֶת עָבֶד: 43 לֹא־

תִרְדֶּה בוֹ בְּפָרֶךְ וְיָרֵאתָ מֵאֱלֹהֶיךָ ילה: 44 וְעַבְדְּךָ פו׳ וַאֲמָתְךָ אֲשֶׁר יִהְיוּ

אל־לָךְ מֵאֵת הַגּוֹיִם אֲשֶׁר סְבִיבֹתֵיכֶם מֵהֶם תִּקְנוּ עֶבֶד וְאָמָה

דמב, מלוי ע״ב: 45 וְגַם יג״ל מִבְּנֵי הַתּוֹשָׁבִים הַגָּרִים עִמָּכֶם מֵהֶם תִּקְנוּ

וּמִמִּשְׁפַּחְתָּם אֲשֶׁר עִמָּכֶם אֲשֶׁר הוֹלִידוּ בְּאַרְצְכֶם וְהָיוּ לָכֶם

לַאֲחֻזָּה: 46 וְהִתְנַחַלְתֶּם אֹתָם לִבְנֵיכֶם אַחֲרֵיכֶם לָרֶשֶׁת אֲחֻזָּה לְעֹלָם

ריבוע ס״ג + י׳ אותיות בָּהֶם תַּעֲבֹדוּ וּבְאַחֵיכֶם בְּנֵי־יִשְׂרָאֵל אִישׁ ע״ה קנ״א קס״א

בְּאָחִיו לֹא־תִרְדֶּה בוֹ בְּפָרֶךְ:

ON A LEAP YEAR: SEVENTH READING - DAVID - MALCHUT

[47] And if a stranger who is a settler among you becomes rich and one of your brethren beside him becomes poor and sells himself to the stranger living among you or to a member of the stranger's family,

[48] he retains the right of redemption after he has sold himself, one of his brethren may redeem him:[49] or his uncle or his uncle's son may redeem him, or any blood relative in his family may redeem him; or if he prospers, he may redeem himself.

[50] And he and his buyer are to count the time from the year he sold himself up to the Year of Jubilee, and the price for his release is to be based on the rate paid to a hired man for that number of years.

[51] And if many years remain, he must pay for his redemption a larger share of the price that he was bought for. [52] And if only a few years remain until the Year of Jubilee, he is to compute that and pay for his redemption accordingly.

[53] He is to be treated as a servant hired from year to year; you must see to it that his owner does not rule over him ruthlessly.

[54] And if he is not redeemed by any of these means, he and his children are to be released in the Year of Jubilee,

ON A LEAP YEAR: MAFTIR

[55] for the children of Israel belong to Me as servants; they are My servants, whom I brought out of land of Egypt. I am the Lord, your God.

[26:1] Do not make for yourselves idols or set up a graven image or a pillar for yourselves, and do not place any figured stone in your land to bow down before it, for I am the Lord your God. [2] You shall keep My Sabbaths and have reverence for My Sanctuary. I am the Lord.

Leviticus 25:48 – If we see someone being treated as a slave, either physically or spiritually, we have a responsibility to intervene. Slavery is so wrong that we must not only avoid practicing it, we must also take action against it if we see it being practiced.

ON A LEAP YEAR: SEVENTH READING - DAVID - MALCHUT

47 וְכִי תַשִּׂיג יַד גֵּר בּ״ן קּנ״א וְתוֹשָׁב עִמָּךְ ה׳ הוייות, גמם וּמָךְ אָחִיךָ עִמּוֹ וְנִמְכַּר לְגֵר בּ״ן קּנ״א תּוֹשָׁב עִמָּךְ ה׳ הוייות, גמם אוֹ לְעֵקֶר מִשְׁפַּחַת גֵּר בּ״ן קּנ״א:

48 אַחֲרֵי נִמְכַּר גְּאֻלָּה תִּהְיֶה־לּוֹ אֶחָד אהבה, דאגה מֵאֶחָיו יִגְאָלֶנּוּ 49 אוֹ־ דֹדוֹ אוֹ בֶן־דֹּדוֹ יִגְאָלֶנּוּ אוֹ־מִשְּׁאֵר בְּשָׂרוֹ מִמִּשְׁפַּחְתּוֹ יִגְאָלֶנּוּ אוֹ־ הִשִּׂיגָה יָדוֹ וְנִגְאָל: 50 וְחִשַּׁב עִם־קֹנֵהוּ מִשְּׁנַת הִמָּכְרוֹ לוֹ עַד שְׁנַת הַיֹּבֵל וְהָיָה יהוה כֶּסֶף מִמְכָּרוֹ בְּמִסְפַּר שָׁנִים כִּימֵי שָׂכִיר יִהְיֶה ⋯ עִמּוֹ:

51 אִם יוהך, ע״ה מ״ב ־עוֹד רַבּוֹת בַּשָּׁנִים לְפִיהֶן יָשִׁיב גְּאֻלָּתוֹ מִכֶּסֶף מִקְנָתוֹ: 52 וְאִם יוהך, ע״ה מ״ב ־מְעַט נִשְׁאַר בַּשָּׁנִים עַד־שְׁנַת הַיֹּבֵל וְחִשַּׁב־ לוֹ כְּפִי שָׁנָיו יָשִׁיב אֶת־גְּאֻלָּתוֹ: 53 כִּשְׂכִיר שָׁנָה בְּשָׁנָה יִהְיֶה ⋯ עִמּוֹ לֹא־יִרְדֶּנּוּ בְּפֶרֶךְ לְעֵינֶיךָ ע״ה קס״א: 54 וְאִם יוהך, ע״ה מ״ב ־לֹא יִגָּאֵל בְּאֵלֶּה וְיָצָא בִּשְׁנַת הַיֹּבֵל הוּא וּבָנָיו עִמּוֹ:

ON A LEAP YEAR: MAFTIR

55 כִּי־לִי בְנֵי־יִשְׂרָאֵל עֲבָדִים עֲבָדַי הֵם אֲשֶׁר־הוֹצֵאתִי אוֹתָם מֵאֶרֶץ אלהים דאלפין מִצְרָיִם מצר אֲנִי אני, טדהד כוזו יְהוָֹה אדניאהדונהי אֱלֹהֵיכֶם ילה:

26 1 לֹא־תַעֲשׂוּ לָכֶם אֱלִילִם וּפֶסֶל וּמַצֵּבָה לֹא־תָקִימוּ לָכֶם וְאֶבֶן מַשְׂכִּית לֹא תִתְּנוּ בְּאַרְצְכֶם לְהִשְׁתַּחֲוֹת עָלֶיהָ פהל כִּי אֲנִי אני, טדהד כוזו יְהוָֹה אדניאהדונהי אֱלֹהֵיכֶם ילה: 2 אֶת־שַׁבְּתֹתַי תִּשְׁמֹרוּ וּמִקְדָּשִׁי תִּירָאוּ אֲנִי אני, טדהד כוזו יְהוָֹה אדניאהדונהי:

ON A LEAP YEAR: HAFTARAH OF BEHAR

The prophet Jeremiah was told by God to take a piece of land and redeem it as his own, even while the city he resided in was under imminent threat of being conquered by the Chaldeans.

There is a story that helps us understand this concept. A man stopped in the rain to pray in the shelter of a castle. Following his prayer, the building collapsed. The man then said that the castle had been created for the sole purpose of providing shelter for him to pray that one prayer.

Jeremiah 32:6-27

32:⁶ And Jeremiah said, "The word of the Lord came to me, saying:

⁷ 'See, Hanamel, the son of Shallum your uncle shall come to you and say, "Buy my field at Anathoth, for the right of redemption is yours to buy it."

⁸ So, Hanamel, my uncle's son came to me in the court of the guard according to the words of the Lord and said to me, 'Buy my field, I pray you, that is in Anathoth, which is in the land of Benjamin, for the right of inheritance is yours, buy it for yourself.' Then I knew that this was the word of the Lord.

⁹ And I bought the field that was at Anathoth of Hanamel, my uncle's son, and weighed out for him seventeen shekels of silver.

¹⁰ And I subscribed the deed, and sealed it and called witnesses, and weighed him the money on the scales.

¹¹ So I took the deed of purchase, both that which was sealed copy containing the terms and conditions, and that which was open;

¹² and I delivered the deed of purchase to Baruch son of Neriah, the son of Mahseiah, in the presence of Hanamel, my uncle's son and in the presence of the witnesses that subscribed the deed of the purchase, before all the Jews that sat in the court of the guard.

ON A LEAP YEAR: HAFTARAH OF BEHAR

Jeremiah's prayer resulted in God's reminder to him of the wondrous power of the Creator. By following Jeremiah's example and elevating our consciousness, we can use our connection with God to elevate other people, animals, and even inanimate objects. We should also remember while reading books and using physical objects, to focus on elevating them as well.

ירמיהו פרק לב

32 6 וַיֹּאמֶר יִרְמְיָהוּ הָיָה יהה דְּבַר ראה ־יְהֹוָהאהדונהי אֵלַי לֵאמֹר: 7 הִנֵּה

מ"ה יה וַחֲנַמְאֵל בֶּן־שַׁלֻּם דֹּדְךָ בָּא אֵלֶיךָ אני לֵאמֹר קְנֵה ע"ה = יוסף, ציון, ר"פ יהוה,

לְךָ אֶת־שָׂדִי אֲשֶׁר בַּעֲנָתוֹת כִּי לְךָ מִשְׁפַּט ע"ה ה"פ אלהים הַגְּאֻלָּה לִקְנוֹת:

8 וַיָּבֹא אֵלַי חֲנַמְאֵל בֶּן־דֹּדִי כִּדְבַר ראה יְהֹוָהאהדונהי אֶל־חֲצַר הַמַּטָּרָה

וַיֹּאמֶר אֵלַי קְנֵה ע"ה = יוסף, ציון, ר"פ יהוה, נָא אֶת־שָׂדִי אֲשֶׁר־בַּעֲנָתוֹת אֲשֶׁר

בְּאֶרֶץ אלהים דאלפין בִּנְיָמִין כִּי־לְךָ מִשְׁפַּט ע"ה ה"פ אלהים הַיְרֻשָּׁה וּלְךָ הַגְּאֻלָּה

קְנֵה ע"ה = יוסף, ציון, ר"פ יהוה, ־לָךְ וָאֵדַע כִּי דְבַר ראה ־יְהֹוָהאהדונהי הוּא:

9 וָאֶקְנֶה אֶת־הַשָּׂדֶה שדי מֵאֵת חֲנַמְאֵל בֶּן־דֹּדִי אֲשֶׁר בַּעֲנָתוֹת

וָאֶשְׁקֲלָה־לּוֹ אֶת־הַכֶּסֶף שִׁבְעָה שְׁקָלִים וַעֲשָׂרָה הַכָּסֶף: 10 וָאֶכְתֹּב

בַּסֵּפֶר וָאֶחְתֹּם וָאָעֵד עֵדִים וָאֶשְׁקֹל הַכֶּסֶף בְּמֹאזְנָיִם: 11 וָאֶקַּח אֶת־

סֵפֶר הַמִּקְנָה אֶת־הֶחָתוּם נתה, קס"א קנ"א קמ"ג הַמִּצְוָה וְהַחֻקִּים וְאֶת־הַגָּלוּי:

12 וָאֶתֵּן אֶת־הַסֵּפֶר הַמִּקְנָה אֶל־בָּרוּךְ יהוה ע"ב ורבוע מ"ה בֶּן־נֵרִיָּה בֶּן־

מַחְסֵיָה לְעֵינֵי ריבוע מ"ה וְחֲנַמְאֵל ריבוע מ"ה דֹּדִי וּלְעֵינֵי ריבוע מ"ה הָעֵדִים הַכֹּתְבִים

בְּסֵפֶר הַמִּקְנָה לְעֵינֵי ריבוע מ"ה כָּל ילי ־הַיְּהוּדִים הַיֹּשְׁבִים בַּחֲצַר הַמַּטָּרָה:

13 *And I charged Baruch before them saying:*

14 *'Thus says the Lord of Hosts, the God of Israel: "Take these deeds, this deed of the purchase, both that which is sealed and this deed which is open, and put them in an earthen vessel, that they may continue many days."*

15 *For thus says the Lord of Hosts, the God of Israel: "Houses and fields and vineyards will again be bought in this land."*

16 *Now after I had delivered the deed of purchase to Baruch the son of Neriah, I prayed to the Lord, saying:*

17 *'Ah, Lord God, see You have made the heaven and the earth by Your Great Power and by Your Outstretched Arm; there is nothing too hard for You;*

18 *Who shows mercy to thousands and recompenses the iniquity of the fathers into the bosom of their children after them; the Great Mighty God, the Lord of Hosts is His Name;*

19 *Great in counsel and Mighty in work; Whose eyes are open to all the ways of the sons of men; to give everyone according to his ways and according to the fruit of his doings;*

20 *You performed signs and wonders in the land of Egypt, even to this day, both in Israel and among other men, and made Yourself a Name, even to this day;*

21 *You brought Your people Israel out of the land of Egypt with signs and with wonders, and with a Strong Hand and with an Outstretched Arm and with great terror;*

22 *and have given them this land, which You had sworn to give their fathers to give them, a land flowing with milk and honey;*

23 *and they came in and took possession of it, but they hearkened not to Your Voice; nor walked in Your Law; they have done nothing of all that You commanded of them to do , therefore You have caused all this evil to befall them.*

24 *See the mounds, they are come to the city to take it; and the city is given into the hands of the Chaldeans who are attacking it. And what You have spoken has come to pass and behold you see it.'*

וָאֲצַוֶּ֗ה אֶת־בָּרוּךְ יהוה ע"ב ורבוע מ"ה לְעֵינֵיהֶ֖ם ריבוע מ"ה לֵאמֹֽר׃ 14 כֹּֽה־ הֵי 13

אָמַר֩ יְהֹוָ֨הֱאֱלֹהִי"אֱלֹהִים"אֲדֹנָי צְבָא֜וֹת נתה ורבוע אהיה אֱלֹהֵ֣י דמב, ילה יִשְׂרָאֵ֗ל לָק֣וֹחַ אֶת־

הַסְּפָרִ֣ים הָאֵ֡לֶּה אֵ֣ת סֵ֩פֶר֩ הַמִּקְנָ֨ה הַזֶּ֜ה וְאֵ֣ת הֶחָת֗וּם נתה, קס"א קנ"א קמ"ג וְהוּ

וְאֵ֨ת סֵ֤פֶר הַגָּלוּי֙ הַזֶּ֔ה וְהוּ וּנְתַתָּ֖ם בִּכְלִי־חָ֑רֶשׂ לְמַ֥עַן יַעַמְד֖וּ יָמִ֥ים נלך

רַבִּֽים׃ 15 כִּ֣י כֹ֣ה הֵי אָמַ֞ר יְהֹוָ֤הֱאֱלֹהִי"אֲדֹנָי צְבָאוֹת֙ נתה ורבוע אהיה אֱלֹהֵ֣י דמב, ילה

יִשְׂרָאֵ֔ל ע֥וֹד יִקָּנ֛וּ בָתִּ֥ים וְשָׂד֖וֹת וּכְרָמִ֑ים בָּאָ֖רֶץ אלהים דאלפין הַזֹּֽאת׃

16 וָאֶתְפַּלֵּ֖ל אֶל־יְהֹוָ֑הֱאֱלֹהִי"אֲדֹנָי אַחֲרֵ֣י תִתִּ֗י אֶת־סֵ֤פֶר הַמִּקְנָה֙ אֶל־בָּר֔וּךְ

בֶּן־נֵרִיָּ֖ה לֵאמֹֽר׃ 17 אֲהָהּ֙ אֲדֹנָ֣י לכלו יְהֹוִ֔הֱאֱלֹהִי"אֲדֹנָי הִנֵּ֣ה יהוה ע"ב ורבוע מ"ה

אַתָּ֣ה | עָשִׂ֗יתָ אֶת־הַשָּׁמַ֙יִם֙ י"פ טל, י"פ כוזו וְאֶת־הָאָ֔רֶץ אלהים דההין ע"ה מ"ה יה

בְּכֹֽחֲךָ֙ הַגָּד֔וֹל לההו, מבה, יזל, אום וּבִֽזְרֹעֲךָ֖ הַנְּטוּיָ֑ה לֹֽא־יִפָּלֵ֥א מִמְּךָ֖ כָּל־ ילי

דָּבָֽר׃ ראה 18 עֹ֤שֶׂה חֶ֙סֶד֙ ע"ב, ריבוע יהוה לַֽאֲלָפִ֔ים קס"א וּמְשַׁלֵּם֙ עֲוֹ֣ן אָב֔וֹת אֶל־

חֵ֖יק בְּנֵיהֶ֣ם אַחֲרֵיהֶ֑ם הָאֵ֤ל לאה (אלד ע"ה) הַגָּדוֹל֙ לההו, מבה, אום הַגִּבּ֔וֹר

יְהֹוָ֥הֱאֱלֹהִי"אֲדֹנָי צְבָא֖וֹת נתה ורבוע אהיה שְׁמֽוֹ מהש ע"ה, אל שדי ע"ה׃ 19 גְּדֹל֙ לההו, מבה, יזל, אום

הָֽעֵצָה֙ ע"ב ורבוע מ"ה וְרַ֣ב הָעֲלִֽילִיָּ֔ה אֲשֶׁר־עֵינֶ֣יךָ ריבוע מ"ה פְקֻח֔וֹת עַל־כָּל־ ילי

דַּרְכֵ֖י בְּנֵ֣י אָדָ֑ם מ"ה לָתֵ֤ת לְאִישׁ֙ ע"ה קנ"א קס"א כִּדְרָכָ֔יו וְכִפְרִ֖י מַעֲלָלָֽיו׃

20 אֲשֶׁר־שַׂ֜מְתָּ אֹת֤וֹת וּמֹֽפְתִים֙ בְּאֶ֣רֶץ אלהים דאלפין בְּמִצְרַ֔יִם מצר עַד־הַיּ֥וֹם

הַזֶּ֖ה וְהוּ וּבְיִשְׂרָאֵ֣ל וּבָֽאָדָ֑ם גגד, זן, מזבח וַתַּֽעֲשֶׂה־לְּךָ֥ שֵׁ֖ם יהוה עדי כַּיּ֥וֹם

הַזֶּֽה וְהוּ׃ 21 וַתֹּצֵ֤א אֶת־עַמְּךָ֙ ה' הוויות, נמם אֶת־יִשְׂרָאֵ֣ל מֵאֶ֣רֶץ גגד, זן, מזבח

מִצְרַ֔יִם מצר בְּאֹת֖וֹת וּבְמֹֽפְתִ֑ים וּבְיָ֤ד חֲזָקָה֙ וּבְאֶזְר֣וֹעַ נְטוּיָ֔ה אלהים דאלפין

וּבְמוֹרָ֖א גָּדֽוֹל לההו, מבה, יזל, אום׃ 22 וַתִּתֵּ֤ן ב"פ כהת לָהֶם֙ אֶת־הָאָ֣רֶץ אלהים דההין ע"ה

הַזֹּ֔את אֲשֶׁר־נִשְׁבַּ֥עְתָּ לַֽאֲבוֹתָ֖ם לָתֵ֣ת לָהֶ֑ם אֶ֛רֶץ אלהים דאלפין זָבַ֥ת חָלָ֖ב

וּדְבָֽשׁ׃ 23 וַיָּבֹ֜אוּ וַיִּֽרְשׁ֣וּ אֹתָ֗הּ וְלֹֽא־שָׁמְע֤וּ בְקוֹלֶ֙ךָ֙ וּבְתֹרָתְךָ֣ ותרתך

(כתיב: וּבְתֹרֹתְךָ) לֹֽא־הָלָ֔כוּ ילי אֵ֤ת מ"ה כָּל־אֲשֶׁ֛ר צִוִּ֥יתָה לָהֶ֖ם לַעֲשׂ֑וֹת לֹ֣א

[25] *And You have said to me Lord God, 'Buy you the field for money and call witnesses, even though the city will be handed over to the Chaldeans. "*

[26] *Then came the word of the Lord to Jeremiah, saying:*

[27] *"Behold, I am the Lord, the God of all flesh; Is anything too hard for Me?"*

עָשׂוּ וַתִּקְרָא אֹתָם אֵת כָּל־הָרָעָה הַזֹּאת: 24 הִנֵּה הַסֹּלְלוֹת

בָּאוּ הָעִיר לְלָכְדָהּ וְהָעִיר נִתְּנָה בְּיַד

הַכַּשְׂדִּים הַנִּלְחָמִים עָלֶיהָ מִפְּנֵי הַחֶרֶב וְהָרָעָב

וְהַדָּבֶר וַאֲשֶׁר דִּבַּרְתָּ הָיָה וְהִנְּךָ רֹאֶה:

25 וְאַתָּה אָמַרְתָּ אֵלַי אֲדֹנָי יֱהֹוִה קְנֵה־לְךָ

הַשָּׂדֶה בַּכֶּסֶף וְהָעֵד עֵדִים וְהָעִיר נִתְּנָה בְּיַד

הַכַּשְׂדִּים: 26 וַיְהִי דְּבַר־יְהֹוָה אֶל־יִרְמְיָהוּ לֵאמֹר: 27 הִנֵּה

אֲנִי יְהֹוָה אֱלֹהֵי כָּל־בָּשָׂר הֲמִמֶּנִּי יִפָּלֵא כָּל־

דָּבָר:

BECHUKOTAI

LESSON OF BECHUKOTAI
(Leviticus 26:3-27:34)

At the end of the previous Chapter of Behar, the Bible spoke about how humanity could curse the Creator. What is the connection between that and everything else that is said about Mount Sinai in the rest of that chapter? If we can reveal this very important concept, we will be able to connect to the power of immortality that was revealed on Mount Sinai when Moses went up to receive the Ten Utterances from God. This Revelation of Light allowed all the deaf to hear, all the blind to see, and all the people who had any kind of defect to be cured. So it behooves us to find a way to connect with that Light.

What is the relationship between cursing God and Mount Sinai? As Rav Ashlag explains in his Introduction to *Ten Luminous Emanations*, "Nothing in this world is really ours, and we don't really deserve anything. Even if we work for something, what we receive as a result is not really a possession. If we find a sum of money on the street and we didn't work for it, and it didn't fall out of our own pocket, either, it came from Heaven. And that is how we should see everything in this world."

Whoever denies that everything comes from the Creator is literally cursing God. These people are saying that they don't need the Creator, that they deserve what they have. But from the moment they say this, they merit nothing. They have disconnected themselves from the Light. Therefore, only negative things can happen to them.

The way to receive Light is to give thanks every single day for what we have and not to cry over what we don't have. If we understand this, then we will merit immortality. This is the first lesson of the Chapter of Bechukotai.

The second lesson concerns our understanding of the "big picture." It's so easy to complain about every little thing that happens: "Why has God done this to me!?" Early in their relationship, Rav Brandwein, Rav Berg's teacher, often told the Rav to undertake certain tasks, and Rav Berg did not necessarily understand why—until he saw the big picture. It is too easy to feel sorry for ourselves and feel that we've been "wronged"—not just by God, but also by our friends, our parents, and even our children.

There is a *Midrash* (discussion amongst the sages) that says that life and death are at the mercy of the tongue. Every minute, the Negative Side is waiting for us to say something it can use against us. So much of the strength of negativity comes from what we say! Therefore, we must take responsibility for each and every word or sound that passes our lips. This is especially true regarding words of self-pity or blame.

Concerning the *shemitah* (the sabbatical)

Why is the *shemitah* the only precept that the Bible says was given on Mount Sinai? What is so important that every seven years we must not work the land? What is so crucial about the sabbatical that we are told how God spoke to Moses on Mount Sinai about this blessing?

Here is the secret. It's as if the Light said, "If you do not work the land during this year, I will give you a blessing for the other years." The Light says to us, "You will be with Me and I will be with you. But first you must get beyond the *Desire to Receive for the Self Alone*. You must get past the distrustful desire that says, 'I am the one who has to eat, so why is the Light telling me not to work?'" Even if it is written in the Bible that there will be a blessing, we have to have certainty in our own hearts that we will be with the Creator and the Creator will be with us.

Regarding the curses

Why are there 98 curses, but far fewer blessings, mentioned in this chapter?

The Light wants the best for us, but there is a reason there are more curses than blessings. If everything was always good, no one would ever think of taking the spiritual path. Sometimes, we need curses to wake us up from our deep sleep. The Light needs to warn us that we don't have much time left.

The Vilna Gaon, Rav Eliyahu ben Shlomo Zalman Kremer (1720–1797) told this story in the temple: Once, there were two friends named Reuben and Simon. They were born at the same time, on the same day, in the same year. They also had the same luck. Whatever happened to one of them also happened to the other, except for one thing: Simon became rich, while Reuben became poor.

One day, Reuben the poor came to Simon the rich and asked to borrow some money. Simon said, "Of course, I will give it to you. You are my closest friend."

But after a few years, Simon became poor and Reuben became rich. This time, it was Simon who went to Reuben to borrow some money for food. But Reuben would not give his friend any money.

Eventually, they both passed away and went to the Upper World. Simon was taken straight to the Garden of Eden because he was a *tzaddik*, (a righteous person), but Reuben was condemned to return to this world.

Simon said, "I will go down with him," and he returned to the world as a poor person who collected money for charity. Eventually, he reached a point where he didn't have anyone left to ask, so he inquired of the people in his city if there was someone new whom he could ask for money. They told him that there was one such person, but he would never give anything. However, even though the miser lived at the top of a high mountain, Simon went anyway. It took Simon hours to go up the mountain. When he finally knocked on the miser's door, a servant opened the door and asked what he wanted. Simon said that he had come to ask for *tzedakah* (charity). The servant told him, "You're a fool! Everybody knows my master does not give charity."

At that moment, the miser (who was the reincarnated soul of Reuben) came to the door to see what was happening. The servant said, "There is someone here asking for *tzedakah.*"

Reuben the miser threw Simon the poor man out, and Simon fell down the stairs and died. At that instant, the angels cried, "How can such a righteous person die like this?"

And in the same second that the Vilna Gaon related this part of the story, one of the people listening to him in the temple cried out, "No! It can't be that I have no chance to fix my terrible sin!" That person was Reuben.

We learn from this parable that we can never know when our last chance to correct something is being presented to us. We must do our best at all times and remember our true goal. Therefore, we need curses to remind us about what is really important in this world so that we can wake up and do our spiritual work.

SYNOPSIS OF BECHUKOTAI

The word *Bechukotai* means "you will follow My decrees and laws." But according to Kabbalah, there aren't any laws—there is only Cause and Effect. Positive actions create positive outcomes, and negative actions create negative ones. In this chapter, we have blessings and curses to show us that what we get in life depends entirely on our actions.

ON A LEAP YEAR: FIRST READING - ABRAHAM - CHESED

26:³ I *f you follow My Statutes and keep My Commandments and do them, ⁴ then I will send you rain in its season, and the ground will yield its crops and the trees of the field will yield their fruit. ⁵ And your threshing will continue until grape harvest and the grape harvest will continue until planting, and you will eat all the food you want and live in safety in your land.*

ON A LEAP YEAR: SECOND READING - ISAAC - GEVURAH

⁶ And I will grant peace in the land, and you will lie down and no one will make you afraid; and I will remove evil beasts from the land, and the sword will not pass through your land.

FROM THE RAV

The War to end all Wars

This is the last chapter of the *Book of Vayikra* (Leviticus), the third book of the Five Books of Moses. In the entire book, all we read about are sacrifices, which we have come to understand are not "sacrifices" in the conventional sense, but refer, instead, to where we sacrifice ourselves. But for whom do we sacrifice ourselves—our parents, our children? The *Zohar* says very clearly that this is a misrepresentation of what this book actually provides us with. Rather, says the *Zohar*, the *Book of Vayikra* contains the rules of war. But if we read the entire book, we'll find no mention of a single war that the Israelites had.

Here, at The Kabbalah Centre, we say this is not a synagogue, but a war room, where we plan and execute our strategy because we realize that in life there is a war. After all, what day goes by without some form of headache from somewhere?

According to the *Zohar*, in Bechukotai, we have the ultimate methodology of war: We learn all about how to conduct ourselves in war—and particularly in this kind of war, which is a war to end all wars. By "war to end all wars," I'm referring here to our personal lives: Once we achieve the end of war in our personal lives, there will be no war out there.

The *Zohar* tells us wars happen because of people—it's always the people. As long as people cannot find internal peace within, there will be the inevitable conflicts with others, whether with a neighbor or within a family, and then these personal conflicts become perpetrated throughout the world. In fact there is more commentary on this section than there are verses. And in Bechukotai there are 78 verses, [which is three times the Tetragrammaton (*Yud, Hei, Vav* and *Hei*)—26 X 3 = 78]

We say in Kabbalah, if anything goes wrong, take responsibility for it. You ask, "Why should I? Just look what this person did to me, stole from me and ruined my

ON A LEAP YEAR: FIRST READING - ABRAHAM - CHESED

3 אִם־בְּחֻקֹּתַי תֵּלֵכוּ וְאֶת־מִצְוֹתַי תִּשְׁמְרוּ וַעֲשִׂיתֶם אֹתָם: יוהך, ע״ה מ״ב

4 וְנָתַתִּי גִשְׁמֵיכֶם בְּעִתָּם וְנָתְנָה הָאָרֶץ אלהים דההין ע״ה יְבוּלָהּ וְעֵץ ע״ה קס״א הַשָּׂדֶה שדי יִתֵּן פִּרְיוֹ: 5 וְהִשִּׂיג לָכֶם דַּיִשׁ אֶת־בָּצִיר וּבָצִיר יַשִּׂיג אֶת־זָרַע וַאֲכַלְתֶּם לַחְמְכֶם לָשֹׂבַע ע״ב ואלהים דיודין וִישַׁבְתֶּם לָבֶטַח בְּאַרְצְכֶם:

ON A LEAP YEAR: SECOND READING - ISAAC - GEVURAH

6 וְנָתַתִּי שָׁלוֹם בָּאָרֶץ אלהים דאלפין וּשְׁכַבְתֶּם וְאֵין מַחֲרִיד וְהִשְׁבַּתִּי חַיָּה רָעָה רהע מִן־הָאָרֶץ אלהים דההין ע״ה וְחֶרֶב רבוע ס״ג ורבוע אהיה לֹא־תַעֲבֹר בְּאַרְצְכֶם:

---

business…" Kabbalah's answer is: "What did you do to him in a last lifetime?" Of course, thinking that way would mean assuming responsibility, and when you assume responsibility, it could seem as if you begin to reverse your fortune. It's a paradox, but through restriction is how we receive. Restricting our acceptance of the illusion of the 1 Percent Reality is how we receive freedom from chaos.

גִשְׁמֵיכֶם

Leviticus 26:4 – The blessing of rain is discussed in this verse. Rain includes not only the water that falls from the sky but all the water in the universe. The world and our bodies exist because of water. If we can control water, we can renew the life of the world. If we can't control water, there is decay and entropy.

"Then I will give you rain in due season." (Leviticus 26:4) Everyone will bestow of his strength upon you. Who are they? The

correction you made, OF THE UNISON of the Holy Name, THE UNISON OF STATUTE AND LAW, ZEIR ANPIN AND MALCHUT, SO THAT THEY WILL BESTOW PLENTY UPON YOU.
— The Zohar, Bechukotai, 5:20

שָׁלוֹם

Leviticus 26:6 – In this verse, we learn that God will provide peace "in the land," meaning the Middle East. When all the different people of the Middle East treat each other with human dignity, there will be peace. But because they don't, there is chaos. Political problems can't be solved without humankind respecting one another and treating everyone with human dignity.

"And I will give you peace in the land, and you shall lie down, and none shall make you afraid." (Leviticus 26:6) Rav Yosi opened the discussion with the verse: "Tremble and sin not…." (Psalms 4:5) This verse has been explained. It behooves man to have his Good Inclination cause his Evil one to tremble.
— The Zohar, Bechukotai 7:25

7 And you will pursue your enemies, and they will fall by the sword before you.

8 And five of you will chase a hundred, and a hundred of you will chase ten thousand, and your enemies will fall by the sword before you.

9 And I will have respect for you and make you fruitful and increase your numbers, and I will establish My Covenant with you.

ON A LEAP YEAR: THIRD READING - JACOB - TIFERET
WHEN CONNECTED: FIFTH READING - AARON - HOD

10 And you shall eat last year's harvest and you will bring forth the old from before the new.

11 And I will set My Tabernacle among you, and My Soul shall not abhor you.

12 And I will walk among you and will be your God, and you will be My People.

13 I am the Lord your God, who brought you out of land of Egypt so that you would no longer be their slaves; and I broke the bars of your yoke and enabled you to walk with heads held high.

14 But if you will not listen to Me and will not do all these commandments,

15 and if you will reject My Statutes and if your soul abhors My Ordinances so that you will not do all My Commandments and break My Covenant,

16 then I will do this to you: I will bring upon you sudden terror, even consumption and fever that will destroy your sight and your soul to languish and you shall sow your seed in vain, for your enemies shall eat it.

17 And I will set My Face against you so that you will be defeated by your enemies; those who hate you will rule over you, and you will flee even when no one is pursuing you.

Leviticus 26:10 – It is said that newer fruits are less spiritually potent for us than older, mature fruits, so we should eat the old fruits before the new ones. "Old" and "new" do not have the same meaning in the spiritual dimension as in the everyday world, because in the Upper World, there is no time—no today and no tomorrow, only an eternal present moment. "New" in the spiritual world denotes something that is not fully actualized, while "old" refers to something that has manifested to completeness.

בְּאַרְצְכֶם: 7 וּרְדַפְתֶּם אֶת־אֹיְבֵיכֶם וְנָפְלוּ לִפְנֵיכֶם לֶחָרֶב

רבוע ס"ג ורבוע אהיה: 8 וְרָדְפוּ מִכֶּם חֲמִשָּׁה מֵאָה דמב, מלוי ע"ב וּמֵאָה דמב, מלוי ע"ב

מִכֶּם רְבָבָה יִרְדֹּפוּ וְנָפְלוּ אֹיְבֵיכֶם לִפְנֵיכֶם לֶחָרֶב רבוע ס"ג ורבוע אהיה:

9 וּפָנִיתִי אֲלֵיכֶם וְהִפְרֵיתִי אֶתְכֶם וְהִרְבֵּיתִי אֶתְכֶם וַהֲקִימֹתִי אֶת־

בְּרִיתִי אִתְּכֶם:

ON A LEAP YEAR: THIRD READING - JACOB - TIFERET
WHEN CONNECTED: FIFTH READING - AARON - HOD

10 וַאֲכַלְתֶּם יָשָׁן נוֹשָׁן וְיָשָׁן מִפְּנֵי חכמה בינה וְחָדָשׁ י"ב הוויות תּוֹצִיאוּ:

11 וְנָתַתִּי מִשְׁכָּנִי בְּתוֹכְכֶם וְלֹא־תִגְעַל נַפְשִׁי אֶתְכֶם: 12 וְהִתְהַלַּכְתִּי

בְּתוֹכְכֶם וְהָיִיתִי לָכֶם לֵאלֹהִים מום, אהיה אדני; ילה וְאַתֶּם תִּהְיוּ־לִי לְעָם

עלם: 13 אֲנִי אני, טדה"ד כוז"ו יְהֹוָ‍ה אלהים יאהדונהי אֱלֹהֵיכֶם ילה אֲשֶׁר הוֹצֵאתִי אֶתְכֶם

מֵאֶרֶץ אלהים דאלפין מִצְרַיִם מצר מִהְיֹת לָהֶם עֲבָדִים וָאֶשְׁבֹּר מֹטֹת עֻלְּכֶם

וָאוֹלֵךְ אֶתְכֶם קוֹמְמִיּוּת: 14 וְאִם לֹא תִשְׁמְעוּ ע"ה מ"ב יוהך, ע"ה מ"ב לִי וְלֹא תַעֲשׂוּ

אֶת כָּל ילי ־הַמִּצְוֺת הָאֵלֶּה: 15 וְאִם ע"ה מ"ב יוהך, ־בְּחֻקֹּתַי תִּמְאָסוּ וְאִם

יוהך, ע"ה מ"ב אֶת־מִשְׁפָּטַי תִּגְעַל נַפְשְׁכֶם לְבִלְתִּי עֲשׂוֹת אֶת־כָּל ילי ־מִצְוֺתַי

לְהַפְרְכֶם אֶת־בְּרִיתִי: 16 אַף־אֲנִי אני, טדה"ד כוז"ו אֶעֱשֶׂה־זֹּאת לָכֶם

וְהִפְקַדְתִּי עֲלֵיכֶם בֶּהָלָה אֶת־הַשַּׁחֶפֶת וְאֶת־הַקַּדַּחַת מְכַלּוֹת עֵינַיִם

וּמְדִיבֹת נָפֶשׁ רמ"ח ‑ ד' הוויות וּזְרַעְתֶּם לָרִיק זַרְעֲכֶם וַאֲכָלֻהוּ אֹיְבֵיכֶם:

לֹא תִשְׁמְעוּ

Leviticus 26:14 – The curses listed here are not always bad for us because they can impel us to change ourselves. If things were always good, we'd never grow spiritually; we'd just stay in the same place forever. There are five sets of curses covered in this section, each one more grievous than the previous one. The message here is: If we don't change, things will become worse and worse for us until we realize we have to transform ourselves. So we had better begin! The *Midrash* says that the curses are given in such detail because the intent is to create awe in the people so that they obey God's Will. (*Ibn Ezra, verse13*)

18 *And if after all this you will not listen to Me, then I will chastise you for your sins seven times over.*

19 *And I will break down your stubborn pride and make your heaven like iron and the ground beneath you like bronze.*

20 *And your strength will be spent in vain, for your soil will not yield her crops, nor will the trees of the land yield their fruit.*

21 *And if you walk contrary to me and do not to listen to me, I will multiply your plagues seven times over, according to your sins.*

22 *And I will send the beast of the field against you, and they will rob you of your children, and destroy your cattle and make you so few in number that your ways shall become desolate.*

23 *And if in spite of these things you will not be corrected unto Me, but continue to walk contrary to Me,*

24 *then I will also walk contrary toward you and will smite you, even I, for your sins seven times over.*

25 *And I will bring a sword upon you to avenge the breaking of the Covenant, and you will withdraw into your cities, and I will send pestilence among you, and you will be delivered into the hand of the enemy.*

26 *When I cut off your supply of bread, ten women will be able to bake your bread in one oven, and they will dole out the bread again by weight, and you will eat, but you will not be satisfied.*

27 *And if in spite of this, you still do not listen to Me but walk contrary unto Me,*

28 *then I will walk contrary unto you in fury, and I will also chastise you for your sins seven times over.*

עַד־אֵלֶּה

Leviticus 26:18 – With the second set of curses, the land suffers as the people do. Just as we can't accomplish anything when cursed, the land can't yield fruit when it is cursed.

וְלֹא תֹאבוּ

Leviticus 26:21 – The third set of curses concerns the destruction of animals. This shows us that if something happens to our livestock or pets, it has to do with our own state of being. We have a deep connection with animals, and if our pet becomes sick, it is a wake-up call that there is something spiritually wrong with us.

17 וְנָתַתִּי פָנַי בָּכֶם וְנִגַּפְתֶּם לִפְנֵי אֹיְבֵיכֶם וְרָדוּ בָכֶם שֹׂנְאֵיכֶם וְנַסְתֶּם וְאֵין־רֹדֵף אֶתְכֶם: 18 וְאִם־

עַד־אֵלֶּה לֹא תִשְׁמְעוּ לִי וְיָסַפְתִּי לְיַסְּרָה אֶתְכֶם שֶׁבַע עַל־חַטֹּאתֵיכֶם: 19 וְשָׁבַרְתִּי אֶת־גְּאוֹן עֻזְּכֶם וְנָתַתִּי אֶת־שְׁמֵיכֶם כַּבַּרְזֶל וְאֶת־אַרְצְכֶם כַּנְּחֻשָׁה: 20 וְתַם לָרִיק כֹּחֲכֶם וְלֹא־תִתֵּן אַרְצְכֶם אֶת־יְבוּלָהּ וְעֵץ הָאָרֶץ לֹא יִתֵּן פִּרְיוֹ: 21 וְאִם־תֵּלְכוּ עִמִּי קֶרִי וְלֹא תֹאבוּ לִשְׁמֹעַ לִי וְיָסַפְתִּי עֲלֵיכֶם מַכָּה שֶׁבַע כְּחַטֹּאתֵיכֶם: 22 וְהִשְׁלַחְתִּי בָכֶם אֶת־חַיַּת הַשָּׂדֶה וְשִׁכְּלָה אֶתְכֶם וְהִכְרִיתָה אֶת־בְּהֶמְתְּכֶם וְהִמְעִיטָה אֶתְכֶם וְנָשַׁמּוּ דַּרְכֵיכֶם: 23 וְאִם־

בְּאֵלֶּה לֹא תִוָּסְרוּ לִי וַהֲלַכְתֶּם עִמִּי קֶרִי: 24 וְהָלַכְתִּי אַף־אֲנִי עִמָּכֶם בְּקֶרִי וְהִכֵּיתִי אֶתְכֶם גַּם־אָנִי שֶׁבַע עַל־חַטֹּאתֵיכֶם: 25 וְהֵבֵאתִי עֲלֵיכֶם חֶרֶב נֹקֶמֶת נְקַם־בְּרִית וְנֶאֱסַפְתֶּם אֶל־עָרֵיכֶם וְשִׁלַּחְתִּי דֶבֶר בְּתוֹכְכֶם וְנִתַּתֶּם בְּיַד־אוֹיֵב: 26 בְּשִׁבְרִי לָכֶם מַטֵּה־לֶחֶם וְאָפוּ עֶשֶׂר נָשִׁים לַחְמְכֶם בְּתַנּוּר אֶחָד וְהֵשִׁיבוּ לַחְמְכֶם בַּמִּשְׁקָל וַאֲכַלְתֶּם וְלֹא תִשְׂבָּעוּ: 27 וְאִם־בְּזֹאת לֹא תִשְׁמְעוּ לִי וַהֲלַכְתֶּם עִמִּי בְּקֶרִי: 28 וְהָלַכְתִּי עִמָּכֶם בַּחֲמַת־קֶרִי וְיִסַּרְתִּי אֶתְכֶם

לֹא תִוָּסְרוּ

Leviticus 26:23 – The fourth set of curses are plagues. If enough people exhibit the same negativity, it unleashes the power of Satan. A critical mass of negativity can create an opening that will allow Satan to attack even those people who don't deserve it.

לֹא תִשְׁמְעוּ

Leviticus 26:27 – The fifth set of curses is the worst. The most deadly kinds of destruction—destruction on the scale of the Holocaust—are promised here for those who do not mend their ways. Since hatred is the root of this kind of destruction, it is vital that we eliminate the hatred inside ourselves so that we can be protected from any kind of chaos.

²⁹ *And you shall eat the flesh of your sons and the flesh of your daughters shall you eat.*

³⁰ *And I will destroy your high places, cut down your sun pillars and cast your carcasses upon the carcasses of your idols, and My Soul shall abhor you.*

³¹ *And I will make your cities a waste and will bring your sanctuaries to desolation, and I will take no delight in the pleasing aroma of your offerings.*

³² *And I will bring the land into desolation, and your enemies who dwell there shall be astonished at it.*

³³ *And I will scatter you among the nations and I will draw out the sword and pursue you; and your land shall be a desolation, and your cities will be laid to waste.*

³⁴ *Then the land will be paid her Sabbaths all the time that it lies desolate and you are in the land of your enemies; even then shall the land rest and repay its Sabbaths.*

³⁵ *As long as it lies desolate, the land will have rest, even the rest which it did not have in your Sabbaths when you dwelled in it.*

³⁶ *And as for those of you who are left, I will make their hearts so fearful in the lands of their enemies that the sound of a windblown leaf will chase them, and they will flee as one fleeing from the sword, and they will fall when no one is pursuing them.*

³⁷ *And they shall stumble over one another as it were before the sword, when no one is pursuing them, and you will have no power to stand before your enemies.*

³⁸ *And you will perish among the nations; and the land of your enemies will devour you.*

³⁹ *And those of you who are left will pine away in their iniquity, in the land of your enemies and also in the iniquities of their fathers shall they pine away with them.*

⁴⁰ *And they shall confess their iniquity, and the iniquity of their fathers, in their treachery against which they committed against Me, and also they have walked contrary to Me.*

⁴¹ *I also will walk contrary to them, and bring them into the land of their enemies; if perchance their uncircumcised hearts be humbled and they then be paid the punishment for their iniquity,*

אַף־אָנִי אני, טדהד כוזו שֶׁבַע עב ואלהים דיורין עַל־וֹחַטֹּאתֵיכֶם: 29 וַאֲכַלְתֶּם

בְּשַׂר בְּנֵיכֶם וּבְשַׂר בְּנֹתֵיכֶם תֹּאכֵלוּ: 30 וְהִשְׁמַדְתִּי אֶת־בָּמֹתֵיכֶם

וְהִכְרַתִּי אֶת־וֹחַמָּנֵיכֶם וְנָתַתִּי אֶת־פִּגְרֵיכֶם עַל־פִּגְרֵי גִּלּוּלֵיכֶם וְגָעֲלָה

נַפְשִׁי אֶתְכֶם: 31 וְנָתַתִּי אֶת־עָרֵיכֶם חָרְבָּה וַהֲשִׁמּוֹתִי אֶת־מִקְדְּשֵׁיכֶם

וְלֹא אָרִיחַ בְּרֵיחַ נִיחֹחֲכֶם: 32 וַהֲשִׁמֹּתִי אֲנִי אני, טדהד כוזו אֶת־הָאָרֶץ

אלהים דההין עה וְשָׁמְמוּ עָלֶיהָ פהל אֹיְבֵיכֶם הַיֹּשְׁבִים בָּהּ: 33 וְאֶתְכֶם אֱזָרֶה

בַגּוֹיִם וַהֲרִיקֹתִי אַחֲרֵיכֶם חָרֶב רבוע סג ורבוע אהיה וְהָיְתָה אַרְצְכֶם שְׁמָמָה

וְעָרֵיכֶם יִהְיוּ אל חָרְבָּה: 34 אָז תִּרְצֶה הָאָרֶץ אלהים דההין עה אֶת־שַׁבְּתֹתֶיהָ

כֹּל יוי יְמֵי הָשַּׁמָּה וְאַתֶּם בְּאֶרֶץ אלהים דאלפין אֹיְבֵיכֶם אָז תִּשְׁבַּת הָאָרֶץ

אלהים דההין עה וְהִרְצָת אֶת־שַׁבְּתֹתֶיהָ: 35 כָּל יוי יְמֵי הָשַּׁמָּה תִּשְׁבֹּת אֵת

אֲשֶׁר לֹא־שָׁבְתָה בְּשַׁבְּתֹתֵיכֶם בְּשִׁבְתְּכֶם עָלֶיהָ: 36 וְהַנִּשְׁאָרִים פהל

בָּכֶם בפ אל וְהֵבֵאתִי מֹרֶךְ בִּלְבָבָם בְּאַרְצֹת אֹיְבֵיהֶם וְרָדַף אֹתָם קוֹל

עב סג עה עָלֶה נִדָּף וְנָסוּ מְנֻסַת־חֶרֶב רבוע סג ורבוע אהיה וְנָפְלוּ וְאֵין רֹדֵף:

37 וְכָשְׁלוּ אִישׁ עה קנ קסא ־בְּאָחִיו כְּמִפְּנֵי־חֶרֶב רבוע סג ורבוע אהיה וְרֹדֵף אַיִן

וְלֹא־תִהְיֶה לָכֶם תְּקוּמָה לִפְנֵי חכמה בינה אֹיְבֵיכֶם: 38 וַאֲבַדְתֶּם בַּגּוֹיִם

וְאָכְלָה אֶתְכֶם אֶרֶץ אלהים דאלפין אֹיְבֵיכֶם: 39 וְהַנִּשְׁאָרִים בָּכֶם בפ אל

יִמַּקּוּ בַּעֲוֹנָם בְּאַרְצֹת אֹיְבֵיכֶם וְאַף בַּעֲוֹנֹת אֲבֹתָם אִתָּם יִמָּקּוּ:

40 וְהִתְוַדּוּ אֶת־עֲוֹנָם וְאֶת־עֲוֹן גיפ מב ־אֲבֹתָם בְּמַעֲלָם אֲשֶׁר מָעֲלוּ־בִי

וְאַף אֲשֶׁר־הָלְכוּ מיה עִמִּי בְּקֶרִי: 41 אַף־אָנִי אני, טדהד כוזו אֵלֵךְ עִמָּם

בְּקֶרִי וְהֵבֵאתִי אֹתָם בְּאֶרֶץ אלהים דאלפין אֹיְבֵיהֶם אוֹ־אָז יִכָּנַע לְבָבָם

הֶעָרֵל אלהים דיורין וְאָז יִרְצוּ אֶת־עֲוֹנָם: 42 וְזָכַרְתִּי אֶת־בְּרִיתִי יַעֲקוֹב וְאַף

אֶת־בְּרִיתִי יִצְחָק דפ בן וְאַף אֶת־בְּרִיתִי אַבְרָהָם רמח, וזפ אל אֶזְכֹּר

וְהָאָרֶץ אלהים דההין עה אֶזְכֹּר: 43 וְהָאָרֶץ אלהים דההין עה תֵּעָזֵב מֵהֶם וְתִרֶץ

42 then I will remember My Covenant with Jacob and also My Covenant with Isaac and also My Covenant with Abraham I will remember, and I will remember the land.

43 For the land shall lie forsaken without them and shall be paid her Sabbaths while she lies desolate without them, and they will be paid the punishment for their iniquity; because even because they rejected My Ordinances and their soul abhorred My Statutes.

44 And yet in spite of all that, when they are in the land of their enemies, I will not reject them nor will I abhor them so as to destroy them completely and to break My Covenant with them, for I am the Lord their God.

45 But for their sake, I will remember the Covenant of their ancestors whom I brought out of the land of Egypt in the sight of the nations, that I might be their God. I am the Lord."

46 These are the statutes and ordinances and laws that the Lord made on Mount Sinai between Him and the children of Israel by the hand of Moses.

ON A LEAP YEAR: FOURTH READING - MOSES – NETZACH
WHEN CONNECTED: SIXTH READING - JOSEPH - YESOD

27: 1 And the Lord spoke to Moses, saying, 2 "Speak to the children of Israel and say to them: When a man utters a vow of persons to the Lord according to your values,

3 then your evaluation shall be for the male between the ages of twenty years old and sixty years old, even your evaluation will be fifty shekels of silver, according to the shekel of the sanctuary.

4 And if it is a female, then your evaluation will be thirty shekels. 5 And if it between the ages of five years old to twenty years old, then your evaluation shall be twenty shekels for the male and ten shekels for the female.

6 And if it from one month old to five years then, then your evaluation shall be five shekels of silver for the male and for the female your evaluation will be three shekels of silver.

עֶרְכְּךָ

Leviticus 27:3 – Value was assigned to the gifts given to the Tabernacle, but a gift's value was relative and depended on the wealth of the person who gave it. The value was based on who the person was and what physical and spiritual resources he or she had. Today, we have to ask

אֶת־שַׁבְּתֹתֶיהָ בְּהָשַׁמָּה מֵהֶם וְהֵם יִרְצוּ אֶת־עֲוֺנָם יַעַן וּבְיַעַן

בְּמִשְׁפָּטַי מָאָסוּ וְאֶת־חֻקֹּתַי גָּעֲלָה נַפְשָׁם: 44 וְאַף־גַּם יִבּל ־זֹאת

בִּהְיוֹתָם בְּאֶרֶץ אלהים דאלפין אֹיְבֵיהֶם לֹא־מְאַסְתִּים וְלֹא־גְעַלְתִּים

לְכַלֹּתָם לְהָפֵר בְּרִיתִי אִתָּם כִּי אֲנִי אני, טדהד כויו יְהֹוָ֒אֲדֹנָיאהדונהי אֱלֹהֵיהֶם

ילה: 45 וְזָכַרְתִּי לָהֶם בְּרִית רִאשֹׁנִים אֲשֶׁר הוֹצֵאתִי־אֹתָם מֵאֶרֶץ

מִצְרַיִם אלהים דאלפין מצר לְעֵינֵי ריבוע מ"ה הַגּוֹיִם לִהְיוֹת לָהֶם לֵאלֹהִים

מום, אהיה אדני; ילה אֲנִי אני, טדהד כויו יְהֹוָ֒אֲדֹנָיאהדונהי: 46 אֵלֶּה הַחֻקִּים וְהַמִּשְׁפָּטִים

וְהַתּוֹרֹת אֲשֶׁר נָתַן יְהֹוָ֒אֲדֹנָיאהדונהי בֵּינוֹ וּבֵין בְּנֵי יִשְׂרָאֵל בְּהַר אור, רז, אין סוף

סִינָי נמם, ה"פ יהוה בְּיַד־מֹשֶׁה מהטע, אל שדי:

ON A LEAP YEAR: FOURTH READING - MOSES – NETZACH
WHEN CONNECTED: SIXTH READING - JOSEPH - YESOD

27 1 וַיְדַבֵּר ראה יְהֹוָ֒אֲדֹנָיאהדונהי מהטע, אל שדי אֶל־מֹשֶׁה לֵּאמֹר: 2 דַּבֵּר ראה

אֶל־בְּנֵי יִשְׂרָאֵל וְאָמַרְתָּ אֲלֵהֶם אִישׁ ע"ה קנ"א קס"א כִּי יַפְלִא נֶדֶר בְּעֶרְכְּךָ

נְפָשֹׁת לַיהֹוָ֒אֲדֹנָיאהדונהי: 3 וְהָיָה יהוה עֶרְכְּךָ הַזָּכָר מִבֶּן עֶשְׂרִים שָׁנָה וְעַד

בֶּן־שִׁשִּׁים שָׁנָה וְהָיָה יהוה עֶרְכְּךָ וַחֲמִשִּׁים שֶׁקֶל כֶּסֶף בְּשֶׁקֶל הַקֹּדֶשׁ:

4 וְאִם יוהך, ע"ה מ"ב ־נְקֵבָה הִוא וְהָיָה יהוה עֶרְכְּךָ שְׁלֹשִׁים שָׁקֶל: 5 וְאִם

יוהך, ע"ה מ"ב מִבֶּן־חָמֵשׁ שָׁנִים וְעַד בֶּן־עֶשְׂרִים שָׁנָה וְהָיָה יהוה עֶרְכְּךָ

הַזָּכָר עֶשְׂרִים שְׁקָלִים וְלַנְּקֵבָה עֲשֶׂרֶת שְׁקָלִים: 6 וְאִם יוהך, ע"ה מ"ב מִבֶּן

חֹדֶשׁ י"ב הוויות וְעַד בֶּן־חָמֵשׁ שָׁנִים וְהָיָה יהוה עֶרְכְּךָ הַזָּכָר וַחֲמִשָּׁה

---

ourselves whether or not we're really sharing. We have to know how much is enough to give and whether we're truly sharing or just giving with our own agenda in mind. For some people, giving money is a sharing act; for others, a sharing act is doing service. Because, today, there is no Tabernacle and no Temple where we can give as the patriarchs did, we have to decide for ourselves what action constitutes true sharing for us.

7 And if it be from sixty years old or more, if it be male, then your evaluation will be fifteen shekels and for the female, ten shekels.

8 But if he be too poor for your evaluation then he shall be set before to the priest, and the priest shall evaluate him, according to the means of him that vowed what the the priest will evaluate him. 9 And if it be a beast that men bring as an offering to the Lord, any such animal given to the Lord shall be holy.

10 He shall not alter it or substitute it, a good for a bad, or a bad for a good; and if he should at all change beast for beast, then both it and that for which it is changed shall be holy.

11 And if it be an unclean beast, of which they may not bring an offering to the Lord, then he shall present the beast before the priest, 12 and the priest shall evaluate it whether it as good or bad, as you the priest evaluates it, so shall it be.

13 But if he will indeed redeem it, then he shall add a fifth part thereof onto its evaluation.

14 And if a man sanctifies his house to be holy to the Lord, then the priest shall evaluate it, whether it be good or bad, as the priest shall evaluate it, so shall it stand.

15 And if he who sanctified it will redeem his house, then he must add a fifth to its value, and it shall be his.

ON A LEAP YEAR: FIFTH READING - AARON – HOD
WHEN CONNECTED: SEVENTH READING - DAVID - MALCHUT

16 And if a man shall sanctify to the Lord part of the field of his possession, then your evaluation shall be according to the sowing thereof, the sowing of a homer of barley, shall be evaluated at fifty shekels of silver.

17 If he sanctifies his field during the Year of Jubilee, according to your evaluation shall it stand.

וְלֹא-יָמִיר

Leviticus 27:10 – People who share by giving away their possessions need to be careful. There is energy in possessions, so if we're giving something away that we are still attached to, we can give away negativity. We have to give with no strings attached; we can't want back what we gave, nor can we feel that the recipient is now in our debt. Unless there are no strings attached to the gift and no hidden agenda, we have given darkness rather than Light.

שְׁקָלִים כֶּסֶף וְלַנְּקֵבָה עֶרְכְּךָ שְׁלֹשֶׁת שְׁקָלִים כָּסֶף: 7 וְאִם יוהך, ע"ה מ"ב

מִבֶּן־שִׁשִּׁים שָׁנָה וָמַעְלָה אִם יוהך, ע"ה מ"ב ־זָכָר וְהָיָה יהוה עֶרְכְּךָ חֲמִשָּׁה

עָשָׂר שָׁקֶל וְלַנְּקֵבָה עֲשָׂרָה שְׁקָלִים: 8 וְאִם יוהך, ע"ה מ"ב ־מָךְ הוּא

מֵעֶרְכֶּךָ וְהֶעֱמִידוֹ לִפְנֵי חכמה בינה הַכֹּהֵן מלה וְהֶעֱרִיךְ אֹתוֹ הַכֹּהֵן מלה עַל־

פִּי אֲשֶׁר תַּשִּׂיג יַד הַנֹּדֵר יַעֲרִיכֶנּוּ הַכֹּהֵן מלה: 9 וְאִם יוהך, ע"ה מ"ב ־בְּהֵמָה

בֵּן, לכבד, יבם אֲשֶׁר יַקְרִיבוּ מִמֶּנָּה קָרְבָּן לַיהוֹוָאדנ"יאהדונהי כֹּל ילי אֲשֶׁר יִתֵּן

מִמֶּנּוּ לַיהוֹוָאדנ"יאהדונהי יִהְיֶה ייי ־קֹּדֶשׁ: 10 לֹא יַחֲלִיפֶנּוּ $\boxed{\text{וְלֹא־יָמִיר אֹתוֹ}}$

טוֹב והו בְּרָע אוֹ־רַע בְּטוֹב והו וְאִם יוהך, ע"ה מ"ב ־הָמֵר יָמִיר בְּהֵמָה בֵּן, לכבד, יבם

בִּבְהֵמָה בֵּן, לכבד, יבם וְהָיָה יהוה ־הוּא וּתְמוּרָתוֹ יִהְיֶה ייי ־קֹּדֶשׁ: 11 וְאִם

יוהך, ע"ה מ"ב כָּל ילי ־בְּהֵמָה בֵּן, לכבד, יבם טְמֵאָה אֲשֶׁר לֹא־יַקְרִיבוּ מִמֶּנָּה קָרְבָּן

לַיהוֹוָאדנ"יאהדונהי וְהֶעֱמִיד אֶת־הַבְּהֵמָה בֵּן, לכבד, יבם לִפְנֵי חכמה בינה הַכֹּהֵן מלה:

12 וְהֶעֱרִיךְ הַכֹּהֵן מלה אֹתָהּ בֵּין טוֹב והו וּבֵין רָע דצ כְּעֶרְכְּךָ דצ הַכֹּהֵן מלה כֵּן

יִהְיֶה ייי: 13 וְאִם יוהך, ע"ה מ"ב ־גָּאֹל יִגְאָלֶנָּה וְיָסַף חֲמִישִׁתוֹ עַל־עֶרְכֶּךָ:

14 וְאִישׁ ע"ה קנ"א קס"א כִּי־יַקְדִּשׁ אֶת־בֵּיתוֹ ב"פ ראה קֹדֶשׁ לַיהוֹוָאדנ"יאהדונהי

וְהֶעֱרִיכוֹ הַכֹּהֵן מלה בֵּין טוֹב והו וּבֵין רָע דצ כַּאֲשֶׁר יַעֲרִיךְ אֹתוֹ הַכֹּהֵן מלה

כֵּן יָקוּם: 15 וְאִם יוהך, ע"ה מ"ב ־הַמַּקְדִּישׁ יִגְאַל אֶת־בֵּיתוֹ ב"פ ראה וְיָסַף

חֲמִישִׁית כֶּסֶף־עֶרְכְּךָ דצ עָלָיו וְהָיָה יהוה לוֹ:

ON A LEAP YEAR: FIFTH READING - AARON – HOD
WHEN CONNECTED: SEVENTH READING - DAVID - MALCHUT

16 וְאִם יוהך, ע"ה מ"ב | מִשְּׂדֵה אֲחֻזָּתוֹ יַקְדִּישׁ אִישׁ ע"ה קנ"א קס"א לַיהוֹוָאדנ"יאהדונהי

וְהָיָה יהוה עֶרְכְּךָ דצ לְפִי זַרְעוֹ זֶרַע חֹמֶר שְׂעֹרִים כתר בַּחֲמִשִּׁים שָׁקֶל

כָּסֶף: 17 אִם יוהך, ע"ה מ"ב ־מִשְּׁנַת הַיֹּבֵל יַקְדִּישׁ שָׂדֵהוּ כְּעֶרְכְּךָ דצ יָקוּם:

18 וְאִם יוהך, ע"ה מ"ב ־אַחַר הַיֹּבֵל יַקְדִּישׁ שָׂדֵהוּ וְחִשַּׁב־לוֹ הַכֹּהֵן מלה אֶת־

[18] *But if he sanctifies his field after the Jubilee, then the priest will determine the value according to the number of years that remain until the next Year of Jubilee, and an abatement shall be made for your evaluation.*

[19] *And if he who sanctifies the field wishes to redeem it, then he shall add a fifth part of the money of your evaluation of it, and the field will again become his.*

[20] *And if he will not redeem the field, or if he has sold the field to another man, it can not be redeemed any more.*

[21] *But when the field is released in the Jubilee, it shall become holy to the Lord; as a field devoted, it will become the possession of the priests.*

ON A LEAP YEAR: SIXTH READING - JOSEPH - YESOD

[22] *And if he sanctifies to the Lord a field he has bought, which is a field of his possession,* [23] *then the priest will determine the worth of your evaluation up to the Year of Jubilee, and he shall give your evaluation on that day as something holy to the Lord.*

[24] *In the Year of Jubilee, the field shall return to him from whom it was bought, even to him to whom the possession of the land belongs.* [25] *And all your evaluations shall be according to the shekel of the sanctuary, twenty gerahs shall be the shekel.*

[26] *However, the firstborn of a beast, which is born as a firstborn to the Lord, no man shall sanctify, whether it is an ox or a sheep, it is the Lord's.*

[27] *And if it is an unclean beast, then he shall ransom it according to your evaluation, and shall add onto it a fifth of the value of it; and if it is not redeemed, then it should be sold according to your evaluation.*

[28] *Notwithstanding, no devoted thing that a man devotes to the Lord, all that he has, whether of man or beast or of the field of his possession, shall be sold or redeemed; every devoted thing is most holy to the Lord.*

בְּכוֹר

Leviticus 27:26 – Just like a first-born human being, a first-born animal also has a certain energy for overcoming death. A first-born offspring is special; he or she should be treated differently from the other siblings and held to a higher standard than they are. The *Zohar* says:

> *"… the firstborn has an added virtue and advantage in everything, and it depends upon his actions."*
> — The Zohar, Beresheet A:459

הַכֶּסֶף עַל־פִּי הַשָּׁנִים הַנּוֹתָרֹת עַד שְׁנַת הַיֹּבֵל וְנִגְרַע מֵעֶרְכֶּךָ׃
19 וְאִם יוהך, ע״ה מ״ב ־גָּאֹל יִגְאַל אֶת־הַשָּׂדֶה שדי הַמַּקְדִּישׁ אֹתוֹ וְיָסַף
חֲמִשִׁית כֶּסֶף־עֶרְכְּךָ עָלָיו וְקָם לוֹ׃ 20 וְאִם יוהך, ע״ה מ״ב ־לֹא יִגְאַל אֶת־
הַשָּׂדֶה שדי וְאִם יוהך, ע״ה מ״ב ־מָכַר אֶת־הַשָּׂדֶה שדי לְאִישׁ ע״ה קנ״א קס״א אַחֵר
לֹא יִגָּאֵל עוֹד׃ 21 וְהָיָה יהוה הַשָּׂדֶה שדי בְּצֵאתוֹ בַיֹּבֵל קֹדֶשׁ
לַיהֹוָהאדניאהדונהי כִּשְׂדֵה הַחֵרֶם לַכֹּהֵן מלה תִּהְיֶה אֲחֻזָּתוֹ׃

ON A LEAP YEAR: SIXTH READING - JOSEPH - YESOD

22 וְאִם יוהך, ע״ה מ״ב אֶת־שְׂדֵה מִקְנָתוֹ אֲשֶׁר לֹא מִשְּׂדֵה אֲחֻזָּתוֹ יַקְדִּישׁ
לַיהֹוָהאדניאהדונהי׃ 23 וְחִשַּׁב־לוֹ הַכֹּהֵן מלה אֵת מִכְסַת הָעֶרְכְּךָ עַד שְׁנַת
הַיֹּבֵל וְנָתַן אבגית״ץ, ושר, אהבת חנם אֶת־הָעֶרְכְּךָ בַּיּוֹם ע״ה = נגד, זן, מזבח הַהוּא
קֹדֶשׁ לַיהֹוָהאדניאהדונהי׃ 24 בִּשְׁנַת הַיּוֹבֵל יָשׁוּב הַשָּׂדֶה שדי לַאֲשֶׁר קָנָהוּ
מֵאִתּוֹ לַאֲשֶׁר־לוֹ אֲחֻזַּת הָאָרֶץ אלהים דההין ע״ה׃ 25 וְכָל ילי ־עֶרְכְּךָ יִהְיֶה ייי
בְּשֶׁקֶל הַקֹּדֶשׁ עֶשְׂרִים גֵּרָה ר״פ ב״ן יִהְיֶה ייי הַשָּׁקֶל׃ 26 אַךְ אהיה ־בְּכוֹר
אֲשֶׁר־יְבֻכַּר לַיהֹוָהאדניאהדונהי בִּבְהֵמָה ב״ן, לכב, יבמ לֹא־יַקְדִּישׁ אִישׁ ע״ה קנ״א קס״א
אֹתוֹ אִם יוהך, ע״ה מ״ב ־שׁוֹר אבגית״ץ, ושר, אהבת חנם אִם יוהך, ע״ה מ״ב ־שֶׂה לַיהֹוָהאדניאהדונהי
הוּא׃ 27 וְאִם יוהך, ע״ה מ״ב בַּבְּהֵמָה ב״ן, לכב, יבמ הַטְּמֵאָה וּפָדָה בְעֶרְכֶּךָ וְיָסַף
חֲמִשִׁתוֹ עָלָיו וְאִם יוהך, ע״ה מ״ב ־לֹא יִגָּאֵל וְנִמְכַּר בְּעֶרְכֶּךָ׃ 28 אַךְ אהיה ־
כָּל ילי ־חֵרֶם אֲשֶׁר יַחֲרִם אִישׁ ע״ה קנ״א קס״א לַיהֹוָהאדניאהדונהי מִכָּל ילי ־אֲשֶׁר־
לוֹ מֵאָדָם מ״ה וּבְהֵמָה ב״ן, לכב, יבמ וּמִשְּׂדֵה אֲחֻזָּתוֹ לֹא יִמָּכֵר וְלֹא יִגָּאֵל
כָּל ילי ־חֵרֶם קֹדֶשׁ־קָדָשִׁים הוּא לַיהֹוָהאדניאהדונהי׃

ON A LEAP YEAR: SEVENTH READING - DAVID - MALCHUT

29 Nothing devoted, that may be devoted of men, shall be ransomed; he shall surely be put to death.

30 And all the tithe of the land, whether of the seed of the land or of the fruit of the tree, is the Lord's; it is holy to the Lord.

31 And if a man will redeem any of his tithe, he must add onto it a fifth part thereof.

MAFTIR

32 And the entire tithe of the herd or the flock that passes under the rod, the tenth shall be holy to the Lord.

33 He shall not inquire whether it be good or bad, nor shall he change it, and if he changes it at all, then both it and that for which it is changed shall be holy, it shall not be redeemed."

34 These are the commandments which the Lord commanded Moses for the children of Israel on Mount Sinai.

מַעֲשֵׂר

Leviticus 27:30 – From the Torah we learn the importance of tithing ten percent of everything we have. This is because what we "own" doesn't really belong to us. It's vitally important not only to give, but also to make sure that we give to the right people and institutions. During the times of the Tabernacle and the Temple, the tithes went to the Tabernacle and then to the Temple. Today, we have to be sure that both our gift and the recipient of the gift are connected solely to the Light and not to darkness.

וזוק

When we conclude our reading of a Book of the Torah, we say chazak (meaning "strength") three times. The numerical value of repeating chazak three times is Mem, Hei, Shin, which gives us healing. We also use one of the 72 Names—Pei, Hei, Lamed—to activate our strength. The spiritual path is not easy, and we require strength and certainty to take advantage of all that is put before us. The 72 Names of God connects us to the source of Light that we need to gain the power of mind over matter. And when we use the tools of the 72 Names, we tap into the dimension where consciousness controls reality.

ON A LEAP YEAR: SEVENTH READING - DAVID - MALCHUT

29 כָּל ילי ־חֵ֫רֶם אֲשֶׁ֨ר יָחֳרַ֜ם מִן־הָֽאָדָ֛ם מ״ה לֹ֥א יִפָּדֶ֖ה מ֥וֹת יוּמָֽת׃

30 וְכָל ילי ־מַעְשַׂ֨ר יֶרֹת הָאָ֜רֶץ אלהים דההין ע״ה מִזֶּ֤רַע הָאָ֨רֶץ֙ אלהים דההין ע״ה מִפְּרִ֣י ע״ה אלהים דאלפין הָעֵ֔ץ ע״ה קס״א לַיהֹוָ֖אדנ״יאהדונהי ה֑וּא קֹ֖דֶשׁ לַֽיהֹוָֽ֑אדנ״יאהדונהי׃

31 וְאִם ־גָּאֹ֥ל יִגְאַ֛ל יוהך, ע״ה מ״ב ־גָּאֹ֥ל יִגְאַ֛ל אִ֖ישׁ ע״ה קנ״א קס״א מִֽמַּעַשְׂר֑וֹ חֲמִֽשִׁית֖וֹ יֹסֵ֥ף עָלָֽיו׃

MAFTIR

32 וְכָל ילי ־מַעְשַׂ֤ר יֶרֹת [מַעְשַׂ֤ר] מלוי אהיה דיודין ע״ה בָּקָר֙ וָצֹ֔אן כֹּ֥ל ילי אֲשֶׁר־יַעֲבֹ֖ר תַּ֣חַת הַשָּׁ֑בֶט הָ֣עֲשִׂירִ֔י יִֽהְיֶ֥ה ־קֹ֖דֶשׁ לַֽיהֹוָֽ֑אדנ״יאהדונהי׃ 33 לֹ֧א יְבַקֵּ֣ר בֵּֽין־ט֣וֹב והו לָרַ֗ע וְלֹ֣א יְמִירֶ֑נּוּ וְאִם ־הָמֵ֤ר יוהך, ע״ה מ״ב ־הָמֵ֤ר יְמִירֶ֨נּוּ֙ וְהָֽיָה־ה֤וּא וּתְמֽוּרָת֔וֹ יִֽהְיֶה־קֹ֔דֶשׁ לֹ֥א יִגָּאֵֽל׃ 34 אֵ֣לֶּה הַמִּצְוֹ֗ת אֲשֶׁ֨ר צִוָּ֧ה יְהֹוָ֛אדנ״יאהדונהי את־מֹשֶׁ֖ה מהע, אל שדי אֶל־בְּנֵ֣י יִשְׂרָאֵ֑ל אור, רז, אין סוף בְּהַ֖ר סִינָֽ֑י נממ, ה״פ יהוה׃

חֲזַק ג הַהֵ (חסד-ימין)   חֲזַק ג הַהֵ (גבורה-שמאל)   חֲזַק ג הַהֵ (תפארת-אמצע) חֲזַק ג הַהֵ, מהע

וְנִתְחַזֵּק (מלכות)

HAFTARAH OF BECHUKOTAI

Jeremiah prayed, "Heal me, God, and I will be healed; save me, and I will be saved; for You are my praise," (*Jeremiah 17:14*) reminding us not to wait for the bad times to try and connect with the

Jeremiah 16:19-17:14

16:[19] Lord, my strength and my fortress, and my refuge in the day of affliction, to You shall the nations come from the ends of the earth and shall say, "Our fathers have inherited nothing but lies, vanity and things wherein there is no profit."

[20] Shall a man make to himself gods, and they are no gods?

[21] Therefore, behold I will cause them to know, this time I will cause them to know My Hand and My Might, and they shall know that my name is the Lord.

17:[1] The sin of Judah is written with a pen of iron, and with the point of a diamond; it is graven on the tablet of their heart and on the horns of their altars.

[2] Like the symbols of their sons are their altars, and their Asherim are by the leafy trees upon the high hills.

[3] My mountain in the field, I will give you substance and all your treasures for a spoil and your high places, because of sin throughout all your borders.

[4] And you, even yourself shall discontinue from your heritage that I gave you; and I will cause you to serve your enemies in a land you do not know, for you have kindled a fire in My Nostril, which shall burn forever."

[5] Thus says the Lord: "Cursed is the man who trusts in man, who depends on flesh for his strength and whose heart turns away from the Lord.

[6] He will be like a tamarisk in the desert, and shall not see when good comes; but shall inhabit the parched places of the wilderness, a salt land and not inhabited.

[7] Blessed is the man who trusts in the Lord, and whose trust the Lord's is.

[8] For he shall be like a tree planted by the waters and that spreads out its roots by the river, and shall not see when comes; but its foliage will be luxuriant; and shall not be anxious in the year of drought and shall never cease from yielding fruit.

HAFTARAH OF BECHUKOTAI

Creator, but rather to desire this connection all the time. Praying to God when we're distressed is a reactive behavior.

ירמיהו פרק טז

16 19 יְהֹוָאַדְנִיאהדנֹהי עֻזִּי אלהים ע״ה, מום ע״ה וּמָעֻזִּי וּמְנוּסִי בְּיוֹם ע״ה = נגד, זן, מזבח

צָרָה אלהים דההין אֵלֶיךָ אני גּוֹיִם יָבֹאוּ מֵאַפְסֵי־אָרֶץ אלהים דאלפין וְיֹאמְרוּ אַךְ

אהיה ־שֶׁקֶר נָחֲלוּ אֲבוֹתֵינוּ הֶבֶל מלוי ס״ג וְאֵין־בָּם מ״ב מוֹעִיל: 20 הֲיַעֲשֶׂה־

לּוֹ אָדָם מ״ה אֱלֹהִים מום, אהיה אדני; ילה וְהֵמָּה לֹא אֱלֹהִים מום, אהיה אדני; ילה:

21 לָכֵן הִנְנִי מוֹדִיעָם בַּפַּעַם הַזֹּאת אוֹדִיעֵם אֶת־יָדִי וְאֶת־גְּבוּרָתִי

וְיָדְעוּ כִּי־שְׁמִי רבוע ע״ב ורבוע ס״ג יְהֹוָאַדְנִיאהדנֹהי: 17 1 וַחַטַּאת יְהוּדָה כְּתוּבָה

בְּעֵט בַּרְזֶל ר״ת בלהה רחל זלפה לאה בְּצִפֹּרֶן שָׁמִיר חֲרוּשָׁה עַל־לוּחַ לִבָּם

וּלְקַרְנוֹת מִזְבְּחוֹתֵיכֶם: 2 כִּזְכֹּר בְּנֵיהֶם מִזְבְּחֹתָם וַאֲשֵׁרֵיהֶם עַל־עֵץ

ע״ה קס״א רַעֲנָן עַל גְּבָעוֹת הַגְּבֹהוֹת: 3 הֲרָרִי בַּשָּׂדֶה וַיִּלֶךְ כָּל־ יל׳

אוֹצְרוֹתֶיךָ לָבַז אֶתֵּן בָּמֹתֶיךָ בְּחַטָּאת בְּכָל־ ב״ן, לכב, יבם ־גְּבוּלֶיךָ:

4 וְשָׁמַטְתָּה וּבְךָ מִנַּחֲלָתְךָ אֲשֶׁר נָתַתִּי לָךְ וְהַעֲבַדְתִּיךָ אֶת־אֹיְבֶיךָ

בָּאָרֶץ אלהים דאלפין אֲשֶׁר לֹא־יָדָעְתָּ כִּי־אֵשׁ אלהים דיודין ע״ה קְדַחְתֶּם בְּאַפִּי

עַד־עוֹלָם תּוּקָד: 5 כֹּה הי״ | אָמַר יְהֹוָאַדְנִיאהדנֹהי אָרוּר הַגֶּבֶר אֲשֶׁר

יִבְטַח בָּאָדָם מ״ה יהוה עדי וְשָׂם בָּשָׂר זְרֹעוֹ וּמִן־יְהֹוָאַדְנִיאהדנֹהי יָסוּר לִבּוֹ:

6 וְהָיָה יהוה כְּעַרְעָר בָּעֲרָבָה וְלֹא יִרְאֶה רי״י, גבורה כִּי־יָבוֹא טוֹב הו׳ וְשָׁכַן

ע״ג וְזֵרִים בַּמִּדְבָּר רמ״ווז, ווׂ״פ אל אָרֶץ אלהים דאלפין מְלֵחָה וְלֹא תֵשֵׁב: 7 בָּרוּךְ

יהוה ע״ב ורבוע מ״ה הַגֶּבֶר אֲשֶׁר יִבְטַח בַּיהֹוָאַדְנִיאהדנֹהי וְהָיָה יהוה יְהֹוָאַדְנִיאהדנֹהי

מִבְטַחוֹ: 8 וְהָיָה יהוה ע״ה קס״א כְּעֵץ יהוה | שָׁתוּל עַל־מַיִם וְעַל־יוּבַל יְשַׁלַּח

⁹ The heart is deceitful above all things and it is exceedingly weak—who can know it?

¹⁰ I, the Lord search the heart; I try the reins, even to give every man according to his ways and according to his doings."

¹² As the partridge sits on eggs and hatches them not, so is the man who gains riches by unjust means; they will desert him, when his life is half gone, and at his end shall a fool.

¹² A glorious high throne from the beginning is the place of our sanctuary.

¹³ Lord, the hope of Israel, all who forsake you shall be ashamed. "And those that depart from Me will be written in the earth because they have forsaken the Lord, the fountain of living water.

¹⁴ Heal me, Lord, and I shall be healed; save me and I shall be saved, for You are my praise.

שָׁרָשָׁיו וְלֹא יִרְאֶה רְיֵי, גבורה (כתיב: ירא) כִּי־יָבֹא חֹם וְהָיָה עָלֵהוּ יהוה רַעֲנָן

וּבִשְׁנַת בַּצֹּרֶת לֹא יִדְאָג וְלֹא יָמִישׁ מֵעֲשׂוֹת פֶּרִי עִה אלהים האלפין: 9 עָקֹב

בִּ"פ מום הַלֵּב מִכֹּל יִלי וְאָנֻשׁ הוּא מִי יְיַ יְדָעֶנּוּ: 10 אֲנִי אני יְהֹוָהּ אדני ואהדונהי

חֹקֵר לֵב בֹּחֵן כְּלָיוֹת וְלָתֵת לְאִישׁ עִה קנ"א קס"א כְּדָרְכָיו (כתיב: כדרכו)

כִּפְרִי עִה אלהים האלפין מַעֲלָלָיו: 11 קֹרֵא דָגַר וְלֹא יָלָד עָשָׂה עֹשֶׂר וְלֹא

בְמִשְׁפָּט עִה ה"פ אלהים בְּחֲצִי יָמָיו (כתיב: ימו) יַעַזְבֶנּוּ וּבְאַחֲרִיתוֹ יִהְיֶה ייי

נָבָל: 12 כִּסֵּא יה אדני עה כְּבוֹד מָרוֹם מֵרִאשׁוֹן מְקוֹם יהוה ברבוע, ר"פ אל

מִקְדָּשֵׁנוּ: 13 מִקְוֵה קנ"א, אלהים יִשְׂרָאֵל אדני יְהֹוָהּ ואהדונהי כָּל יִלי עֹזְבֶיךָ

יֵבֹשׁוּ וְסוּרַי (כתיב: יסורי) בָאָרֶץ אלהים האלפין יִכָּתֵבוּ כִּי עָזְבוּ מְקוֹר מַיִם־

חַיִּים בינה עה אֶת־ יְהֹוָהּ ואהדונהי: 14 רְפָאֵנִי יְהֹוָהּ ואהדונהי וְאֵרָפֵא

הוֹשִׁיעֵנִי וְאִוָּשֵׁעָה כִּי תְהִלָּתִי אָתָּה:

SPECIAL READINGS

MAFTIR OF SHABBAT SHEKALIM

Shekalim is the plural form of the word *shekel*, an ancient currency still used in Israel today. During the month of *Adar* (Pisces), each person paid half a shekel to the Temple. The half-shekel offering teaches us a lesson in consciousness: No matter how smart we think we are, no matter how much we think we see, we only perceive half of the total picture. Knowing that what we see is limited creates a humility that allows the Light to direct and support us. When we think we see everything, we give in to judgment and negativity, and the Creator says, "If you know everything,

Exodus 30:11-16

30:11 Then the Lord spoke to Moses, saying,

12 "When you take a census of the Israelites to count them, each one must pay the Lord a ransom for his life at the time he is counted. Then no plague will come on them when you number them.

13 Each one who passes over to those already counted is to give a half shekel, according to the holy shekel, which weighs twenty gerahs. This half shekel is a contribution to the Lord.

14 All who pass over, those twenty years old or more, are to give a contribution to the Lord.

15 The rich are not to give more than a half shekel and the poor are not to give less when you make the contribution to the Lord to atone for your lives.

16 Take the atonement money from the Israelites and use it for the service of the Tent of Meeting. It will be a memorial for the Israelites before the Lord, making atonement for your lives."

MAFTIR OF SHABBAT SHEKALIM

why do you need Me?" The Maftir of Shabbat Shekalim gives us the ability to see beyond the boundaries that ordinarily limit us.

Scripture says that only people who were at least twenty years old gave the offering. "The rich shall not give more, and the poor shall not give less than half a *shekel*, when they give an offering unto the Lord, to make atonement for your souls." (*Exodus 30:15*)

שֵׁמוֹת פֶּרֶק ל

30 11 וַיְדַבֵּר ראה יְהֹוָואהדניאהדונהי אֶל־מֹשֶׁה מהע, אל שדי לֵּאמֹר: 12 כִּי תִשָּׂא
אֶת־רֹאשׁ ריבוע אלהים ואלהים דיודין ע"ה בְּנֵי־יִשְׂרָאֵל לִפְקֻדֵיהֶם וְנָתְנוּ
אבגית"ץ, ועוֹר, אהבת חנם אִישׁ ע"ה קנ"א כֶפֶר מצפץ נַפְשׁוֹ לַיהֹוָואהדניאהדונהי בִּפְקֹד
רבוע ע"ב אֹתָם וְלֹא־יִהְיֶה יהי בָהֶם נֶגֶף בִּפְקֹד רבוע ע"ב אֹתָם: 13 זֶה | יִתְּנוּ
כָּל־הָעֹבֵר ילי רבוע יהוה ורבוע אלהים עַל־הַפְּקֻדִים מַחֲצִית הַשֶּׁקֶל בְּשֶׁקֶל
הַקֹּדֶשׁ עֶשְׂרִים גֵּרָה ד"פ בן הַשֶּׁקֶל מַחֲצִית הַשֶּׁקֶל תְּרוּמָה לַיהֹוָואהדניאהדונהי:
14 כֹּל ילי הָעֹבֵר רבוע יהוה ורבוע אלהים עַל־הַפְּקֻדִים מִבֶּן עֶשְׂרִים שָׁנָה
וָמָעְלָה יִתֵּן תְּרוּמַת יְהֹוָואהדניאהדונהי: 15 הֶעָשִׁיר לֹא־יַרְבֶּה וְהַדַּל לֹא
יַמְעִיט מִמַּחֲצִית הַשָּׁקֶל לָתֵת אֶת־תְּרוּמַת יְהֹוָואהדניאהדונהי לְכַפֵּר מצפץ
עַל־נַפְשֹׁתֵיכֶם: 16 וְלָקַחְתָּ אֶת־כֶּסֶף הַכִּפֻּרִים מֵאֵת בְּנֵי יִשְׂרָאֵל וְנָתַתָּ
אֹתוֹ עַל־עֲבֹדַת אֹהֶל לאה מוֹעֵד וְהָיָה יהוה, יהה לִבְנֵי יִשְׂרָאֵל לְזִכָּרוֹן
ע"ב קס"א נט"ב לִפְנֵי חכמה בינה יְהֹוָואהדניאהדונהי לְכַפֵּר מצפץ עַל־נַפְשֹׁתֵיכֶם:

HAFTARAH OF SHABBAT SHEKALIM

This Haftarah describes the period when Joash became king of Jerusalem at the age of seven and went on to reign for forty years. Once again, we are reminded that to be a pure channel, like Betzalel, the twelve year old builder of the Tabernacle, one does not need to have lived many

2 Kings 11:17-12:17

11: ¹⁷ Jehoiada then made a covenant between the Lord and the king and people that they would be the Lord's people. He also made a covenant between the king and the people.

¹⁸ All the people of the land went to the temple of Baal and tore it down. They smashed the altars and idols to pieces and killed Mattan the priest of Baal in front of the altars. Then the priest posted guards at the temple of the Lord.

¹⁹ He took with him the commanders of hundreds, the Carites, the guards and all the people of the land, and together they brought the king down from the Temple of the Lord and went into the palace, entering by way of the gate of the guards. The king then took his place on the royal throne,

²⁰ and all the people of the land rejoiced. And the city was quiet, because Athaliah had been slain with the sword at the palace.

12:¹ Joash was seven years old when he began to reign.

² In the seventh year of Jehu, Joash became king, and he reigned in Jerusalem forty years. His mother's name was Zibiah; she was from Beersheba.

³ Joash did what was right in the eyes of the Lord all his years, in the way Jehoiada, the priest, instructed him.

⁴ The high places, however, were not removed; the people continued to offer sacrifices and burn incense there.

⁵ Joash said to the priests, "Collect all the money that is brought as sacred offerings to the Temple of the Lord - the money collected in the census, the money received from personal vows and the money brought voluntarily to the temple.

HAFTARAH OF SHABBAT SHEKALIM

years or studied a great deal. Wisdom does not depend on how much we know or how old we are,
but on how connected we are to the Light.

מלכים ב פרק יא

11 17 וַיִּכְרֹת יְהוֹיָדָע אֶת־הַבְּרִית בֵּין יְהֹוָאדֹנָי וּבֵין הַמֶּלֶךְ וּבֵין הָעָם לִהְיוֹת לְעָם לַיהֹוָאדֹנָי וּבֵין הַמֶּלֶךְ וּבֵין הָעָם: 18 וַיָּבֹאוּ כָל־עַם הָאָרֶץ בֵּית־הַבַּעַל וַיִּתְּצֻהוּ אֶת־מִזְבְּחֹתָיו (כתיב: מזבחתו) וְאֶת־צְלָמָיו שִׁבְּרוּ הֵיטֵב וְאֵת מַתָּן כֹּהֵן הַבַּעַל הָרְגוּ לִפְנֵי הַמִּזְבְּחוֹת וַיָּשֶׂם הַכֹּהֵן פְּקֻדֹּת עַל־בֵּית יְהֹוָאדֹנָי: 19 וַיִּקַּח אֶת־שָׂרֵי הַמֵּאוֹת וְאֶת־הַכָּרִי וְאֶת־הָרָצִים וְאֵת | כָּל־עַם הָאָרֶץ וַיֹּרִידוּ אֶת־הַמֶּלֶךְ מִבֵּית יְהֹוָאדֹנָי וַיָּבוֹאוּ דֶרֶךְ־שַׁעַר הָרָצִים בֵּית הַמֶּלֶךְ וַיֵּשֶׁב עַל־כִּסֵּא הַמְּלָכִים: 20 וַיִּשְׂמַח כָּל־עַם־הָאָרֶץ וְהָעִיר שָׁקָטָה וְאֶת־עֲתַלְיָהוּ הֵמִיתוּ בַחֶרֶב בֵּית הַמֶּלֶךְ: (כתיב: מלך) 12 1 בֶּן־שֶׁבַע שָׁנִים יְהוֹאָשׁ בְּמָלְכוֹ: 2 בִּשְׁנַת־שֶׁבַע לְיֵהוּא מָלַךְ יְהוֹאָשׁ וְאַרְבָּעִים שָׁנָה מָלַךְ בִּירוּשָׁלַ͏ִם וְשֵׁם אִמּוֹ צִבְיָה מִבְּאֵר שָׁבַע: 3 וַיַּעַשׂ יְהוֹאָשׁ הַיָּשָׁר בְּעֵינֵי יְהֹוָאדֹנָי כָּל־יָמָיו אֲשֶׁר הוֹרָהוּ יְהוֹיָדָע הַכֹּהֵן: 4 רַק הַבָּמוֹת לֹא־סָרוּ עוֹד הָעָם מְזַבְּחִים וּמְקַטְּרִים בַּבָּמוֹת: 5 וַיֹּאמֶר יְהוֹאָשׁ אֶל־הַכֹּהֲנִים כֹּל כֶּסֶף הַקֳּדָשִׁים אֲשֶׁר־יוּבָא בֵית־ יְהֹוָאדֹנָי כֶּסֶף עוֹבֵר אִישׁ כֶּסֶף נַפְשׁוֹת עֶרְכּוֹ כָּל־כֶּסֶף אֲשֶׁר יַעֲלֶה עַל לֶב־אִישׁ לְהָבִיא בֵּית

[6] *Let every priest receive the money from one of the treasurers, and let it be used to repair whatever damage is found in the Temple."*

[7] *But by the twenty-third year of King Joash the priests still had not repaired the Temple.*

[8] *King Joash summoned Jehoiada, the priest, and the other priests and asked them, "Why aren't you repairing the damage done to the Temple? Take no more money from your treasurers, but hand it over for repairing the Temple."*

[9] *The priests agreed that they would not collect any more money from the people and that they would not repair the Temple themselves.*

[10] *Jehoiada, the priest, took a chest and bored a hole in its lid. He placed it beside the altar, on the right side as one enters the Temple of the Lord. The priests who guarded the entrance put into the chest all the money that was brought to the Temple of the Lord.*

[11] *Whenever they saw that there was a large amount of money in the chest, the royal secretary and the High Priest came, counted the money that had been brought into the temple of the Lord and put it into bags.*

[12] *When the amount had been determined, they gave the money to the men appointed to supervise the work on the Temple. With it they paid those who worked on the Temple of the Lord - the carpenters and builders,*

[13] *the masons and stonecutters. They purchased timber and dressed stone for the repair of the Temple of the Lord, and met all the other expenses of restoring the temple.*

[14] *The money brought into the Temple was not spent for making silver basins, wick trimmers, sprinkling bowls, trumpets or any other articles of gold or silver for the Temple of the Lord;*

[15] *it was paid to the workmen, who used it to repair the Temple.*

[16] *They did not require an accounting from those to whom they gave the money to pay the workers, because they acted with complete honesty.*

[17] *The money from the guilt offerings and sin offerings was not brought into the Temple of the Lord; it belonged to the priests.*

יְהֹוָאדנָי יאהדונהי׃ 6 יִקְחוּ וזעם לָהֶם הַכֹּהֲנִים מלה אִישׁ ע״ה קנ״א קס״א מֵאֵת מַכָּרוֹ
וְהֵם יְחַזְּקוּ אֶת־בֶּדֶק הַבַּיִת ב״פ ראה לְכֹל יה אדני אֲשֶׁר־יִמָּצֵא שָׁם יהוה שדי
בָּדֶק׃ 7 וַיְהִי אל, ייא״י בִּשְׁנַת עֶשְׂרִים וְשָׁלֹשׁ שָׁנָה לַמֶּלֶךְ יְהוֹאָשׁ לֹא־
חִזְּקוּ הַכֹּהֲנִים מלה אֶת־בֶּדֶק הַבָּיִת ב״פ ראה׃ 8 וַיִּקְרָא ב״פ קס״א - ה׳ אותיות
הַמֶּלֶךְ יְהוֹאָשׁ לִיהוֹיָדָע הַכֹּהֵן מלה וְלַכֹּהֲנִים וַיֹּאמֶר אֲלֵהֶם מַדּוּעַ
אֵינְכֶם מְחַזְּקִים אֶת־בֶּדֶק הַבָּיִת ב״פ ראה וְעַתָּה אַל־תִּקְחוּ־כֶסֶף מֵאֵת
מַכָּרֵיכֶם כִּי־לְבֶדֶק הַבַּיִת ב״פ ראה תִּתְּנֻהוּ׃ 9 וַיֵּאֹתוּ הַכֹּהֲנִים מלה לְבִלְתִּי
קְחַת־כֶּסֶף מֵאֵת הָעָם וּלְבִלְתִּי חַזֵּק פהל אֶת־בֶּדֶק הַבָּיִת ב״פ ראה׃
10 וַיִּקַּח וזעם יְהוֹיָדָע הַכֹּהֵן מלה אֲרוֹן ע״ה ג״פ אלהים אֶחָד אהבה, דאגה וַיִּקֹּב חֹר
בְּדַלְתּוֹ וַיִּתֵּן י״פ מלוי ע״ב אֹתוֹ אֵצֶל הַמִּזְבֵּחַ זן, נגד מִיָּמִין (כתיב: בימין) בְּבוֹא־
אִישׁ ע״ה קנ״א קס״א בֵּית ב״פ ראה יְהֹוָאדנָי יאהדונהי וְנָתְנוּ־שָׁמָּה מהש, משה, אל שדי
הַכֹּהֲנִים מלה שֹׁמְרֵי הַסַּף אֶת־כָּל ילי ־הַכֶּסֶף הַמּוּבָא בֵית ב״פ ראה ־
יְהֹוָאדנָי יאהדונהי׃ 11 וַיְהִי אל, ייא״י כִּרְאוֹתָם כִּי־רַב ע״ב ורבוע מ״ה הַכֶּסֶף בָּאָרוֹן
ע״ה ג״פ אלהים וַיַּעַל סֹפֵר הַמֶּלֶךְ וְהַכֹּהֵן מלה הַגָּדוֹל להח, מבה, יזל, אום וַיָּצֻרוּ וַיִּמְנוּ
אֶת־הַכֶּסֶף הַנִּמְצָא בֵית ב״פ ראה ־יְהֹוָאדנָי יאהדונהי׃ 12 וְנָתְנוּ אֶת־הַכֶּסֶף
הַמְתֻכָּן עַל־יְדֵי (כתיב: יד) עֹשֵׂי הַמְּלָאכָה אל אדני הַמֻּפְקָדִים (כתיב: הפקדים)
בֵּית ב״פ ראה יְהֹוָאדנָי יאהדונהי וַיּוֹצִיאֻהוּ לְחָרָשֵׁי הָעֵץ ע״ה קס״א וְלַבֹּנִים הָעֹשִׂים
בֵּית ב״פ ראה יְהֹוָאדנָי יאהדונהי׃ 13 וְלַגֹּדְרִים וּלְחֹצְבֵי הָאֶבֶן וְלִקְנוֹת עֵצִים
וְאַבְנֵי מַחְצֵב לְחַזֵּק פהל אֶת־בֶּדֶק בֵּית ב״פ ראה יְהֹוָאדנָי יאהדונהי וּלְכֹל יה אדני
אֲשֶׁר־יֵצֵא עַל־הַבַּיִת ב״פ ראה לְחָזְקָה׃ 14 אַךְ לֹא יֵעָשֶׂה בֵּית ב״פ ראה
יְהֹוָאדנָי יאהדונהי סִפּוֹת כֶּסֶף מְזַמְּרוֹת מִזְרָקוֹת חֲצֹצְרוֹת כָּל ילי ־כְּלִי כלי
זָהָב וּכְלִי כלי ־כֶסֶף מִן־הַכֶּסֶף הַמּוּבָא בֵית ב״פ ראה ־יְהֹוָאדנָי יאהדונהי׃ 15 כִּי־
לְעֹשֵׂי הַמְּלָאכָה אל אדני יִתְּנֻהוּ וְחִזְּקוּ־בוֹ אֶת־בֵּית ב״פ ראה יְהֹוָאדנָי יאהדונהי׃
16 וְלֹא יְחַשְּׁבוּ אֶת־הָאֲנָשִׁים אֲשֶׁר יִתְּנוּ אֶת־הַכֶּסֶף עַל־יָדָם לָתֵת
לְעֹשֵׂי הַמְּלָאכָה אל אדני כִּי בֶאֱמֻנָה הֵם עֹשִׂים׃ 17 כֶּסֶף אָשָׁם וְכֶסֶף
חַטָּאוֹת לֹא יוּבָא בֵּית ב״פ ראה יְהֹוָאדנָי יאהדונהי לַכֹּהֲנִים יִהְיוּ אל׃

MAFTIR OF SHABBAT ZACHOR

Uncertainty is our greatest opportunity for positive change because it gives us a chance to confront and overcome the negative power of doubt. When we overcome doubt, we overcome all our fears at the seed level—which is the source of unhappiness in our lives. This reading deals with the war against the nation of Amalek. The *Zohar* tells us that Amalek is not a nation, but a concealed

Deuteronomy 25:17-19

25:*17* "Remember what Amalek did to you along the way, when you came out from Egypt,

18 how he met you along the way and attacked among you all the stragglers at your rear when you were faint and weary; and he did not fear God.

19 It shall come about when the Lord, your God has given you rest from all your surrounding enemies, in the land which the Lord, your God gives you as an inheritance to possess, you shall blot out the memory of Amalek from under heaven. You must not forget.

HAFTARAH OF SHABBAT ZACHOR

This Haftarah recounts the war against Amalek. The Talmud says that King David sinned twice and King Saul only once, yet King David was forgiven and King Saul was killed and his kingdom taken away. When God came to King Saul and said, "Go and kill Amalek," King Saul thought to

1 Samuel 15:1-34

15:*1* Samuel said to Saul, "I am the one the Lord sent to anoint you king over His people Israel; so listen now to the message from the Lord.

2 This is what the Lord of Hosts says: 'I will punish the Amalekites for what they did to Israel when they waylaid them as they came up from Egypt.

MAFTIR OF SHABBAT ZACHOR

truth about life. The word *amalek* has the same numerical value as the Aramaic word *safek*, which means "doubt." According to Kabbalah, words of equivalent numerical value share the same meaning. With this reading, we receive the power of certainty to overcome our own Amalek (doubt).

דברים פרק כה

25 17 זָכוֹר ע״ב קס״א אֵת אֲשֶׁר־עָשָׂה לְךָ עֲמָלֵק ב״פ ק״ך בַּדֶּרֶךְ ב״פ יב״ק

בְּצֵאתְכֶם מִמִּצְרָיִם מצר: 18 אֲשֶׁר קָרְךָ בַּדֶּרֶךְ ב״פ יב״ק וַיְזַנֵּב בְּךָ כָּל ילי

הַנֶּחֱשָׁלִים אַחֲרֶיךָ וְאַתָּה עָיֵף וְיָגֵעַ וְלֹא יָרֵא אלף למד יהוה אֱלֹהִים

מום, אהיה אדני ; ילה: 19 וְהָיָה יהוה, יהה בְּהָנִיחַ יְהוָֹאהדונהי אֱלֹהֶיךָ ילה | לְךָ

מִכָּל ילי ־אֹיְבֶיךָ מִסָּבִיב בָּאָרֶץ אלהים דאלפין אֲשֶׁר יְהוָֹאהדונהי אֱלֹהֶיךָ

נֹתֵן אבגית״ץ, ושר, אהבת חנם לְךָ נַחֲלָה לְרִשְׁתָּהּ תִּמְחֶה אֶת־זֵכֶר עֲמָלֵק ילה

מִתַּחַת הַשָּׁמָיִם ב״פ ק״ך י״פ טל, י״פ כוזו לֹא תִּשְׁכָּח ע״ה קרעשטן:

HAFTARAH OF SHABBAT ZACHOR

himself that maybe God wanted him to kill all the people but not the animals. The problem for King Saul was not that he was wrong, but that he made a calculation.

שמואל א פרק טו

15 1 וַיֹּאמֶר שְׁמוּאֵל אֶל־שָׁאוּל אֹתִי שָׁלַח יְהוָֹאהדונהי לִמְשָׁחֲךָ

לְמֶלֶךְ עַל־עַמּוֹ עַל־יִשְׂרָאֵל וְעַתָּה שְׁמַע לְקוֹל ע״ב ס״ג ע״ה דִּבְרֵי ראה

יְהוָֹאהדונהי: 2 כֹּה היי אָמַר יְהוָֹאהדונהי צְבָאוֹת נתה ורבוע אהיה; פני שכינה

³ Now go, attack the Amalekites and totally destroy everything that belongs to them. Do not spare them; put to death men and women, children and infants, cattle and sheep, camels and donkeys.' "

⁴ So Saul summoned the men and mustered them at Telaim—two hundred thousand foot soldiers and ten thousand men from Judah.

⁵ Saul went to the city of Amalek and set an ambush in the ravine.

⁶ Then he said to the Kenites, "Go away, leave, go down from the Amalekites so that I do not destroy you along with them; for you showed kindness to all the Israelites when they came up out of Egypt." So the Kenites moved away from the Amalekites.

⁷ Then Saul attacked the Amalekites all the way from Havilah to Shur, to the east of Egypt.

⁸ He captured Agag, king of the Amalekites, alive and all his people he totally destroyed with the sword.

⁹ But Saul and the army spared Agag and the best of the sheep and cattle, the fat calves and lambs—everything that was good. These they were unwilling to destroy completely, but everything that was despised and weak they totally destroyed.

¹⁰ Then the word of the Lord came to Samuel:

¹¹ "I am grieved that I have made Saul king, because he has turned away from Me and has not carried out my instructions." Samuel was troubled, and he cried out to the Lord all that night.

¹² Early in the morning Samuel got up and went to meet Saul, but Samuel was told, "Saul has gone to Carmel. There he has set up a monument in his own honor and has turned and gone on down to Gilgal."

¹³ When Samuel reached Saul, Saul said, "The Lord bless you! I have carried out the Lord's instructions."

¹⁴ But Samuel said, "What then is this bleating of sheep in my ears? What is this lowing of cattle that I hear?"

¹⁵ Saul answered, "They brought them from the Amalekites; they spared the best of the sheep and cattle to sacrifice to the Lord your God, but we totally destroyed the rest." ¹⁶ "Stop!" Samuel said to Saul. "Let me tell you what the Lord said to me last night." "Speak," Saul replied.

פָּקַ֣דְתִּי אֵ֧ת אֲשֶׁר־עָשָׂ֛ה עֲמָלֵ֖ק לְיִשְׂרָאֵ֑ל אֲשֶׁר־שָׂ֥ם ל֛וֹ

בַּדֶּ֖רֶךְ בַּעֲלֹת֣וֹ מִמִּצְרָֽיִם: 3 עַתָּה֩ לֵ֨ךְ וְהִכִּיתָ֜ה אֶת־עֲמָלֵ֗ק

וְהַחֲרַמְתֶּם֙ אֶת־כָּל־אֲשֶׁר־ל֔וֹ וְלֹ֥א תַחְמֹ֖ל עָלָ֑יו וְהֵמַתָּ֞ה מֵאִ֣ישׁ

עַד־אִשָּׁ֗ה מֵֽעֹלֵל֙ וְעַד־יוֹנֵ֔ק מִשּׁ֣וֹר וְעַד־שֶׂ֔ה

מִגָּמָ֖ל וְעַד־חֲמֽוֹר: 4 וַיְשַׁמַּ֤ע שָׁאוּל֙ אֶת־הָעָ֔ם וַֽיִּפְקְדֵם֙ בַּטְּלָאִ֔ים

מָאתַ֣יִם אֶ֔לֶף רַגְלִ֑י וַעֲשֶׂ֥רֶת אֲלָפִ֖ים אֶת־אִ֥ישׁ

יְהוּדָֽה: 5 וַיָּבֹ֥א שָׁא֖וּל עַד־עִ֣יר עֲמָלֵ֑ק

וַיָּ֖רֶב בַּנָּֽחַל: 6 וַיֹּ֣אמֶר שָׁא֣וּל אֶל־הַקֵּינִ֡י לְכוּ֩ סֻּ֨רוּ רְד֜וּ מִתּ֣וֹךְ

עֲמָ֣לֵקִ֗י פֶּן־אֹֽסִפְךָ֙ עִמּ֔וֹ וְאַתָּ֞ה עָשִׂ֤יתָה חֶ֙סֶד֙ עִם־כָּל־בְּנֵ֣י

יִשְׂרָאֵ֔ל בַּעֲלוֹתָ֖ם מִמִּצְרָ֑יִם וַיָּ֥סַר קֵינִ֖י מִתּ֥וֹךְ עֲמָלֵֽק: 7 וַיַּ֥ךְ

שָׁא֖וּל אֶת־עֲמָלֵ֑ק מֵֽחֲוִילָ֙ה בּוֹאֲךָ֣ שׁ֔וּר אֲשֶׁ֖ר

עַל־פְּנֵ֥י מִצְרָֽיִם: 8 וַיִּתְפֹּ֛שׂ אֶת־אֲגַ֥ג מֶֽלֶךְ־עֲמָלֵ֖ק וָזֶ֥י

וְאֶת־כָּל־הָעָ֖ם הֶחֱרִ֣ים לְפִי־חָֽרֶב: 9 וַיַּחְמֹל֩ שָׁא֨וּל

וְהָעָ֜ם עַל־אֲגָ֗ג וְעַל־מֵיטַ֣ב הַצֹּאן֩ וְהַבָּקָ֨ר וְהַמִּשְׁנִ֤ים וְעַל־

הַכָּרִים֙ וְעַל־כָּל־הַטּ֔וֹב וְלֹ֥א אָב֖וּ הַחֲרִימָ֑ם וְכָל־הַמְּלָאכָ֛ה

נְמִבְזָ֥ה וְנָמֵ֖ס אֹתָ֥הּ הֶחֱרִֽימוּ: 10 וַֽיְהִי֙ דְּבַר־יְהוָ֔ה

אֶל־שְׁמוּאֵ֖ל לֵאמֹֽר: 11 נִחַ֗מְתִּי כִּֽי־הִמְלַ֤כְתִּי אֶת־שָׁאוּל֙ לְמֶ֔לֶךְ כִּֽי־שָׁ֞ב

מֵאַֽחֲרַ֗י וְאֶת־דְּבָרַ֖י לֹ֣א הֵקִ֑ים וַיִּ֙חַר֙ לִשְׁמוּאֵ֔ל וַיִּזְעַ֥ק אֶל־

יְהוָ֖ה כָּל־הַלָּֽיְלָה: 12 וַיַּשְׁכֵּ֧ם שְׁמוּאֵ֛ל לִקְרַ֥את שָׁא֖וּל

בַּבֹּ֑קֶר וַיֻּגַּ֙ד לִשְׁמוּאֵ֜ל לֵאמֹ֗ר בָּֽא־שָׁא֣וּל הַכַּרְמֶ֔לָה וְהִנֵּ֙ה מַצִּ֥יב

ל֣וֹ יָ֔ד וַיִּסֹּב֙ וַֽיַּעֲבֹ֔ר וַיֵּ֖רֶד הַגִּלְגָּֽל: 13 וַיָּבֹ֥א שְׁמוּאֵ֖ל אֶל־

שָׁא֑וּל וַיֹּ֧אמֶר ל֣וֹ שָׁא֗וּל בָּר֤וּךְ אַתָּה֙ לַֽיהוָ֔ה

הֲקִמֹ֖תִי אֶת־דְּבַ֥ר יְהוָֽה: 14 וַיֹּ֣אמֶר שְׁמוּאֵ֔ל וּמֶ֛ה ק֥וֹל

הַצֹּאן֙ הַזֶּ֣ה בְּאָזְנָ֑י וְק֣וֹל הַבָּקָ֖ר אֲשֶׁ֥ר

¹⁷ Samuel said, "Although you were once small in your own eyes, did you not become the head of the tribes of Israel? The Lord anointed you king over Israel.

¹⁸ And He sent you on a mission, saying, 'Go and completely destroy those wicked people, the Amalekites; make war on them until you have wiped them out.'

¹⁹ Why did you not obey the Lord's voice? Why did you pounce on the plunder and do evil in the eyes of the Lord?"

²⁰ "But I did obey the Lord," Saul said to Samuel. "I went on the mission the Lord assigned me. I completely destroyed the Amalekites and brought back Agag their king.

²¹ The soldiers took sheep and cattle from the plunder, the best of what was devoted to God, in order to sacrifice them to the Lord, your God at Gilgal."

²² But Samuel replied: "Does the Lord delight in burnt offerings and sacrifices as much as in obeying the voice of the Lord? To obey is better than sacrifice, and to heed is better than the fat of rams.

²³ For rebellion is like the sin of divination, and arrogance like the evil of idolatry. Because you have rejected the word of the Lord, he has rejected you as king."

²⁴ Then Saul said to Samuel, "I have sinned. I violated the Lord's command and your instructions. I was afraid of the people and so I gave in to them.

²⁵ Now I beg you, forgive my sin and come back with me, so that I may worship the Lord."

²⁶ But Samuel said to Saul, "I will not go back with you. You have rejected the word of the Lord, and the Lord has rejected you as king over Israel!"

²⁷ As Samuel turned to leave, he caught hold of the hem of his robe, and it tore.

²⁸ Samuel said to him, "The Lord has torn the kingdom of Israel from you today and has given it to one of your neighbors—to one better than you.

²⁹ He who is the Glory of Israel does not lie or change his mind; for he is not a man, that he should change his mind."

15 וַיֹּאמֶר שָׁאוּל מֵעֲמָלֵקִי הֱבִיאוּם אֲשֶׁר חָמַל הָעָם עַל־מֵיטַב הַצֹּאן וְהַבָּקָר לְמַעַן זְבֹחַ לַיהֹוָה אֱלֹהֶיךָ וְאֶת־הַיּוֹתֵר הֶחֱרַמְנוּ׃ 16 וַיֹּאמֶר שְׁמוּאֵל אֶל־שָׁאוּל הֶרֶף וְאַגִּידָה לְּךָ אֵת אֲשֶׁר דִּבֶּר יְהֹוָה אֵלַי הַלָּיְלָה וַיֹּאמֶר (כתיב: ויאמרו) לוֹ דַּבֵּר׃ 17 וַיֹּאמֶר שְׁמוּאֵל הֲלוֹא אִם־קָטֹן אַתָּה בְּעֵינֶיךָ רֹאשׁ שִׁבְטֵי יִשְׂרָאֵל אָתָּה וַיִּמְשָׁחֲךָ יְהֹוָה לְמֶלֶךְ עַל־יִשְׂרָאֵל׃ 18 וַיִּשְׁלָחֲךָ יְהֹוָה בְּדָרֶךְ וַיֹּאמֶר לֵךְ וְהַחֲרַמְתָּה אֶת־הַחַטָּאִים אֶת־עֲמָלֵק וְנִלְחַמְתָּ בוֹ עַד כַּלּוֹתָם אֹתָם׃ 19 וְלָמָּה לֹא־שָׁמַעְתָּ בְּקוֹל יְהֹוָה וַתַּעַט אֶל־הַשָּׁלָל וַתַּעַשׂ הָרַע בְּעֵינֵי יְהֹוָה׃ 20 וַיֹּאמֶר שָׁאוּל אֶל־שְׁמוּאֵל אֲשֶׁר שָׁמַעְתִּי בְּקוֹל יְהֹוָה וָאֵלֵךְ בַּדֶּרֶךְ אֲשֶׁר־שְׁלָחַנִי יְהֹוָה וָאָבִיא אֶת־אֲגַג מֶלֶךְ עֲמָלֵק וְאֶת־עֲמָלֵק הֶחֱרַמְתִּי׃ 21 וַיִּקַּח הָעָם מֵהַשָּׁלָל צֹאן וּבָקָר רֵאשִׁית הַחֵרֶם לִזְבֹּחַ לַיהֹוָה אֱלֹהֶיךָ בַּגִּלְגָּל׃ 22 וַיֹּאמֶר שְׁמוּאֵל הַחֵפֶץ לַיהֹוָה בְּעֹלוֹת וּזְבָחִים כִּשְׁמֹעַ בְּקוֹל יְהֹוָה הִנֵּה שְׁמֹעַ מִזֶּבַח טוֹב לְהַקְשִׁיב מֵחֵלֶב אֵילִים׃ 23 כִּי חַטַּאת־קֶסֶם מֶרִי וְאָוֶן וּתְרָפִים הַפְצַר יַעַן מָאַסְתָּ אֶת־דְּבַר יְהֹוָה וַיִּמְאָסְךָ מִמֶּלֶךְ׃ 24 וַיֹּאמֶר שָׁאוּל אֶל־שְׁמוּאֵל חָטָאתִי כִּי־עָבַרְתִּי אֶת־פִּי־יְהֹוָה וְאֶת־דְּבָרֶיךָ כִּי יָרֵאתִי אֶת־הָעָם וָאֶשְׁמַע בְּקוֹלָם׃ 25 וְעַתָּה שָׂא נָא אֶת־חַטָּאתִי וְשׁוּב עִמִּי וְאֶשְׁתַּחֲוֶה לַיהֹוָה׃ 26 וַיֹּאמֶר שְׁמוּאֵל אֶל־שָׁאוּל לֹא אָשׁוּב עִמָּךְ כִּי מָאַסְתָּה אֶת־דְּבַר יְהֹוָה וַיִּמְאָסְךָ יְהֹוָה מִהְיוֹת מֶלֶךְ עַל־יִשְׂרָאֵל׃ 27 וַיִּסֹּב שְׁמוּאֵל לָלֶכֶת וַיַּחֲזֵק בִּכְנַף

[30] He replied, "I have sinned. But please honor me before the elders of my people and before Israel; come back with me, so that I may worship the Lord, your God."

[31] So Samuel went back with Saul, and Saul worshiped the Lord.

[32] Then Samuel said, "Bring me Agag king of the Amalekites." Agag came to him confidently, thinking, "Surely the bitterness of death is past."

[33] But Samuel said, "As your sword has made women childless, so will your mother be childless among women." And Samuel put Agag to death before the Lord at Gilgal.

[34] Then Samuel left for Ramah, but Saul went up to his home in Gibeah-Saul.

ע״ה קנ״א, אלהים אדני ־מֵעָלָיו וַיִּקָּרַע: 28 וַיֹּאמֶר אֵלָיו שְׁמוּאֵל קָרַע ב״פ אלף לכזר, ש״ע

יְהֹוָ֗ה אדניאהדונהי אֶת־מַמְלְכוּת יִשְׂרָאֵל מֵעָלֶיךָ הַיּוֹם ע״ה = נגד, זך, מזבח וּנְתָנָהּ

לְרֵעֲךָ הַטּוֹב יהו מִמֶּךָּ: 29 וְגַם יג״ל נֵצַח יִשְׂרָאֵל לֹא יְשַׁקֵּר וְלֹא יִנָּחֵם

כִּי לֹא אָדָם מ״ה הוּא לְהִנָּחֵם: 30 וַיֹּאמֶר חָטָאתִי עַתָּה כַּבְּדֵנִי נָא נֶגֶד

זך נגד, מזבח זִקְנֵי־עַמִּי וְנֶגֶד זך נגד, מזבח יִשְׂרָאֵל וְשׁוּב עִמִּי וְהִשְׁתַּחֲוֵיתִי

לַיהֹוָ֗ה אדניאהדונהי אֱלֹהֶיךָ ילה: 31 וַיָּשָׁב שְׁמוּאֵל אַחֲרֵי שָׁאוּל וַיִּשְׁתַּחוּ

שָׁאוּל לַיהֹוָ֗ה אדניאהדונהי: 32 וַיֹּאמֶר שְׁמוּאֵל הַגִּישׁוּ אֵלַי אֶת־אֲגַג מֶלֶךְ

עֲמָלֵק ב״פ קד וַיֵּלֶךְ כלי אֵלָיו אֲגַג מַעֲדַנֹּת וַיֹּאמֶר אֲגָג אָכֵן יהוה מ״ה סָר

י הויות מַר ב״פ קד ־הַמָּוֶת: 33 וַיֹּאמֶר שְׁמוּאֵל כַּאֲשֶׁר שִׁכְּלָה נָשִׁים חַרְבֶּךָ

כֵּן־תִּשְׁכַּל מִנָּשִׁים אִמֶּךָ וַיְשַׁסֵּף שְׁמוּאֵל אֶת־אֲגָג לִפְנֵי וזכמה בינה

יְהֹוָ֗ה אדניאהדונהי בַּגִּלְגָּל: 34 וַיֵּלֶךְ כלי שְׁמוּאֵל הָרָמָתָה וְשָׁאוּל עָלָה אֶל־

בֵּיתוֹ ב״פ ראה גִּבְעַת שָׁאוּל:

MAFTIR OF SHABBAT PARAH

This reading connects us with the power to cleanse our negativity. According to the *Zohar*, the Red Heifer is the mother of the Golden Calf. Therefore, by sacrificing the Red Heifer, we correct the sin of worshipping the Golden Calf. The *Zohar* tells us that before the creation of Golden Calf, we achieved the consciousness where immortality was a reality. Through reading this Bible passage, we can connect with the taste of immortality once again, reminding us that it is in our destiny.

> *...after the giving of Torah, the Shechinah was a mere Tent, as it is written: "A Tabernacle that shall not be taken down, not one of the stakes thereof shall ever be removed," (Isaiah 33:20)*

Numbers 19:1-22

19:¹ Then the Lord spoke to Moses and Aaron, saying,

² "This is the statute of the law which the Lord has commanded, saying, 'Speak to the sons of Israel and they will bring you an unblemished red heifer in which there is no defect and on which a yoke has never been placed.

³ You shall give it to Eleazar, the priest, and it shall be brought outside the camp and be slaughtered in his presence.

⁴ Next, Eleazar, the priest, shall take some of its blood with his finger and sprinkle some of its blood toward the front of the tent of meeting seven times.

⁵ Then the heifer shall be burnt in his sight; its hide and its flesh and its blood, with its refuse, shall be burned.

⁶ The priest shall take cedar wood and hyssop and scarlet material and cast it into the midst of the burning heifer.

⁷ The priest shall then wash his clothes and bathe his body in water, and afterward come into the camp, but the priest shall be unclean until evening.

⁸ The one who burns it shall also wash his clothes in water and bathe his body in water, and shall be unclean until evening.

⁹ Now a man who is clean shall gather up the ashes of the heifer and deposit them outside the camp in a clean place, and the congregation of the sons of Israel shall keep it as water to remove impurity; it is purification from sin.

MAFTIR OF SHABBAT PARAH

and it was continuously illuminated. But now, after the sin of the Calf, it was called the Tabernacle of Appointment [or the Tent of Meeting], because it was only illuminated periodically. Before, it had given long life to the world, and death was powerless. After the giving of the Torah, there was freedom from the Angel of Death. But, after the sin of the Calf, the Shechinah became the Tabernacle of Periodic Congregation, as it is written: "the house of appointment to all the living." (Job 30:33) Now it is governed by time, and life is limited in the world.

> — *The Zohar, Beresheet B 57:297*

בְּמִדְבַּר פֶּרֶק יט

19 1 וַיְדַבֵּר רָאה יְהֹוָ֨ה וֵאלֹהֵינוּ מהע, אל שדי אֶל־מֹשֶׁה וְאֶל־אַהֲרֹ֖ן ע״ב ורבוע ע״ב

לֵאמֹֽר: 2 זֹ֚את חֻקַּ֣ת הַתּוֹרָ֔ה אֲשֶׁר־צִוָּ֖ה פוי יְהֹוָ֨ה וֵאלֹהֵינוּ לֵאמֹ֑ר

דַּבֵּ֣ר ראה | אֶל־בְּנֵ֣י יִשְׂרָאֵ֗ל וְיִקְח֣וּ חום אֵלֶ֩יךָ֩ פָרָ֨ה אֲדֻמָּ֜ה אני עסמ״ב ורבוע עסמ״ב

תְּמִימָ֗ה אֲשֶׁ֤ר אֵֽין־בָּהּ֙ מ֔וּם מום, אלהים, אהיה אדני אֲשֶׁ֛ר לֹא־עָלָ֥ה עָלֶ֖יהָ פהל

עֹֽל: 3 וּנְתַתֶּ֣ם אֹתָ֔הּ אֶל־אֶלְעָזָ֖ר הַכֹּהֵ֑ן מלה וְהוֹצִ֤יא אֹתָהּ֙ אֶל־מִח֣וּץ

לַֽמַּחֲנֶ֔ה וְשָׁחַ֥ט אֹתָ֖הּ לְפָנָֽיו: 4 וְלָקַ֞ח ב״פ יהוה אדני אהיה אֶלְעָזָ֧ר הַכֹּהֵ֛ן מלה

מִדָּמָ֖הּ בְּאֶצְבָּע֑וֹ וְהִזָּ֞ה ג״פ יהוה פְנֵ֨י וחכמה בינה אֶל־נֹ֧כַח אֹֽהֶל־לאה מוֹעֵ֛ד

מִדָּמָ֖הּ שֶׁ֥בַע ע״ב ואלהים דיודין פְּעָמִֽים: 5 וְשָׂרַ֥ף אֶת־הַפָּרָ֖ה לְעֵינָ֑יו ריבוע מ״ה

אֶת־עֹרָ֤הּ וְאֶת־בְּשָׂרָהּ֙ וְאֶת־דָּמָ֔הּ עַל־פִּרְשָׁ֖הּ יִשְׂרֹֽף: 6 וְלָקַ֣ח

הַכֹּהֵ֗ן מלה ב״פ יהוה אדני אהיה עֵ֣ץ ע״ה קס״א אֶ֔רֶז ד״פ בן וְאֵז֖וֹב וּשְׁנִ֣י תוֹלָ֑עַת שקוצי״ת

וְהִשְׁלִ֕יךְ אֶל־תּ֖וֹךְ שְׂרֵפַ֥ת הַפָּרָֽה: 7 וְכִבֶּ֨ס בְּגָדָ֜יו הַכֹּהֵ֗ן מלה וְרָחַ֤ץ

בְּשָׂרוֹ֙ בַּמַּ֔יִם וְאַחַ֖ר יָבֹ֣א אֶל־הַֽמַּחֲנֶ֑ה וְטָמֵ֥א הַכֹּהֵ֖ן מלה עַד־הָעָֽרֶב

8 וְהַשֹּׂרֵ֣ף אֹתָ֔הּ יְכַבֵּ֤ס בְּגָדָיו֙ בַּמַּ֔יִם וְרָחַ֥ץ בְּשָׂר֖וֹ רבוע יהוה ורבוע אלהים

בַּמָּ֑יִם וְטָמֵ֖א עַד־הָעָֽרֶב: רבוע יהוה ורבוע אלהים 9 וְאָסַ֣ף | אִ֣ישׁ ע״ה קנ״א קס״א

טָה֗וֹר י״פ אכא אֵ֚ת אֵ֣פֶר אחר ע״ה סזהד״ך הַפָּרָ֔ה וְהִנִּ֥יחַ מִח֣וּץ לַֽמַּחֲנֶ֖ה בְּמָק֣וֹם

10 The one who gathers the ashes of the heifer shall wash his clothes and be unclean until evening; and it shall be a perpetual statute to the sons of Israel and to the alien who sojourns among them.

11 The one who touches the corpse of any person will be unclean for seven days,

12 that one shall purify himself from uncleanness with it on the third day and on the seventh day, and then he will be clean; but if he does not purify himself on the third day and on the seventh day, he will not be clean.

13 Anyone who touches a corpse, the body of a man who has died, and does not purify himself, defiles the Tabernacle of the Lord; and that person shall be cut off from Israel. Because the water for impurity was not sprinkled on him, he shall be unclean; his uncleanness is still on him.

14 This is the law when a man dies in a tent: everyone who comes into the tent and everyone who is in the tent shall be unclean for seven days.

15 Every open vessel, which has no covering tied down on it, shall be unclean.

16 Also, anyone who in the open field touches one who has been slain with a sword or who has died naturally, or a human bone or a grave, shall be unclean for seven days.

17 Then for the unclean person they shall take some of the ashes of the burnt purification from sin and flowing water shall be added to them in a vessel.

18 A clean person shall take hyssop and dip it in the water, and sprinkle it on the tent and on all the furnishings and on the souls who were there, and on the one who touched the bone, or the one slain or the one dying naturally, or on the grave.

19 Then the clean person shall sprinkle on the unclean on the third day and on the seventh day; and on the seventh day he shall purify him, and he shall wash his clothes and bathe himself in water and shall be clean by evening.

20 But the man who is unclean and does not purify himself, that person shall be cut off from the midst of the assembly, because he has defiled the Sanctuary of the Lord; the water for impurity has not been sprinkled on him; he is unclean.

טָהוֹר וְהָיְתָה לַעֲדַת בְּנֵי־יִשְׂרָאֵל לְמִשְׁמֶרֶת לְמֵי

נִדָּה חַטָּאת הִוא: 10 וְכִבֶּס הָאֹסֵף אֶת־אֵפֶר הַפָּרָה אֶת־בְּגָדָיו

וְטָמֵא עַד־הָעָרֶב וְהָיְתָה לִבְנֵי יִשְׂרָאֵל וְלַגֵּר הַגָּר

בְּתוֹכָם לְחֻקַּת עוֹלָם: 11 הַנֹּגֵעַ בְּמֵת לְכָל־

נֶפֶשׁ אָדָם וְטָמֵא שִׁבְעַת יָמִים: 12 הוּא יִתְחַטָּא־

בוֹ בַּיּוֹם הַשְּׁלִישִׁי וּבַיּוֹם הַשְּׁבִיעִי יִטְהָר וְאִם

לֹא יִתְחַטָּא בַּיּוֹם הַשְּׁלִישִׁי וּבַיּוֹם

הַשְּׁבִיעִי לֹא יִטְהָר: 13 כָּל־הַנֹּגֵעַ בְּמֵת בְּנֶפֶשׁ

הָאָדָם אֲשֶׁר־יָמוּת וְלֹא יִתְחַטָּא אֶת־מִשְׁכַּן

יְהוָה טִמֵּא וְנִכְרְתָה הַנֶּפֶשׁ הַהִוא מִיִּשְׂרָאֵל כִּי מֵי

נִדָּה לֹא־זֹרַק עָלָיו טָמֵא יִהְיֶה עוֹד טֻמְאָתוֹ בוֹ: 14 זֹאת הַתּוֹרָה

אָדָם כִּי־יָמוּת בְּאֹהֶל כָּל־הַבָּא אֶל־הָאֹהֶל וְכָל־

אֲשֶׁר בָּאֹהֶל יִטְמָא שִׁבְעַת יָמִים: 15 וְכֹל כְּלִי פָתוּחַ אֲשֶׁר

אֵין־צָמִיד פָּתִיל עָלָיו טָמֵא הוּא: 16 וְכֹל אֲשֶׁר־יִגַּע עַל־פְּנֵי

הַשָּׂדֶה בַּחֲלַל־חֶרֶב אוֹ בְמֵת

אוֹ־בְעֶצֶם אָדָם אוֹ בְקָבֶר יִטְמָא שִׁבְעַת יָמִים:

17 וְלָקְחוּ לַטָּמֵא מֵעֲפַר שְׂרֵפַת הַחַטָּאת וְנָתַן עָלָיו

מַיִם חַיִּים אֶל־כֶּלִי: 18 וְלָקַח אֵזוֹב וְטָבַל בַּמַּיִם

אִישׁ טָהוֹר וְהִזָּה עַל־הָאֹהֶל וְעַל־כָּל־הַכֵּלִים

וְעַל־הַנְּפָשׁוֹת אֲשֶׁר הָיוּ־שָׁם וְעַל־הַנֹּגֵעַ בַּעֶצֶם אוֹ

בֶחָלָל אוֹ בַמֵּת אוֹ בַקָּבֶר: 19 וְהִזָּה הַטָּהֹר

עַל־הַטָּמֵא בַּיּוֹם הַשְּׁלִישִׁי וּבַיּוֹם הַשְּׁבִיעִי

וְחִטְּאוֹ בַּיּוֹם הַשְּׁבִיעִי וְכִבֶּס בְּגָדָיו וְרָחַץ בַּמַּיִם וְטָהֵר

בָּעֶרֶב: 20 וְאִישׁ אֲשֶׁר־יִטְמָא וְלֹא

21 So it shall be a perpetual statute for them. And he who sprinkles the water for impurity shall wash his clothes, and he who touches the water for impurity shall be unclean until evening.

22 Furthermore, anything that the unclean person touches shall be unclean; and the person who touches it shall be unclean until evening.' "

HAFTARAH OF SHABBAT PARAH

Ezekiel tells the people that God will gather them from their exile and cleanse them of their iniquities so that they may once again dwell in the Land of Israel. This was not because the people had transformed, but rather because God wanted it so. We have an opportunity during this reading to

Ezekiel 36:16-36

36:16 The word of the Lord was to me:

17 "Son of man, when the people of Israel were living in their own land, they defiled it by their conduct and their actions. Their conduct was like a woman's monthly uncleanness in My sight.

18 So I poured out My wrath on them because they had shed blood in the land and because they had defiled it with their idols.

19 I dispersed them among the nations, and they were scattered through the countries; I judged them according to their conduct and their actions.

20 And wherever they went among the nations they profaned My Holy Name, for it was said of them, 'These are the Lord's people, and yet they had to leave his land.'

21 I had concern for My Holy Name, which the house of Israel profaned among the nations where they had gone.

יִתְוַחֲטָא וְנִכְרְתָה הַנֶּפֶשׁ רמ״ח ־ ז׳ הויות הַהִוא מִתּוֹךְ הַקָּהָל ע״ב ס״ג כִּי אֶת־

מִקְדַּשׁ יְהֹוָ‏אהדונהי טִמֵּא מֵי ילי נִדָּה לֹא־זֹרַק עָלָיו טָמֵא הוּא:

21 וְהָיְתָה לָהֶם לְחֻקַּת עוֹלָם וּמַזֵּה מֵי ילי הַנִּדָּה יְכַבֵּס בְּגָדָיו וְהַנֹּגֵעַ

בְּמֵי ילי הַנִּדָּה יִטְמָא עַד־הָעָרֶב רבוע יהוה ורבוע אלהים: 22 וְכֹל ילי אֲשֶׁר־יִגַּע־

בּוֹ הַטָּמֵא יִטְמָא וְהַנֶּפֶשׁ רמ״ח ־ ז׳ הויות הַנֹּגַעַת תִּטְמָא עַד־הָעָרֶב

רבוע יהוה ורבוע אלהים:

HAFTARAH OF SHABBAT PARAH

search within and identify those areas where we worship idols—addictions, our need for approval, the voyeurism of our society—and ask for the Creator's help to cleanse them. Only then can we transform and connect more closely to the true source of fulfillment—the Light of the Creator.

יחזקאל פרק לו

36 16 וַיְהִי אל , ייא״י דְבַר רעה ־יְהֹוָ‏אהדונהי אֵלַי לֵאמֹר: 17 בֶּן־אָדָם מ״ה

בֵּית ב״פ רעה יִשְׂרָאֵל יֹשְׁבִים עַל־אַדְמָתָם וַיְטַמְּאוּ אוֹתָהּ בְּדַרְכָּם

וּבַעֲלִילוֹתָם כְּטֻמְאַת הַנִּדָּה הָיְתָה דַרְכָּם לְפָנָי חכמה בינה: 18 וָאֶשְׁפֹּךְ

חֲמָתִי עֲלֵיהֶם עַל־הַדָּם רבוע אהיה אֲשֶׁר־שָׁפְכוּ עַל־הָאָרֶץ אלהים דההין ע״ה

וּבְגִלּוּלֵיהֶם טִמְּאוּהָ: 19 וָאָפִיץ אֹתָם בַּגּוֹיִם וַיִּזָּרוּ בָּאֲרָצוֹת כְּדַרְכָּם

וְכַעֲלִילוֹתָם שְׁפַטְתִּים: 20 וַיָּבוֹא אֶל־הַגּוֹיִם אֲשֶׁר־בָּאוּ שָׁם וַיְחַלְּלוּ

אֶת־שֵׁם יהוה שדי קָדְשִׁי בֶּאֱמֹר לָהֶם עַם־יְהֹוָ‏אהדונהי אֵלֶּה וּמֵאַרְצוֹ

יָצָאוּ: 21 וָאֶחְמֹל עַל־שֵׁם יהוה שדי קָדְשִׁי אֲשֶׁר חִלְּלֻהוּ בֵּית ב״פ רעה

יִשְׂרָאֵל בַּגּוֹיִם אֲשֶׁר־בָּאוּ שָׁמָּה מהע, מעה, אל שדי: 22 לָכֵן אֱמֹר לְבֵית

ב״פ רעה ־יִשְׂרָאֵל כֹּה הי אָמַר אֲדֹנָי יְהֹוִ‏אהדונהי לֹלה לֹא לְמַעַנְכֶם אֲנִי

²² Therefore say to the house of Israel, this is what the Lord, God, says: 'It is not for your sake, house of Israel, that I am going to do these things, but for the sake of My Holy Name, which you have profaned among the nations where you have gone.

²³ I will show the holiness of My great Name, which has been profaned among the nations, the Name you have profaned among them. Then the nations will know that I am the Lord,' declares the Lord, God, 'when I show Myself holy through you before their eyes.

²⁴ For I will take you out of the nations; I will gather you from all the countries and bring you into your own land.

²⁵ I will sprinkle pure water on you, and you will be pure; I will purify you from all your impurities and from all your idols.

²⁶ I will give you a new heart and put a new spirit in you; I will remove from you your heart of stone and give you a heart of flesh.

²⁷ And I will put My spirit in you and move you to follow My decrees and be careful to keep My laws.

²⁸ You will live in the land I gave your forefathers; you will be My people, and I will be your God.

²⁹ I will save you from all your uncleanness. I will call for the grain and make it plentiful and will not bring famine upon you.

³⁰ I will increase the fruit of the trees and the crops of the field, so that you will no longer suffer disgrace among the nations because of famine.

³¹ Then you will remember your evil ways and wicked deeds, and you will loathe yourselves for your sins and detestable practices.

³² I want you to know that I am not doing this for your sake,' declares the Lord, God. 'Be ashamed and disgraced for your conduct, house of Israel!'

³³ This is what the Lord, God, says: 'On the day I purify you from all your sins, I will resettle your towns, and the ruins will be rebuilt.

³⁴ The desolate land will be cultivated instead of lying desolate in the sight of all who pass through it.

עֲשֶׂה בֵית יִשְׂרָאֵל כִּי אִם ־לְשֵׁם קָדְשִׁי אֲשֶׁר חִלַּלְתֶּם בַּגּוֹיִם אֲשֶׁר־בָּאתֶם שָׁם: 23 וְקִדַּשְׁתִּי אֶת־שְׁמִי הַגָּדוֹל הַמְחֻלָּל בַּגּוֹיִם אֲשֶׁר חִלַּלְתֶּם בְּתוֹכָם וְיָדְעוּ הַגּוֹיִם כִּי־אֲנִי יְהֹוָה נְאֻם אֲדֹנָי יֱהֹוִה בְּהִקָּדְשִׁי בָכֶם לְעֵינֵיהֶם: 24 וְלָקַחְתִּי אֶתְכֶם מִן־הַגּוֹיִם וְקִבַּצְתִּי אֶתְכֶם מִכָּל־הָאֲרָצוֹת וְהֵבֵאתִי אֶתְכֶם אֶל־אַדְמַתְכֶם: 25 וְזָרַקְתִּי עֲלֵיכֶם מַיִם טְהוֹרִים וּטְהַרְתֶּם מִכֹּל טֻמְאוֹתֵיכֶם וּמִכָּל־גִּלּוּלֵיכֶם אֲטַהֵר אֶתְכֶם: 26 וְנָתַתִּי לָכֶם לֵב חָדָשׁ וְרוּחַ חֲדָשָׁה אֶתֵּן בְּקִרְבְּכֶם וַהֲסִרֹתִי אֶת־לֵב הָאֶבֶן מִבְּשַׂרְכֶם וְנָתַתִּי לָכֶם לֵב בָּשָׂר: 27 וְאֶת־רוּחִי אֶתֵּן בְּקִרְבְּכֶם וְעָשִׂיתִי אֵת אֲשֶׁר־בְּחֻקַּי תֵּלֵכוּ וּמִשְׁפָּטַי תִּשְׁמְרוּ וַעֲשִׂיתֶם: 28 וִישַׁבְתֶּם בָּאָרֶץ אֲשֶׁר נָתַתִּי לַאֲבֹתֵיכֶם וִהְיִיתֶם לִי לְעָם וְאָנֹכִי אֶהְיֶה לָכֶם לֵאלֹהִים: 29 וְהוֹשַׁעְתִּי אֶתְכֶם מִכֹּל טֻמְאוֹתֵיכֶם וְקָרָאתִי אֶל־הַדָּגָן וְהִרְבֵּיתִי אֹתוֹ וְלֹא־אֶתֵּן עֲלֵיכֶם רָעָב: 30 וְהִרְבֵּיתִי אֶת־פְּרִי הָעֵץ וּתְנוּבַת הַשָּׂדֶה לְמַעַן אֲשֶׁר לֹא תִקְחוּ עוֹד חֶרְפַּת רָעָב בַּגּוֹיִם: 31 וּזְכַרְתֶּם אֶת־דַּרְכֵיכֶם הָרָעִים וּמַעַלְלֵיכֶם אֲשֶׁר לֹא־טוֹבִים וּנְקֹטֹתֶם בִּפְנֵיכֶם עַל עֲוֺנֹתֵיכֶם וְעַל תּוֹעֲבוֹתֵיכֶם: 32 לֹא לְמַעַנְכֶם אֲנִי־עֹשֶׂה נְאֻם אֲדֹנָי יֱהֹוִה יִוָּדַע לָכֶם בּוֹשׁוּ וְהִכָּלְמוּ מִדַּרְכֵיכֶם בֵּית יִשְׂרָאֵל: 33 כֹּה אָמַר אֲדֹנָי יֱהֹוִה בְּיוֹם טַהֲרִי אֶתְכֶם מִכֹּל עֲוֺנוֹתֵיכֶם וְהוֹשַׁבְתִּי אֶת־הֶעָרִים וְנִבְנוּ הֶחֳרָבוֹת: 34 וְהָאָרֶץ הַנְּשַׁמָּה תֵּעָבֵד תַּחַת אֲשֶׁר הָיְתָה שְׁמָמָה לְעֵינֵי כָּל־עוֹבֵר: 35 וְאָמְרוּ הָאָרֶץ הַלֵּזוּ הַנְּשַׁמָּה

35 They will say, "This land that was laid waste has become like the Garden of Eden; the cities that were lying in ruins, desolate and destroyed, are now fortified and inhabited."

36 Then the nations around you that remain will know that I, the Lord, have rebuilt what was destroyed and have replanted what was desolate. I, the Lord, have spoken, and I will do it.' "

MAFTIR OF SHABBAT HACHODESH

The first month of the year from an astrological point of view is the month of Aries (*Nissan*). As the first month, Aries is also the seed of the year. This means that the whole year is contained within it. The first twelve days of Aries control all the other months and all zodiac signs of the

Exodus 12:1-20

12:¹ The Lord said to Moses and Aaron in Egypt,

2 "This month is to be for you the first month, the first of the months of the year.

3 Speak to the entire Congregation of Israel, saying that on the tenth day of this month each man is to take a lamb for his family, one for each household.

4 If any household is too small for a whole lamb, they must share one with their nearest neighbor, accounting for each person according to how much of the lamb he would consume.

5 The lamb must be a pure, year-old male lamb, from the lambs and the goats you shall take.

6 You will guard them until the fourteenth day of the month, and slaughter it – the entire assembly of the Congregation of Israel – at twilight.

7 And you shall take from the blood and put it on the two doorposts and on the frame of the houses where the lambs are eaten.

הָיְתָה כְּגַן־עֵדֶן יהוה אלהים אדני עכ״ה, ה״פ אדני הֶחֳרָבֹות וְהַנְשַׁמֹּות

וְהַנֶּהֱרָסֹות בְּצוּרֹות יֵשֵׁבוּ: 36 וְיָדְעוּ הַגֹּויִם אֲשֶׁר יִשָּׁאֲרוּ סְבִיבֹותֵיכֶם

כִּי | אֲנִי אני, טדהד כוז״י יְהֹוָ֒אֳדֹנִֹיאֳהֳדֹונֵֹהי בָּנִיתִי הַנֶּהֱרָסֹות נָטַעְתִּי הַנְּשַׁמָּה אֲנִי

אני, טדהד כוז״י יְהֹוָ֒אֳדֹנִֹיאֳהֳדֹונֵֹהי דִּבַּרְתִּי ראה וְעָשִֹיתִי:

MAFTIR OF SHABBAT HACHODESH

year: The first day controls Aries, the second controls Taurus, the third controls Gemini, and so on. By connecting to this Maftir we connect to and control the month of Aries, and thus, we control the whole year.

שמות פרק יב

12 1 וַיֹּאמֶר יְהֹוָ֒אֳדֹנִֹיאֳהֳדֹונֵֹהי מהע, אל שדי אֶל־מֹשֶׁה וְאֶל־אַהֲרֹן ע״ב רבוע ע״ב

בְּאֶרֶץ אלהים דאלפין מִצְרַיִם מצר לֵאמֹר: 2 הַחֹדֶשׁ י״ב הוויות הַזֶּה והו לָכֶם

רֹאשׁ ריבוע אלהים ואלהים דיודין ע״ה חֳדָשִׁים רִאשֹׁון הוּא לָכֶם לְחָדְשֵׁי הַשָּׁנָה:

3 דַּבְּרוּ ראה אֶל־כָּל־ ילי עֲדַת יִשְֹרָאֵל לֵאמֹר בֶּעָשֹׂר לַחֹדֶשׁ י״ב הוויות

הַזֶּה והו וְיִקְחוּ וחם לָהֶם אִישׁ ע״ה קנ״א קס״א שֶֹה לְבֵית ב״פ ראה ־אָבֹת שֶֹה

לַבָּיִת ב״פ ראה: 4 וְאִם ע״ה מ״ב ־יִמְעַט הַבַּיִת ב״פ ראה מִהְיֹת מִשֶֹּה וְלָקַח

ב״פ יהוה אדני אהיה הוּא וּשְׁכֵנֹו הַקָּרֹב אֶל־בֵּיתֹו ב״פ ראה בְּמִכְסַת נְפָשֹׁת

אִישׁ ע״ה קנ״א קס״א לְפִי אָכְלֹו תָּכֹסּוּ עַל־הַשֶּׂה: 5 שֶֹה תָמִים זָכָר בֶּן־שָׁנָה

יִהְיֶה ייי לָכֶם מִן־הַכְּבָשִֹים וּמִן־הָעִזִּים תִּקָּחוּ: 6 וְהָיָה יהוה, יהה לָכֶם

לְמִשְׁמֶרֶת עַד אַרְבָּעָה עָשָֹר יֹום ע״ה = נגד, זן, מזבח לַחֹדֶשׁ י״ב הוויות הַזֶּה והו

וְשָׁחֲטוּ אֹתֹו כֹּל ילי קְהַל ע״ב ס״ג עֲדַת־יִשְֹרָאֵל בֵּין הָעַרְבָּיִם: 7 וְלָקְחוּ

מִן־הַדָּם רבוע אהיה וְנָתְנוּ עַל־שְׁתֵּי הַמְּזוּזֹת וְעַל־הַמַּשְׁקֹוף עַל הַבָּתִּים

8 And you shall eat the meat on that night roasted over fire, and unleavened bread with bitter herbs you shall eat.

9 Do not eat the meat raw or cooked in water, but roast it over the fire—head, legs and inner parts.

10 Do not leave any of it till morning; if some is left till morning, you must burn it.

11 This is how you are to eat it: with your cloak tucked into your belt, your sandals on your feet and your staff in your hand. Eat it in haste; it is the Lord's Passover.

12 I will pass through Egypt on that same night and strike every firstborn in Egypt—both men and animals—and I will bring judgment on all the gods of Egypt. I am the Lord.

13 The blood will be a sign for you on the houses where you are; and when I see the blood, I will pass over you. No deadly plague will touch you when I strike Egypt.

14 This is a day you are to commemorate; for the generations to come you shall celebrate it as a festival to the Lord—a lasting ordinance.

15 For seven days you are to eat unleavened bread, but on the first day you shall remove grain from your houses, for whoever eats anything leavened must be cut off from Israel, from the first day through the seventh day.

16 On the first day hold a sacred assembly, and another one on the seventh day. You shall do no work at all on these days, except to prepare food for everyone to eat—that is all you may do.

17 And you shall guard the unleavened bread, because it was on this very day that I brought your legions out of Egypt. You shall keep this day as a lasting ordinance for the generations to come.

18 From the beginning of the fourteenth day, in the evening, you shall eat unleavened bread until the twenty-first day of the month in the evening.

אֲשֶׁר־יֵאָכֵל אֹתוֹ בָּהֶם: 8 וְאָכְלוּ אֶת־הַבָּשָׂר בַּלַּיְלָה מלה הַזֶּה וה צְלִי־

אֵשׁ אלהים דיודין ע״ה וּמַצּוֹת עַל־מְרֹרִים יֹאכְלֻהוּ: 9 אַל־תֹּאכְלוּ מִמֶּנּוּ נָא

וּבָשֵׁל מְבֻשָּׁל בַּמָּיִם כִּי אִם־צְלִי־אֵשׁ יוהך, ע״ה מ״ב אלהים דיודין ע״ה רֹאשׁוֹ

עַל־כְּרָעָיו וְעַל־קִרְבּוֹ: 10 וְלֹא־תוֹתִירוּ מִמֶּנּוּ עַד־בֹּקֶר וְהַנֹּתָר מִמֶּנּוּ

עַד־בֹּקֶר בָּאֵשׁ אלהים דיודין ע״ה תִּשְׂרֹפוּ: 11 וְכָכָה תֹּאכְלוּ אֹתוֹ מָתְנֵיכֶם

חֲגֻרִים נַעֲלֵיכֶם בְּרַגְלֵיכֶם וּמַקֶּלְכֶם בְּיֶדְכֶם וַאֲכַלְתֶּם אֹתוֹ בְּחִפָּזוֹן

פֶּסַח הוּא לַיהֹוָ֥ה֙ואדניאהדונהי: 12 וְעָבַרְתִּי בְאֶרֶץ־מִצְרַיִם מצר אלהים דאלפין

בַּלַּיְלָה מלה הַזֶּה וה וְהִכֵּיתִי כָל־בְּכוֹר יוי בְּאֶרֶץ מִצְרַיִם מצר אלהים דאלפין

מֵאָדָם מ״ה וְעַד־בְּהֵמָה ב״ן, לכב, יבמ וּבְכָל בן, לכב, יבמ אֱלֹהֵי דמב, ילה מִצְרַיִם

אֶעֱשֶׂה שְׁפָטִים אֲנִי אני, טדהד כו״ו יְהֹוָ֥ה֙ואדניאהדונהי: 13 וְהָיָה יהוה; יהה הַדָּם

רבוע אהיה לָכֶם לְאֹת עַל הַבָּתִּים אֲשֶׁר אַתֶּם שָׁם יהוה שדי וְרָאִיתִי אֶת־

הַדָּם רבוע אהיה וּפָסַחְתִּי עֲלֵכֶם וְלֹא־יִהְיֶה יוי בָכֶם ב״פ אל נֶגֶף לְמַשְׁחִית

בְּהַכֹּתִי בְּאֶרֶץ אלהים דאלפין מִצְרָיִם מצר: 14 וְהָיָה יהוה, יהה הַיּוֹם ע״ה = נגד, זן, מזבח

הַזֶּה וה לָכֶם לְזִכָּרוֹן ע״ב קס״א נט״ב וְחַגֹּתֶם אֹתוֹ חַג לַיהֹוָ֥ה֙ואדניאהדונהי לְדֹרֹתֵיכֶם

חֻקַּת עוֹלָם תְּחָגֻּהוּ: 15 שִׁבְעַת יָמִים נלך מַצּוֹת תֹּאכֵלוּ אַךְ אהיה בַּיּוֹם

ע״ה = נגד, זן, מזבח הָרִאשׁוֹן תַּשְׁבִּיתוּ שְּׂאֹר ג׳ מווזין דאלהים דקטנות מִבָּתֵּיכֶם כִּי |

כָל־אֹכֵל יוי חָמֵץ וְנִכְרְתָה הַנֶּפֶשׁ רמ״ח ∴ ד׳ הוויות הַהִוא מִיִּשְׂרָאֵל מִיּוֹם

ע״ה = נגד, זן, מזבח הָרִאשֹׁן עַד־יוֹם ע״ה = נגד, זן, מזבח הַשְּׁבִעִי: 16 וּבַיּוֹם ע״ה = נגד, זן, מזבח

הָרִאשׁוֹן מִקְרָא־שם ע״ה, הויה שדי קֹדֶשׁ וּבַיּוֹם ע״ה = נגד, זן, מזבח הַשְּׁבִיעִי

מִקְרָא־שם ע״ה, הויה שדי קֹדֶשׁ יִהְיֶה יוי לָכֶם כָּל יוי מְלָאכָה אל אדני לֹא־

יֵעָשֶׂה בָהֶם אהיה אַךְ אֲשֶׁר יֵאָכֵל לְכָל יה אדני נֶפֶשׁ רמ״ח ∴ ד׳ הוויות הוּא

לְבַדּוֹ יֵעָשֶׂה לָכֶם: 17 וּשְׁמַרְתֶּם אֶת־הַמַּצּוֹת כִּי בְּעֶצֶם הַיּוֹם

ע״ה = נגד, זן, מזבח הַזֶּה וה הוֹצֵאתִי אֶת־צִבְאוֹתֵיכֶם מֵאֶרֶץ אלהים דאלפין מִצְרָיִם

מצר וּשְׁמַרְתֶּם אֶת־הַיּוֹם ע״ה = נגד, זן, מזבח הַזֶּה וה לְדֹרֹתֵיכֶם חֻקַּת עוֹלָם:

18 בָּרִאשֹׁן בְּאַרְבָּעָה עָשָׂר יוֹם ע״ה = נגד, זן, מזבח לַחֹדֶשׁ י״ב הוויות בָּעֶרֶב

19 For seven days no grain shall be found in your houses, because anyone who eats that which is leavened shall be cut off from the Congregation of Israel, whether he is a stranger or native-born.

20 Eat nothing that is leavened; in all of your habitations, you shall eat unleavened bread."

HAFTARAH OF SHABBAT HACHODESH

This Haftarah is read the Shabbat before or on Rosh Chodesh *Nissan* (Aries). *Nissan* is the first month of the year, and is also known as the *Rosh Hashanah* for Kings. Not that we are kings, but this tells us that we can connect to the power of renewal, to become a new person, open to receive the Light of the Creator.

Reb Menachem Mendel of Kotzk said: "If you pray and nothing changes and you are the same person as you were before you prayed, it is not only as if you had not prayed, but you are called evil." Evil in this case does not mean getting into evil affairs; it's about being given an opportunity to change and not doing so. For example each Shabbat we have an opportunity to connect to and receive Light of the Torah so that every one of us can find the Light of Creator that lies within. But if we do not open ourselves to receive the Light of Shabbat, nothing will come in.

Ezekiel 45:18-46:15

45:18 This is what the Lord, God says: "In the first month on the first day you are to take a young bull without defect and purify the sanctuary.

19 The priest is to take some of the blood of the sin offering and put it on the doorposts of the Temple, on the four corners of the upper ledge of the altar and on the gateposts of the inner court.

20 You are to do the same on the seventh day of the month for anyone who sins unintentionally or through ignorance; so you are to make atonement for the temple. 21 In the first month on the fourteenth day will be to you the Passover, a feast lasting seven days, during which you shall eat unleavened bread.

רבוע יהוה ורבוע אלהים תֹּאכְלוּ מַצֹּת עַד יֹום ע״ה = נגד, זך, מזבח הָאֶחָד אהבה, דאגה

וְעֶשְׂרִים לַחֹדֶשׁ י״ב הוויות בָּעֶרֶב רבוע יהוה ורבוע אלהים: 19 שִׁבְעַת יָמִים גלך

שְׂאֹר ג' מווין דאלהים דקטנות לֹא יִמָּצֵא בְּבָתֵּיכֶם כִּי | כָּל יכי ־אֹכֵל מַחְמֶצֶת

וְנִכְרְתָה הַנֶּפֶשׁ רמ״ח ~ ז' הוויות הַהִוא מֵעֲדַת יִשְׂרָאֵל בַּגֵּר בין קס״א ־וּבְאֶזְרַח

הָאָרֶץ אלהים דההין ע״ה: 20 כָּל יכי ־מַחְמֶצֶת לֹא תֹאכֵלוּ בְּכֹל בין, לכב, יבם

מֹושְׁבֹתֵיכֶם תֹּאכְלוּ מַצֹּות:

HAFTARAH OF SHABBAT HACHODESH

As the Rav says, the month of *Nissan* is the best concealed secret in the world—it is about eliminating chaos from our lives at the seed level. It is an opportunity to change our destiny; everything of a physical nature is in the palm of your hands. However, Satan's most potent weapon is that he has us convinced that we can not extricate ourselves from chaos; he makes us think that we can not do it alone.

The Haftarah of Shabbat haChodesh, gives us this opening and makes it possible for us to transform and be different on a seed level, and when our consciousness is different create a new destiny for the coming year, for ourselves and the world.

יחזקאל פרק מה

45 18 כֹּה היי ־אָמַר אֲדֹנָי ללה יְהֹוִאהדונהי בָּרִאשֹׁון בְּאֶחָד אהבה, דאגה

לַחֹדֶשׁ י״ב הוויות תִּקַּח רבוע אהיה דאלפין פַּר מזווזר, ערי, סנדלפון ־בֶּן־בָּקָר תָּמִים

וְחִטֵּאתָ אֶת־הַמִּקְדָּשׁ: 19 וְלָקַח יהוה אהיה אדני יהוה הַכֹּהֵן מלה מִדַּם רבוע אהיה

הַחַטָּאת וְנָתַן אבגית״ץ, ושר, אהבת חנם אֶל־מְזוּזַת נית, זו מות הַבַּיִת ב״פ ראה וְאֶל־

אַרְבַּע פִּנֹּות הָעֲזָרָה לַמִּזְבֵּחַ זך, נגד וְעַל־מְזוּזַת נית, זו מות שַׁעַר הֶחָצֵר

הַפְּנִימִית: 20 וְכֵן תַּעֲשֶׂה בְּשִׁבְעָה בַחֹדֶשׁ מֵאִישׁ ע״ה קנ״א קס״א שֹׁגֶה

וּמִפֶּתִי וְכִפַּרְתֶּם אֶת־הַבָּיִת ב״פ ראה: 21 בָּרִאשֹׁון בְּאַרְבָּעָה עָשָׂר יֹום

²² On that day the prince is to provide a bull as a sin offering for himself and for all the people of the land.

²³ Every day during the seven days of the Feast he is to provide seven bulls and seven rams without defect as a burnt offering to the Lord, and a male goat for a sin offering.

²⁴ He is to provide as a grain offering an ephah for each bull and an ephah for each ram, along with a hin of oil for each ephah.

²⁵ During the seven days of the Feast, which begins in the seventh month on the fifteenth day, he is to make the same provision for sin offerings, burnt offerings, grain offerings and oil."

46:¹ This is what the Lord, God says: "The gate of the inner court facing east is to be shut on the six working days, but on the Sabbath day and on the day of the New Moon it is to be opened.

² The prince is to enter from the outside through the portico of the gateway and stand by the gatepost. The priests are to sacrifice his burnt offering and his fellowship offerings. He is to worship at the threshold of the gateway and then go out, but the gate will not be shut until evening.

³ On the Sabbaths and New Moons the people of the land are to worship in the presence of the Lord at the entrance to that gateway.

⁴ The burnt offering the prince brings to the Lord on the Sabbath day is to be six male lambs without defect and a ram without defect.

⁵ The grain offering given with the ram is to be an ephah, and the grain offering with the lambs is to be as much as he pleases, along with a hin of oil for each ephah.

⁶ On the day of the New Moon he is to offer a young bull, six lambs and a ram, all without defect.

⁷ He is to provide as a grain offering one ephah with the bull, one ephah with the ram, and with the lambs as much as his hand can reach, along with a hin of oil with each ephah.

⁸ When the prince enters, he is to go in through the portico of the gateway, and he is to come out the same way.

⁹ When the people of the land come before the Lord at the appointed feasts, whoever enters by the north gate to worship is to go out the south gate; and whoever enters

בַּחֹדֶשׁ יֵ״ב הוויות יִהְיֶ֣ה יי לָכֶ֔ם הַפָּ֑סַח וְחַ֗ג שְׁבֻע֣וֹת יָמִ֔ים גלך

מַצּ֥וֹת יֵאָכֵֽל: 22 וְעָשָׂ֣ה הַנָּשִׂ֣יא בַּיּ֣וֹם עֵ״ה = נגד, זן, מזבח הַה֗וּא בַּעֲד֖וֹ וּבְעַ֥ד

כָּל־עַ֣ם הָאָ֑רֶץ אלהים דההין ע״ה פַּ֖ר בזחזרך, ערי, סנדלפון אלהים דההין ע״ה וְחַטָּֽאת: 23 וְשִׁבְעַ֣ת

יְמֵֽי־הֶחָ֡ג יַעֲשֶׂ֣ה עוֹלָ֣ה לַֽיהֹוֵ֣אֱהֹדִֽוִֽילֹהְדֹונֵֽהֹי שִׁבְעַ֣ת פָּרִ֣ים וְשִׁבְעַ֣ת אֵילִ֣ים

תְּמִימִם֩ לַיּ֨וֹם עֵ״ה = נגד, זן, מזבח שִׁבְעַ֣ת הַיָּמִ֑ים גלך וְחַטָּ֗את שְׂעִ֥יר עִזִּ֖ים לַיּֽוֹם

עֵ״ה = נגד, זן, מזבח : 24 וּמִנְחָ֗ה עֵ״ה ב״פ בן אֵיפָ֣ה לַפָּ֗ר בזחזרך, ערי, סנדלפון וְאֵיפָ֣ה לָאַ֣יִל

יַעֲשֶׂ֔ה וְשֶׁ֖מֶן י״פ טל, י״פ כוזו; ביט הִ֥ין לָאֵיפָֽה: 25 בַּשְּׁבִיעִ֗י בַּחֲמִשָּׁ֨ה עָשָׂ֥ר י֣וֹם

בַּחֹ֡דֶשׁ יֵ״ב הוויות בֶּחָ֣ג יַעֲשֶׂ֣ה כָּאֵ֔לֶּה שִׁבְעַ֖ת הַיָּמִ֑ים גלך

כַּֽחַטָּ֣את כָּֽעֹלָ֗ה וְכַמִּנְחָ֖ה וְכַשָּֽׁמֶן י״פ טל, י״פ כוזו; ביט : 46 1 כֹּֽה־ היי אָמַר֩

אֲדֹנָ֨י ללה יְהֹוִ֣אֱהֹדִֽוִֽילֹהְדֹונֵֽהֹי שַׁ֜עַר הֶחָצֵ֤ר הַפְּנִימִ֙ית֙ הַפֹּנֶ֣ה קָדִ֔ים יי

סָג֗וּר שֵׁ֚שֶׁת יְמֵ֣י הַֽמַּעֲשֶׂ֔ה וּבְי֨וֹם עֵ״ה = נגד, זן, מזבח הַשַּׁבָּ֛ת יִפָּתֵ֖חַ וּבְי֥וֹם

הַחֹ֖דֶשׁ יֵ״ב הוויות יִפָּתֵֽחַ: 2 וּבָ֣א הַנָּשִׂ֡יא דֶּרֶךְ֩ ב״פ יב״ק אוּלָ֨ם

הַשַּׁ֜עַר מִח֗וּץ וְעָמַד֙ עַל־מְזוּזַ֣ת נית, זן מות הַשַּׁ֔עַר וְעָשׂ֣וּ הַכֹּֽהֲנִ֗ים מלה אֶת־

עֽוֹלָתוֹ֙ וְאֶת־שְׁלָמָ֔יו וְהִֽשְׁתַּֽחֲוָה֙דומ עַל־מִפְתַּ֣ן הַשַּׁ֔עַר וְיָצָ֑א וְהַשַּׁ֥עַר לֹֽא־

יִסָּגֵ֖ר עַד־הָעָֽרֶב רבוע יהוה ורבוע אלהים: 3 וְהִשְׁתַּחֲו֣וּ עַם־הָאָ֗רֶץ אלהים דההין ע״ה

פֶּ֚תַח הַשַּׁ֣עַר הַה֔וּא בַּשַּׁבָּת֖וֹת וּבֶֽחֳדָשִׁ֑ים לִפְנֵ֖י יְהֹוָֽאֱהֹדִֽוִֽילֹהְדֹונֵֽהֹי: 4 וְהָ֣עֹלָ֔ה

אֲשֶׁר־יַקְרִ֥ב הַנָּשִׂ֖יא לַֽיהֹוָֽאֱהֹדִֽוִֽילֹהְדֹונֵֽהֹי בְּי֣וֹם עֵ״ה = נגד, זן, מזבח הַשַּׁבָּ֑ת שִׁשָּׁ֧ה

כְבָשִׂ֛ים תְּמִימִ֖ם וְאַ֥יִל תָּמִֽים: 5 וּמִנְחָה֙ עֵ״ה ב״פ בן אֵיפָה֙ לָאַ֔יִל וְלַכְּבָשִׂ֥ים

מִנְחָ֖ה עֵ״ה ב״פ בן מַתַּ֣ת יָד֑וֹ וְשֶׁ֖מֶן י״פ טל, י״פ כוזו, ביט הִ֥ין לָאֵיפָֽה: 6 וּבְי֣וֹם

הַחֹ֗דֶשׁ יֵ״ב הוויות עֵ״ה = נגד, זן, מזבח פַּ֧ר בזחזרך, ערי, סנדלפון בֶּן־בָּקָ֛ר תְּמִימִ֖ם וְשֵׁ֣שֶׁת

כְבָשִׂ֥ים וָאַ֖יִל תְּמִימִ֣ם יִהְי֑וּ אל: 7 וְאֵיפָ֨ה לַפָּ֜ר בזחזרך, ערי, סנדלפון וְאֵיפָ֤ה

לָאַ֙יִל֙ יַעֲשֶׂ֣ה מִנְחָ֔ה עֵ״ה ב״פ בן וְלַ֨כְּבָשִׂ֔ים כַּאֲשֶׁ֥ר תַּשִּׂ֖יג יָד֑וֹ וְשֶׁ֕מֶן

הִ֥ין לָאֵיפָֽה: 8 וּבְב֥וֹא הַנָּשִׂ֖יא דֶּ֣רֶךְ ב״פ יב״ק אוּלָ֤ם הַשַּׁ֙עַר֙

יָב֔וֹא וּבְדַרְכּ֖וֹ יֵצֵֽא: 9 וּבְב֨וֹא עַם־הָאָ֜רֶץ אלהים דההין ע״ה לִפְנֵ֣י חכמה בינה

by the south gate is to go out the north gate. No one is to return through the gate by which he entered, but each is to go out the opposite gate.

[10] *The prince is to be among them, going in when they go in and going out when they go out.*

[11] *At the festivals and the appointed feasts, the grain offering is to be an ephah with a bull, an ephah with a ram, and with the lambs as much as one pleases, along with a hin of oil for each ephah.*

[12] *When the prince provides a freewill offering to the Lord - whether a burnt offering or fellowship offerings—the gate facing east is to be opened for him. He shall offer his burnt offering or his fellowship offerings as he does on the Sabbath day. Then he shall go out, and after he has gone out, the gate will be shut.*

[13] *Every day you are to provide a year-old lamb without defect for a burnt offering to the Lord; morning by morning you shall provide it.*

[14] *You are also to provide with it morning by morning a grain offering, consisting of a sixth of an ephah with a third of a hin of oil to moisten the flour. The presenting of this grain offering to the Lord is a lasting ordinance.*

[15] *So the lamb and the grain offering and the oil shall be provided morning by morning for a regular burnt offering."*

יְהֹוָ֨אֲדֹנָי֙ בַּמּֽוֹעֲדִ֔ים בַּבָּ֖א הַבָּ֥א דֶ֣רֶךְ ב"פ יב"ק ־שַׁ֙עַר֙ צָפ֣וֹן לְהִֽשְׁתַּחֲוֺ֔ת יֵצֵ֖א

דֶ֑רֶךְ ב"פ יב"ק ־שַׁ֣עַר נֶ֗גֶב וְהַבָּא֙ דֶּ֣רֶךְ ב"פ יב"ק ־שַׁ֤עַר נֶ֙גֶב֙ יֵצֵ֣א דֶ֔רֶךְ ב"פ יב"ק

־שַׁ֣עַר צָפ֑וֹנָה ע"ה עסמ"ב לֹ֥א יָשׁ֖וּב דֶּ֑רֶךְ ב"פ יב"ק הַשַּׁ֙עַר֙ אֲשֶׁר־בָּ֣א ב֔וֹ כִּ֖י

נִכְח֥וֹ יֵצֵֽא (כתיב: יצאו)׃ 10 וְהַנָּשִׂ֖יא בְּתוֹכָ֑ם בְּבוֹאָ֣ם יָב֔וֹא וּבְצֵאתָ֖ם

יֵצֵֽאוּ׃ 11 וּבַֽחַגִּ֣ים וּבַמּֽוֹעֲדִ֗ים תִּֽהְיֶ֤ה הַמִּנְחָה֙ ע"ה ב"פ בן אֵיפָ֣ה לַפָּ֔ר

מזבח, ערי, סנדלפון ־וְאֵיפָ֣ה לָאַ֗יִל וְלַכְּבָשִׂ֛ים מַתַּ֥ת יָד֖וֹ וְשֶׁ֣מֶן י"פ טל, י"פ כוו"ו; ביט הִ֥ין

לָֽאֵיפָֽה׃ 12 וְכִֽי־יַעֲשֶׂה֩ הַנָּשִׂ֨יא נְדָבָ֜ה בינה ע"ה וחיים, עוֹלָ֣ה אֽוֹ־שְׁלָמִים֮ נְדָבָה֒

וחיים, בינה ע"ה לַֽיהֹוָ֨אֲדֹנָי֙ וּפָ֣תַֽח ל֗וֹ אֶת־הַשַּׁ֙עַר֙ הַפֹּנֶ֣ה קָדִ֔ים וְעָשָׂ֣ה אֶת־

עֹֽלָת֗וֹ וְאֶת־שְׁלָמָיו֙ כַּאֲשֶׁ֣ר יַעֲשֶׂ֣ה בְּי֣וֹם ע"ה = נגד, זן, מזבח הַשַּׁבָּ֑ת וְיָצָ֕א וְסָגַ֣ר

אֶת־הַשַּׁ֖עַר אַחֲרֵ֥י צֵאתֽוֹ׃ 13 וְכֶ֨בֶשׂ ב"פ קס"א בֶּן־שְׁנָת֜וֹ תָּמִ֗ים תַּעֲשֶׂ֥ה

עוֹלָ֛ה לַיּ֖וֹם ע"ה = נגד, זן, מזבח לַֽיהֹוָ֨אֲדֹנָי֙ בַּבֹּ֥קֶר בַּבֹּ֖קֶר תַּעֲשֶׂ֥ה אֹתֽוֹ׃

14 וּמִנְחָה֩ ע"ה ב"פ בן תַעֲשֶׂ֨ה עָלָ֜יו בַּבֹּ֤קֶר בַּבֹּ֙קֶר֙ שִׁשִּׁ֣ית הָֽאֵיפָ֔ה וְשֶׁ֗מֶן

י"פ טל, י"פ כוו"ו, ביט שְׁלִישִׁ֤ית הַהִין֙ לָרֹ֣ס אֶת־הַסֹּ֑לֶת מִנְחָה֙ ע"ה ב"פ בן

לַֽיהֹוָ֨אֲדֹנָי֙ חֻקּ֥וֹת עוֹלָ֖ם תָּמִֽיד ע"ה נתה, ע"ה קס"א קנ"א קמ"ג׃ 15 יַעֲשׂ֨וּ

(כתיב: ועשו) אֶת־הַכֶּ֤בֶשׂ ב"פ קס"א וְאֶת־הַמִּנְחָה֙ ע"ה ב"פ בן וְאֶת־הַשֶּׁ֔מֶן

י"פ טל, י"פ כוו"ו; ביט בַּבֹּ֥קֶר בַּבֹּ֖קֶר עוֹלַ֣ת אבגיתצ, ועיר, אהבת חנם תָּמִֽיד

ע"ה נתה, ע"ה קס"א קנ"א קמ"ג׃

HAFTARAH OF SHABBAT HAGADOL

This is the Shabbat before *Pesach* (Passover), the most powerful Shabbat of the whole year. Passover gives us freedom from all the forces that enslave us, from all of the beliefs that keep us in bondage and limit our potential. The energy of this particular Shabbat empowers us and fortifies

Malachi 3:4-24

3:4 "Then the offering of Judah and Jerusalem will be pleasant to the Lord as in the days of old; as in former years.

5 And I will come near you for judgment; I will be a swift witness against sorcerers, against adulterers, against perjurers, against those who exploit wage earners and widows and orphans, and against those who turn away an alien—because they do not fear Me," says the Lord of Hosts.

6 "For I am the Lord, I do not change; you are not consumed, sons of Jacob.

7 Yet from the days of your fathers you have gone away from My ordinances and have not kept them. Return to Me, and I will return to you," says the Lord of Hosts. But you said, 'In what way shall we return?'

8 Will a man rob God? Yet you have robbed Me! But you say, 'In what way have we robbed You?' In tithes and offerings.

9 You are cursed with a curse, for you have robbed Me, even this whole nation.

10 Bring all the tithes into the storehouse, that there may be food in My house, and try Me now in this," says the Lord of Hosts, "If I will not open for you the windows of heaven and pour out for you such blessing that there will not be room enough to receive it.

11 And I will rebuke the devourer for your sakes, so that he will not destroy the fruit of your ground, nor shall the vine fail to bear fruit for you in the field," says the Lord of Hosts;

12 and all nations will call you blessed, for you will be a delightful land," says the Lord of Hosts.

HAFTARAH OF SHABBAT HAGADOL

our Passover connection so that we can more powerfully connect to the week that can remove the chains of our bondage. Without connecting to this Shabbat, it is very difficult to really receive all the benefit of Passover and the freedom that it offers.

מלאכי פרק גֹ

וְעָרְבָה לַיהוָׁהᵃʰᵈⁱ מִנְחַת יְהוּדָה וִירוּשָׁלָם ᵣⁱⁱ ˢⁱˢ כִּימֵי עוֹלָם 4 3

וּכְשָׁנִים קַדְמֹנִיֹּת: 5 וְקָרַבְתִּי אֲלֵיכֶם לַמִּשְׁפָּט ᵉʰ ʰˢ ᵃˡʰⁱᵐ וְהָיִיתִי | עֵד

מְמַהֵר בַּמְכַשְׁפִים וּבַמְנָאֲפִים וּבַנִּשְׁבָּעִים לַשָּׁקֶר וּבְעֹשְׁקֵי שְׂכַר

ᵗⁱˢ ᵇⁿ ־שָׂכִיר אַלְמָנָה ᵏᵘᵏ, ʳᵇᵘᵃ ᵃᵈⁿⁱ וְיָתוֹם ʸᵒˢᵖ וּמַטֵּי־גֵר ᵇⁿ ᵏⁿᵃ וְלֹא יְרֵאוּנִי

אָמַר יְהוָׁהᵃʰᵈⁱ צְבָאוֹת ⁿᵗʰ ᵘʳᵇᵘᵃ ᵃʰⁱʰ; ᵖⁿⁱ ˢᵏⁱⁿʰ 6 כִּי אֲנִי ᵃⁿⁱ, ᵗᵈʰᵈ ᵏᵘᵘ

יְהוָׁהᵃʰᵈⁱ לֹא שָׁנִיתִי וְאַתֶּם בְּנֵי־יַעֲקֹב ᵘⁱ ʸʰᵛʰ, ʸᵃʰᵈᵘⁿʰⁱ ᵃⁱʳʰⁿᵘⁱʰ לֹא

כְלִיתֶם: 7 לְמִימֵי אֲבֹתֵיכֶם סַרְתֶּם מֵחֻקַּי וְלֹא שְׁמַרְתֶּם שׁוּבוּ אֵלַי

וְאָשׁוּבָה אֲלֵיכֶם אָמַר יְהוָׁהᵃʰᵈⁱ צְבָאוֹת ⁿᵗʰ ᵘʳᵇᵘᵃ ᵃʰⁱʰ; ᵖⁿⁱ ˢᵏⁱⁿʰ

וַאֲמַרְתֶּם בַּמֶּה ᵐ"ʰ נָשׁוּב: 8 הֲיִקְבַּע אָדָם ᵐᵘᵐ, ᵃʰⁱʰ ᵃᵈⁿⁱ אֱלֹהִים ᵐ"ʰ; ʸˡʰ כִּי

אַתֶּם קֹבְעִים אֹתִי וַאֲמַרְתֶּם בַּמֶּה ᵐ"ʰ קְבַעֲנוּךָ הַמַּעֲשֵׂר ʸʳᵗ וְהַתְּרוּמָה:

9 בַּמְּאֵרָה אַתֶּם נֵאָרִים וְאֹתִי אַתֶּם קֹבְעִים הַגּוֹי כֻּלּוֹ: 10 הָבִיאוּ אֶת־

כָּל ʸˡⁱ ־הַמַּעֲשֵׂר ʸʳᵗ אֶל־בֵּית ᵇ"ᵖ ʳᵃʰ הָאוֹצָר אֵˡ, ʸⁱᵃ"ⁱ וִיהִי טֶרֶף ʳᵖⁱʰ ᵉ"ʰ

בְּבֵיתִי וּבְחָנוּנִי נָא בָּזֹאת אָמַר יְהוָׁהᵃʰᵈⁱ צְבָאוֹת ⁿᵗʰ ᵘʳᵇᵘᵃ ᵃʰⁱʰ; ᵖⁿⁱ ˢᵏⁱⁿʰ

אִם ʸᵘʰᵏ, ᵉ"ʰ ᵐ"ᵇ ־לֹא אֶפְתַּח לָכֶם אֵת אֲרֻבּוֹת הַשָּׁמַיִם ʸ"ᵖ ᵗˡ, ʸ"ᵖ ᵏᵘᵘ

וַהֲרִיקֹתִי לָכֶם בְּרָכָה עַד־בְּלִי־דָי: 11 וְגָעַרְתִּי לָכֶם בָּאֹכֵל וְלֹא־

יַשְׁחִת לָכֶם אֶת־פְּרִי ᵉ"ʰ ᵃˡʰⁱᵐ ᵈᵃˡᵖⁱⁿ הָאֲדָמָה וְלֹא־תְשַׁכֵּל לָכֶם הַגֶּפֶן

בַּשָּׂדֶה אָמַר יְהוָׁהᵃʰᵈⁱ צְבָאוֹת ⁿᵗʰ ᵘʳᵇᵘᵃ ᵃʰⁱʰ, ᵖⁿⁱ ˢᵏⁱⁿʰ: 12 וְאִשְּׁרוּ אֶתְכֶם

כָּל ʸˡⁱ ־הַגּוֹיִם כִּי־תִהְיוּ אַתֶּם אֶרֶץ ᵃˡʰⁱᵐ ᵈᵃˡᵖⁱⁿ חֵפֶץ אָמַר יְהוָׁהᵃʰᵈⁱ

צְבָאוֹת ⁿᵗʰ ᵘʳᵇᵘᵃ ᵃʰⁱʰ; ᵖⁿⁱ ˢᵏⁱⁿʰ: 13 חָזְקוּ עָלַי דִּבְרֵיכֶם ʳᵃʰ אָמַר יְהוָׁהᵃʰᵈⁱ

13 "Your words have been harsh against Me," says the Lord, "yet you say, 'What have we spoken against You?'

14 You have said, 'It is useless to serve God; what profit is it that we have kept His ordinance, and that we have walked as mourners before the Lord of Hosts?

15 So now we call the proud blessed, for those who do wickedness are raised up; they even tempt God and go free.'"

16 Then those who feared the Lord spoke to one another, and the Lord listened and heard them; so a book of remembrance was written before Him for those who fear the Lord and who meditate on His name.

17 "They shall be Mine," says the Lord of Hosts, "on the day that I make them My jewels. And I will spare them as a man spares his own son who serves him."

18 Then you shall again discern between the righteous and the wicked, between one who serves God and one who does not serve Him.

19 For, behold, the day comes, it burns as a furnace; and all the proud, and all that work wickedness, shall be stubble; and the day that cometh shall set them ablaze," said the Lord of Hosts, "that it shall leave them neither root nor branch.

20 But unto you that fear My name shall the sun of righteousness arise with healing in its wings; and you shall go forth, and gambol as calves of the stall.

21 And you shall tread down the wicked; for they shall be ashes under the soles of your feet in the day that I do make," said the Lord of Hosts.

22 "Remember you the law of Moses My servant, which I commanded unto him in Horeb for all Israel, even statutes and ordinances.

23 Behold, I will send you Elijah the prophet before the coming of the great and terrible day of the Lord.

24 And he shall turn the heart of the fathers to the children, and the heart of the children to their fathers; lest I come and smite the land with utter destruction.

Behold, I will send you Elijah the prophet before the coming of the great and terrible day of the Lord.

14 אֲמַרְתֶּם שָׁוְא עֲבֹד אֱלֹהִים וָאֲמַרְתֶּם מַה־נִּדְבַּרְנוּ עָלֶיךָ: וּמַה־בֶּצַע כִּי שָׁמַרְנוּ מִשְׁמַרְתּוֹ וְכִי הָלַכְנוּ קְדֹרַנִּית מִפְּנֵי יְהוָה צְבָאוֹת: 15 וְעַתָּה אֲנַחְנוּ מְאַשְּׁרִים זֵדִים גַּם־נִבְנוּ עֹשֵׂי רִשְׁעָה גַּם בָּחֲנוּ אֱלֹהִים וַיִּמָּלֵטוּ: 16 אָז נִדְבְּרוּ יִרְאֵי יְהוָה אִישׁ אֶל־רֵעֵהוּ וַיַּקְשֵׁב יְהוָה וַיִּשְׁמָע וַיִּכָּתֵב סֵפֶר זִכָּרוֹן לְפָנָיו לְיִרְאֵי יְהוָה וּלְחֹשְׁבֵי שְׁמוֹ: 17 וְהָיוּ לִי אָמַר יְהוָה צְבָאוֹת לַיּוֹם אֲשֶׁר אֲנִי עֹשֶׂה סְגֻלָּה וְחָמַלְתִּי עֲלֵיהֶם כַּאֲשֶׁר יַחְמֹל אִישׁ עַל־בְּנוֹ הָעֹבֵד אֹתוֹ: 18 וְשַׁבְתֶּם וּרְאִיתֶם בֵּין צַדִּיק לְרָשָׁע בֵּין עֹבֵד אֱלֹהִים לַאֲשֶׁר לֹא עֲבָדוֹ: 19 כִּי־הִנֵּה הַיּוֹם בָּא בֹּעֵר כַּתַּנּוּר וְהָיוּ כָל־זֵדִים וְכָל־עֹשֵׂה רִשְׁעָה קַשׁ וְלִהַט אֹתָם הַיּוֹם הַבָּא אָמַר יְהוָה צְבָאוֹת אֲשֶׁר לֹא־יַעֲזֹב לָהֶם שֹׁרֶשׁ וְעָנָף: 20 וְזָרְחָה לָכֶם יִרְאֵי שְׁמִי שֶׁמֶשׁ צְדָקָה וּמַרְפֵּא בִּכְנָפֶיהָ וִיצָאתֶם וּפִשְׁתֶּם כְּעֶגְלֵי מַרְבֵּק: 21 וְעַסּוֹתֶם רְשָׁעִים כִּי־יִהְיוּ אֵפֶר תַּחַת כַּפּוֹת רַגְלֵיכֶם בַּיּוֹם אֲשֶׁר אֲנִי עֹשֶׂה אָמַר יְהוָה צְבָאוֹת: 22 זִכְרוּ תּוֹרַת מֹשֶׁה עַבְדִּי אֲשֶׁר צִוִּיתִי אוֹתוֹ בְחֹרֵב עַל־כָּל־יִשְׂרָאֵל חֻקִּים וּמִשְׁפָּטִים: 23 הִנֵּה אָנֹכִי שֹׁלֵחַ לָכֶם אֵת אֵלִיָּה הַנָּבִיא לִפְנֵי בּוֹא יוֹם יְהוָה הַגָּדוֹל וְהַנּוֹרָא: 24 וְהֵשִׁיב לֵב־אָבוֹת עַל־בָּנִים וְלֵב בָּנִים עַל־אֲבוֹתָם פֶּן־אָבוֹא וְהִכֵּיתִי אֶת־הָאָרֶץ חֵרֶם: הִנֵּה אָנֹכִי שֹׁלֵחַ לָכֶם אֵת אֵלִיָּה הַנָּבִיא לִפְנֵי בּוֹא יוֹם יְהוָה הַגָּדוֹל וְהַנּוֹרָא:

HAFTARAH OF THE EVE OF ROSH CHODESH

On one level, this Haftarah concerns the eve of Rosh Chodesh, the eve of a new lunar (astrological) month. In a deeper sense, it speaks of the love between David and Jonathan. Although Jonathan was heir to the throne, he knew that David might become king. Yet Jonathan loved David and felt

1 Samuel 20:18-42

20:[18] Then Jonathan said to him, "Tomorrow is the New Moon, and you will be missed because your seat will be empty.

[19] When you have stayed for three days, you shall go down quickly and come to the place where you hid yourself on that eventful day, and you shall remain by the stone Ezel.

[20] I will shoot three arrows to the side, as though I shot at a target.

[21] And behold, I will send the lad, saying, 'Go, find the arrows.' If I specifically say to the lad, 'Behold, the arrows are on this side of you, get them,' then come; for there is safety for you and no harm, as the Lord lives.

[22] "But if I say to the youth, 'Behold, the arrows are beyond you,' go, for the Lord has sent you away.

[23] As for the agreement of which you and I have spoken, behold, the Lord is between you and me forever."

[24] So David hid in the field; and when the New Moon came, the king sat down to eat food.

[25] The king sat on his seat as usual, the seat by the wall; then Jonathan rose up and Abner sat down by Saul's side, but David's place was empty.

[26] Nevertheless Saul did not speak anything that day, for he thought, "It is an accident, he is not clean, surely he is not clean."

[27] It came about the next day, the second day of the New Moon, that David's place was empty; so Saul said to Jonathan his son, "Why has the son of Jesse not come to the meal, either yesterday or today?"

[28] Jonathan then answered Saul, "David earnestly asked leave of me to go to Bethlehem, [29] for he said, 'Please let me go, since our family has a sacrifice in the

HAFTARAH OF THE EVE OF ROSH CHODESH

no jealousy. To truly feel love for another person, we must give up our own selfish desires. To have a successful relationship of any kind, we must be willing to sacrifice something.

שמואל 1 פרק 20

20 18 וַיֹּאמֶר־לוֹ יְהוֹנָתָן מָחָר חֹדֶשׁ וְנִפְקַדְתָּ כִּי יִפָּקֵד
מוֹשָׁבֶךָ: 19 וְשִׁלַּשְׁתָּ תֵּרֵד מְאֹד וּבָאתָ אֶל־הַמָּקוֹם אֲשֶׁר־
נִסְתַּרְתָּ שָּׁם בְּיוֹם הַמַּעֲשֶׂה וְיָשַׁבְתָּ אֵצֶל הָאֶבֶן
הָאָזֶל: 20 וַאֲנִי שְׁלֹשֶׁת הַחִצִּים צִדָּה אוֹרֶה לְשַׁלַּח־לִי
לְמַטָּרָה: 21 וְהִנֵּה אֶשְׁלַח אֶת־הַנַּעַר לֵךְ מְצָא אֶת־הַחִצִּים
אִם־אָמֹר אֹמַר לַנַּעַר הִנֵּה הַחִצִּים | מִמְּךָ וָהֵנָּה
קָחֶנּוּ | וָבֹאָה כִּי־שָׁלוֹם לְךָ וְאֵין דָּבָר חַי־יְהֹוָה: 22 וְאִם־
כֹּה אֹמַר לָעֶלֶם הִנֵּה הַחִצִּים מִמְּךָ וָהָלְאָה לֵךְ כִּי שִׁלֵּחֲךָ
יְהֹוָה: 23 וְהַדָּבָר אֲשֶׁר דִּבַּרְנוּ אֲנִי וָאָתָּה הִנֵּה
יְהֹוָה בֵּינִי וּבֵינְךָ עַד־עוֹלָם: [ס] 24 וַיִּסָּתֵר דָּוִד בַּשָּׂדֶה
וַיְהִי הַחֹדֶשׁ וַיֵּשֶׁב הַמֶּלֶךְ אֶל־ (כתיב: עַל־) הַלֶּחֶם לֶאֱכוֹל:
25 וַיֵּשֶׁב הַמֶּלֶךְ עַל־מוֹשָׁבוֹ כְּפַעַם | בְּפַעַם אֶל־מוֹשַׁב הַקִּיר וַיָּקָם
יְהוֹנָתָן וַיֵּשֶׁב אַבְנֵר מִצַּד שָׁאוּל וַיִּפָּקֵד מְקוֹם דָּוִד: 26 וְלֹא־
דִבֶּר שָׁאוּל מְאוּמָה בַּיּוֹם הַהוּא כִּי אָמַר מִקְרֶה הוּא
בִּלְתִּי טָהוֹר הוּא כִּי־לֹא טָהוֹר: [ס] 27 וַיְהִי מִמָּחֳרַת
הַחֹדֶשׁ הַשֵּׁנִי וַיִּפָּקֵד מְקוֹם דָּוִד [פ] וַיֹּאמֶר שָׁאוּל אֶל־
יְהוֹנָתָן בְּנוֹ מַדּוּעַ לֹא־בָא בֶן־יִשַׁי גַּם־תְּמוֹל גַּם־הַיּוֹם
אֶל־הַלָּחֶם: 28 וַיַּעַן יְהוֹנָתָן אֶת־שָׁאוּל נִשְׁאֹל נִשְׁאַל דָּוִד מֵעִמָּדִי
עַד־בֵּית לָחֶם: 29 וַיֹּאמֶר שַׁלְּחֵנִי נָא כִּי זֶבַח מִשְׁפָּחָה לָנוּ

city, and my brother has commanded me to attend. And now, if I have found favor in your sight, please let me get away that I may see my brothers.' For this reason he has not come to the king's table."

³⁰ Then Saul's anger burned against Jonathan and he said to him, "You son of a perverse, rebellious woman! Do I not know that you are choosing the son of Jesse to your own shame and to the shame of your mother's nakedness?

³¹ For as long as the son of Jesse lives on the Earth, neither you nor your kingdom will be established. Now, send and bring him to me, for he must surely die."

³² But Jonathan answered Saul, his father, and said to him, "Why should he be put to death? What has he done?"

³³ Then Saul hurled his spear at him to strike him down: so Jonathan knew that his father had decided to put David to death.

³⁴ Then Jonathan arose from the table in fierce anger, and did not eat food on the second day of the New Moon, for he was grieved over David because his father had dishonored him.

³⁵ Now it came about in the morning that Jonathan went out into the field for the appointment with David, and a little lad was with him.

³⁶ He said to his lad, "Run, find now the arrows which I am about to shoot." As the lad was running, he shot an arrow past him.

³⁷ When the lad reached the place of the arrow which Jonathan had shot, Jonathan called after the lad and said, "Is not the arrow beyond you?"

³⁸ And Jonathan called after the lad, "Hurry, be quick, do not stay!" And Jonathan's lad picked up the arrow and came to his master.

³⁹ The lad was not aware of anything; only Jonathan and David knew about the matter.

⁴⁰ Then Jonathan gave his weapons to his lad and said to him, "Go; bring them to the city."

⁴¹ When the lad was gone, David rose from the south side and fell on his face to the ground and bowed three times, and they kissed each other and wept together, but David wept more.

⁴² Jonathan said to David, "Go in safety, inasmuch as we have sworn to each other in the Name of the Lord, saying, 'The Lord will be between me and you, and between my descendants and your descendants forever.' "

אלהים, מום בָּעִיר מזדלפורן, עֵרי, מזדלפורן וְהוּא צִוָּה פּיי ־לֵי אָוֶי וְעַתָּה אִם־ יהוך

מָצָאתִי חֵן מווי בְּעֵינֶיךָ ע"ה קס"א אִמָּלְטָה נָּא וְאֶרְאֶה אֶת־אֶחָי עַל־כֵּן

לֹא־בָא אֶל־שֻׁלְחַן הַמֶּלֶךְ: [ס] 30 וַיִּחַר־אַף שָׁאוּל בִּיהוֹנָתָן וַיֹּאמֶר לוֹ

בֶּן־נַעֲוַת הַמַּרְדּוּת הֲלוֹא יָדַעְתִּי כִּי־בֹחֵר אַתָּה לְבֶן־יִשַׁי לְבָשְׁתְּךָ

וּלְבֹשֶׁת עֶרְוַת אִמֶּךָ: 31 כִּי כָל־ ילי ־הַיָּמִים גלך אֲשֶׁר בֶּן־יִשַׁי חַי עַל־

הָאֲדָמָה לֹא תִכּוֹן אַתָּה וּמַלְכוּתֶךָ וְעַתָּה שְׁלַח וְקַח אֹתוֹ אֵלַי כִּי

בֶן־מָוֶת הוּא: [ס] 32 וַיַּעַן יְהוֹנָתָן אֶת־שָׁאוּל אָבִיו וַיֹּאמֶר אֵלָיו לָמָּה

יוּמַת מֶה מ"ה עָשָׂה: 33 וַיָּטֶל שָׁאוּל אֶת־הַחֲנִית עָלָיו לְהַכֹּתוֹ וַיֵּדַע

יְהוֹנָתָן כִּי־כָלָה הִיא מֵעִם עמם אָבִיו לְהָמִית אֶת־דָּוִד: [ס] 34 וַיָּקָם

יְהוֹנָתָן מֵעִם עמם הַשֻּׁלְחָן בָּחֳרִי־אָף וְלֹא־אָכַל בְּיוֹם גנד, זך, מזבוי ־הַחֹדֶשׁ

הַשֵּׁנִי לֶחֶם י"ב הוויות ג"פ יהוה כִּי נֶעְצַב אֶל־דָּוִד כִּי הִכְלִמוֹ אָבִיו: [ס]

35 וַיְהִי אל בַבֹּקֶר וַיֵּצֵא יְהוֹנָתָן הַשָּׂדֶה ע"די לְמוֹעֵד דָּוִד וְנַעַר ע"ך קָטֹן

עִמּוֹ: 36 וַיֹּאמֶר לְנַעֲרוֹ רֻץ מְצָא נָא אֶת־הַחִצִּים אֲשֶׁר אָנֹכִי איע מוֹרֶה

הַנַּעַר ע"ך רָץ וְהוּא־יָרָה הַחֵצִי לְהַעֲבִרוֹ: 37 וַיָּבֹא הַנַּעַר ע"ך עַד־מְקוֹם

יהוה ברבוע הַחֵצִי אֲשֶׁר יָרָה יְהוֹנָתָן וַיִּקְרָא עם ה' אותיות = ב"פ קס"א יְהוֹנָתָן אַחֲרֵי

הַנַּעַר ע"ך וַיֹּאמֶר הֲלוֹא הַחֵצִי מִמְּךָ וָהָלְאָה: 38 וַיִּקְרָא עם ה' אותיות = ב"פ קס"א

יְהוֹנָתָן אַחֲרֵי הַנַּעַר ע"ך מְהֵרָה חוּשָׁה אַל־תַּעֲמֹד וַיְלַקֵּט נַעַר ע"ך

יְהוֹנָתָן אֶת־הַחִצִּים (כתיב: החצי) וַיָּבֹא אֶל־אֲדֹנָיו: 39 וְהַנַּעַר ע"ך לֹא־

יָדַע מְאוּמָה אַךְ אהיה יְהוֹנָתָן וְדָוִד יָדְעוּ אֶת־הַדָּבָר ראה: [ס] 40 וַיִּתֵּן י"פ

מלוי ע"ב יְהוֹנָתָן אֶת־כֵּלָיו כלי אֶל־הַנַּעַר ע"ך אֲשֶׁר־לוֹ וַיֹּאמֶר לוֹ לֵךְ הָבֵיא

הָעִיר מזדלפור, עֵרי, מזדלפורן: 41 הַנַּעַר ע"ך בָּא וְדָוִד קָם מֵאֵצֶל הַנֶּגֶב וַיִּפֹּל

לְאַפָּיו אַרְצָה אלהים דההין ע"ה וַיִּשְׁתַּחוּ שָׁלֹשׁ פְּעָמִים וַיִּשְּׁקוּ | אִישׁ ע"ה קס"א

קס"א אֶת־רֵעֵהוּ וַיִּבְכּוּ אִישׁ ע"ה קס"א קס"א אֶת־רֵעֵהוּ עַד־דָּוִד הִגְדִּיל:

42 וַיֹּאמֶר יְהוֹנָתָן לְדָוִד לֵךְ לְשָׁלוֹם אֲשֶׁר נִשְׁבַּעְנוּ שְׁנֵינוּ אֲנַחְנוּ בְּשֵׁם

שדי יהוה יְהוָֹה אלהים יאהדונהי לֵאמֹר יְהוָֹה אלהים יאהדונהי יִהְיֶה יי | בֵּינִי וּבֵינֶךָ וּבֵין זַרְעִי

וּבֵין זַרְעֶךָ עַד־עוֹלָם: [פ]

MAFTIR OF SHABBAT ROSH CHODESH

In this Maftir, we read about the tribes of Reuben, Shimon and Gad, which were stationed in the south. The *Zohar* in *Terumah* says that the south signifies *Chesed*, or love and mercy, and is a place of quiet that is protected by the angel Michael. And that the south is where everything is

Numbers 28:9-15

28:9 *"On the Sabbath day, make an offering of two lambs a year old without defect, together with its drink offering and a grain offering of two-tenths of an ephah of fine flour mixed with oil.*

10 This is the burnt offering for every Sabbath, in addition to the regular burnt offering and its drink offering.

11 On the first of every month, present to the Lord a burnt offering of two young bulls, one ram and seven male lambs a year old, all without defect.

12 With each bull there is to be a grain offering of three-tenths of an ephah of fine flour mixed with oil; with the ram, a grain offering of two-tenths of an ephah of fine flour mixed with oil;

13 and with each lamb, a grain offering of a tenth of an ephah of fine flour mixed with oil. This is for a burnt offering, a pleasing aroma, an offering made to the Lord by fire.

14 With each bull there is to be a drink offering of half a hin of wine; with the ram, a third of a hin; and with each lamb, a quarter of a hin. This is the monthly burnt offering to be made at each new moon during the year.

15 Besides the regular burnt offering with its drink offering, one male goat is to be presented to the Lord as a sin offering."

MAFTIR OF SHABBAT ROSH CHODESH

manifested once we've completed our spiritual connections. By listening to this reading, we have an opportunity to go within ourselves, finding the clarity to manifest all our spiritual connections and imbuing the coming month with Light.

בּמדבּר פּרק 28

28 9 וּבְיוֹם נגד, זן, מזבח הַשַּׁבָּת שְׁנֵי־כְבָשִׂים בְּנֵי־שָׁנָה תְּמִימִם וּשְׁנֵי עֶשְׂרֹנִים סֹלֶת מִנְחָה ע״ה ב״פ ב״ן בְּלוּלָה בַשֶּׁמֶן י״פ טל, י״פ כוזו, ביט וְנִסְכּוֹ: 10 עֹלַת שַׁבַּת בְּשַׁבַּתּוֹ עַל־עֹלַת אבגיתצ, וער, אהבת חנם הַתָּמִיד נתה, קס״א ג קנ״א ג קמ״ג וְנִסְכָּהּ: [פ] 11 וּבְרָאשֵׁי ריבוע אלהים ג אלהים דיודין ע״ה חָדְשֵׁיכֶם י״ב הוויות תַּקְרִיבוּ עֹלָה לַיהֹוָהאדניאהדונהי פָּרִים בְּנֵי־בָקָר שְׁנַיִם וְאַיִל אֶחָד אהבה, דאגה כְּבָשִׂים בְּנֵי־שָׁנָה שִׁבְעָה תְּמִימִם: 12 וּשְׁלֹשָׁה עֶשְׂרֹנִים סֹלֶת מִנְחָה ע״ה ב״פ ב״ן בְּלוּלָה בַשֶּׁמֶן י״פ טל, י״פ כוזו, ביט לַפָּר מזוזר, ערי הָאֶחָד אהבה, דאגה וּשְׁנֵי עֶשְׂרֹנִים סֹלֶת מִנְחָה ע״ה ב״פ ב״ן בְּלוּלָה בַשֶּׁמֶן י״פ טל, י״פ כוזו, ביט לָאַיִל הָאֶחָד אהבה, דאגה: 13 וְעִשָּׂרֹן עִשָּׂרוֹן סֹלֶת מִנְחָה ע״ה ב״פ ב״ן בְּלוּלָה בַשֶּׁמֶן י״פ טל, י״פ כוזו, ביט לַכֶּבֶשׂ ב״פ קס״א הָאֶחָד אהבה, דאגה עֹלָה רֵיחַ נִיחֹחַ אִשֶּׁה לַיהֹוָהאדניאהדונהי: 14 וְנִסְכֵּיהֶם חֲצִי הַהִין יְהֹוָה ייי לַפָּר מזוזר, ערי וּשְׁלִישִׁת הַהִין לָאַיִל וּרְבִיעִת הַהִין לַכֶּבֶשׂ ב״פ קס״א יַיִן מ״ך, י״פ האא קס״א אַת עֹלַת אבגיתצ, וער, אהבת חנם זֹאת עֹלַת חֹדֶשׁ י״ב הוויות בְּחָדְשׁוֹ י״ב הוויות לְחָדְשֵׁי י״ב הוויות הַשָּׁנָה: 15 וּשְׂעִיר עִזִּים אֶחָד אהבה, דאגה לְחַטָּאת לַיהֹוָהאדניאהדונהי עַל־עֹלַת אבגיתצ, וער, אהבת חנם הַתָּמִיד נתה, קס״א ג קנ״א ג קמ״ג יֵעָשֶׂה ייי וְנִסְכּוֹ: [ס]

HAFTARAH OF SHABBAT ROSH CHODESH

Just as Shabbat cools the fires of Hell, these same fires are shut down on Rosh Chodesh giving us the power to deflect and avoid judgment

Isaiah 66:1-24

66:[1] This is what the Lord says: "Heaven is My Throne, and the Earth is My Footstool. Where is the House you will build for Me? Where will My Resting Place be?

[2] Has not My hand made all these things, and so they came into being?" declares the Lord. "This is the one I esteem: he who is humble and contrite in spirit, and trembles at My Word.

[3] But whoever sacrifices a bull is like one who kills a man, and whoever offers a lamb, like one who breaks a dog's neck; whoever makes a grain offering is like one who presents pig's blood, and whoever burns memorial incense, like one who worships an idol. They have chosen their own ways, and their souls delight in their abominations;

[4] so I also will choose harsh treatment for them and will bring upon them what they dread. For when I called, no one answered, when I spoke, no one listened. They did evil in My sight and chose what displeases Me."

[5] Hear the Word of the Lord, you who tremble at His Word: "Your brothers who hate you, and exclude you because of My Name, have said, 'Let the Lord be glorified, that we may see your joy!' Yet they will be put to shame.

[6] Hear that uproar from the city, hear that noise from the temple! It is the sound of the Lord repaying His enemies all they deserve.

[7] Before she goes into labor, she gives birth; before the pains come upon her, she delivers a son.

[8] Who has ever heard of such a thing? Who has ever seen such things? Can a country be born in a day or a nation be brought forth in a moment? Yet no sooner is Zion in labor than she gives birth to her children.

HAFTARAH OF SHABBAT ROSH CHODESH

ישעיהו פרק 66

66 1 כֹּה הי אָמַר יְהֹוָה יאהדונהי הַשָּׁמַיִם י"פ טל, י"פ כוזו כִּסְאִי וְהָאָרֶץ
אלהים דההין ע"ה הֲדֹם רַגְלָי אֵי־זֶה בַיִת ב"פ ראה אֲשֶׁר תִּבְנוּ־לִי וְאֵי־זֶה מָקוֹם
יהוה ברבוע מְנוּחָתִי: 2 וְאֶת־כָּל ילי ־אֵלֶּה יָדִי עָשָׂתָה וַיִּהְיוּ מלוי ס"ג כָל ילי ־
אֵלֶּה נְאֻם־יְהֹוָה יאהדונהי וְאֶל־זֶה אַבִּיט אֶל־עָנִי ריבוע מ"ה וּנְכֵה־רוּחַ מלוי
אלהים דיודין וְחָרֵד עַל־דְּבָרִי ראה: 3 שׁוֹחֵט הַשּׁוֹר אבגיתצ, ושר, אהבת חנם מַכֵּה־
אִישׁ ע"ה קנ"א קס"א זוֹבֵחַ הַשֶּׂה עֹרֵף כֶּלֶב מַעֲלֵה מִנְחָה ע"ה ב"פ ב"ן דַּם רבוע אהיה
־חֲזִיר מַזְכִּיר לְבֹנָה מְבָרֵךְ אָוֶן גַּם יגל ־הֵמָּה בָּחֲרוּ בְּדַרְכֵיהֶם ב"פ יב"ק
וּבְשִׁקּוּצֵיהֶם נַפְשָׁם חָפֵצָה: 4 גַּם יגל ־אֲנִי אני אֶבְחַר בְּתַעֲלֻלֵיהֶם
וּמְגוּרֹתָם אָבִיא לָהֶם יַעַן קָרָאתִי וְאֵין עוֹנֶה דִּבַּרְתִּי ראה וְלֹא שָׁמֵעוּ
וַיַּעֲשׂוּ הָרַע רהע בְּעֵינַי ריבוע מ"ה וּבַאֲשֶׁר לֹא־חָפַצְתִּי בָּחָרוּ: [ס] 5 שִׁמְעוּ
דְּבַר ראה ־יְהֹוָה יאהדונהי הַחֲרֵדִים אֶל־דְּבָרוֹ ראה אָמְרוּ אֲחֵיכֶם שֹׂנְאֵיכֶם
מְנַדֵּיכֶם לְמַעַן שְׁמִי ריבוע ע"ב ורבוע ס"ג יִכְבַּד יְהֹוָה יאהדונהי וְנִרְאֶה
בְשִׂמְחַתְכֶם וְהֵם יֵבֹשׁוּ: 6 קוֹל ע"ב ס"ג ע"ה שָׁאוֹן מֵעִיר מנצפך, ערי, סנדלפון קוֹל
ע"ב ס"ג ע"ה מֵהֵיכָל אדני, ללה קוֹל ע"ב ס"ג ע"ה יְהֹוָה יאהדונהי מְשַׁלֵּם גְּמוּל לְאֹיְבָיו:
7 בְּטֶרֶם רפ"ח ע"ה תָּחִיל יָלָדָה בְּטֶרֶם רפ"ח ע"ה יָבוֹא חֵבֶל לָהּ וְהִמְלִיטָה
זָכָר: 8 מִי ילי ־שָׁמַע כָּזֹאת מִי ילי רָאָה ראה כָּאֵלֶּה הֲיוּחַל אֶרֶץ
אלהים דאלפין בְּיוֹם נגד, זן, מזבח אֶחָד אהבה, דאגה אִם יוהך ־יִוָּלֵד גּוֹי פַּעַם אֶחָת
כִּי־חָלָה לכה גַּם יגל ־יָלְדָה צִיּוֹן יוסף, ו"פ יהוה אֶת־בָּנֶיהָ: 9 הַאֲנִי אני אַשְׁבִּיר

⁹ Do I bring to the moment of birth and not give delivery?" says the Lord. "Do I close up the womb when I bring to delivery?" says your God.

¹⁰ "Rejoice with Jerusalem and be glad for her, all you who love her; rejoice greatly with her, all you who mourn over her.

¹¹ For you will nurse and be satisfied at her comforting breasts; you will drink deeply and delight in her overflowing abundance."

¹² For this is what the Lord says: "I will extend peace to her like a river, and the wealth of nations like a flooding stream; you will nurse and be carried on her arm and dandled on her knees.

¹³ As a mother comforts her child, so will I comfort you; and you will be comforted over Jerusalem."

¹⁴ When you see this, your heart will rejoice and you will flourish like grass; the hand of the Lord will be made known to His servants, but his fury will be shown to His foes.
¹⁵ See, the Lord is coming with fire, and His chariots are like a whirlwind; He will bring down His anger with fury, and His rebuke with flames of fire.

¹⁶ For with fire and with his sword the Lord will execute judgment upon all men, and many will be those slain by the Lord.

¹⁷ "Those who consecrate and purify themselves to go into the gardens, following the one in the midst of those who eat the flesh of pigs and rats and other abominable things—they will meet their end together," declares the Lord.

¹⁸ "And I, because of their actions and their imaginations, am about to come and gather all nations and tongues, and they will come and see My glory.

¹⁹ I will set a sign among them, and I will send some of those who survive to the nations—to Tarshish, to the Libyans and Lydians (famous as archers), to Tubal and Greece, and to the distant islands that have not heard of My fame or seen My glory. They will proclaim My glory among the nations.

²⁰ And they will bring all your brothers, from all the nations, to My Holy Mountain in Jerusalem as an offering to the Lord—on horses, in chariots and wagons, and on mules and camels," says the Lord. "They will bring them, as the Israelites bring their grain offerings, to the Temple of the Lord in ceremonially clean vessels.

וְלֹא אוֹלִיד יֹאמַר יְהֹוָׁה אִם ־אֲנִ֣י אֲנִי הַמּוֹלִ֥יד וְעָצַ֖רְתִּי אָמַ֥ר

אֱלֹהָֽיִךְ ילה: [ס] 10 שִׂמְח֣וּ אֶת־יְרוּשָׁלַ֗ם ריי שיע וְגִ֣ילוּ בָ֔הּ כָּל ־יל ־אֹהֲבֶ֑יהָ

שִׂ֥ישׂוּ אִתָּ֖הּ מָשׂ֑וֹשׂ כָּל ־יל ־הַמִּֽתְאַבְּלִ֖ים עָלֶֽיהָ׃ פהל: 11 לְמַ֤עַן תִּֽינְקוּ֙

וּשְׂבַעְתֶּ֔ם מִשֹּׁ֖ד תַּנְחֻמֶ֑יהָ לְמַ֥עַן תָּמֹ֛צּוּ וְהִתְעַנַּגְתֶּ֖ם מִזִּ֥יז כְּבוֹדָֽהּ׃ [ס]

12 כִּי־כֹ֣ה היי | אָמַ֣ר יְהֹוָ֗ה הִנְנִ֣י נֹטֶֽה־אֵ֠לֶ֠יהָ כְּנָהָ֨ר שָׁל֜וֹם וּכְנַ֧חַל

שׁוֹטֵ֛ף כְּב֥וֹד לב ־גּוֹיִ֖ם וִֽינַקְתֶּ֑ם עַל־צַד֙ תִּנָּשֵׂ֔אוּ וְעַל־בִּרְכַּ֖יִם תְּשָׁעֳשָֽׁעוּ׃

13 כְּאִ֕ישׁ עה קנא קסא אֲשֶׁ֥ר אִמּ֖וֹ תְּנַחֲמֶ֑נּוּ כֵּ֚ן אָנֹכִ֣י איע אֲנַ֣חֶמְכֶ֔ם

וּבִירֽוּשָׁלַ֖ם ריי שיע תְּנֻחָֽמוּ׃ 14 וּרְאִיתֶם֙ וְשָׂ֣שׂ לִבְּכֶ֔ם וְעַצְמוֹתֵיכֶ֖ם

כַּדֶּ֣שֶׁא תִפְרַ֑חְנָה וְנוֹדְעָ֤ה יַד־יְהֹוָה֙ אֶת־עֲבָדָ֔יו וְזָעַ֖ם אֶת־

אֹיְבָֽיו׃ [ס] 15 כִּֽי־הִנֵּ֤ה מה יה יְהֹוָה֙ אלהים דיודין עה בָּאֵ֣שׁ יָב֔וֹא וְכַסּוּפָ֖ה

מַרְכְּבֹתָ֑יו לְהָשִׁ֤יב בְּחֵמָה֙ אַפּ֔וֹ וְגַעֲרָת֖וֹ בְּלַֽהֲבֵי־אֵֽשׁ אלהים דיודין עה ׃

16 כִּ֤י בָאֵשׁ֙ אלהים דיודין עה יְהֹוָ֣ה אהדונהי עה נִשְׁפָּ֔ט וּבְחַרְבּ֖וֹ ריי, גבורה אֶת־כָּל־

יל ־בָּשָׂ֑ר וְרַבּ֖וּ חַֽלְלֵ֥י יְהֹוָֽה אהדונהי ׃ 17 הַמִּתְקַדְּשִׁ֨ים וְהַמִּטַּהֲרִ֜ים אֶל־

הַגַּנּ֗וֹת אַחַ֤ר אַחַ֣ד (כתיב: אחוד) בַּתָּ֙וֶךְ֙ אֹֽכְלֵי֙ בְּשַׂ֣ר הַחֲזִ֔יר וְהַשֶּׁ֖קֶץ

וְהָעַכְבָּ֑ר יַחְדָּ֥ו יָסֻ֖פוּ נְאֻם־יְהֹוָֽה אהדונהי ׃ 18 וְאָנֹכִ֗י איע מַעֲשֵׂיהֶ֣ם

וּמַחְשְׁבֹֽתֵיהֶ֔ם בָּ֕אָה לְקַבֵּ֥ץ אֶת־כָּל ־יל ־הַגּוֹיִ֖ם וְהַלְּשֹׁנ֑וֹת וּבָ֖אוּ וְרָא֥וּ

אֶת־כְּבוֹדִֽי׃ 19 וְשַׂמְתִּ֨י בָהֶ֜ם א֗וֹת וְשִׁלַּחְתִּ֣י מֵהֶ֣ם | פְּלֵיטִים֮ אֶל־הַגּוֹיִם֒

תַּרְשִׁ֨ישׁ פּ֥וּל וְל֛וּד מֹ֥שְׁכֵי קֶ֖שֶׁת תֻּבַ֣ל בפ ריי, בפ גבורה וְיָוָ֑ן אתזר הָאִיִּ֣ים

הָרְחֹקִ֗ים אֲשֶׁ֨ר לֹא־שָׁמְע֤וּ אֶת־שִׁמְעִי֙ וְלֹא־רָא֣וּ אֶת־כְּבוֹדִ֔י וְהִגִּ֥ידוּ

אֶת־כְּבוֹדִ֖י בַּגּוֹיִֽם׃ 20 וְהֵבִ֣יאוּ אֶת־כָּל ־יל ־אֲחֵיכֶ֣ם מִכָּל ־יל ־הַגּוֹיִ֣ם |

מִנְחָ֣ה עה בפ בן | לַֽיהֹוָ֡ה בַּסּוּסִ֣ים ריבוע אדני, כוק וּבָרֶ֩כֶב֩ וּבַצַּבִּ֨ים

וּבַפְּרָדִ֜ים וּבַכִּרְכָּר֗וֹת עַ֣ל הַ֥ר רבוע אלהים יה קָדְשִׁ֛י יְרוּשָׁלַ֖ם ריין שיע אָמַ֣ר

יְהֹוָ֑ה אהדונהי כַּֽאֲשֶׁ֣ר יָבִ֣יאוּ בְנֵי֩ יִשְׂרָאֵ֨ל אֶת־הַמִּנְחָ֜ה עה בפ בן בִּכְלִ֥י כלי

טָה֖וֹר יפ אכא בֵּ֥ית בפ ראה יְהֹוָֽה אהדונהי ׃ 21 וְגַם ־יגל ־מֵהֶ֛ם אֶקַּ֥ח לַכֹּֽהֲנִ֥ים

²¹ *And I will select some of them also to be priests and Levites," says the Lord.*

²² *"As the New Heavens and the New Earth that I make will endure before Me," declares the Lord, "so will your name and descendants endure.*

²³ *From one New Moon to another and from one Sabbath to another, all mankind will come and bow down before Me," says the Lord.*

²⁴ *"And they will go out and look upon the dead bodies of those who rebelled against Me; their worm will not die, nor will their fire be quenched, and they will be loathsome to all mankind."*

From one New Moon to another and from one Sabbath to another, all mankind will come and bow down before Me," says the Lord.

22 כִּי כַאֲשֶׁר הַשָּׁמַיִם אָמַר יְהֹוָה
עֹשֶׂה אֲנִי אֲשֶׁר הֶחָדָשָׁה וְהָאָרֶץ הֶחֳדָשִׁים
וְהָיָה נֶאֻם־יְהֹוָה זַרְעֲכֶם וְשִׁמְכֶם כֵּן יַעֲמֹד עֹמְדִים לְפָנַי 23
כָּל־ בָּשָׂר יָבוֹא בְשַׁבַּתּוֹ וּמִדֵּי שַׁבָּת בְּחָדְשׁוֹ מִדֵּי־חֹדֶשׁ
24 וְיָצְאוּ וְרָאוּ בְּפִגְרֵי אָמַר יְהֹוָה לְהִשְׁתַּחֲוֺת לְפָנַי בָּשָׂר
וְהָיוּ תִכְבֶּה לֹא וְאִשָּׁם תָמוּת לֹא תוֹלַעְתָּם כִּי בִי הַפֹּשְׁעִים הָאֲנָשִׁים
וּמִדֵּי בְּחָדְשׁוֹ מִדֵּי־חֹדֶשׁ וְהָיָה לְכָל־בָּשָׂר׃ דֵרָאוֹן לְכָל־
אָמַר לְפָנַי לְהִשְׁתַּחֲוֺת כָל־בָּשָׂר יָבוֹא בְשַׁבַּתּוֹ שַׁבָּת
יְהֹוָה׃

This work is dedicated to the memory of my parents—
Itzkhak ben Avraham and Tzivia bat Tovah.

May their souls be elevated to a higher level and may their
spirits reside among the tzadikim.